United Confederate Veterans of Limestone and Freestone Counties Texas

Patricia Bennett McGinty

HERITAGE BOOKS
2013

HERITAGE BOOKS
AN IMPRINT OF HERITAGE BOOKS, INC.

Books, CDs, and more—Worldwide

For our listing of thousands of titles see our website
at
www.HeritageBooks.com

Published 2013 by
HERITAGE BOOKS, INC.
Publishing Division
100 Railroad Ave. #104
Westminster, Maryland 21157

Copyright © 2001 Patricia Bennett McGinty

All rights reserved. No part of this book may be reproduced or transmitted in any form or by any means, electronic or mechanical, including photocopying, recording or by any information storage and retrieval system without written permission from the author, except for the inclusion of brief quotations in a review.

International Standard Book Numbers
Paperbound: 978-0-7884-1989-8
Clothbound: 978-0-7884-6978-7

PREFACE

This book was compiled from the original United Confederate Veterans' JOE JOHNSTON CAMP NO. 94 of Limestone and Freestone Counties Minute Records. The two books are in very fragile condition and the ink is sometimes faint or smeared. The names in the books are spelled numerous ways that I have not attempted to systemize in any way except for the generals. Many of the units were moved from brigade to brigade, division to division, corps to corps, and army to army. The commanders in the field were changed as promotions, deaths or disabilities occurred.

The books were used at different times and sometimes concurrent. Pages were glued into the Roster book from an unknown source and unfortunately some pages were missing from each book.

To supply the reader with as much information as possible, if a death date was found, then it has been added to the names.

Abbreviations used to preserve space: Pvt. – private; Lt. – lieutenant; Capt. – captain; Mus. – musician; Sgt. – sergeant; Qr. Mtr. – quartermaster; Brig. Gen'l. – Brigadier General; Col. Br. – color bearer; Battn – battalion; Batty – battery; H. Arty – heavy artillery; Lt. Arty – light artillery; Det. Ser. – detached service; Mtd. Infy – mounted infantry; Dis. Cav. – dismounted cavalry; T-MS. – Trans-Mississippi Department; N. VA. – Army of Northern Virginia; TN. – Army of the Tennessee.

Any italicized name was not found during research and cannot be verified. Also, there were numerous officers named Stewart, Stuart, Johnson, Johnston, etc. When using the information concerning the brigade, division or corp generals, additional research material should be utilized.

The "Confederate Veteran" published numerous articles written by members of the Joe Johnston Camp and are another source of information on the battles the veterans fought and the conditions of the times.

The last two surviving Confederate veteran members of the Joe Johnston Camp No. 94 from the last reunion held in July 1940 at the Confederate Park at Jack's Creek Reunion grounds were M. B. Douglas of Mart and William Wesley Asbury Frost of the Nebo Community near Wortham. W. W. A. Frost was born the 10th of September 1845, Macon, Georgia, and died at his home the 16th of May 1941. He was buried in Wortham Cemetery.

TABLE OF CONTENTS

Roster of Ex-Confederates of Limestone County, Texas, 1889..1

Roster of Ex-Confederates of Limestone County, Texas, August 1, 1890..11

Roster of Ex-Confederates of Limestone County, Texas, July 22, 1891..15

Roster of Ex-Confederates of Limestone County, Texas, August 2-5, 1892...17

Roster of Ex-Confederates of Limestone County, Texas, 1894-1895..23

Roster of Ex-Confederates of Limestone County, Texas, July 22-24, 1896..28

Roster of Ex-Confederates of Limestone County, Texas, 1903...34

Constitution of Joe Johnston Camp No. 94...40

Camp Minutes..43

Roster of Ex-Confederates of Limestone County, Texas..55

New Constitution of Joe Johnston Camp No. 94...77

Camp Minutes..78

List of Confederate Veterans Living July 27, 1926..116

List of Confederate Widows Living July 27, 1926...117

List of Sons and Daughters..117

Possible Civil War Veterans buried in Limestone County..121

CSA Veterans Not Listed on Rosters Buried in Limestone County...129

Death Dates of Deceased Members of Joe Johnston Camp No. 94...130

Index..132

ROSTER OF EX-CONFEDERATE VETERANS OF LIMESTONE COUNTY, TEXAS

1889

NAMES	RANK	CO.	REGT.	STATE	SERVICE	BRIGADE	DIVISION	CORPS	ARMY OF	POST OFFICE
Adair, S. M.		C	10th	AL.						Big Hill
Adams, L. A.	Pvt.	G	11th	TN.	Cavalry	Beale	W. H. Jackson	Forrest	TN.	Armour
Adams, M.	1st Lt.	D	20th	TX.	Infantry	Harrison			T-MS.	Mexia
Adams, W. H.	Capt.	F	33rd	TN.	Infantry	Strahl	Cheatham	Polk/Hardee	TN.	Mexia
Alford, N. W.	Pvt.	K	20th	TX.	Cavalry	Maxey	Hindman	E. K. Smith	T-MS.	Groesbeck
Allen, B. W.	Pvt.	K	20th	TX.	Cavalry	Maxey	Hindman	E. K. Smith	T-MS.	Kosse
Allen, J. H.		F	9th	AL.	Infantry					Kosse
Anderson, C. A.			Bledsmir Batty							Shiloh
Anderson, T. M.	Mus.		82nd	TX.	Cavalry		French	Polk	TN.	Frosa
Anglin, E. W.	Pvt.	McNelly	Scouts	TX.	Cavalry	Horton	Green		T-MS.	Groesbeck
Anglin, J. C.	Pvt.	McNelly	Scouts	TX.	Cavalry	Horton	Green		T-MS.	Groesbeck
Anglin, John	Pvt.	McNelly	Scouts	TX.	Cavalry	Horton	Green		T-MS.	Groesbeck
Archer, Geo. W.	Pvt.	C	8th	TX.	Cavalry	Wharton	Wheeler	Wheeler	TN.	Mexia
Archer, J. H.	Pvt.	F	36th	MS.	Infantry	Sears				Mt. Calm
Archibald, E. L.	Pvt.	B	Rucker's	MS.	Cavalry	Rucker	Chalmers			Groesbeck
Armour, James	Pvt.	C	Bradford	TX.	Cavalry	McCulloch		E. K. Smith	TN.	Armour
Arnett, S. T.	Pvt.	I	21st	TX.	Cavalry	Parsons	Green		T-MS.	Kosse
Arvin, J. A.			9th	VA.	Infantry	Corse	Pickett	Wharton	N. VA.	Mexia
Athey, J. H.	Pvt.	E	6th	AL.	Cavalry	Clanton	Johnson	Longstreet	TN.	Armour
Adkinson, T. H.	Pvt.	E	38th	AL.	Infantry	Holtzclaw	Clayton	Hood	TN.	Mexia
Bailey, D. H.		F	32nd	GA.	Infantry	Harrison	McLaws	Stewart	TN.	Horn Hill
Ball, W. A.	Scout					Loring				Kosse
Banks, A. H.		I		ARK.	Infantry	Cabell		Price	T-MS.	Big Hill
Barnard, A. G.	Pvt.	B	22nd	ARK.	Infantry	Fagan		Price	T-MS.	Horn Hill
Barrey, J. M.		D	Willis' Batty	TX.		Waul	Green		T-MS.	Mexia
Barton, W. M.	Pvt.	E	13th	NC	H. Arty	Dixon			N. VA.	Mexia
Batchelor, T. J.	Pvt.	E	62nd	AL.	Infantry	Thomas			T-MS.	Horn Hill
Bates, C. S.	1st Sgt.	H	20th	TX.	Cavalry	Maxey	Hindman	E. K. Smith	T-MS.	Mexia
Beaty, J. F.	Scout	F		TX.	Cavalry					Kosse
Bell, J. H.				TX.						Tehuacana
Bell, J. M.	Pvt.	A	6th	AL.	Infantry	Waul	Green	Ewell	T-MS.	Horn Hill
Bell, J. W.		H	20th	TX.		Battle	Rodes		N. VA.	Tehuacana
Bell, W. N.	Capt.	A				Marmaduke	Cooper		T-MS.	Tehuacana
Berry, Frank		H	1st	MS.			Hindman		TN.	Honest Ridge
Berry, J. W.		H	31st	MS.		Featherston	Loring	Hardee	TN.	Honest Ridge
Berry, Warren		H	1st	MS.						Honest Ridge
Berryman, H. C.	Pvt.	H	20th	TX.	Infantry	Elmore		E. K. Smith	T-MS.	Prairie Grove
Bishop, John		A	33rd	AL.						Farrar
Black, B. F.		C	3rd	LA.	Infantry	Thomas	Mouton			Kirk
Blackmon, H. C.		D	8th	AL.	Cavalry				T-MS.	Kosse

1

ROSTER OF EX-CONFEDERATE VETERANS OF LIMESTONE COUNTY, TEXAS

Name	Rank	Co.	Regt.	State	Branch	Brigade	Division	Corps/Army	Community
Booth, S.									Armour
Booth, W. P.	Col. Br.	E	36th	ARK.	Infantry	McRae	Churchill	T-MS.	Armour
Bower, Chris J.	Pvt.	C	8th	TX.	Infantry	Young	Walker	T-MS.	Mexia
Boyd, A. R.		C	7th			Elmore		T-MS.	Mt. Calm
Boyd, H. A.	1st Lt.	E	35th	TX.	Cavalry	Bee	Walker	T-MS.	Tehuacana
Boykin, W. P.	Pvt.	K	1st	TX.	Artillery		Magruder	T-MS.	Mexia
Boyle, G. C.	Pvt.	C	2nd	MS.	Infantry	McCown	Johnson	N. VA.	Tehuacana
Bradford, C. M.	Pvt.	D	20th	TX.	Infantry				Groesbeck
Bradshaw, John	Pvt.	A	33rd	AL.	Infantry	Wood		Lee	Personville
Bridges, J. J.		I	55th	GA.	Infantry		Hardee	TN.	Kosse
Briggs, L. M.		B	15th	TX.	Infantry				Kosse
Brooks, F.		K	Swet						Head's Prairie
Brooks, J. H.		E	19th	TX.	Infantry				Kosse
Brooks, T. W.		E	19th	TX.	Infantry				
Brooks, W. F.	2nd Sgt.	K	1st	TX.	Infantry	Hood	Whiting	Longstreet	Tehuacana
Browder, W. H.		A	1st	AL.	Cavalry				Groesbeck
Brown, J. M.	Pvt.	E	3rd	TX.	Cavalry	Green	Green	T-MS.	Mexia
Brown, J. P.	Capt.	K	12th	TX.	Cavalry	Parsons		T-MS.	Kosse
Brown, McN.			3rd	LA.	Cavalry	Cabell			Mt. Calm
Brown, W. P.	Capt.	K	20th	TX.	Dis. Cav.	Maxey	Hindman		Groesbeck
Bryan, E.		C	Gurley	TX.	Cavalry	Law		T-MS.	Mt. Calm
Bryant, R. J.	Sgt.	B	Speight's	TX.	Infantry	Waul		T-MS.	Mexia
Bryant, Thomas	2nd Sgt.	B	60th	AL.	Infantry	Gracie		T-MS.	Horn Hill
Bryant, W. M. C.		A	9th	VA.	Cavalry	W. H. F. Lee	Walker	TN.	Point Enterprise
Buckner, W. A.	2nd Lt.	B	11th	TN.	Cavalry	Forrest		Stuart	Mexia
Bugg, J. R.		C	18th	TX.	Cavalry			N. VA.	Mt. Calm
Burditt, W. R.		H	8th	TX.	Cavalry	Harrison	Wharton	TN.	Big Hill
Burney, Thomas	Pvt.	C	15th	TX.	Cavalry		Holmes	Wheeler	Honest Ridge
Burney, W. A.		F	Owens' Batty	ARK.	Det. Ser.				Armour
Butler, J. E.		McNelly	Scouts	TX.	Cavalry	Horton	Green	T-MS.	Mt. Calm
Butrall, T. E.	Pvt.	A	Steven's	ARK.	Cavalry	Pike	Holmes	T-MS.	Head's Prairie
Byars, T. W.	2nd Lt.	C	2nd Battn	GA.		Wright	Mahone	Longstreet	Mexia
Calhoun, R. H.	Pvt.		Confuit's Batty	GA.	Lt. Arty	Cherokee	Stevenson	Hardee	Mexia
Camp, L. E.	Pvt.		8th	MS.	Cavalry				Mexia
Carpenter, G. W.		D	11th	MS.	Infantry				Farrar
Carpenter, W. L.	Pvt.	F	1st	TN.	Infantry	Archer	Heth	A. P. Hill	N. VA.
Cashion, A. J.	Capt.	H	Lewis	TX.	Infantry	Elmore			Mexia
Castellow, C. A.	Pvt.		17th	TX.	Cavalry				
Chandler, H. J.		I		TX.	Cavalry	Baylor			Farrar
Chatham, J. R.		E	4th	MO.		Clark	Marmaduke		Prairie Grove
Chisholm, D. H.			21st	MS.	Infantry	Humphreys	McLaws	Longstreet	Shiloh
Clanahan, James	Pvt.		Willis' Battery	TX.	Artillery	Waul		N. VA.	Mexia
Clark, M. H.	Pvt.	E	5th	SC	Infantry	Jenkins		TN.	Groesbeck
Cline, A. J.		D							Mt. Calm
Clinton, A. M.	Pvt.	A	38th	TN.	Infantry	Wright	Cheatham	Bragg	TN.	Mexia

ROSTER OF EX-CONFEDERATE VETERANS OF LIMESTONE COUNTY, TEXAS

Name	Rank	Co.	Regt.	State	Branch	Brigade	Division	Army	Town
Cockran, J. W.		E	6th	MS.	Cavalry				Kosse
Coker, W. M.			Taylor	TX.					Kosse
Collins, T. J.	Pvt.	A	7th	LA.	Infantry	Peck	Gordon	N. VA.	Honest Ridge
Collum, George	Pvt.	I	9th	TX.	Cavalry	Ross	W. H. Jackson		Armour
Cook, J. P.	Pvt.	B	30th	AL.	Infantry	Pettus	Stevenson	TN.	Mexia
Cooper, W. R.	Pvt.		47th	TN.	Infantry	Maney	Cheatham	TN.	Groesbeck
Cotton, S. M.	Pvt.	C	19th	ARK.	Infantry	Tappan	Churchill	TN.	Honest Ridge
Cox, A. J.		H	38th	AL.	Infantry	Holtzclaw		T-MS.	Mexia
Cox, M. B.		G	18th	AL.			Stewart	TN.	Prairie Grove
Crawford, F. M.	Pvt.	E	58th	AL.	Infantry	Holtzclaw	A. P. Stewart	TN.	Armour
Curry, W. E.	Pvt.	E	Baylor's	TX.	Cavalry	Lane	Hunt	T-MS.	Mexia
Davidson, J. M.	Pvt.	B	30th	MS.	Infantry	Walthall	Anderson	TN.	Hubbard City
Davis, J. I.	Pvt.	E	Baylor's	TX.	Cavalry	Lane	Green	T-MS.	Mexia
Davis, J. W.	Pvt.	K	10th	TX.	Cavalry	Cooper	Wharton	T-MS.	Forrest Glade
Davis, R. E.	Pvt.	C	1st	AL.	Legion	Gracie	B. R. Johnson	N. VA.	Armour
Transferred to		H	60th	AL.					
Davis, S. A.		A		ARK.	Infantry	Cabell			Big Hill
Davis, W. A.	Mus.	H	33rd	ARK.	Infantry	Tappan	Churchill	T-MS.	Hancock
Day, R. N.	Pvt.	F	55th	GA.				TN.	Horn Hill
Deis, J. M.	Pvt.		Sanders' Batty	MO.	Artillery	1st Missouri		TN.	Mexia
Doke, F. J.		F	9th	MO.	Infantry				Kosse
Douglass, P. O.	Pvt.	A	15th	ARK.	Infantry	Dockery	Churchill	T-MS.	Mart, McLennan Co.
Doyle, W. E.	Pvt.	G	7th	SC	Cavalry	Gary	Field	N. VA.	Mexia
Duncan, N. G.	Pvt.	G	10th	MS.	Infantry		Longstreet		Prairie Grove
Durham, C. A.	Pvt.	K	6th	SC	Cavalry	Hampton			Armour
Durham, F. M.	Pvt.	K	20th	TX.	Dis. Cav.	Maxey	Hindman	T-MS.	Headville
Durst, W. E.	Pvt.	A	5th	TX.	Infantry	Young	Walker	T-MS.	Prairie Grove
Dyer, J. G.					Artillery	Tappan	E. K. Smith		Prairie Grove
Eady, L.	1st Lt.	I	33rd	AL.	Infantry	Lowrey	Cleburne	TN.	Groesbeck
Ellison, Samuel	Pvt.	C	25th	AL.	Infantry	Deas	Withers	TN.	Prairie Hill
Elzy, F. M.	Pvt.	K	12th	LA.	Infantry	Scott	Loring	TN.	Honest Ridge
Erwin, J. C.	Pvt.	K	48th	AL.	Infantry	Taliaferro	Jackson	N. VA.	Elem Ridge
Ethridge, B. R.		B	7th	LA.	Infantry	Maxey	Longstreet		Mt. Calm
Eubanks, John	Pvt.	B	9th	MS.	Cavalry	Ferguson		TN.	Mexia
Evans, G. M. T.	Sgt.	B	5th	LA.	Infantry			T-MS.	Prairie Hill
Farmer, W. L.		D	34th			Anderson			Mexia
Farnsworth, W. T.	Pvt.	I	13th	TN.	Infantry	Vaughn	Cheatham	TN.	Armour
Farrar, T. J.		C	12th	TX.	Cavalry	Parsons		T-MS.	Groesbeck
Farrington, W. O.		K	15th	ARK.		Beale		TN.	Point Enterprise
Farrow, R. E.		C	28th	LA.		Mouton	Polignac		Armour
Fitzgerald, James M	Pvt.	A	2nd	LA.	Infantry	Hays	Jackson	N. VA.	Mexia
Flanagan, J. C.	Pvt.	E	9th	TN.	Infantry	Maney	Cheatham	TN.	Tehuacana
Flanagan, J. D.		E	7th	AL.	Cavalry				Prairie Hill
Foster, Moses W.	Pvt.	G	Hardeman	TX.	Cavalry				Kosse
Foster, S. C.	Pvt.	D	7th	MS.	Cavalry	Chalmers	Forrest	TN.	Mexia

ROSTER OF EX-CONFEDERATE VETERANS OF LIMESTONE COUNTY, TEXAS

Name	Rank	Co.	Unit	State	Branch	Brigade	Division	Corps/Army	Home
Franks, T. L.	Pvt.	F	10th	TX.	Cavalry	Cooper		Longstreet	T-MS.	Mexia
Frazier, W. D.	Pvt.	I	59th	AL.	Infantry	Gracie			N. VA.	Armour
Fullinwider, A. E.	Pvt.	I		TX.	Mtd. Infy	Hardeman		Magruder	T-MS.	Mexia
Fuqua, M. P.	Pvt.	B	22nd	ARK.	Infantry	Hawthorn	Churchill	E. K. Smith	T-MS.	Tehuacana
Furguson, W. H.		D	Elmon	TX.	Infantry					Kosse
Gardiner, H. J.		I	24th	MS.					TN.	Prairie Grove
Gatlin, T. S.		A	33rd	ARK.		Tappan			T-MS.	Point Enterprise
George, T.		E	10th	TX.	Cavalry	Parsons			T-MS.	Tehuacana
Gibson, T. J.	Pvt.	B	12th	GA.	Infantry	Doles	Ewell	T. J. Jackson	N. VA.	Mexia
Gilbert, B. F.	Pvt.	A	17th	TX.	Cavalry	Polignac	Walker	E. K. Smith	T-MS.	Mexia
Gilmore, R. D.	Pvt.	B	4th	TX.	Infantry	Hood	Ewell	T. J. Jackson	N. VA.	Thornton
Glass, A. P.		G	1st	MS.	Cavalry					Kosse
Glass, W. S.		B	20th	GA.						Personville
Gorden, James		A	38th	TN.		Wright	Cheatham			Armour
Graham, J. A.	Pvt.	I	31st	MS.	Infantry	Featherston	Loring	Stewart	TN.	Tehuacana
Graves, W. A.										Kosse
Gray, H. W.	Pvt.	D	37th	VA.	Infantry	Stewart/3rd		Jackson	N. VA.	Mexia
Gray, J. T. L.	Pvt.	A	33rd	TN.	Infantry	Strahl	Cheatham	Hardee	TN.	Mexia
Grice, Jacob	Scout	I	15th							Head's Prairie
Griffis, J. L.	Pvt.	C	24th	MS.	Infantry	Walthall	Withers	Polk	TN.	Kirk
Grover, J. S.	Pvt.	G	Madison	TX.	Cavalry	Law	Green		T-MS.	Mexia
Grooves, J. R.		C	15th	ARK.	Infantry					Honest Ridge
Grooves, J. S. [Rev.	Pvt.	E	15th	TX.	Infantry				T-MS.	
Groves, Noble	Pvt.	G	15th	ARK.	Infantry				TN.	Mexia
Guynes, J. F.	Pvt.	F	6th	MS.	Infantry					Mexia
Hall, J. C.		B	40th	AL.						Point Enterprise
Hamich, S. H.	Pvt.	K	15th	MS.	Infantry	Adams	Loring	A. P. Stewart	TN.	Groesbeck
Hammond, B. F.		D	20th	TX.	Infantry					Kosse
Hammond, D. P.		D	1st Batty	MS.						Kosse
Hammond, W. R.		K	12th	TX.	Cavalry					Kosse
Hamca, A. W.	Pvt.	F	22nd	TX.	Infantry	Waul	Walker		T-MS.	Kirk
Hancock, B. J.	Pvt.	I	19th	TX.	Cavalry	Parsons	Marmaduke		T-MS.	Mexia
Hardy, David	Capt.	G	28th	LA.	Infantry	Mouton	Polignac	Taylor	T-MS.	Prairie Hill
Harper, W. M.		G	Speight's	TX.	Scouts					Head's Prairie
Harrington, R.		H	20th	TX.	Infantry					Farrar
Harthcock, J. L.	Pvt.	C	15th	MS.	Infantry	Adams	Loring	Stewart	TN.	Mexia
Harvey, J. W.	Pvt.	F	38th	AL.	Infantry	Holtzclaw	Cheatham	Hood	TN.	Mexia
Hayes, A. J.		F	56th	GA.		Cumming				Armour
Henderson, N. G.		F	1st	TX.		McCulloch			T-MS.	Forest Glade
Henry, J. R.										Mexia
Henson, W. S.		D	Wood's	MS.		Adams				Mexia
Herring, E.	Sgt.	K	36th	AL.	Infantry	Clayton	Cheatham	Hardee	TN.	Mexia
Herring, E. R.		F	15th	TX.						Prairie Hill
Herring, M.		A	1st	AL.	Infantry		Johnson	Hood	TN.	Mexia
Herring, W. H.	2nd Sgt.	G	18th	AL.	Infantry	Holtzclaw	Clayton	Hardee	TN.	Prairie Grove

4

ROSTER OF EX-CONFEDERATE VETERANS OF LIMESTONE COUNTY, TEXAS

Name	Rank	Co.	Reg.	State	Branch	Commander	Army	Battles	Burial
Hicks,	Pvt.	F	20th	TX.					Honest Ridge
Hillyen, W. S.		B	27th	LA.					Mt. Calm
Hines, J. H.	Pvt.	E	31st	LA.	Infantry		Shoup	Johnston	TN. Prairie Grove
Hodges, B.		E	17th	AL.			Baldwin	Hardee	TN. Armour
Hollaway, G. W.	Pvt.	E	8th	TX.			Holtzclaw	A. P. Stewart	T-MS. Prairie Hill
Holloway, J. V.		A	7th	TX.	Infantry	Gregg			Mt. Calm
Holt, A. R. T.									Mexia
Hord, T. A.									Mexia
Howell, Robert		H	5th	TN.	Infantry	Featherston			Mt. Calm
Howze, J. G.	Pvt.	H	4th	SC	Cavalry	Butler	Hampton	Longstreet	N. VA. Groesbeck
Hughes, D. F.									Mexia
Hughes, S.		E	53rd	AL.	Cavalry	Roddey			Point Enterprise
Hughes, W. J.	Pvt.	G	28th	TX.	Cavalry	King	Walker		TN. Elem Ridge/Prairie Hill
Hughes, W. P.		G		TX.	Cavalry				T-MS. Mt. Calm
Hunt, David	Pvt.	F	16th Battn	GA.	Infantry				Shiloh
Hunt, Bennett	Pvt.	H	38th	AL.	Infantry	Clayton			Point Enterprise
Hunter, T. B.		G	12th	TX.	Cavalry				Big Hill
Hunter, T. R.	Col. Br.	G	12th	TX.	Cavalry	Parsons			Groesbeck
Ingram, John	Pvt.	G	13th	AL.	Infantry	Colquitt	Hill	Longstreet	N. VA. Mexia
Ingram, S. C.	Pvt.	B	13th	AL.	Infantry	Magruder		Johnston	N. VA. Mexia
Irwin, J. C.	Pvt.	R	48th	AL.	Infantry	Taliaferro	Hood	Longstreet	N. VA. Kirk
Jackson, F. M.	Pvt.	G	6th	TX.	Cavalry	Ross			T-MS. Groesbeck
Jackson, N. H.			13th	TX.	Cavalry				Mexia
Jackson, T. E.		I	7th	TX.	Cavalry				Groesbeck
Jennings, G. L.	Capt.	H	31st	MS.	Infantry	Featherston	Loring		TN. Honest Ridge
Johnson, D. C.	Pvt.	H	Alexander's	TX.	Infantry	Polignac	Mouton		T-MS. Forest Glade
Johnson, J. C.	Pvt.	A	4th	GA.	Infantry	Morgan	Allen	Wheeler	TN. Mexia
Johnson, J. G.		C	Hubbard's	TX.	Cavalry	Waul	Walker		T-MS. Prairie Hill
Johnson, Jas. R.		D	2nd	KY.	Infantry	Morgan			Mexia
Johnson, W. M.	Pvt.	A	32nd	TX.	Cavalry	Buchel	Dagley		T-MS. Thornton
Joiner, H. C.	O. Sgt.	E	19th	TX.	Infantry	Scurry	Walker	E. K. Smith	T-MS. Groesbeck
Jones, J. A.	Bugler	K	5th	NC	Cavalry	Barringer	A. P. Stewart	Hampton	N. VA. Kosse
Jones, N. M.	Sgt. Maj.	H	1st	NC	Infantry	Armistead	Hoke		N. VA. Kosse
Jourdan, E. J.		C	22nd	TX.	Infantry				Farrar
Jordan, G. L.		B	12th	TX.		Parsons	Green	Wharton	T-MS. Shiloh
Justice, William	Pvt.	B	10th	TX.	Infantry	Granbury	Cleburne	Hardee	TN. Personville
Kamsler, William	Pvt.	I	25th	TX.	Infantry	Harrison	Walker		T-MS. Mexia
Kaufman, M.	Capt.	B	45th	AL.	Infantry	Lowrey	Cleburne	Hardee	TN. Mexia
Keirbow, W. H.			2nd	GA.	Cavalry				Prairie Grove
Kemp, M. W.	1st Lt.	D	13th	AL.	Infantry	Archer	A. P. Hill	Jackson	N. VA. Mexia
Kendall, P. L.		C	8th	TX.					Armour
Kennedy, A. W.		F				Bradford		E. K. Smith	T-MS. Honest Ridge
Kenner, James	Pvt.	E	19th	AL.	Infantry	Scurry	Walker		Groesbeck
Kenney, G. W.		G	6th	TX.	Infantry	Battle	Rodes	Ewell	N. VA. Wortham
Kincaid, D. C.	Qr. Master								T-MS. Tehuacana

ROSTER OF EX-CONFEDERATE VETERANS OF LIMESTONE COUNTY, TEXAS

Name	Rank	Co.	Regt.	State	Branch	Brigade	Division	Army	Theater	Residence
Kirkpatrick, W. R.*	Ch. Eng.									Prairie Hill
Langston, J. M.	Pvt.	A	1st	FL.	Cavalry		Longstreet		N. VA.	Mexia
Lanning, S. R.		K	1st	TN.	Cavalry				T-MS.	Mexia
Lanning, W. D.	Pvt.	K	18th	AL.	Infantry	Holtzclaw				Mexia
Lansford, G. W.			10th	MS.	Infantry			State Service		Farrar
Le Noir, J. Y.	Pvt.	B	1st Batty	SC	Infantry					Horn Hill
Leach, H. A.	Pvt.	B	62nd	AL.	Infantry					Big Hill
Lee, G. W.	1st Lt.		Forrest	AL.	Cavalry					Groesbeck
Lee, Isaac		I	9th	TX.	Cavalry					Personville
Lester, H. E.				ARK.	Artillery	Tappan				Mt. Calm
Lewis, H.	Pvt.	G	24th	TX.	Cavalry	Granbury	Cleburne		TN.	Thornton
Lumday, W. C.			2nd	FL.	Artillery					Mt. Calm
Lindly, T. P.	Pvt.	C	20th	TX.	Infantry	Frost	Hindman		T-MS.	Tehuacana
Lindsay, W. H.	Pvt.	K	23rd	AL.	Infantry	Pettus	Stevenson	Lee	TN.	Mexia
Lindsley, J. T.										Tehuacana
Linebarger, J. M.	Pvt.	A	34th	ARK.	Infantry	Fagan			T-MS.	Horn Hill
Love, S. B.	Pvt.	G	6th	TX.	Cavalry	Ross	Jackson		TN.	Tehuacana
Loveutte, R. N.	2d Lt.	A	1st			McLaws		Longstreet	N. VA.	Calvert, Robertson Co.
Lowery, M. S. P.		K			Cavalry	Parsons				Head's Prairie
Mahoney, D. A.		A	60th	AL.	Infantry	Gracie			TN.	Point Enterprise
Mahoney, J. T.	Pvt.	E	1st	AL.	Infantry	Walthall			TN.	Mexia
McAnelly, G. W.		I	4th	TX.	Cavalry					Farrar
McCain, J. H.	Capt.	B	30th	AL.	Infantry	Pettus	Stevenson	Lee	N. VA.	Mexia
McCullough, Ben	Pvt.	D	Perrin's	MS.	Cavalry	Ferguson			TN.	Armour
McDonald, J. C.			20th	TX.						Prairie Grove
McDonald, J. E.	Pvt.	A	2nd	AL.	Cavalry	Ferguson	Wheeler		TN.	Prairie Hill
McDonald, M. L.	Pvt.	D	Wood's	MS.	Cavalry	Adams	Wheeler		TN.	Mexia
McKinney, J. W.	Cpl.	H.	55th	AL.	Infantry	Buford	Loring	Stewart	T-MS.	Billington
McPherson, Joseph		B	3rd	AL.	Cavalry					Groesbeck
Meeks, T. M.		D	New Orleans		Scouts					Kosse
Merrie, R. T.		C		TX.		Speight				Personville
Michard, J. S.	Cpl.	A	1st	VA.	Infantry	Huger			N. VA.	Mexia
Miller, J. L.		D		TX.	Infantry	Waterhouse		E. K. Smith	T-MS.	Mt. Calm/Mt. Antioch
Miller, J. M.		I	23rd	MS.						Mexia
Moffett, S. B.		E	2nd	TX.	Infantry					Big Hill
Monroe, S. S.		A	1st Batty	NC	H. Arty					Kosse
Montgomery, J. R.	Pvt.	F	4th	LA.	Cavalry	Harrison			T-MS.	Prairie Grove [Dead]
Moody, P.		B			Infantry					
Moody, J. N.		G	13th	AL.						Prairie Grove
Moody, N. R.	Pvt.	C	37th	MS.	Infantry	Martin	Maury	Price		Mexia
Moody, T.			3rd Battn			Hellian Legion			TN.	Personville
Moore, Jas.	Pvt.	K		TX.	Cavalry	Green	Walker		T-MS.	Forest Glade
Morgan, W. J.	Pvt.	A		TX.	Cavalry	Whitfield	Price		TN.	Tehuacana
Morris, H. T.		E	20th		Infantry					Groesbeck
Morrow, G. M.		K	36th	AL.						Shiloh

ROSTER OF EX-CONFEDERATE VETERANS OF LIMESTONE COUNTY, TEXAS

Name	Rank	Co.	Regt.	State	Branch	Brigade	Division	Corps/Army	Town
Morton, Z. T.	Pvt.	A	5th	GA.	Infantry	Cumming			Personville
Moss, J. W.		K	12th	TX.	Cavalry				Kosse
Mullins, J. H.		H	26th	AL.		Deas	Withers	TN.	Shiloh
Myers, R. E.		H	11th	GA.	Infantry				Kosse
Nash, J. W.	Pvt.		Styles'	VA.	H. Arty				Forest Glade
Nelson, A. J.		E	29th	AL.	Infantry	Cantey			Tehuacana
Nelson, T. J.	Pvt.	G	20th	AL.	Infantry				Personville
Newberry, W. W.		D	23rd	NC				N. VA.	Armour
Newcomb, E. T.		I	7th		Cavalry	A. P. Stewart			Mt. Calm/Mt. Antioch
Newton, J. S.		C	41st	MS.	Infantry				Kosse
Nickels, J. N.		C	10th	TX.	Cavalry	Parsons			Mt. Calm/Mt. Antioch
Norwood, T. A.		A	14th	LA.					Prairie Grove
O'Neal, R.		E	35th	TX.	Cavalry				Kosse
Oaks, G. W.		K	8th	AL.	Infantry				Personville
Oaks, J. D.		A	62nd	AL.					Personville
Oaks, J. M.	Pvt.	K	8th	AL.	Infantry				Personville
Outzs, B. F.	Asst. Surg.	I	2nd	SC		Hampton			Kosse
Owens, Sam		H	67th	AL.	Infantry	Scott	Loring	A. P. Stewart	Groesbeck
Palmer, J. W.		B	60th	GA.	Infantry	Gordon	Ewell	Jackson	Forest Glade
Parker, D. H.		K	53rd	AL.	Cavalry				Kosse
Parker, J. E.	Pvt.	I	3rd	AL.	Infantry	Battle	Rodes	Ewell	Mexia
Parker, J. F.*		B	3rd	LA.	Cavalry			N. VA.	Honest Ridge
Parten, J. G.		E	20th	GA.	Infantry				Kosse
Patterson, John	Pvt.	B	10th	TX.	Infantry	Granbury	Cleburne	Hardee	Groesbeck
Payne, J. S.**		A	16th	TX.	Infantry		Walker		Bonner
Payne, R. W.	Pvt.	H	12th	MS.	Cavalry	Ferguson	Jackson	Wheeler	Forest Glade
Perkins, S. P.									Armour
Persons, L. R.		F	15th	TX.	Infantry				Personville
Pitt, R. E.		H	3rd	KY.	Infantry				Kosse
Pleasant, J. L.		H	2nd	TX.	Cavalry				Groesbeck
Poindexter, J. K. P.		H	9th	TX.	Cavalry				Kosse
Polk, E. D.	Capt.	B	4th	TN.	Infantry	Maney	Cheatham	Polk	Kosse
Pope, E. D.		B	21st	TN.	Cavalry				Kosse
Powell, J. G.	Pvt.	K	35th	TX.	Cavalry	Buchel	Green	Early	Mexia
Powell, W. L.	Pvt.	F	9th	LA.	Infantry	Hays	Gordon		Hubbard City
Price, J. E.		E	35th	TX.	Cavalry	Terrill	Bagby	Horton	Kosse
Prichard, G. M. D.		G	9th	TX.				T-MS.	Prairie Grove
Prince, J. H.	Pvt.	C	10th	GA.	Infantry	Simms	McLaws	Longstreet	Armour
Pringle, A. K.		I	37th	MS.	Infantry			N. VA.	Kosse
Rambo, J. M.	O. Sgt.	F	9th	MS.	Cavalry	Ferguson	Wheeler	Jackson	Personville
Rambo, W. L.		E	8th	MS.	Infantry				Farrar
Ramsey, J. B.		A	1st	NC	Cavalry	Hill			Mt. Calm/Mt. Antioch
Raseo, Jno.	Pvt.	B	20th	TX.	Cavalry	Cooper		T-MS.	Thornton
Ratliff, C. C.	Sgt.	A	19th	TX.	Cavalry	Parsons			Honest Ridge
Richardson, J. A. T.	Pvt.	H	1st	TN.	Infantry	Maney	Cheatham	Polk	Tehuacana

ROSTER OF EX-CONFEDERATE VETERANS OF LIMESTONE COUNTY, TEXAS

Name	Rank	Co.	Regt.	State	Branch	Brigade	Division	Corps	Army	Residence
Richardson, S. H.		I	1st Conf Battn	VA	Infantry	Johnson	F. Lee	Hampton	N. VA.	Kosse
Richardson, Wm. H.	1st Lt.	F	12th	MD	Cavalry	Johnson	F. Lee	Hampton	N. VA.	Mexia
Richardson, W. H.	1st Lt.	F	2nd	AL.		Clayton	Cheatham	Hardee	TN.	Mexia
Riddle, J. E.	Pvt.	B	36th	MS.						Elem Ridge
Rivers, N. P.		B	3rd	AL.	Infantry	Johnson	Walker			Personville
Roberts, H. W.		L	16th	AL.						Mexia/Mt. Calm
Roberts, J. J.		A	42nd	TX.	Cavalry	Green				Armour
Roberts, W. G.		F	7th	TX.						Mt. Calm/Mt. Antioch
Rodgers, M. C.		K	20th	TX.	Dis. Cav.	Maxey	Hindman			Prairie Grove
Rogers, A. J.	Sgt.	K	20th	TX.	Infantry	Granbury	Cleburne	Hardee	TN.	Personville
Rogers, M. C.	Pvt.	F	10th	TX.	Infantry	Forney	Walker		T-MS.	Prairie Grove
Rogers, M. L.	Pvt.	K	22nd	TX.	Infantry	Ector	Cheatham	Polk	TN.	Tehuacana
Rogers, R.	Pvt.	I	9th	TX.						Marlin, Falls Co.
Roper, W. M.		I	4th	TX.						Honest Ridge
Ross, G. W.	Pvt.	H	4th	MO.	Cavalry	Cockrell	French	Polk	TN.	Mexia
Rucker, H. P.	Pvt.	D	12th	KY.	Cavalry	Forrest	Wheeler		TN.	Groesbeck
Ruff, J. W.	Sgt.	G	36th	MS.	Infantry	Anderson	French	A. P. Stewart		Mexia
Sanders, R. E.	Capt.	E	19th	TX.	Cavalry					Tehuacana
Sanders, T. F.		A	27th	ARK.		McLaws				Honest Ridge
Sanders, W. M.		E	1st	LA.						Honest Ridge
Sandifer, J. S.		H	12th	ARK.						Personville
Sawyer, J. P.	Pvt.	D	12th	MS.	Cavalry	Ferguson	Wheeler	Polk	TN.	Mexia
Scarborough, S. R.	Pvt.	K	40th	MS.	Infantry	Featherston	Loring		TN.	Forest Glade
Scott, A. V.		C	44th	AL.	Infantry	McLaws	Field	Longstreet	N. VA.	Wortham
Scroggin, M.*		E	46th	GA.						Honest Ridge
Sellers, T. M.	Pvt.	I	3rd	AL.	Cavalry	Morgan	Allen	Wheeler	TN.	Thornton
Shaffer, G. H.		K	36th	MS.	Infantry	Sears				Mt. Calm/Mt. Antioch
Shead, C. B.		A	7th	TX.	Infantry	Grigg				Mt. Calm/Mt. Antioch
Shell, C. C.		G	8th	AL.						Personville
Shilling, C. T.		I		LA.						Mt. Calm/Mt. Antioch
Shriver, Adair	Pvt.	D	Richmond Batty	LA.	Artillery	Adams	Anderson	A. P. Hill	N. VA.	Elem Ridge
Simmons, H. F.	Pvt.	E	Wood's	MS.	Cavalry	Walthall	Johnson	Lee	N. VA.	Mexia
Simmons, J. W.	Pvt.	C	27th	MS.	Infantry		Johnson	Lee	N. VA.	Mexia
Sims, B. R.		A	40th	MS.						Prairie Grove
Sims, J. R.	2nd Lt.	E	8th	MS.	Infantry	Lowrey	Cleburne	Hardee	TN.	Personville
Skillern, T. W.	Pvt.	C	36th	ARK.	Infantry	McRae	Churchill	Price	T-MS.	Frosa
Skruggs, S. K.		C	8th	TX.						Mexia
Sloan, A. J.		E	Flannagan's	AL.		McNair	Walker	Bragg	TN.	Tehuacana
Smith, Alex*		I	Young's	TX.						Shiloh
Smith, J. B.		I	30th	AL.						Big Hill
Smythe, E. B.	Pvt.		7th	TX.	Cavalry	Sibley				Mexia
Squyres, A. S.	Pvt.			TX.	Cavalry	Shelby				Thornton
Stafford, G. F.				AL.						Armour
Stanford, J. T.		G	27th	AL.	Infantry					Point Enterprise
Stanford, David	Pvt.					Home Guards				Mexia

ROSTER OF EX-CONFEDERATE VETERANS OF LIMESTONE COUNTY, TEXAS

Name	Rank	Co.	Regt.	State	Branch	Brigade	Division	Dept.	Residence
Stanford, L. A.	Pvt.	B							Mexia
Starkey, J.		A	Shaver's	AL.					Kosse
Steele, Rado	Pvt.			ARK.					Forest Glade
Stephens, B. C.		D	10th	TX.	Infantry	Granbury	Cleburne	TN.	Prairie Grove
Stephens, W. M.		H	4th	TN.		Hardee			Kosse
Stewart, F. M.			51st	AL.	Cavalry				Honest Ridge
Stewart, W. O.			28th	TX.					Forest Glade
Stitt, J. T.	Pvt.	E	17th	AL.	Infantry	Slaughter		TN.	Mexia
Storey, J. M.	O. Sgt.	H	28th	TX.	Infantry	Randal	Walker	T-MS.	Mexia
Strahorn, F. B.		D	3rd	ARK.		Cabell	Fagan	T-MS.	Groesbeck
Sturdivant, J. H.	Pvt.	G	38th	TN.	Infantry		Cheatham	TN.	Mexia
Suttle, J. M.	1st Sgt.	H	23rd	GA.	Infantry	Colquitt	Hoke	N. VA.	Tehuacana
Tackett, C. V.	Pvt.	C	3rd	LA.	Cavalry				Honest Ridge
Taylor, J. L.	Pvt.	A	7th	TX.	Infantry	Granbury	Cleburne	TN.	Hubbard City
Teakell, J. S.		G	2nd	AL.	Cavalry	Ferguson			Mt. Calm/Mt. Antioch
Thomas, G. I.		G	42nd	TN.	Infantry				Farrar
Thomas, J. W.	Cpl.	H	43rd	NC	Infantry	Daniel	Rodes	N. VA.	Tehuacana
Thompson, J. B.		I	18th	AL.					Mexia
Thompson, J. W.		C	4th	AL.		Law		N. VA.	Groesbeck
Thompson, L. E.	Pvt.	B	3rd	MO.	Cavalry	Marmaduke	Hood		Thornton
Tiles, C. E.			20th	TX.	Infantry		Price	T-MS.	Farrar
Trammell, F. E.	Capt.	B	17th	ARK.	Infantry	Hubbard	Van Dorn		Armour
Tribble, B. F.				TX.	Cavalry				Kosse
Tucker, M. A.	Sgt. Major	F	15th	TX.	Infantry	Granbury	Cleburne	TN.	Horn Hill
Tucker, M. T.	Pvt.	G	8th	TX.	Infantry	Waul	Walker		Thornton
Turner, B. W.		E	30th	AL.	Infantry	Pettus	Stevenson		Shiloh
Turner, G. W.	Sgt.	I	28th	TX.		Randal	Walker		
Ushe,									
Usry, B. M. F.			15th	GA.	Cavalry	Deshler		T-MS.	Groesbeck
Vickers, J. H.	Cpl.	E	9th	LA.	Infantry	Moore	Smith	Militia	Groesbeck
Vinson, G. B.	Col.	A	2nd	GA.	Infantry	Wofford	Jackson	N. VA.	Mexia
Wacaster, G. W.	Pvt.	H	24th	TX.	Infantry		McLaws	N. VA.	Prairie Grove
Wade, T. W.			20th		Cavalry		Longstreet		Thornton
Wait, G. D.			Wood's		Cavalry				Tehuacana
Walker, L. D.	Pvt.	B	10th	TX.	Infantry	Bee	E. K. Smith	T-MS.	Groesbeck
Walker, S. S.	Pvt.	I	2nd	TX.	Cavalry	Granbury	Cleburne	TN.	Groesbeck
Wallace, B. F.	Pvt.	F	15th	TX.	Cavalry	Stone	Major	T-MS.	Groesbeck
Wallace, J. D.		F	23rd	MS.	Infantry	Granbury	Cleburne	TN.	Armour
Waller, N. L.									Kosse
Walling, J. G.	Pvt.	C	15th	TX.	Infantry	Polignac	Mouton	T-MS.	Mexia
Ward, J. J.		K	Terry's	TX.	Cavalry				Thornton
Ward, R. P.	Pvt.	F	12th	TX.	Cavalry	Parsons			Mexia
Ward, W. J.	Pvt.	D	7th	SC	Cavalry	Gary	Lee	N. VA.	Honest Ridge
Washam, M. L.	Pvt.	G	5th	TX.	Cavalry	Green		T-MS.	Tehuacana
Watkins, R. L.		G	12th	TX.	Cavalry	Parsons	Walker	T-MS.	Tehuacana

ROSTER OF EX-CONFEDERATE VETERANS OF LIMESTONE COUNTY, TEXAS

Name	Rank	Co.	Regt.	State	Branch	Brigade	Division	Corps	Army	Town
Watson, C. L.	2nd Sgt.	D	10th	TX.	Infantry	Granbury	Cleburne	Hardee	TN.	Mexia
Watson, W. A.	Pvt.	A	4th	TX.	Infantry	Hood	Field	Longstreet	N. VA.	Groesbeck
Webb, J. C.	Sgt.	K	20th	TX.	Infantry	Maxey	Hindman			Honest Ridge
Webb, Jacob	Pvt.	B	10th	TX.	Infantry	Granbury	Cleburne	Hardee	TN.	Groesbeck/Thornton
White, J. B.	Pvt.	A	Johnson's	TX.	Cavalry				T-MS.	Mexia
Wilder, J. L.	2nd Sgt.	K	2nd	LA.	Infantry	Stafford	Walker	Jackson	T-MS.	Mexia
Wilder, V. S.	Pvt.	E	29th	AL.	Infantry		Johnson	Johnson	TN.	Groesbeck
Wilder, W. M.	Pvt.	B	10th	TX.	Infantry	Granbury	Cleburne	Hardee	TN.	Cade, Navarro Co.
Williams, D. C.	Pvt.	C	16th	TX.	Infantry	Gibson		Hardee	TN.	Prairie Grove
Williams, E. W.	Pvt.	C	3rd	TX.	Cavalry	Ross	Jackson	Hardee	TN.	Tehuacana
Williams, H. W.	Pvt.	C	36th	NC	H. Arty	Post Duty		Ft. Fisher, N.C.		Mexia
Wilson, David		C				Parsons				Head's Prairie
Wilson, T. M.		A	16th	NC	Infantry					Kosse
Wood, Arthur	3rd Sgt.	D	20th	TX.	Cavalry	Granbury	Cleburne	Hardee	TN.	Kosse
Wood, C. H. F.	2nd Sgt.	F	15th	TX.	Cavalry	Granbury	Cleburne	Hardee	TN.	Point Enterprise
Wood, Ira E.		F	15th	TX.	Dis. Cav.	Wheeler				Tehuacana
Wood, J. H.		C	Lewis Battn							Kosse
Wood, W. O.	Pvt.		Reserves	ARK.			Cobb	E. K. Smith	T-MS.	Mexia
Wootan, W. S.		G		GA.						Mexia
Word, G. M.	Pvt.	McAnally	Scouts							Mexia
Wright, J. H.	Pvt.	I	2nd	ARK.	Infantry	Govan	Cleburne	Hardee	TN.	Wortham
Wright, Joel J/T.		B	20th	TX.	Cavalry	Speight				Mt. Calm/Mt. Antioch
Wright, W. Z.		D	8th	ARK.	Cavalry	McRae				Mt. Calm/Mt. Antioch
Wright, Z. T.	Pvt.	F	31st	AL.	Infantry	Pettus	Stevenson	Hood	TN.	Mexia
Wylie, Oscar		K	5th	AL.	Infantry	Rodes				Groesbeck
Yates, M. D.		F	49th	TN.						Honest Ridge

ROSTER OF EX-CONFEDERATE VETERANS OF LIMESTONE COUNTY, TEXAS

AUGUST 1, 1890

NAMES	RANK	CO.	REGT.	STATE	SERVICE	BRIGADE	DIVISION	CORPS	ARMY OF	POST OFFICE
Adkinson, T. H.	Pvt.	E	38th	AL.	Infantry	Holtzclaw	Clayton	Hood	TN.	Mexia
Anderson, T. M.	Mus.	I	82nd	TX.	Cavalry		Hindman		TN.	Frosa
Anglin, J. C.	Pvt.			TX.	Cavalry	Ind. Scouts	Green		T-MS.	Groesbeck
Anglin, John	Pvt.			TX.	Cavalry	Ind. Scouts	Green		T-MS.	Groesbeck
Archibald, E. L.	Pvt.	B	Rucker's	MS.	Cavalry	Rucker	Chalmers		TN.	Groesbeck
Barton, W. M.	Pvt.	E	13th		H. Arty				N. VA.	Mexia
Batchelor, T. J.	Pvt.	E	62nd	AL.	Infantry	Thomas			T-MS.	Horn Hill
Bates, C. S.	1st Sgt.	?	20th	TX.	Cavalry	Maxey		E. K. Smith	T-MS.	Mexia
Bell, J. M.	Pvt.	A	6th	AL.	Infantry	Battle	Rodes	Ewell	N. VA.	Horn Hill
Berryman, H. C.	Pvt.	H	20th	GA.	Infantry	Elmore			T-MS.	Prairie Grove
Bower C. J.	Pvt.	C	8th	TX.	Infantry	Young	Walker	E. K. Smith	T-MS.	Mexia
Boyd, H. A.	1st Lt.	E	35th	TX.	Cavalry	Bee	Walker	E. K. Smith	T-MS.	Tehuacana
Boykin, W. P.	Pvt.	K	1st	TX.	Artillery		Magruder	E. K. Smith	T-MS.	Mexia
Bradford, C. M.	Pvt.	D	20th	TX.	Infantry		Magruder		T-MS.	Groesbeck
Bradshaw, John	Pvt.	A	33rd	AL.	Infantry	Harrison			T-MS.	Personville
Brooks, W. F.	2nd Sgt.	K	1st	TX.	Infantry	Wood	Whiting	Hardee	TN.	Tehuacana
Brown, J. M.	Pvt.	E	3rd	TX.	Cavalry	Hood		Longstreet	N. VA.	Mexia
Brown, W. P.	Capt.	K	20th	TX.	Dis. Cav.	Green			T-MS.	Groesbeck
Bryant, R. J.	Sgt.	B		TX.	Infantry	Maxey	Hindman		T-MS.	Mexia
Bryant, Thomas	2nd Sgt.	B	Speight's	TX.	Infantry	Waul				Horn Hill
Buckner, W. A.	2nd Lt.	B	9th	VA.	Cavalry	W. H. F. Lee	Bee	A. P. Stewart	T-MS.	Mexia
Byars, T. W.	2nd Lt.	A	Steven's	ARK.	Cavalry	Pike	Holmes		N. VA.	Mexia
Calhoun, R. H.	Pvt.	C	2nd	GA.	Infantry	Wright	Mahone	Longstreet	T-MS.	Mexia
Camp, L. E.	Pvt.		Confuit's Batty	GA.	Artillery		Stevenson	Hardee	N. VA.	Mexia
Cashion, A. J.	Capt.	A	1st	TN.	Infantry	Archer	Heth	Hill	TN.	Mexia
Clanahan, James	Pvt.	I	21st	MS.	Infantry	Humphreys	McLaws	Longstreet	N. VA.	Mexia
Clinton, A. M.	Pvt.	A	38th	TN.	Infantry	Wright	Cheatham	Bragg	N. VA.	Mexia
Collum, George	Pvt.	I	9th	TX.	Cavalry	Ross	Jackson		TN.	Armour
Cook, J. P.	Pvt.	B	30th	AL.	Infantry	Pettus	Stevenson	Lee	TN.	Mexia
Cooper, W. R.	Pvt.		47th	TN.	Infantry	Maney	Cheatham	Lee		Groesbeck
Cotton, S. M.	Pvt.		19th	ARK.	Infantry	Tappan	Churchill	Bragg	T-MS.	Horn Hill
Cox, A. J.	Pvt.	H	38th	AL.	Infantry	Holtzclaw		Price	TN.	Mexia
Curry, W. E.	Pvt.	E	Baylor's	TX.	Cavalry	Walthall	Green	Stewart	T-MS.	Mexia
Davidson, J. M.	Pvt.	B	30th	MS.	Infantry	Lane	Anderson	Polk	TN.	Hubbard City
Davis, J. I.	Pvt.	E	Baylor's	TX.	Cavalry	Lane	Green		T-MS.	Mexia
Davis, J. W.	Pvt.	K	10th	TX.	Cavalry	Cooper	Gano		T-MS.	Mexia
Davis, W. A.	Mus.	H	33rd	ARK.	Infantry	Tappan	Churchill	E. K. Smith	T-MS.	Hancock
Day, R. M.	Pvt.	F	55th	GA.	Infantry				TN.	Horn Hill
Deis, J. M.	Pvt.			MO.	Artillery	1st Missouri	Price	Hardee	TN.	Mexia
Doyle, W. E.	Pvt.	G	7th	SC	Cavalry	Gary	Field	Longstreet	N. VA.	Mexia

ROSTER OF EX-CONFEDERATE VETERANS OF LIMESTONE COUNTY, TEXAS

Name	Rank	Co.	Regt.	State	Branch	Brigade	Division	Army	Residence
Durham, F. M.	Pvt.	K	20th	TX.	Dis. Cav.	Maxey	Hindman	T-MS.	Headville
Durst, W. E.	Pvt.	A	5th	TX.	Infantry	Young	Walker	T-MS.	Mexia
Eady, L.	1st Lt.	I	33rd	AL.	Infantry	Lowrey	Cleburne	TN.	Groesbeck
Eubanks, John	Pvt.	B	9th	MS.	Cavalry	Ferguson	Jackson	TN.	Mexia
Farnsworth, W. T.	Pvt.	I	13th	TN.	Infantry	Vaughn	Cheatham	TN.	Armour
Fitzgerald, James	Pvt.	A	2nd	LA.	Infantry	Hays		N. VA.	Mexia
Flanagan, J. C.	Pvt.	E	9th	TN.	Infantry	Massa	Cheatham	TN.	Tehuacana
Foster, S. C.	Pvt.	D	7th	MS.	Cavalry	Chalmers	Forrest	TN.	Mexia
Franks, T. L.	Pvt.	F	10th	TX.	Cavalry	Cooper		T-MS.	Mexia
Frazier, W. D.	Pvt.	I	59th	AL.	Infantry	Gracie	Longstreet	N. VA.	Armour
Fullinwider, A. E.	Pvt.	I		TX.	Mtd. Infy	Hardeman	Magruder	T-MS.	Mexia
Fuqua, M. P.	Pvt.	B	22nd	ARK.	Infantry	Hawthorn	Churchill	E. K. Smith	Tehuacana
Gibson, T. J.	Pvt.	B	12th	GA.	Infantry	Doles	Ewell	N. VA.	Mexia
Gilbert, B. F.	Pvt.	A	17th	TX.	Cavalry	Polignac	Walker	T-MS.	Mexia
Gilmore, R. D.	Pvt.	B	4th	TX.	Infantry	Hood	Ewell	N. VA.	Thornton
Gray, H. W.	Pvt.	D	37th	VA	Infantry	Stewart	Johnson	N. VA.	Mexia
Gray, J. I. L.	Pvt.	A	33rd	TN.	Infantry	Strahl	Cheatham	TN.	Mexia
Groves, Noble	Pvt.	G	15th	ARK.	Infantry		Hardee	TN.	Mexia
Hamich, S. H.	Pvt.	K	15th	MS.	Infantry	Adams	Loring	TN.	Groesbeck
Hancock, B. J.	Pvt.	I	19th	TX.	Cavalry	Parsons		TN.	Mexia
Harthcock, J. L.	Pvt.	C	15th	MS.	Infantry	Adams	Loring	T-MS.	Mexia
Harvey, J. W.	Pvt.	F	38th	AL.	Infantry	Holtzclaw	Hood	TN.	Mexia
Herring, E.	Sgt.	K	36th	AL.	Infantry	Clayton	Cheatham	TN.	Mexia
Herring, W. H.	2nd Sgt.	G	18th	AL.	Infantry	Holtzclaw	Clayton	TN.	Prairie Grove
Ingram, John	Pvt.	G	13th	AL.	Infantry	Colquitt	Hill	N. VA.	Mexia
Ingram, S. C.	Pvt.	B	13th	AL.	Infantry	Magruder	Johnston	N. VA.	Mexia
Irwin, J. C.	Pvt.	K	48th	AL.	Infantry	Taliaferro	Hood	N. VA.	Kirk
Jackson, F. M.	Pvt.	G	6th	TX.	Cavalry	Ross		T-MS.	Groesbeck
Johnson, J. C.	Pvt.	A	4th	GA.	Cavalry	Morgan	Allen	TN.	Mexia
Johnson, W. M.	Pvt.	A	32nd	TX.	Cavalry	Buchel	Dagley	T-MS.	Thornton
Joiner, H. C.	Sgt.	E	19th	TX.	Infantry	Scurry	Walker	T-MS.	Groesbeck
Jones, J. A.	Bugler	K	5th	NC	Cavalry	Barringer	Stuart	N. VA.	Kosse
Jones, N. M.	Sgt. Major		1st	NC	Infantry	Armstrong	Hoke	N. VA.	Kosse
Kaufman, M.	Capt.	B	45th	AL.	Infantry	Lowrey	Cleburne	TN.	Mexia
Kemp, M. W.	1st Lt.	D	13th	AL.	Infantry	Archer	A. P. Hill	N. VA.	Mexia
Kenney, G. W.	Pvt.	G	6th	AL.	Infantry	Battle	Rodes	N. VA.	Wortham
Kincaid, D. C.	Qr. Master			TX.				T-MS.	Tehuacana
Le Noir, J. Y.	Pvt.	B	1st Battn	SC			State Service		Horn Hill
Lewis, H.	Pvt.	G	24th	TX.	Cavalry	Granbury	Cleburne	TN.	Thornton
Lindly, T. P.	Pvt.	C	20th	TX.	Infantry	Frost	Hindman	T-MS.	Wortham
Lindsay, W. H.	Pvt.	K	23rd	AL.	Infantry	Pettus	Stevenson	TN.	Mexia
Linebarger, J. M.	Pvt.	A	34th	ARK.	Infantry	Fagan		Lee	T-MS.	Horn Hill
Love, R. M.	Pvt.	G	6th	TX.	Cavalry	Ross	Jackson	TN.	Groesbeck
Love, S. B.	Pvt.	G	6th	TX.	Cavalry	Ross	Jackson	TN.	Tehuacana
Mahoney, S. T.	Pvt.	E	1st	AL.	Infantry	Walthall		TN.	Mexia

ROSTER OF EX-CONFEDERATE VETERANS OF LIMESTONE COUNTY, TEXAS

Name	Rank	Co.	Reg.	Branch	Brigade	Division	State	Town
McDonald, J. E.	Pvt.	A	2nd	Cavalry	Ferguson	Wheeler	AL.	TN.	Prairie Hill
McDonald, M. L.	Pvt.	D	Wood's	Cavalry	Adams	Wheeler	MS.	TN.	Mexia
McKinney, J. W.	Cpl.	H	55th	Infantry	Buford	Loring	AL.	T-MS.	Billington
Montgomery, J. R.*	Pvt.	F	4th	Cavalry	Harrison	Stewart	LA.	T-MS.	Prairie Grove
Moody, N. R.	Pvt.	C	37th	Infantry	Martin	Price	MS.	TN.	Mexia
Morgan, W. I.	Pvt.	A		Cavalry	Whitfield	Maury	TX.	TN.	Tehuacana
Parker, J. E.	Pvt.	I	3rd	Infantry	Battle	Rodes	AL.	N. VA.	Mexia
Patterson, John	Pvt.	B	10th	Infantry	Granbury	Cleburne	TX.	TN.	Groesbeck
Payne, R. W.	Pvt.	H	12th	Cavalry	Ferguson	Jackson	MS.	TN.	Mexia
Polk, E. D.	Capt.	B	4th	Infantry	Maney	Cheatham	TN.	TN.	Kosse
Powell, I. G.	Pvt.	K	35th	Cavalry	Buchel	Cheatham	TX.	TN.	Mexia
Powell, W. L.	Pvt.	F	9th	Infantry	Hays	Green	LA.	N. VA.	Hubbard City
Prince, J. H.	Pvt.	C	10th	Infantry	Simms	Gordon	GA.	N. VA.	Armour
Rambo, J. M.	O. Sgt.	F	9th	Infantry	Ferguson	McLaws	MS.	TN.	Personville
Raseo, Jno.	Pvt.	B	20th	Cavalry	Cooper	Jackson	TX.	T-MS.	Thornton
Richardson, J. A. T.	Pvt.	H	1st	Infantry	Maney	Cheatham	TN.	TN.	Tehuacana
Richardson, M. A.	1st Lt.	F	2nd	Cavalry	Johnson	F. Lee	MD.	N. VA.	Mexia
Rogers, M. C.	Pvt.	F	10th	Infantry	Granbury	Cleburne	TX.	TN.	Prairie Grove
Rogers, M. L.	Pvt.	K	22nd	Infantry	Forney	Walker	TX.		Tehuacana
Rogers, R.	Pvt.	I	9th	Infantry	Ector	Cheatham	TX.	TN.	Marlin
Ross, G. W.	Pvt.	H	4th	Cavalry	Cockrell	French	MO.	TN.	Mexia
Rucker, H. P.	Pvt.	D	12th	Cavalry	Forrest	Polk	KY.	TN.	Groesbeck
Sawyer, J. T.	Pvt.	D	12th	Cavalry	Ferguson	Wheeler	MS.	TN.	Mexia
Scarborough, S. R.	Pvt.	K	40th	Infantry	Featherston	Loring	MS.	TN.	Mexia
Sellers, F. M.	Pvt.	I	3rd	Cavalry	Morgan	Allen	AL.	TN.	Thornton
Simmons, J. W.	Pvt.	E	27th	Infantry	Walthall	Johnson	MS.	TN.	Mexia
Sims, J. R.	2nd Lt.	E	8th	Infantry	Lowrey	Cleburne	MS.	TN.	Personville
Skillern, T. W.	Pvt.	C	36th	Infantry	Gray	Churchill	ARK.	T-MS.	Frosa
Stanford, David	Pvt.			Infantry	Home Guards		AL.		Mexia
Stanford, T. A.	Pvt.			Infantry	Home Guards		AL.		Mexia
Steele, Rado	Pvt.	B	10th	Infantry	Granbury	Cleburne	TX.	TN.	Mexia
Stitt, J. T.	Pvt.	E	17th	Infantry	Slaughter	Hardee	AL.	TN.	Mexia
Storey, J. M.	Orderly	H	28th	Infantry	Randal	Walker	TX.	T-MS.	Mexia
Sturdivant, I. H.	Pvt.	G	38th	Infantry	Cheatham		TN.		Mexia
Suttle, J. M.	1st Sgt.	H	23rd	Infantry	Colquitt	Hoke	GA.	N. VA.	Tehuacana
Taylor, J. L.	Pvt.	A	7th	Infantry	Granbury	Cleburne	TX.	TN.	Hubbard City
Thomas, J. W.	Cpl.	H	43rd	Infantry	Daniel	Ewell	NC	N. VA.	Tehuacana
Thompson, L. E.	Pvt.	B	3rd	Cavalry	Marmaduke	Rodes	MO.	T-MS.	Thornton
Tidwell, D. K.	Pvt.	A	11th	Cavalry	Roddey	Marmaduke	AL.	TN.	Mart, McLennan Co.
Tubb, C. G.	Pvt.	G	12th	Infantry	Smith	Forrest	TX.	T-MS.	Mexia
Tucker, M. A.	Sgt. Major	F	15th	Infantry	Granbury	Magruder	TX.	TN.	Horn Hill
Vickers, J. H.	Cpl.	E	9th	Militia	Smith	Hardee	GA.	GA.	Mexia
Vinson, G. B.	Col.	A	2nd	Infantry	Jackson	Smith	LA.	N. VA.	Prairie Grove
Walker, L. D.	Pvt.	B	10th	Infantry	Moore	Jackson	TX.	TN.	Groesbeck
Walker, S. S.	Pvt.	I	2nd	Cavalry	Stone	Cleburne	TX.	T-MS.	Groesbeck
						Taylor			
						Major			

ROSTER OF EX-CONFEDERATE VETERANS OF LIMESTONE COUNTY, TEXAS

Wallace, S. F.	Pvt.	F	15th	TX.	Cavalry	Granbury	Cleburne	Hardee	TN.	Hancock
Walling, J. G.	Pvt.	C	15th	TX.	Infantry	Polignac	Mouton	Taylor	T-MS.	Thornton
Ward, R. P.	Pvt.	F	12th	TX.	Cavalry	Parsons			T-MS.	Mexia
Ward, W. J.	Pvt.	D	7th	SC	Cavalry	Gary			N. VA.	Tehuacana
Watly, M. B.	Pvt.	D	Clanton's	AL.	Cavalry	Hadson	Forrest		TN.	Prairie Hill
Watson, C. L.	2nd Sgt.	D	10th	TX.	Infantry	Granbury	Cleburne	Hardee	TN.	Mexia
White, J. B.	Pvt.		Johnson's	TX.	Cavalry				T-MS.	Mexia
Wilder, W. M.	Pvt.	B	10th	TX.	Infantry	Granbury	Cleburne	Hardee	TN.	Cade, Navarro Co.
Wiley, O.	1ST Sgt.	K	5th	AL.	Infantry	Rodes	Early	Jackson	N. VA.	Groesbeck
Williams, E. W.	Pvt.	C	3d	TX.	Cavalry	Ross	Jackson	Hardee	TN.	Tehuacana
Williams, H. W.	Pvt.	C	36th	NC	H. Arty	Ft. Duty		Ft. Fisher		Mexia
Wood, C. H. F.	3rd Sgt.	F	15th	TX.	Cavalry	Granbury	Cleburne	Hardee	TN.	Mexia
Wood, Ira	2nd Sgt.	F	15th	TX.	Dis. Cav.	Granbury	Cleburne	Hardee	TN.	Mexia
Wright, J. H.	Pvt.	I	2nd	ARK.	Infantry	Govan	Cleburne	Hardee	TN.	Wortham
Wright, Z. T.	Pvt.	F	31st	AL.	Infantry	Pettus	Stevenson	Hood	TN.	Mexia

* Dead

ROSTER OF EX-CONFEDERATE VETERANS OF LIMESTONE COUNTY, TEXAS

JULY 22, 1891

NAMES	RANK	CO.	REGT.	STATE	SERVICE	BRIGADE	DIVISION	CORPS	ARMY OF	POST OFFICE
Allen, Willie	Sgt.	K	Bass'	MS.	Infantry	Cooper	Steele		T-MS.	Kosse
Archibald, E. L.	Pvt.	B	Rucker's	TX.	Cavalry	Chalmers	Outlaw	Forrest	TN.	Groesbeck
Bailey, Ed	Pvt.	A	11th	MS.	Cavalry					Prairie Hill
Baisden, G. C.		B	10th	GA.	Cavalry	Gholson		Forrest	TN.	Groesbeck
Barkwell, W. E.	Pvt.	B	Anderson's	AL.	Artillery		Breckinridge	Hardee	TN.	Kirk
Bell, J. M.	1st Lt.	A	6th	VA.	Infantry	Rodes	A. P. Hill	Gordon	N. VA.	Horn Hill
Bolton, D. H.	Pvt.	H	10th	MO.	Infantry	Taliaferro	Jackson	Ewell	N. VA.	Prairie Hill
Brooks, W. T.	Capt.	I	22nd	TX.	Infantry	Early			TN.	Prairie Hill
Bryan, E. R.	Pvt.	G	6th	TX.	Cavalry	Ross	Hood		TN.	Prairie Hill
Burns, John	Pvt.	H	6th	TX.	Infantry	Granbury	Cleburne	Hardee	TN.	Groesbeck
Drinkard, A. M.	Pvt.	I	7th	LA.	Cavalry	Sibley			T-MS.	Kirk
Duke, W. H.	Pvt.	C	15th	MS.	Infantry	Gray	Polignac	Buckner	T-MS.	Prairie Hill
Dumis, R. M.	Pvt.	A	13th	TX.	Infantry	Ferguson	Loring	Stewart	TN.	Prairie Hill
Durst, W. E.	Pvt.	A	25th	AL.	Infantry	Young	Walker		T-MS.	Mexia
Ellison, Sam	Pvt.	C	12th	LA.	Infantry	Gordon	Withers	Hardee	TN.	Prairie Hill
Elzy, T. M.	Pvt.	A		LA.	Infantry	Scott	Loring	Hood	TN.	Horn Hill
Evans, G. M. T.	Sgt.	B	8th	LA.	Cavalry	Brint			T-MS.	Prairie Hill
Fontinott, E. T.	Pvt.	G	22nd	TX.	Cavalry	Gano			T-MS.	Prairie Hill
Foster, M. W.	Pvt.	G	1st	MS.	Artillery				T-MS.	Kirk
Garner, F. M.	Pvt.	B	9th	MS.	Cavalry	Ferguson			T-MS.	Prairie Hill
Gibson, H.	Pvt.	A	31st	MS.	Infantry	Featherston	Loring	A. P. Stewart	TN.	Mexia
Graham, W. A.	Pvt.	I	24th	MS.	Infantry	Walthall	Johnson	Lee	TN.	Kirk
Griffin, J. L.	Pvt.	C		MS.	Cavalry	Armstrong			TN.	Kirk
Griffin, T. H.	Pvt.	B		TX.	Cavalry	Lane	Green		T-MS.	Kirk
Groover, J. S.		G	16th	MS.	Infantry	Harris	Anderson	Hill	N. VA.	Mexia
Guy, W. J.	Pvt.	E	12th	TX.	Cavalry	Parsons	Couples		T-MS.	Groesbeck
Hancock, L. R.	Pvt.	B	28th	LA.	Infantry	Gray	Mouton	Taylor	T-MS.	Mexia
Hardy, David	Capt.	G	1st	TX.	Infantry	Fagan	Churchill		T-MS.	Prairie Hill
Harris, C. T.	Pvt.	G	Benevides'	TX.	Cavalry				T-MS.	Mexia
Henry, Wm.	Pvt.		Scouts	TX.	Cavalry				T-MS.	Mexia
Holladay, J. W.	Pvt.	B	8th	TX.	Infantry	Young	Walker	Hardee	TN.	Prairie Hill
Hollaway, G. W.	Pvt.	E	McCardle's	TX.	Infantry	Elmore		Magruder	T-MS.	Prairie Hill
Hooker, Robert	Pvt.	E	30th	TX.	Cavalry					Hubbard
Hughes, E. C.	Pvt.	A	38th	AL.	Infantry	Holtzclaw	Stewart	Hood	TN.	Prairie Hill
Hunt, Bennett	Pvt.	H	7th	AL.	Cavalry	Farris			T-MS.	Mexia
Jackson, J. G.	Pvt.	G	Scouts							Kirk
Jayne, A. A.		Harvey								
Jennings, G. L.	Capt.	H	31st	MS.	Infantry	Featherston	Loring	Hardee	TN.	Kirk
Johnston, C. W.	3rd Sgt.	H	11th	TX.	Infantry	Runnels	Walker		T-MS.	Buena Vista
Joiner, H. C.	Sgt.	E	19th	TX.	Infantry	Scurry	Walker		T-MS.	Groesbeck

15

ROSTER OF EX-CONFEDERATE VETERANS OF LIMESTONE COUNTY, TEXAS

Name	Rank	Co.	Regt.	State	Branch				State	Cemetery
Justice, Wm.	Pvt.	B	10th	TX.	Infantry	Granbury	Cleburne		TN.	Personville
Kemper, P. H.	Pvt.	B	8th	TN.	Cavalry	Morgan			TN.	Prairie Hill
Kirkpatric, V. R.	Major		Engineers						T-MS.	Prairie Hill
Little, W. H. H.	Pvt.	E		TX.	Artillery				T-MS.	Kirk
Loving, D. H.	Pvt.	A	52nd	VA.	Infantry	Pegram	Early	Jackson	N. VA.	Prairie Hill
Lumpkin, J. B.	Pvt.	E	8th	TX.	Infantry	Young	Walker		T-MS.	Kirk
Macom,				GA.		Cobb		Wooten		
McCullough, Ben	Pvt.	D	Perrin's	MS.	Cavalry	Ferguson			TN.	Armour
McDonald, J. E.	Pvt.	G	2nd	AL.	Cavalry	Ferguson	Jackson		TN.	Prairie Hill
McElroy, C. W.	Pvt.		Seldon's	AL.	Artillery					Kirk
McKinney, J. W.	Cpl.	H	55th	AL.	Infantry	Buford	Loring	A. P. Stewart	TN.	Prairie Hill
Michum, W. D.	Pvt.	E	28th	TX.	Infantry	Ferguson	Loring	A. P. Stewart	TN.	Prairie Hill
Morris, G. W.	Pvt.	E	4th	ARK.	Infantry	Runnels	McNair		TN.	Prairie Hill
Powers, W. A.	Pvt.			GA.	Infantry	McCoy			TN.	
Price, B. F.	Pvt.	E	8th	LA.				State Troops	T-MS.	Kirk
Reed, J. B.	Pvt.	E	8th	LA.				State Troops	T-MS.	Kirk
Reed, J. M.		F	5th	LA.		Hanson				
Riddle, J. E.	Pvt.	I	36th	AL.					TX.	Kirk
Shelton, W. A.	Pvt.	A		TX.	Cavalry					Prairie Hill
Shriver, A.			Donaldsonville		Artillery					
Steele, A. L.	Sgt.	F	15th	TX.	Infantry	Granbury	Cleburne	Hardee	N. VA.	Groesbeck
Stutesma, Oliver		E	5th	ARK.	Infantry	McRea	Hindman		TN.	Mexia
Swaim, R. H.	Pvt.	F	15th	TX.	Cavalry	Granbury	Cleburne	Hardee	T-MS.	Kirk
Swinney, W. B.	Pvt.	A	12th	MS.	Cavalry	Farris			TN.	Prairie Hill
Tipton, S. H.	Pvt.	F	15th	TX.	Cavalry	Granbury	Cleburne	Hardee	T-MS.	Prairie Hill
Trammell, F. E.	Capt.	B	17th	ARK.	Infantry	L. Hébert	Little	Price	TN.	Mexia
Watkins, R. L.	Pvt.	I	12th	TX.	Cavalry	Parsons			TN.	Armour
Whattley, W. B.	Pvt.	B	7th	AL.	Cavalry	Farris			T-MS.	Kirk

ROSTER OF EX-CONFEDERATE VETERANS OF LIMESTONE COUNTY, TEXAS

AUGUST 2 - 5, 1892

NAMES	RANK	CO.	REGT.	STATE	SERVICE	BRIGADE	DIVISION	CORPS	ARMY OF	POST OFFICE
Adair, Sam	Pvt.	C	10th	AL.	Infantry	Holtzclaw	Clayton	Hood	TN.	Big Hill
Adkinson, T. H.	Pvt.	E	38th	AL.	Cavalry	Maxey		E. K. Smith	T-MS.	Kosse
Allen, B. U.	Pvt.	K	20th	TX.	Infantry	Hood	Whiting	Longstreet	N. VA.	Oletha
Allison, A. B.	Pvt.	C	5th	TX.						Groesbeck
Anderson, Jas.	Pvt.									Groesbeck
Anderson, W. R.	Capt.	D	22nd	TX.	Infantry	Waul	Walker	E. K. Smith	T-MS.	Tehuacana
Anglin, J. A.	Pvt.	McNelly	Scouts	TX.	Cavalry	Green		E. K. Smith	T-MS.	Groesbeck
Anglin, J. C.	Pvt.	McNelly	Scouts	TX.	Cavalry	Green		E. K. Smith	T-MS.	Groesbeck
Archer, G. W.	Pvt.	C	8th	TX.	Cavalry	Wharton	Wheeler	Wheeler	TN.	Mexia
Archer, J. H.	Pvt.	F	36th	MS.		Sears				Billington
Armour, Jas.	Pvt.	C	Bradford's	TX.						Armour
Barry, J. M.	Pvt.	D	Willis'	TX.	Artillery	Waul	Walker	E. K. Smith	T-MS.	Mexia
Barton, W. M.	Pvt.	E	13th	NC	Artillery				T-MS.	Mexia
Batchelor, T. J.	Pvt.	E	62nd	AL.	Infantry	Thomas			N. VA.	Horn Hill
Bates, C. S.	1st Sgt.	K	20th	TX.	Dis. Cav.	Maxey	Hindman	E. K. Smith	T-MS.	Mexia
Beene, Obi	Sgt.	B	4th	MS.	Cavalry	Adams	Forrest		TN.	Luna, Freestone Co.
Bennett, E. G.	C. Sgt.	F	15th	TX.	Cavalry	Granbury	Cleburne	Hardee	TN.	Groesbeck
Bertymore, H. C.	Pvt.	H	20th	TX.	Infantry	Elmore			T-MS.	Prairie Grove
Bond, S. F.	Pvt.	G		TX.	Cavalry					Mexia
Booth, W. P.	Col. Br.	E	36th	ARK.	Infantry	McRae	Churchill	State Troops		Mexia
Bower, Chris	Pvt.	C	8th	TX.	Infantry	Young	Walker	E. K. Smith	T-MS.	Mexia
Bower, W. E.	Pvt.								T-MS.	Mexia
Boyd, H. A.	1st Lt.	E	35th	TX.	Cavalry	Bee	Walker	E. K. Smith	T-MS.	Tehuacana
Boykin, W. P.	Pvt.	K	1st	TX.	Artillery		Magruder	E. K. Smith	T-MS.	Hancock
Boyle, G. C.	Pvt.	C	2nd	MS.	Infantry	Law		Longstreet	N. VA.	Tehuacana
Bradshaw, J.	Pvt.	A	33rd	AL.	Infantry	Wood		Hardee	TN.	Personville
Browder, W. H.	Pvt.	A	1st	AL.	Cavalry	Allen	Johnson	Wheeler	TN.	Groesbeck
Brown, J. P.	Capt.	K	12th	TX.	Cavalry	Parsons	Green	Wharton	T-MS.	Kosse
Brown, W. P.	Capt.	K	20th	TX.	Dis. Cav.	Maxey	Hindman	E. K. Smith	T-MS.	Groesbeck
Bryan, E.	Pvt.	C	Gurley's	TX.	Cavalry	Gano		E. K. Smith	T-MS.	Hubbard City
Bryant, R. J.	Sgt.	B	9th	TX.	Infantry	Waul	Walker	E. K. Smith	T-MS.	Mexia
Buckner, W. A.	2nd Lt.	B	9th	VA.	Cavalry	W. H. F. Lee	Lee	Stuart	N. VA.	Mexia
Burgess, J. J.	Pvt.	H	20th	MS.	Infantry	Adams	Loring	Polk	TN.	Mexia
Burleson, A. J.	Pvt.	K	12th	TX.	Infantry	Parsons	Loring	Polk	TN.	Kosse
Burton, J. I.	Pvt.	A	2nd	TX.	Cavalry	Sibley	Green	E. K. Smith	T-MS.	Kosse
Calhoun, R. H.	Pvt.	C	2nd	GA.	Infantry	Wright	Mahone	Longstreet	N. VA.	Wortham
Camp, L. E.	Pvt.		Confuit's Batty	GA.	Artillery		Stevenson	Hardee	TN.	Mexia
Carleton, W. L.	Surgeon		2nd	ARK.	Infantry	McCulloch			TN.	Frosa
Carroll, J. G.	Pvt.	A	22nd	ARK.	Cavalry	Dockery	Walker	E. K. Smith	T-MS.	Mexia
Carruth, W. A.	Pvt.	F	11th	MS.	Infantry	Davis	Heth	A. P. Hill	N. VA.	Mexia

ROSTER OF EX-CONFEDERATE VETERANS OF LIMESTONE COUNTY, TEXAS

Name	Rank	Co.	Regt.	State	Branch	Brigade	Division	Corps	Army	Residence
Cashion, A. J.	Capt.	H	1st	TN.	Infantry	Archer	Heth	A. P. Hill	N. VA.	Wortham
Castleton, C. A.	Pvt.	C	9th	TX.						Inquire at Honest Ridge
Chambers, E. C.	Pvt.	Lewis	Elmore	TX.						Thornton
Clanahan, Jas.	Pvt.	I	21st	MS.	Infantry	Magruder	McLaws	Longstreet	N. VA.	Mexia
Clark, M. H.	Pvt.	E	Willis'	TX.	Infantry	Humphreys				Groesbeck
Coker, W. J.	Cpl.	E	7th	MS.	Infantry	Waul	French	Hardee	TN.	Mart, McLennan Co.
Collier, B. W.	Pvt.	I	7th	AL.	Cavalry	Sears	Forrest	Hood	TN.	Groesbeck
Collum, Geo.	Pvt.	I	9th	TX.	Cavalry	Rucker	Jackson		TN.	Armour
Cook, J. P.	Pvt.	B	30th	AL.	Infantry	Ross			TN.	Mexia
Cotton, S. M.	Pvt.		19th	ARK.	Infantry	Pettus	Stevenson	Lee	TN.	Horn Hill
Cox, A. J.	Pvt.	H	38th	AL.	Infantry	Tappan	Churchill	Price	T-MS.	Prairie Grove
Cox, M. P.	1st Sgt.	B	22nd	MO.	Infantry	Holtzclaw	A. P. Stewart	Hardee	TN.	Armour
Crawford, F. M.	Pvt.	E	32nd	AL.	Infantry		Breckinridge	Hardee	TN.	Armour
Curtis, W. J.	Pvt.	B	9th	GA.	Lt. Arty	Holtzclaw	A. P. Stewart	Hardee	TN.	Hancock
Dallis, S. F.	Pvt.	B	20th	TX.	Cavalry	Marshall	Buckner	Bragg	TN.	Battle, McLennan Co.
Davidson, J. M.	Pvt.	B	30th	MS.	Infantry	Broughton				
Davis, J. W.	Pvt.	K	10th	TX.	Cavalry	Walthall	Anderson	Polk	TN.	Navarro Co.
Davis, R. E.	Col. Br.	H	60th	AL.	Infantry	Cooper	Gano	E. K. Smith	T-MS.	Mexia
Davis, W. A.	Bugler	H	33rd	ARK.	Infantry	Gracie	B. R. Johnson	Longstreet	N. VA.	Armour
Deis, J. M.	Bugler		1st Missouri	MO.	Artillery	Tappan	Churchill	E. K. Smith	T-MS.	Hancock
Douglass, N. B.	Cpl.	A	15th	ARK.	Cavalry	1st Missouri	Price	Hardee	TN.	Mexia
Douglass, P. O.	Pvt.	C	15th	ARK.	Infantry	Dockery	Walker	E. K. Smith	T-MS.	Mart, McLennan Co.
Douglass, W. C.	Pvt.	G	2nd	TN.	Cavalry	Dockery	Churchill	E. K. Smith	T-MS.	Mart, McLennan Co.
Doyle, W. E.	Pvt.	C	7th	SC	Cavalry	Bell	Forrest		TN.	Mt. Calm
Duke, L. W. [Rev.]	Cpl.	K	5th	AL.	Infantry	Gary	Field	Longstreet	N. VA.	Mexia
Durham, C. A.	Pvt.	K	6th	SC	Cavalry	Battle	Rodes	Jackson	N. VA.	Mexia
Durham, F. M.	Pvt.	K	20th	TX.	Dis. Cav.	Butler	Hampton	Stewart	N. VA.	Armour
Durst, W. E.	Pvt.	A	5th	TX.	Infantry	Maxey	Hindman	E. K. Smith	T-MS.	Headville
Eady, L.	1st Lt.	I	33rd	AL.	Infantry	Young	Walker	E. K. Smith	T-MS.	Mexia
East, Elias	Pvt.	I	13th	AL.	Infantry	Lowrey	Cleburne	Hardee	TN.	Groesbeck
Ellison, Sam	Pvt.	C	25th	AL.	Infantry	Archer				Armour
Elzy, F. M.	Pvt.	A	12th	LA.	Infantry	Deas	Withers	Hardee	TN.	Prairie Hill
Eubank, John	Pvt.	B	9th	MS.	Cavalry	Scott	Loring	Hood	TN.	Horn Hill
Farrar, L. J.	Major		12th	TX.	Cavalry	Ferguson	Jackson		TN.	Mexia
Fife, J. A.	Pvt.	H	31st	MS.	Infantry	Parsons		E. K. Smith	T-MS.	Groesbeck
Flanekin, J. C.	Pvt.	E	9th	TN.	Infantry	Featherston	Loring	Hardee	TN.	Horn Hill
Franks, T. H.	Pvt.	F	10th	TX.	Cavalry	Maney	Cheatham	Polk	T-MS.	Tehuacana
Frazier, W. D.	Pvt.	I	59th	AL.	Infantry	Cooper	Gano	E. K. Smith	T-MS.	Mexia
Fullenwider, A. E.	Pvt.			TX.	Mtd. Infy	Gracie			N. VA.	Armour
Fuqua, M. P.	Pvt.	B	22nd	ARK.	Infantry	Hardeman	Magruder	E. K. Smith	T-MS.	Palestine, Anderson Co
Gibson, Hiram	Pvt.	A	5th	MS.	Cavalry	Hawthorn	Churchill	E. K. Smith	T-MS.	Tehuacana
Gibson, T. J.	Pvt.	B	12th	GA.	Infantry	Ferguson	Jackson	Wheeler	TN.	Mexia
Gilbert, B. F.	Pvt.	A	17th	TX.	Cavalry	Doles	Ewell	Jackson	N. VA.	Mexia
Gilbert, J. S.	Capt.	A	6th	LA.	Cavalry	Polignac	Walker	E. K. Smith	T-MS.	Gone to Ellis Co.
					Infantry	Hays				Cade, Navarro Co.
Goodman, J. H.	Pvt.	P	4th	TX.	Infantry	Hood	Hill		N. VA.	Mart, McLennan Co.

ROSTER OF EX-CONFEDERATE VETERANS OF LIMESTONE COUNTY, TEXAS

Name	Rank	Co.	Reg.	State	Branch	Commander	Division	Corps	State	Residence
Graham, W. A.	Pvt.	I	31st	MS.	Infantry	Featherston	Loring	A. P. Stewart	TN.	Kirk
Graves, Noble	Pvt.	G	15th	ARK.	Infantry				TN.	Mexia
Gray, H. W.	Pvt.	D	37th	VA.	Infantry	Stuart			N. VA.	Mexia
Gray, J. I. L.	Pvt.	A	33rd	TN.	Infantry	Strahl	Johnston	Hardee	TN.	Mexia
Griffis, J. L.	Pvt.	C	24th	MS.	Infantry	Walthall	Cheatham	Hardee	TN.	Kirk
Groover, J. S.	Pvt.	G		TX.	Cavalry	Lane			T-MS.	Mexia
Groves, J. S. [Rev.]	Pvt.	E	15th	TX.	Infantry	Polignac	Green	E. K. Smith	T-MS.	Mexia
Guy, W. J.	Pvt.	E	16th	MS.	Infantry	Harris	Mouton	E. K. Smith	N. VA.	Groesbeck
Guynes, J. F.	Pvt.	F	6th	MS.	Infantry		Anderson	A. P. Hill	TN.	Mexia
Hancock, B. J.	Pvt.	I	19th	TX.	Cavalry	Parsons	Marmaduke	E. K. Smith	T-MS.	Mexia
Hancock, L. R.	Pvt.	B	12th	TX.	Cavalry	Parsons	Couples	E. K. Smith	T-MS.	Mexia
Hanna, A. W.	Pvt.	F	22nd	TX.	Infantry	Waul	Walker	E. K. Smith	T-MS.	Kirk
Harris, C. T.	Sgt.	G	1st	TX.	Detached	Fagan	Churchill	E. K. Smith	T-MS.	Mexia
Harvey, J. W.	Pvt.	F	38th	AL.	Infantry	Holtzclaw	Cheatham	Hardee	TN.	Mexia
Henry, Wm.	Pvt.		Benevides'	TX.	Cavalry				T-MS.	Mexia
Herbert, J. H.	Pvt.		4th	TX.	Infantry	Hood		A. P. Hill	N. VA.	Unknown
Herring, W. H.	1st Sgt.	G	18th	AL.	Infantry	Gladden	Clayton	A. P. Stuart	TN.	Prairie Grove
Hickman, J. P.				AL.	Infantry					Mexia
Holladay, J. W.	Pvt.	A	30th	AL.	Infantry	Armstrong		Hardee	TN.	Mexia
Hood, W. F.	Sgt.	B	1st	ARK.	Infantry	Reynolds				Cade, Navarro Co.
Howard, F. M.	O. Sgt.	A	1st	TN.	Infantry	Archer	Hill	Jackson	N. VA.	Cade, Navarro Co.
Howze, J. G.	Pvt.	H	4th	SC	Cavalry	Butler	Hampton	Stuart	N. VA.	Horn Hill
Hughes, D. F.	Pvt.			AL.						Mexia
Hughes, S.	Pvt.	E	53rd	AL.	Cavalry	Hannon	Wheeler	Hardee	TN.	Mexia
Hunt, Bennett	Pvt.	H	38th	AL.	Infantry	Holtzclaw	Stuart	Hood	TN.	Mexia
Hyatt, J. J.	Pvt.	K	34th	GA.	Infantry	Cumming				Horn Hill
Ingram, John	Pvt.	G	13th	AL.	Infantry	Colquitt	Hill	Longstreet	N. VA.	Mexia
Ingram, S. C.	Pvt.	G	13th	AL.	Infantry	Archer	A. P. Hill	Jackson	N. VA.	
Jackson, F. M.	Pvt.	G	6th	TX.	Cavalry	Ross	Jackson		T-MS.	Groesbeck
Jennings, G. L. [Rev	Capt.	H	31st	MS.	Infantry	Featherston	Loring	E. K. Smith	T-MS.	Kirk
Johnson, J. B.	Pvt.	F	6th	MS.	Cavalry		Forrest		TN.	Mexia
Johnson, W. M.	Pvt.	A	32nd	TX.	Cavalry	Buchel	Dagley	E. K. Smith	T-MS.	Thornton
Joiner, H. C.	O. Sgt.	E	19th	TX.	Infantry	Scurry	Walker	E. K. Smith	T-MS.	Groesbeck
Jones, Jno. A.	Bugler	G	5th	NC	Cavalry	Barringer	W. H. F. Lee	Stuart	N. VA.	Kosse
Jones, Nat. M.	Sgt. Major		1st	NC	Infantry	Armistead	Hoke		N. VA.	Kosse
Jordan, J. B.	Capt.	G	36th	AL.	Infantry	Holtzclaw	Clayton	Hardee	TN.	Groesbeck
Justice, Wm.	Pvt.	B	10th	TX.	Cavalry	Granbury	Cleburne	Hardee	TN.	Personville
Kamsler, Wm.	Pvt.	I	25th	TX.	Cavalry	Harrison	Walker	E. K. Smith	T-MS.	Mexia
Kaufman, M.	Capt.	B	45th	AL.	Infantry	Lowrey	Cleburne	Hardee	TN.	Mexia
Keene, N. A. [Rev.]	Pvt.	C	6th	TX.	Cavalry	Ross	Jackson		N. VA.	Mexia
Kemp, M. W.	1st Lt.	D	13th	AL.	Infantry	Archer	A. P. Hill	Jackson	N. VA.	Mexia
Kenney, G. W.	Pvt.	G	6th	AL.	Infantry	Battle	Rodes	Ewell	N. VA.	Mexia
Kinney, G. E.										Not known
Lanning, W. D.	Pvt.	K	18th	AL.	Infantry	Holtzclaw	Clayton	Hardee	TN.	Mexia
Le Noir, J. Y.	Pvt.	B	1st	SC	Artillery		State Service			Horn Hill

ROSTER OF EX-CONFEDERATE VETERANS OF LIMESTONE COUNTY, TEXAS

Name	Rank	Co.	Regt.	State	Branch	Brigade	Division	Army	Town
Lee, G. W.	1st Lt.	K	5th	AL.	Cavalry	Hood	Forrest	TN.	Groesbeck
Lewis, G. W.	Pvt.	C	20th	TX.	Infantry	Frost	F. H. Robertson	N. VA.	Thornton
Lindley, J. P.	Pvt.	K	23rd	TX.	Infantry	Pettus	Hindman	T-MS.	Wortham
Lindsey, W. H. H.	Pvt.	A	34th	AL.	Infantry	Fagan	Stevenson	Lee	Mexia
Lineberger, J. M.	Pvt.	G	6th	ARK.	Cavalry	Ross	Churchill	E. K. Smith	Horn Hill
Love, R. M.	Pvt.	G	6th	TX.	Cavalry	Ross	Jackson	TN.	Groesbeck
Love, S. B.	Pvt.	A	1st Richmond Howitzers	TX.	Cavalry	Ross	Jackson	TN.	Tehuacana
Loverette, R. H.	2nd Lt.					McLaws	Longstreet	N. VA.	Calvert, Robertson Co.
Loving, D. H.	Pvt.	A	52nd	VA.	Infantry	Pegram	Early	Jackson	N. VA.	Prairie Hill
Martin, Jno. T.	Pvt.	B	7th	AL.	Cavalry			Wheeler	TN.	Groesbeck
McCollough, Ben	Pvt.	D	Perrys'	MS.	Cavalry	Ferguson			TN.	Armour
McDonald, J. C.	Pvt.	K	20th	TX.	Cavalry	Maxey	Wheeler	E. K. Smith	T-MS.	Prairie Grove
McDonald, J. E.	Pvt.	A	2nd	AL.	Cavalry	Ferguson	Wheeler		TN.	Mexia
McDonald, M. L.	Pvt.	D	Woods'	MS.	Cavalry	Adams	Wheeler		TN.	Mexia
McDonald, W. W.	Pvt.	F	15th	TX.	Cavalry	Granbury	Cleburne	Hardee	TN.	Abbott, Hill Co.
McKinney, J. W.	Cpl.	H	55th	AL.	Infantry	Buford	Loring	A. P. Stewart	TN.	Prairie Hill
Miller, A. L.	Pvt.	A		MS.	Cavalry	Powers			TN.	Mexia
Morton, J. M.	Pvt.	I	38th	TN.	Infantry	Wright	Cheatham	Polk	TN.	Mt. Calm
Mullins, J. H.	3rd Sgt.	H	26th	AL.	Infantry	Deas	Withers	Polk	TN.	Armour
Nash, J. W.	Pvt.		Styles' Battn	VA.	H. Artillery				N. VA.	Mexia
Nelson, A. J.	Pvt.	E	29th	AL.	Infantry				TN.	Tehuacana
Nelson, T. J.	Pvt.	G	20th	AL.	Infantry	Pettus	Stevenson	Hood	TN.	Personville
Norwood, T. A. [Re'	Pvt.	A	14th	LA.	Infantry					Personville
Oakes, J. M.	Pvt.	K	8th	AL.						Personville
Parker, J. E.	Pvt.	I	3rd	AL.	Infantry	Battle	Rodes	Ewell	N. VA.	Mexia
Partin, J. G.	Pvt.	E	20th	GA.	Infantry	Toombs	Hood	Longstreet	N. VA.	Horn Hill
Patterson, John	Pvt.	B	10th	TX.	Infantry	Granbury	Cleburne	Hardee	TN.	Groesbeck
Payne, R. W.	Pvt.	N	12th	MS.	Cavalry	Ferguson	Jackson	Wheeler	TN.	Mexia
Phillips, J. B.	Pvt.	K	13th	AL.	Infantry	Archer	A. P. Hill	Jackson	N. VA.	Mt. Calm, Hill Co.
Powell, G. W.										Hubbard City
Powell, J. G.	Pvt.	K	35th	TX.	Cavalry	Buchel	Green	E. K. Smith	T-MS.	Mexia
Powell, W. L.	Pvt.	F	9th	LA.	Infantry	Hays	Gordon	Early	N. VA.	Hubbard City
Prince, J. H.	Pvt.	C	10th	GA.	Infantry	Simms	McLaws	Longstreet	N. VA.	Armour
Rabom, Isaac	2nd Sgt.	C	19th	LA.	Cavalry	Gibson	Stewart		TN.	Groesbeck
Rambo, J. W.	O. Sgt.	F	9th	MS.	Cavalry	Ferguson	Jackson	Wheeler	TN.	Personville
Rasco, John	Pvt.	B	20th	TX.	Cavalry	Cooper	Gano	E. K. Smith	T-MS.	Groesbeck
Reed, T. L.	Pvt.	F	3rd	MO.	Cavalry	Shelby	Marmaduke	Price	T-MS.	Battle, McLennan Co.
Reeves, W. J.										Not known
Reynolds, M. P.	Pvt.	D	7th	AL.	Cavalry	Rucker	Forrest	Hood	TN.	Tehuacana
Richardson, J. A. T.	Pvt.	H	1st	TN.	Infantry	Maney	Cheatham	Polk	TN.	Tehuacana
Richardson, W. H.	1st Lt.	F	2nd	MD.	Cavalry	Johnson	F. Lee	Hampton	N. VA.	Austin, Travis Co.
Riddle, J. E.	Pvt.	B	36th	AL.	Infantry	Clayton	Cheatham	Hardee	TN.	Kirk
Riley, P. O.	Pvt.			TX.				Home Guards	T-MS.	Prairie Hill
Rogers, A. J.	Sgt.	K	20th	TX.	Dis. Cav.	Maxey	Hindman	E. K. Smith	T-MS.	Personville

ROSTER OF EX-CONFEDERATE VETERANS OF LIMESTONE COUNTY, TEXAS

Name	Rank	Co.	Regt.	State	Branch	Brigade	Division	Army	Town
Rogers, R.	Pvt.	I	9th	TX.	Infantry	Ector	Cheatham	Polk	TN.	Marlin
Ross, G. W.	Pvt.	H	4th	MO.	Cavalry	Cockrell	French	Polk	TN.	Mexia
Rucker, H. P.	Pvt.	D	12th	KY.	Cavalry		Forrest	Wheeler	TN.	Groesbeck
Salter, J. G.	Pvt.	B	60th	AL.	Infantry	Gracie	Preston	Hardee	TN.	Cade, Navarro Co.
Sanches, F. M.	Pvt.	H	6th	TX.	Cavalry	Granbury	Cleburne	Hardee	TN.	Axtell, McLennan Co.
Sanders, J. S.	Pvt.			TX.	Det. Ser.				T-MS.	Mexia
Sanderson, N. J.		D		LA.	Engineer			E. K. Smith	T-MS.	Billington
Sawyer, J. P.	Pvt.	D	12th	MS.	Cavalry	Ferguson	Wheeler		TN.	Tehuacana
Scarborough, S. R.	Pvt.	A	15th	MS.	Infantry	Adams	Loring	Polk	TN.	Mexia
Sellers, F. M.	Pvt.	I	3rd	AL.	Cavalry	Morgan	Allen	Wheeler	TN.	Thornton
Shriver, Adam	Pvt.		Rich's Batty	LA.	Artillery		Anderson	Hill	N. VA.	Horn Hill
Simmons, H. F.	Pvt.	D	Woods'	MS.	Cavalry	Adams	Wheeler		TN.	Mexia
Simmons, J. W.	Pvt.	E	27th	MS.	Infantry	Walthall	Johnson	Lee	TN.	Mexia
Sims, J. R.	2nd Lt.	E	8th	MS.	Infantry	Lowrey	Cleburne	Hardee	TN.	Mexia
Skillern, T. W.	Pvt.	C	36th	ARK.	Infantry	Gray	Churchill	Price	T-MS.	Frosa
Sloan, A. J.	2nd Sgt.	I	20th	MS.	Infantry	Floyd	Loring	Jackson	N. VA.	Mexia
Sloan, J. T.	2nd Lt.	E	2nd	ARK.	Infantry	McIntosh	McCulloch		T-MS.	Tehuacana
Smyth, E. B.	Pvt.			TX.	Cavalry	Ross		E. K. Smith	T-MS.	Horn Hill
Spruill, J. A.	Pvt.	H	Whitfield's	TX.	Infantry	Home Guard			TN.	Mexia
Stanford, S. A.	Pvt.			AL.	Infantry					
Steddum, N. B.	Pvt.	F	22nd	TX.	Cavalry	Wharton	Mouton		T-MS.	Mt. Calm
Steele, J. Warren	Pvt.	G	7th	TX.	Infantry	Granbury	Cleburne	E. K. Smith	TN.	Mexia
Steele, Rado	Pvt.	B	10th	TX.	Infantry	Granbury	Cleburne	Hardee	TN.	Mexia
Storey, J. M.	O. Sgt.	H	28th	TX.	Infantry	Randal	Walker	Hardee	T-MS.	Mexia
Sturdivant, I. H.	Pvt.	G	38th	TN.	Infantry		Cheatham	E. K. Smith	TN.	Prairie Grove
Stutesman, O.	Pvt.	E	5th	ARK.	Infantry	McRae	Hindman	E. K. Smith	T-MS.	Mexia
Suttle, J. M.	1st Sgt.	H	23rd	GA.	Infantry	Colquitt	Hoke	Longstreet	N. VA.	Tehuacana
Taylor, J. L.	Pvt.	A	7th	TX.	Infantry	Granbury	Cleburne	Hardee	TN.	Hancock
Thomas, J. W.	Cpl.	H	43rd	NC	Infantry	Daniel	Rodes	Ewell	N. VA.	Tehuacana
Thompson, J. W.	Pvt.	C	4th	AL.	Cavalry	Law	Hood	Longstreet	N. VA.	Groesbeck
Thompson, L. E.	Pvt.	B	3rd	MO.	Cavalry	Marmaduke	Price		N. VA.	Thornton
Thornton, A. N.	O. Sgt.	C	39th	GA.	Infantry	Cumming	Stevenson	Hardee	TN.	Tehuacana
Tomkins, John										Prairie Grove
Trammell, F. E.	Capt.	B	17th	ARK.	Infantry	Hébert	Little	Price	TN.	Armour
Tubb, C. G.	Pvt.	G	12th	TX.	Cavalry	Parsons	Walker	E. K. Smith	T-MS.	Mexia
Tucker, M. A.	Sgt. Major	F	15th	TX.	Cavalry	Johnson	Cleburne	Hardee	TN.	Horn Hill
Usry, B. M.		F	15th	TX.	Cavalry	Dashler		E. K. Smith	T-MS.	Groesbeck
Vickers, J. H.	Cpl.	E	9th	GA.				Home Guards		Mexia
Wade, T. W.	Capt.		20th	TX.	Infantry					Tehuacana
Waite, G. D.	Pvt.	E	Woods'	TX.	Cavalry	Bee		E. K. Smith	T-MS.	Groesbeck
Walker, G. H.	Pvt.	A	9th	LA.	Infantry	Hays	Ewell	Jackson	N. VA.	Shiloh
Walker, S. S.	Pvt.	I	2nd	TX.	Cavalry	Major	Green	E. K. Smith	T-MS.	Groesbeck
Wallace, B. F.	Pvt.	F	15th	TX.	Cavalry	Granbury	Cleburne	Hardee	TN.	Hancock
Walling, J. G.	Pvt.	C	15th	TX.	Infantry	Polignac	Mouton	Taylor	T-MS.	Thornton
Ward, R. P.	Pvt.	F	12th	TX.	Cavalry	Parsons	Walker	E. K. Smith	T-MS.	Mexia

ROSTER OF EX-CONFEDERATE VETERANS OF LIMESTONE COUNTY, TEXAS

Name	Rank	Co.	Reg.	State	Branch	Brigade	Division	Army	Town
Watkins, R. L.	Pvt.	G	12th	TX.	Cavalry	Parsons	Walker	E. K. Smith	Tehuacana
Watson, C. L.	2nd Sgt.	D	10th	TX.	Infantry	Granbury	Cleburne	Hardee	Mexia
Watson, W. A.	Pvt.	H	4th	TX.	Infantry	Hood	Field	Longstreet	Thornton
Whatley, M. B.	Pvt.	D	7th	AL.	Cavalry	*Hodsen*	Forrest		Cotton Gin, Freestone Co.
Wickder, J. W.	O. Sgt.	B	7th	FL.	Infantry		Breckinridge		Mt. Calm
Wilder, J. L.	Pvt.	K	2nd	LA.	Infantry	Stafford	Ewell	Jackson	N. VA.
Wilder, W. M.	Pvt.	B	10th	TX.	Infantry	Granbury	Cleburne	Hardee	Cade, Navarro Co.
Wiley, Oscar	1st Sgt.	K	5th	AL.	Cavalry	Rodes	Early	Jackson	N. VA. Groesbeck
Williams, E. W.	Pvt.	C	3rd	TX.	Cavalry	Ross	Jackson	Hardee	Tehuacana
Williams, H. W.	Pvt.	C	36th	NC	H. Arty	Ft. Duty	Ft. Fisher, N.C.		Mexia
Wood, C. H. F.	3rd Sgt.	F	15th	TX.	Cavalry	Granbury	Cleburne	Hardee	Mexia
Wood, E. B.	Capt.	B	34th	AL.	Infantry	Manigault	Hindman	Polk	Hubbard City
Wood, Ira E.	2nd Sgt.	F	15th	TX.	Cavalry	Granbury	Cleburne	Hardee	Mexia
Wooten, W. S.	Pvt.	E		GA.	Infantry				Mexia
Wright, G. H.	Pvt.	I	2nd	ARK.	Infantry	Govan	Cleburne	Hardee	Mexia
Wright, Jas. A.	Pvt.	F	31st	AL.	Infantry	Pettus	Stevenson	Hood	Prairie Grove
Wright, Joel T.	Pvt.	B	20th	TX.	Cavalry	Roan	Steele	E. K. Smith	T-MS. Mt. Calm
Wright, Z. T.	Pvt.	F	31st	AL.	Infantry	Pettus	Stevenson	Hood	Mexia
Wyatt, W. W.	Pvt.	G	11th	MS.	Infantry	Davis	Heth	A. P. Hill	N. VA. Groesbeck

ROSTER OF EX-CONFEDERATE VETERANS OF LIMESTONE COUNTY, TEXAS

1894-1895

NAME	RANK	CO.	REGT.	STATE	SERVICE	BRIGADE	DIVISION	CORPS	ARMY OF	POST OFFICE
Allen, B. W.	Pvt.	K	20th	TX.	Cavalry	Maxey		E. K. Smith	T-MS.	Kosse
Allen, O. E.	O. Sgt.	F	4th	TX.	Cavalry	Hardeman	Green	E. K. Smith	T-MS.	Mart, McLennan Co.
Anderson, W. R.	Capt.	D	22nd	TX.	Infantry	Waul	Walker	E. K. Smith	T-MS.	Tehuacana
Anglin, J. A.	Pvt.	McNelly		TX.	Scouts	Green		E. K. Smith	T-MS.	Groesbeck
Anglin, J. C.	Pvt.	McNelly		TX.	Scouts	Green		E. K. Smith	T-MS.	Groesbeck
Archer, G. W.	Pvt.	C	8th	TX.	Cavalry	Wharton	Wheeler		TN.	Mexia
Archer, J. H.	Pvt.	F	36th	MS.	Infantry	Sears			T-MS.	Billington
Armour, Jas.	Pvt.	C	Bradford	TX.					T-MS.	Armour
Arnett, S. T.	Pvt.	I	21st	TX.	Cavalry	Parsons		E. K. Smith	T-MS.	Kosse
Arvin, J. A.	Pvt.	H	9th	VA.	Infantry	Corse	Pickett	Longstreet	N. VA.	Mexia
Bailey, Ed										Prairie Hill
Barry, J. M.	Pvt.	D	Willis'		Artillery	Waul			TN.	Mexia
Barton, W. M.	Pvt.	E	13th	NC	Artillery				N. VA.	Mexia
Bates, C. S.	1st Sgt.	K	20th	TX.	Dis. Cav.	Maxey	Hindman	E. K. Smith	T-MS.	Mexia
Beene, S. H.	Pvt.	G	Madison	TX.	Cavalry	Lane	Major	E. K. Smith	T-MS.	Mexia
Bennett, E. G.	C. Sgt.	F	15th	TX.	Cavalry	Granbury	Cleburne	Hardee	TN.	Groesbeck
Bennett, M. M.	Pvt.	I	35th	AL.	Infantry	Scott			TN.	Tehuacana
Berryman, H. C.	Pvt.	H	20th	TX.	Infantry	Elmore		E. K. Smith	T-MS.	Prairie Grove
Bishop, John	Pvt.	A	33rd	AL.	Infantry	Lowrey	Cleburne	Hardee	TN.	Farrar
Bond, S. F.	Pvt.	G		TX.	Cavalry	State Troops			T-MS.	Mexia
Bowder, W. H.	Pvt.	A	1st	AL.	Cavalry	Allen	Johnson	Wheeler	TN.	Groesbeck
Bower, Chris	Pvt.	C	8th	TX.	Infantry	Young	Walker	E. K. Smith	T-MS.	Mexia
Boyd, H. A.	1st Lt.	E	35th	TX.	Cavalry	Bee	Walker	E. K. Smith	T-MS.	Tehuacana
Boyd, G. C.	Pvt.	C	2nd	MS.	Infantry	Law		Longstreet	N. VA.	Tehuacana
Brooks, C. N.	Pvt.	D	Bird's	TX/LA	Cavalry			E. K. Smith	T-MS.	Thornton
Brown, J. P.	Capt.	K	12th	TX.	Cavalry	Parsons	Green	Wharton	T-MS.	Groesbeck
Brown, W. P.	Capt.	K	20th	TX.	Dis. Cav.	Maxey	Hindman	E. K. Smith	T-MS.	Groesbeck
Bryant, R. J.	Sgt.	B		TX.	Infantry	Waul			TN.	Mexia
Buckner, W. A.	2nd Lt.	B	9th	VA.	Cavalry	W. H. F. Lee	Lee	Stewart	N. VA.	Mexia
Bunn, J. G.	Pvt.	H	19th	MS.	Infantry	Posey	A. P. Hill	Longstreet	N. VA.	Frosa
Burgess, J. J.	Pvt.	H	20th	MS.	Infantry	Adams	Loring	Polk	TN.	Mexia
Burleson, A. J.	Pvt.	K	12th	TX.	Cavalry	Parsons	Green	Wharton	T-MS.	Kosse
Burton, J. I.	Pvt.	A	2nd	TX.	Cavalry	Sibley	Green	E. K. Smith	T-MS.	Mexia
Cashion, A. J.	Capt.	H	1st	TN.	Infantry	Archer	Heath	A. P. Hill	N. VA.	Wortham
Camp, L. E.	Pvt.	Confuit's		GA.	Artillery		Stevenson	Hardee	TN.	Mexia
Carleton, W. L.	Surgeon		2nd	ARK.	Infantry	McCulloch			TN.	Frosa
Carroll, J. G.	Pvt.	A	22nd	ARK.	Cavalry	Dockery	Walker	E. K. Smith	T-MS.	Mexia
Carruth, W. A.	Pvt.	F	11th	MS.	Infantry	Davis	Heath	A. P. Hill	N. VA.	Mexia
Chambers, E. C.	Pvt.	Lewis'	Elmore	TX.	Infantry	Magruder				Thornton

ROSTER OF EX-CONFEDERATE VETERANS OF LIMESTONE COUNTY, TEXAS

Name	Rank	Co.	Regt.	State	Branch	Brigade	Division	Corps	Army	Residence
Clanahan, Jas.	Pvt.	I	21st	MS.	Infantry	Waul	Humphreys	McLaws	Longstreet	N. VA.	Mexia
Clark, M. H.	Pvt.	E	Willis'	TX.							Groesbeck
Collum, Geo.	Pvt.	I	9th	TX.	Cavalry	Ross	Jackson			TN.	Tehuacana
Conley, A. B.	Pvt.	I	12th	TN.	Cavalry	Bell	forrest			TN.	Mexia
Cook, J. P.	Pvt.	B	30th	AL.	Infantry	Pettus	Stevenson			TN.	Mexia
Cowart, L. E.	Pvt.	D	12th	GA.	Infantry	Dole	Rodes	Jackson	Lee	N. VA.	Groesbeck
Cox, A. J.	Pvt.	H	38th	AL.	Infantry	Holtzclaw	Stuart	Hardee		TN.	Prairie Grove
Cox, M. B.	Pvt.	G	18th	AL.	Infantry	Holtzclaw	Stuart	Hardee		TN.	Prairie Grove
Crawford, F. M.	Pvt.	E	32nd	AL.	Infantry	Holtzclaw	Stuart	Hardee		TN.	Armour
Davis, J. W.	Pvt.	K	10th	TX.	Cavalry	Cooper	Gano	E. K. Smith		T-MS.	Groesbeck
Davis, W. A.	Bugler	H	33rd	ARK.	Infantry	Tappan	Churchill	E. K. Smith		T-MS.	Hancock
DeCaussey, C. B.	Pvt.	A	5th	FL.	Cavalry		Forrest			TN.	Tehuacana
Deis, J. M.	Bugler		1st	MO.	Artillery		Price				Mexia
Dellis, S. F.	Pvt.	B	20th	TX.	Dis. Cav.	Maxey	Hindman	Hardee		TN.	Hancock
Doke, F. Y.	Capt.	F	9th	MO.	Infantry	1st	Parsons			TN.	Kosse
Douglas, N. B.	Cpl.		15th	ARK.	Cavalry	Dockery	Walker	E. K. Smith		T-MS.	Mart, McLennan Co.
Douglas, P. O.	Pvt.	A	15th	ARK.	Infantry	Doctor	Churchill	E. K. Smith		T-MS.	Mart, McLennan Co.
Douglas, W. C.	Pvt.	C	2nd	TN.	Cavalry	Bell	Forrest			TN.	Mt. Calm
Doyle, W. E.	Pvt.	G	7th	SC.	Cavalry	Gary	Field	Longstreet		N. VA.	Mexia
Duke, L. W. (Rev.)	Cpl.	C	5th	AL.	Infantry	Battle	Rodes	Jackson		N. VA.	Mexia
Duncan, N. Y.	Pvt.	G	10th	MS.	Infantry	Sharp	Hindman	E. K. Smith		T-MS.	Prairie Grove
Durst, W. E.	Pvt.	A	5th	TX.	Infantry	Young	Walker	E. K. Smith		T-MS.	Mexia
East, Elias	Pvt.	I	13th	AL.	Infantry	Archer	A. P. Hill	Jackson		N. VA.	Armour
Ellison, Sam	Pvt.	C	25th	AL.	Infantry	Day	Withers	Hardee		TN.	Prairie Hill
Farrar, L. J.	Major		12th	TX.	Cavalry	Parsons	Walker	E. K. Smith		T-MS.	Groesbeck
Fife, J. A.	Pvt.	H	31st	MS.	Infantry	Featherston	Loring			TN.	Horn Hill
Flanikin, J. C.	Pvt.	E	9th	TN.	Infantry	Mana	Cheatham	Polk		TN.	Tehuacana
Franks, T. L.	Pvt.	F	10th	TX.	Cavalry	Cooper	Gano	E. K. Smith		T-MS.	Mexia
Frazier, W. D.	Pvt.	I	59th	AL.	Infantry	Gracie		Longstreet		N. VA.	Armour
Fuqua, M. P.	Pvt.	B	22nd	ARK.	Infantry	Hawthorn	Churchill	E. K. Smith		T-MS.	Tehuacana
Germany, T. A.	Pvt.	G	12th	TX.	Cavalry	Parsons	Gano	E. K. Smith		T-MS.	Mexia
Gibson, Hiram	Pvt.	A	5th	MS.	Cavalry	Ferguson	Jackson	Wheeler		TN.	Mexia
Gibson, T. J.	Pvt.	B	12th	GA.	Infantry	Dole	Ewell	Jackson		N. VA.	Mexia
Gilbert, C. T.	Pvt.	C	21st	TX.	Cavalry	Parsons	Ewell	E. K. Smith		T-MS.	Cade, Navarro Co.
Gilbert, J. S.	Capt.	A	6th	LA.	Infantry	Hayes	Ewell	Jackson		N. VA.	Cade, Navarro Co.
Goodman, J. H.	Pvt.		4th	TX.	Infantry	Hood		Hill		N. VA.	Mart, McLennan Co.
Gray, H. W.	Pvt.	D	37th	VA.	Infantry	Stewart	Johnston	Jackson		TN.	Mexia
Groover, J. S.	Pvt.	G		TX.	Cavalry	Lane	Green	E. K. Smith		T-MS.	Mexia
Groves, J. S. Rev.	Pvt.	E	15th	TX.	Infantry	Polignac	Mouton	E. K. Smith		T-MS.	Mexia
Groves, Noble	Pvt.	G	15th	ARK.	Infantry	Hood				TN.	Mexia
Hancock, B. J.	Pvt.	I	19th	TX.	Cavalry	Parsons	Marmaduke	E. K. Smith		T-MS.	Mexia
Harris, C. T.	Sgt.	G	1st	TX.	Detached	Fagan	Churchill	E. K. Smith		T-MS.	Cade, Navarro Co.
Hartfield, J. A.	Pvt.	B	13th	TX.							Not Known
Herbert, J. H.	Pvt.		4th	TX.	Infantry	Hood	Gladden	Clayton	A. P. Hill	N. VA.	Mexia
Herring, W. H.	1st Sgt.	G	18th	AL.	Infantry				A. P. Stewart	TN.	Prairie Grove

ROSTER OF EX-CONFEDERATE VETERANS OF LIMESTONE COUNTY, TEXAS

Name	Rank	Co.	State	Unit	Branch	Brigade	Division	Corps/Army	Home
Hickman, J. P.			AL.		Infantry				Mexia
High, R. A.	Pvt.	B	TX.		Infantry	Waul		TN.	Blooming Grove, Navarro Co.
Holloway, G. W.	Pvt.	F	TX.	8th	Infantry	Young	Walker	E. K. Smith	Prairie Hill
Hood, C. B.	Pvt.	E	AL.	51st	Cavalry		Wheeler	T-MS.	Groesbeck
Hood, W. F.	O. Sgt.	B	ARK.	1st	Infantry	Reynolds		TN.	Cade, Navarro Co.
Howard, F. M.	O. Sgt.	A	TN.	1st	Infantry	Archer	Jackson	N. VA.	Cade, Navarro Co.
Howze, J. G.	Pvt.	H	SC.	4th	Cavalry	Butler	Hampton	N. VA.	Horn Hill
Hughes, D. F.	Pvt.		AL.						Mexia
Hughes, S.	Pvt.	E	AL.	53rd	Cavalry		Wheeler	Hardee	Mexia
Ingram, S. C.	Pvt.	G	AL.	13th	Infantry	Archer	A. P. Hill	TN.	
Jayne, A. A.	Scout	G	MS.	28th		*Hannon*		N. VA.	
Jennings, G. L. Rev.	Capt.	H	MS.	31st	Infantry	*Harvey*			Groesbeck
Johnson, J. B.	Pvt.	F	MS.	6th	Cavalry	Featherston	Loring	TN.	Kirk
Johnson, W. M.	Pvt.	A	TX.	32nd	Cavalry		forrest	TN.	Mexia
Joiner, H. C.	O. Sgt.	E	TX.	19th	Cavalry	Scurry	*Dagley*	T-MS.	Thornton
Jolley, J. S.	Pvt.	G	ARK.	3rd	Infantry	Hood	Walker	T-MS.	Groesbeck
Jones, Jno. A.	Bugler	G	NC	5th	Cavalry	Barringer	W. H. F. Lee	N. VA.	Kosse
Jones, Nat. M.	Sgt. Major		NC	1st	Infantry	Armistead	Hoke	N. VA.	Kosse
Jordan, J. B.	Capt.	G	AL.	36th	Infantry	Holtzclaw	Clayton	N. VA.	Kosse
Justice, Wm.	Pvt.	B	TX.	10th	Infantry	Granbury	Cleburne	Hardee	Groesbeck
Kamsler, Wm.	Pvt.	I	TX.	25th	Infantry	Harrison	Walker	Hardee	Personville
Kaufman, M.	Capt.	B	AL.	45th	Infantry	Lowrey	Cleburne	E. K. Smith	Mexia
Keeling, B. D.		I	ARK.	1st	Cavalry	Cabell	Fagan	Hardee	Mexia
Keene, N. A. Rev.	Pvt.	C	TX.	6th	Cavalry	Ross	Jackson	TN.	Kosse
Kemp, M. W.	1st Lt.	D	AL.	13th	Infantry	Archer	A. P. Hill	N. VA.	Mexia
Kenney, G. W.	Pvt.	G	AL.	6th	Infantry	Battle	Rodes	N. VA.	Mexia
Kimbrough, J. S.								N. VA.	Wortham
Knowls, A. R.	Pvt.	D	LA.	12th	Infantry	Buford	Loring	A. P. Stewart	Cade, Navarro Co.
Kynerd, A. J.	Pvt.	A	MS.	27th	Infantry	Walthall	Johnson	Lee	Mexia/Cotton Gin
Lambkin, G. W.	Bugler							TN.	Kirk
Lanning, W. D.	Pvt.	K	AL.	18th	Infantry	Holtzclaw	Clayton	Hardee	Mexia
Lansford, G. W.	Pvt.	C	MS.	10th	Infantry	Tucker	Johnson	Hood	Farrar
Lee, G. W.	1st Lt.		AL.		Cavalry		Forrest	TN.	Groesbeck
Lindley, J. P.	Pvt.	C	TX.	20th	Infantry	Frost	Hindman	E. K. Smith	Wortham
Lindsey, W. H. H.	Pvt.	K	AL.	23rd	Infantry	Pettus	Stevenson	T-MS.	Mexia
Love, R. M.	Pvt.	G	TX.	6th	Cavalry	Ross	Jackson	TN.	Tehuacana
Love, S. B.	Pvt.	G	TX.	6th	Cavalry	Ross	Jackson	TN.	Tehuacana
Martin, L. H	Pvt.	E	LA.	3rd	Infantry			TN.	Kosse
McCorkle, Jas.	Pvt.	F	TX.	15th	Cavalry	Granbury	Cleburne	Hardee	Armour
McDonald, J. E.	Pvt.	A	AL.	2nd	Cavalry	Ferguson	Wheeler	N. VA.	Mexia
McDonald, M. L.	Pvt.	D	MS.	Wood's	Cavalry	Adams	Wheeler	TN.	Mexia
McKinney, J. W.	Cpl.	H	AL.	55th	Infantry	Buford	Loring	A. P. Stewart	Groesbeck
McNeese, G. W.	2nd Lt.	F	TX.	5th	Cavalry	Green		Taylor	Hubbard
Miller, R. S.	Pvt.	I	TX.	4th	Infantry	Hood	Whiting	Longstreet	Hubbard City

ROSTER OF EX-CONFEDERATE VETERANS OF LIMESTONE COUNTY, TEXAS

Name	Rank	Co.	Regt.	State	Branch	Commander	Division	Army	Location
Morton, J. M.	Pvt.	I	38th	TN.	Infantry	Wright	Cheatham	Polk	TN.	Mt. Calm
Mullins, J. H.	3rd Sgt.	H	26th	AL.	Infantry	Day	Withers	Polk	TN.	Armour
Nash, J. W.	Pvt.	Style's		VA.	H. Arty				N. VA.	Mexia
Nelson, A. J.	Pvt.			AL.						Tehuacana
Nelson, T. J.	Pvt.	G	20th	AL.	Infantry	Pettus	Stevenson	Hood	TN.	Personville
Norwood, T. A. Rev	Pvt.	A	14th	LA.						Prairie Grove
Oakes, J. M.	Pvt.	K	8th	AL.						Personville
Ouzts, B. F.	Asst. Surg.			SC.	Cavalry	Butler				Kosse
Parker, J. E.	Pvt.	I	2nd	AL.	Infantry	Battle	Rodes	Ewell	N. VA.	Mexia
Payne, R. W.	Pvt.	I	3rd	MS.	Cavalry	Ferguson	Jackson	Wheeler	TN.	Mexia
Phillips, J. B.	Pvt.	H	12th	AL.	Infantry	Archer	A. P. Hill	Jackson	N. VA.	Mt. Calm
Powell, J. G.	Pvt.	K	13th	TX.	Cavalry	Buchelle	Green	E. K. Smith	T-MS.	Mexia
Powell, W. L.	Pvt.	K	35th	LA.	Infantry	Hayes	Gordon	Early	N. VA.	Hubbard
Raborn, Isaac	2nd Sgt.	F	9th	LA.	Infantry	Gibson	Stuart	Hardee	TN.	Groesbeck
Rambo, J. M.	O. Sgt.	C	19th	MS.	Cavalry	Ferguson	Jackson	Wheeler	TN.	Personville
Reed, T. L.	Pvt.	F	9th	MO.	Cavalry	Shelby	Marmaduke	Price	T-MS.	Battle
Reynolds, M. P.	Pvt.	F	3rd	AL.	Cavalry	Rucker	Forrest	Hood	TN.	Tehuacana
Richardson, J. A. T.	Pvt.	D	7th	TN.	Infantry	Manning	Cheatham	Polk	TN.	Tehuacana
Richardson, W. H.	1st Lt.	H	1st	MD.	Cavalry	Johnson	Fitz Lee	Hampton	TN.	Austin, Travis Co.
Roberts, W. F.	Capt.	F	2nd	TX.	Cavalry	Randall	Walker	E. K. Smith	T-MS.	Mexia
Ross, G. W.	Pvt.	G	28th	MO.	Cavalry	Cockrell	French	Polk	TN.	Mexia
Sawyer, J. P.	Pvt.	H	4th	MS.	Cavalry	Ferguson	Wheeler			
Scarborough, S. R.	Pvt.	D	12th	MS.	Infantry	Adams	Loring	Polk	TN.	Mexia
Sellers, F. M.	Pvt.	A	15th	AL.	Cavalry	Morgan	Allen	Wheeler	TN.	Thornton
Sharp, Tom A.	Pvt.	I	3rd	TX.	Infantry	Granbury	Cleburne	Hardee	TN.	Horn Hill
Shriver, Adam	Pvt.	B	10th	LA.	Artillery		Anderson	Hill	N. VA.	Horn Hill
Simmons, H. F.	Pvt.	Rich's	Wood's	MS.	Cavalry	Adams	Wheeler		TN.	Mexia
Simmons, J. W.	Pvt.	D	27th	MS.	Infantry	Walthall	Johnson	Lee	TN.	Mexia
Skillern, T. W.	Pvt.	E	36th	ARK.	Infantry	Cray	Churchill	Price	T-MS.	Frosa
Sloan, A. J.	2nd Sgt.	C	20th	MS.	Infantry	Floyd	Loring	Jackson	N. VA.	Mexia
Smyth, E. B.	Pvt.	I		TX.	Cavalry			E. K. Smith	T-MS.	Mexia
Spruill, J. A.	Pvt.		Whitfield	TX.	Cavalry	Ross			TN.	Horn Hill
Steddum, N. B.	Pvt.	H	22nd	TX.	Cavalry	Wharton	Mouton	E. K. Smith	T-MS.	Mt. Calm
Steele, J. Warren	Pvt.	F	7th	TX.	Infantry	Granbury	Cleburne	Hardee	TN.	Mexia
Steele, R. E.	1st Lt.	G	7th	TX.	Infantry	Granbury	Cleburne	Hardee	TN.	Mexia
Steele, Rado	Pvt.	G	10th	TX.	Infantry	Granbury	Cleburne	Hardee	TN.	Mexia
Storey, J. M.	O. Sgt.	B	28th	TX.	Infantry	Randall	Walker	E. K. Smith	T-MS.	Mexia
Sturdivant, I. H.	Pvt.	H	38th	TN.	Infantry		Cheatham			Mexia
Suttle, J. M.	1st Sgt.	G	23rd	GA.	Infantry	Colquitt	Hoke	Longstreet	N. VA.	Prairie Grove
Swain, J.	Pvt.	H	43rd	MS.	Infantry	Green	Price	Hardee	TN.	Tehuacana
Tennison, T. F.		I								Prairie Grove
Thomas, J. W.	Cpl.	H	43rd	NC	Infantry	Daniel	Rodes	Ewell	N. VA.	Tehuacana
Thompson, J. W.	Pvt.	C	4th	AL.	Infantry	Law	Hood	Longstreet	N. VA.	Groesbeck
Thornton, A. N.	O. Sgt.	C	39th	GA.	Infantry	Cumming	Stevenson	Hardee	TN.	Tehuacana
Trammell, F. E.	Capt.	B	17th	ARK.	Infantry	Herbert	Little	Price	TN.	Armour

26

ROSTER OF EX-CONFEDERATE VETERANS OF LIMESTONE COUNTY, TEXAS

Tucker, M. A.	Sgt. Major	F	15th	TX.	Cavalry		Cleburne	Hardee	TN.	Horn Hill
Vickers, J. H.	Cpl.	E	9th	GA.				Home Guards		Mexia
Ward, R. P.	Pvt.	F	12th	TX.	Cavalry	Parsons	Walker	E. K. Smith	T-MS.	Mexia
Wood, C. H. F.	3rd Sgt.	F	15th	TX.	Cavalry	Granbury	Cleburne	Hardee	TN.	Mexia
Wallace, B. F.	Pvt.	F	15th	TX.	Cavalry	Granbury	Cleburne	Hardee	TN.	Hancock
Walling, J. J.	Pvt.	C	15th	TX.	Infantry	Polignac	Mouton	Taylor	T-MS.	Thornton
Watson, C. L.	2nd Sgt.	D	10th	TX.	Infantry	Granbury	Cleburne	Hardee	TN.	Mexia
Williams, E. W.	Pvt.	C	3rd	TX.	Cavalry	Ross	Jackson	Jackson	TN.	Tehuacana
Wiley, Oscar	1st Sgt.	K	5th	AL.	Infantry	Rodes	Early	Ft. Fisher	N. VA.	Groesbeck
Williams, H. W.	Pvt.	C	36th	NC	H. Arty.	Fort Duty			NC	Mexia
Wood, Ira E.	2nd Sgt.	F	15th	TX.	Cavalry	Granbury	Cleburne	Hardee	TN.	Mexia
Wilder, W. M.	Pvt.	B	10th	TX.	Infantry	Granbury	Cleburne	Hardee	TN.	Cade, Navarro Co.
Wright, Z. T.	Pvt.	F	31st	AL.	Infantry	Pettus	Stevenson	Hood	TN.	Mexia
Watkins, R. L.	Pvt.	G	12th	TX.	Cavalry	Parsons	Walker	E. K. Smith	T-MS.	Tehuacana
Walker, S. S.	Pvt.	I	2nd	TX.	Cavalry	Major	Green	E. K. Smith	T-MS.	Groesbeck
Wilder, J. L.	Pvt.	K	2nd	LA.	Infantry	Stafford	Ewell	Jackson	N. VA.	Mexia
Wood, E. B.	Capt.	B	34th	AL.	Infantry	Manigault	Hindman	Polk	TN.	Hubbard
Wright, Jas. A.	Pvt.	F	31st	AL.	Infantry	Pettus	Stevenson	Hood	TN.	Prairie Grove
Washum, M. L.	Pvt.	G	2nd	TX.	Cavalry	Green		E. K. Smith	T-MS.	Farrar
Walker, G. H.	Pvt.	A	9th	LA.	Infantry	Hays	Ewell	Jackson	N. VA.	Shiloh
Wyatt, W. W.	Pvt.	G	11th	MS.	Infantry	Davis	Heath	A. P. Hill	N. VA.	Groesbeck
Williams, L. H.	Pvt.	I	Phillips	TX.	Cavalry	Major	Green	E. K. Smith	T-MS.	Mt. Calm
Wright, Joel T.	Pvt.	B	20th	TX.	Cavalry	Roane	Steele	E. K. Smith	T-MS.	Mt. Calm
Welch, J. H.	Pvt.	K	20th	TX.	Dis. Cav.	Maxey	Hindman	E. K. Smith	T-MS.	Kosse
Wickdir, J. W.	O. Sgt.	B	7th	FL.	Infantry		Breckinridge	Hardee	TN.	Mt. Calm

ROSTER OF EX-CONFEDERATE VETERANS OF LIMESTONE COUNTY, TEXAS

JULY 22, 23, 24, 1896

NAME	RANK	CO.	REGT.	STATE	SERVICE	BRIGADE	DIVISION	CORPS	ARMY OF	POST OFFICE
Adams, L. A.	Pvt.	G	11th	TN.	Cavalry	Beale	Jackson	Forrest	TN.	Armour
Allen, B. W.	Pvt.	K	20th	TX.	Cavalry	Maxey	Hindman	E. K. Smith	T-MS.	Kosse
Allen, O. E.	O. Sgt.	F	4th	TX.	Cavalry	Hardeman	Green	E. K. Smith	T-MS.	Mart, McLennan Co.
Allison, A. B.	Pvt.	C	5th	TX.	Infantry	Hood	Whiting	Longstreet	N. VA.	Groesbeck
Anderson, F. M.	Pvt.	B	39th	MS.	Infantry		Gardner	Hardee	TN.	Mexia
Anderson, W. R.	Capt.	D	22nd	TX.	Cavalry	Waul		E. K. Smith	T-MS.	Tehuacana
Anglin, J. C.	Pvt.		McNelly's	TX.	Cavalry	Independent				Groesbeck
Archer, G. W.	Pvt.	C	8th	TX.	Cavalry	Wharton	Wheeler		TN.	Mexia
Archer, J. H.	Pvt.	F	36th	MS.	Infantry	Sears				Billington
Arnett, S. T.	Pvt.	I	21st	TX.	Cavalry	Parsons	Walker	E. K. Smith	T-MS.	Kosse
Arvin, J. A.	Pvt.	H	9th	VA.	Infantry	Corse	Pickett	Longstreet	N. VA.	Mexia
Barrett, J. D.**	Pvt.	I	59th	AL.	Infantry	Gracie	B. Johnson	Gordon	N. VA.	Cotton Gin, Freestone Co.
Barton, W. M.	Pvt.	E	13th	NC	Lt. Arty				N. VA.	Mexia
Batchelor, T. J.	Pvt.	E	62nd	AL.	Infantry	Thomas				Horn Hill
Beene, R. O.	O. Sgt.	G	45th	MS.	Infantry	Hébert	Maury	Hardee	TN.	Beene, Freestone Co.
Beene, S. H.	Pvt.	G	Madison's	TX.	Cavalry	Lane	Major	E. K. Smith	T-MS.	Mexia
Berryman, H. C.	Pvt.	H	20th	TX.	Infantry	Elmore		E. K. Smith	T-MS.	Prairie Grove
Blake, T. W.	Brig. Gen'l.				Infantry	Blake	Magruder	E. K. Smith	T-MS.	Mexia
Bond, S. F.	Pvt.	G	State Troops	TX.	Cavalry					Mexia
Bower, Chris	Pvt.	C	8th	TX.	Infantry	Young	Walker	E. K. Smith	T-MS.	Mexia
Boyd, H. A.	1st Lt.	E	35th	TX.	Cavalry	Bee	Walker	E. K. Smith	T-MS.	Tehuacana
Boyle, Y. C.	Pvt.	C	2nd	MS.	Infantry	Law		Longstreet	N. VA.	Tehuacana
Brady, J. T.	Pvt.		Seaman		Navy					Kosse
Bridges, J. J.	Cpl.	K	55th	GA.	Infantry	Gracie	Bragg			Ben Hur
Brooks, C. N.	Pvt.	D	Byrd's Battn	TX/LA	Cavalry			E. K. Smith	T-MS.	Thornton
Browder, W. H	Pvt.	A	1st	AL.	Cavalry	Allen	Johnson	Wheeler	TN.	Groesbeck
Brown, G. T.	Pvt.	K	12th	TX.	Cavalry	Parsons	Walker	E. K. Smith	T-MS.	Thornton
Brown, J. P.	Capt.	K	12th	TX.	Cavalry	Parsons	Walker	E. K. Smith	T-MS.	Groesbeck
Brown, W. P.	Capt.	K	20th	TX.	Cavalry	Maxey	Hindman	E. K. Smith	T-MS.	Groesbeck
Bryant, R. J.	Sgt.	B		TX.	Infantry	Waul				Mexia
Buckner, W. A.	2nd Lt.	B	9th	VA.	Cavalry	W. H. F. Lee	Fitz Lee	Stuart	N. VA.	Mexia
Bunn, J. G.	Pvt.	H	19th	MS.	Infantry	Posey	A. P. Hill	Longstreet	N. VA.	Frosa
Burch, J. A.	Pvt.	D	29th	GA.	Infantry	Stephens	Walker	Hardee	TN.	Mart, McLennan Co.
Burford, A. W.	Pvt.	A	7th	AL.	Cavalry	Rucker	Chalmers	Forrest	TN.	Mexia
Burleson, A. J.	Pvt.	K	12th	TX.	Cavalry	Parsons	Walker	E. K. Smith	T-MS.	Kosse
Burney, J. S. [Dr.]	Sgt.	C	4th	GA.	Infantry	Cook	Rodes	Jackson	N. VA.	Armour
Byers, Wm.	Sgt.	I	1st	GA.	Cavalry	Ross	Price	Bragg	TN.	Mexia
Camp, L. E.	Pvt.		Confuit's Batty	GA.	Lt. Arty		Stevenson	Hardee	TN.	Mexia
Carroll, J. G.	Pvt.	A	22nd	ARK.	Cavalry	Dockery	Walker	E. K. Smith	T-MS.	Mexia
Carruth, W. A.	Pvt.	F	11th	MS.	Infantry	Davis	Heth	A. P. Hill	N. VA.	Mexia

ROSTER OF EX-CONFEDERATE VETERANS OF LIMESTONE COUNTY, TEXAS

Name	Rank	Co.	Regt.	State	Branch	Brigade	Division	Corps/Army	Residence
Carter, Oliver	2nd Lt.	F	53rd	AL.	Cavalry	Hannon	Kelly	Wheeler	Hubbard
Cashion, A. J.	Capt.	H	1st	TN.	Infantry	Archer	Heth	A. P. Hill	Mexia
Castilow, C. A.	Cpl.	C	9th	TX.	Cavalry	Ross	Jackson		Thornton
Cates, J. B.	Pvt.	D	45th	TN.	Infantry	Brown	Breckinridge	Hardee	Mt. Calm
Clanahan, Jas.	Pvt.	I	21st	MS.	Infantry	Humphreys	McLaws	Longstreet	Mexia
Clark, M. H.	Pvt.	E	Willis'	TX.	Lt. Arty	Waul			Groesbeck
Collier, B. W.	Pvt.	I	7th	AL.	Cavalry	Rucker	Chalmers	Forrest	Mexia
Collum, Geo.	Pvt.	I	9th	TX.	Cavalry	Ross	Jackson		Groesbeck
Cook, J. P.	Pvt.	B	30th	AL.	Infantry	Pettus	Stevenson	Lee	Mexia
Cowart, L. E.	Pvt.	D	12th	GA.	Infantry	Doles	Ewell		Groesbeck
Cox, A. J.	Pvt.	H	38th	AL.	Infantry	Holtzclaw	A. P. Stewart		Prairie Grove
Cox, M. B.	Pvt.	G	18th	AL.	Infantry	Holtzclaw	A. P. Stewart	Hardee	Prairie Grove
Curry, T. J.	Pvt.	G		TN.	Cavalry	Beale	Jackson	Forrest	Kosse
Dailey, W. J.	Cpl.	G	9th	AL.	Cavalry	Allen	Jackson	Wheeler	Kosse
Davie, Wm. R.	Capt.	C	59th	AL.	Infantry	Gracie	B. Johnson	Gordon	Mexia
Deis, J. M.	Bugler		1st	MO.	Lt. Arty		Price	Hardee	Mexia
Dellis, S. F.	Pvt.	B	20th	TX.	Cavalry	Maxey	Hindman	E. K. Smith	Collina
Dickson, J. R.	O. Sgt.	D		SC	Cavalry	Hampton		Longstreet	Mart, McLennan Co.
Doke, F. Y.	Capt.	F		MO.	Infantry	1st Brigade			Kosse
Douglass, N. B.	Cpl.		9th	ARK.	Cavalry	Dockery	Parsons	E. K. Smith	Mart, McLennan Co.
Douglass, P. O.	Pvt.	A	15th	ARK.	Infantry	Dockery	Walker	E. K. Smith	Mart, McLennan Co.
Douglass, W. C.	Pvt.	C	15th		Infantry	Dockery	Churchill	E. K. Smith	Mart, McLennan Co.
Doyle, W. E.	Pvt.		2nd	TN.	Cavalry	Beale	Forrest		Mt. Calm
Duke, L. W. [Rev.]	Cpl.	G	7th	SC	Cavalry	Gary	Field	Longstreet	Mexia
Duncan, N. Y.	Pvt.	C	5th	AL.	Infantry	Battle	Rodes	Jackson	Mexia
Durham, C. A.	Pvt.	G	10th	MS.	Infantry	Sharp	Hindman	E. K. Smith	Prairie Grove
Durham, M. T.	Sgt.	K	6th	SC	Cavalry	Butler	Hampton	Stuart	Armour
Ezell, G. M.	Capt.	B	30th	AL.	Infantry	Pettus	Stevenson	Lee	Kosse
Farrar, L. J.	Major	G	4th	KY.	Infantry	Breckinridge		Hardee	Mart, McLennan Co.
Flaniken, J. C.	Pvt.	E	12th	TX.	Cavalry	Parsons	Walker	E. K. Smith	Groesbeck
Franks, T. L.	Pvt.	F	9th	TN.	Infantry	Maney	Cheatham	Polk	Tehuacana
Frazier, W. D.	Pvt.	I	10th	TX.	Cavalry	Cooper	Gano	E. K. Smith	Mexia
Friley, W. C. [Rev.]	Pvt.	B	59th	AL.	Infantry	Gracie	B. Johnson	Gordon	Yarbroville
Fuqua, M. P.	Pvt.	B	18th	MS.	Infantry	Barksdale			Mexia
Gardner, A. E.	Pvt.	E	22nd	ARK.	Infantry	Hawthorn	Churchill	E. K. Smith	Tehuacana
Germany, T. A.	Pvt.	G	4th	MS.	Cavalry	Mabry	Chalmers	Forrest	Thornton
Gibson, T. J.	Pvt.	B	12th	TX.	Cavalry	Parsons	Walker	E. K. Smith	Mexia
Gilbert, C. T.	Pvt.	C	12th	GA.	Infantry	Doles	Ewell		Mexia
Gordon, Sandy	Pvt.	I	21st	TX.	Cavalry	Parsons	Walker	E. K. Smith	Cade, Navarro Co.
Gray, H. W.	Pvt.	D	8th	VA.	Infantry	Young	Johnston	Jackson	Mexia
Groover, J. S.	Pvt.	G	37th	TX.	Cavalry	Stuart	Green		Mexia
Groves, J. S. [Rev.]	Pvt.	E	15th	TX.	Infantry	Lane	Mouton	E. K. Smith	Mexia
Groves, Noble	Pvt.	G	15th	ARK.	Infantry	Polignac	Churchill	E. K. Smith	Mexia
Hammond, B. F.	Cpl.	B	20th	TX.	Infantry	Dockery	Magruder	E. K. Smith	Kosse
Hammond, D. P.	Pvt.	D	1st	MS.	Infantry	Featherston	Loring	A. P. Stewart	Kosse

ROSTER OF EX-CONFEDERATE VETERANS OF LIMESTONE COUNTY, TEXAS

Name	Rank	Co.	Regt.	State	Branch	Brigade	Division	Corps	Army	Town
Hancock, B. J.	Pvt.	I	19th	TX.	Cavalry	Parsons	Marmaduke	E. K. Smith	T-MS.	Mexia
Hardwick, J. V.	Capt.	H	6th	AL.	Cavalry	Roddey	Forrest	Hardee	TN.	Mart, McLennan Co.
Harris, C. T.	Sgt.	G	1st	TX.	Detached	Fagan	Churchill	E. K. Smith	T-MS.	Mexia
Herbert, J. H.	Pvt.		4th	TX.	Infantry	Hood		Longstreet	N. VA.	Hubbard City
Herring, Elisha	Sgt.	K	36th	AL.	Infantry	Holtzclaw		Hardee	TN.	Prairie Grove
Herring, W. H.	1st Sgt.	G	18th	AL.	Infantry	Gladden	A. P. Stewart		TN.	Prairie Grove
Hickman, J. P.	Pvt.	B	10th	AL.	Infantry	Wilcox	Clayton	A. P. Stewart		Mexia
High, R. A.	Pvt.	B		TX.	Infantry	Waul	Anderson	Longstreet	N. VA.	Blooming Grove, Navarro
Hillis, B. D.	Pvt.	B	1st	ARK.	Cavalry	Fife			TN.	Delia
Hodges, B.	Pvt.	E	17th	AL.	Infantry	Slaughter	Price	Hood	TN.	Armour
Hogue, J. M.	Pvt.	H	13th	ARK.	Infantry	Govan	Cleburne	Hardee	TN.	Groesbeck
Hood, C. B.	Pvt.	E	51st	AL.	Cavalry	Allen	Wheeler	Hardee	TN.	Groesbeck
Hood, W. F.	Sgt.	B	1st	ARK.	Infantry	Reynolds	Walthall	Hood	TN.	Cade, Navarro Co.
Howard, F. M.	O. Sgt.	A	1st	TN.	Infantry	Archer	A. P. Hill	A. P. Stewart	N. VA.	Cade, Navarro Co.
Hughes, S.	Pvt.	E	53rd	AL.	Cavalry	Hannon	Wheeler	Hardee	TN.	Mexia
Ingram, S. C.	Pvt.	G	13th	AL.	Infantry	Archer	A. P. Hill		N. VA.	Luther, Howard Co.
Jackson, J. A.	Pvt.	K	14th	GA.	Infantry	Wilcox	Anderson	Longstreet	N. VA.	Thelma
Jayne, A. A.	Qr. Mtr.	G	28th	MS.	Cavalry	Harvey's Scouts				Groesbeck
Jennings, G. L.	Capt.	H	31st	MS.	Infantry	Featherston	Loring	A. P. Stewart	TN.	Kirk
Johnson, T. J.	Pvt.	B		MO.	Cavalry	Merrick	Price		TN.	Mexia
Johnson, W. M.	Pvt.	A	32nd	TX.	Cavalry	Buchel	Dagley	E. K. Smith	T-MS.	Thornton
Joiner, H. C.	O. Sgt.	E	19th	TX.	Infantry	Scurry	Walker	E. K. Smith	T-MS.	Groesbeck
Jolley, J. S.	Pvt.	G	3rd	ARK.	Infantry	Hood		Longstreet	N. VA.	Kosse
Jones, Jno. A.	Bugler	G	5th	NC	Cavalry	Barringer	W. H. F. Lee	Stuart	N. VA.	Kosse
Jones, Nat. M.	Sgt. Major		1st	NC	Infantry	Armistead	Hoke			Kosse
Jordan, G. L.	Pvt.	B	12th	TX.	Cavalry	Parsons	Walker	E. K. Smith	T-MS.	Luther, Howard Co.
Justice, Wm.	Pvt.	B	10th	TX.	Infantry	Granbury	Cleburne	Hardee	TN.	Personville
Kamsler, Wm.	Pvt.	I	25th	AL.	Infantry	Harrison	Walker	E. K. Smith	T-MS.	Mexia
Kaufman, M.	Capt.	B	45th	AL.	Infantry	Lowrey	Cleburne	Hardee	TN.	Mexia
Keeling, B. D.	Pvt.	I	1st	ARK.	Cavalry	Cabell	Fagan		TN.	Kosse
Kell, J. S.	Pvt.	G	3rd	TN.	Cavalry	Wharton	Wheeler	Hardee	TN.	Tehuacana
Kemp, M. W.	1st Lt.	D	13th	AL.	Infantry	Archer	A. P. Hill	A. P. Hill	N. VA.	Mexia
Kenney, G. W.	Pvt.	G	6th	AL.	Infantry	Battle	Rodes	Ewell	N. VA.	Mexia
Keys, J. C. C.	Pvt.	G	34th	TX.	Cavalry	Buchel	Bagby	E. K. Smith	T-MS.	Cotton Gin, Freestone Co.
Kidd, E. Z.	Sgt.	C	28th	LA.	Infantry	Polignac	Mouton	E. K. Smith	T-MS.	Thornton
Knott, G. W.	Pvt.	C	5th	TX.	Cavalry	Sibley	Green	E. K. Smith	T-MS.	Mexia
Knowls, A. R.	Pvt.	D	12th	LA.	Infantry	Buford	Loring	A. F. Stewart	TN.	Cade, Navarro Co.
Kynerd, A. J.	Pvt.	A	27th	MS.	Infantry	Walthall	Johnson	Lee	TN.	Dallas, Dallas Co.
Lanning, W. D.	Pvt.	K	18th	AL.	Infantry	Holtzclaw	Clayton	Hardee	TN.	Mexia
Lee, G. W.	Adjt.			AL.	Cavalry		Forrest		TN.	Thornton
Lewis, W. B.	Sgt.	C	2nd	FL.	Cavalry		Finegan		TN.	Armour
Lindley, J. P.	Pvt.	C	20th	TX.	Infantry	Frost	Hindman	E. K. Smith	T-MS.	Wortham
Love, R. M.	Pvt.	G	6th	TX.	Cavalry	Ross	Jackson		TN.	Austin, Travis Co.
Love, S. B.	Pvt.	G	6th	TX.	Cavalry	Ross	Jackson		TN.	Richland, Navarro Co.
Mahoney, J. T.	Pvt.	E	1st	AL.	Infantry	Walthall	Johnson	Lee	TN.	Mexia

ROSTER OF EX-CONFEDERATE VETERANS OF LIMESTONE COUNTY, TEXAS

Name	Rank	Co.	Regt.	State	Branch	Col.	Brig.	Div.	Dept.	Residence
Mallard, W. L.	Sgt.	A	4th	TN.	Cavalry		Wheeler		TN.	Tehuacana
Marshall, Calvin	Pvt.	B	Byrd's Battn	TX/LA	Cavalry			E. K. Smith	T-MS.	Mexia
Martin, L. H.	Pvt.	E	3rd	LA.	Infantry				N. VA.	Kosse
McClellan, J. W.	Pvt.	F	28th	LA.	Infantry	Polignac	Mouton		T-MS.	Prairie Hill
McClinlock, J. T.	Pvt.	A	2nd	MS.	Cavalry	Beale	Buford	E. K. Smith	TN.	Hubbard
McCorkle, Jas.	Pvt.	F	15th	TX.	Cavalry	Granbury	Cleburne	Forrest	TN.	Wortham
McDonald, J. E.	Pvt.	A	2nd	AL.	Cavalry	Ferguson	Wheeler	Hardee	TN.	Mexia
McDonald, M. L.	Pvt.	D	Woods'	MS.	Cavalry	Adams	Wheeler		TN.	Mexia
McKinney, J. W.	Cpl.	H	55th	AL.	Infantry	Buford	Loring		TN.	Watt
McNeese, G. W.	2nd Lt.	F	5th	TX.	Cavalry	Green	R. Taylor	A. P. Stewart	T-MS.	Hubbard City
Menifee, R. A.	Pvt.	I	28th	TX.	Infantry	Randal	Walker	E. K. Smith	T-MS.	Tehuacana
Miller, R. S.	Pvt.	I	4th	TX.	Infantry	Hood	Whiting	E. K. Smith	N. VA.	Hubbard City
Milligan, B. F.	Pvt.	A	16th	TN.	Cavalry	Beale	Buford	Longstreet	TN.	Armour
Monroe, J. M.	Pvt.	B	22nd	GA.	Infantry	Elliott	A. P. Stewart	Forrest	TN.	Condor
Moore, W. F. [Dr.]	Pvt.	K	15th	MS.	Infantry	Adams	Loring		TN.	Mexia
Morgan, H. W.	Major		32nd	GA.	Infantry	Cobb		A. P. Stewart	N. VA.	Mexia
Moroe, Louis	Pvt.	E	19th	TX.	Infantry	Waterhouse	Walker		T-MS.	Armour
Morton, J. M.	Pvt.	I	38th	TN.	Infantry	Wright	Cheatham	E. K. Smith	TN.	Mt. Calm
Morton, Z. T.	Pvt.	A	5th	GA.	Infantry	Cumming		Polk	TN.	Personville
Moss, J. W.	Pvt.	K	12th	TX.	Cavalry	Parsons	Walker		T-MS.	Mexia
Mulley, J. W.	Sgt.	B	19th	ARK.	Infantry	Tappan	Churchill	E. K. Smith	T-MS.	Kosse
Mullins, J. H.	3rd Sgt.	H	26th	AL.	Infantry	Deas	Withers	E. K. Smith	TN.	Mart, McLennan Co.
Nash, J. W.	Pvt.		Style's Battn	VA.	H. Arty				N. VA.	Armour
Neill, Geo. A.	Pvt.	Scouts	McAnally	TX.	Cavalry					Mexia
Nelson, A. J.	Pvt.			AL.						Tehuacana
Nelson, T. J.	Pvt.	G	20th	AL.	Infantry	Pettus	Stevenson	Hood	TN.	Tehuacana
Oakes, J. M.	Pvt.	K	8th	AL.	Infantry	Wilcox	Anderson	A. P. Hill	N. VA.	Groesbeck
Ouzts, B. F.	Asst. Surg.	I	2nd	SC	Cavalry	Butler				Personville
Owens, J. M.	Pvt.	I	22nd	GA.	Infantry	Elliott	McLaws	Hardee	TN.	Kosse
Parker, J. E.	Pvt.	I	3rd	AL.	Infantry	Battle	Rodes	Ewell	N. VA.	Armour
Parsons, M. J.	Sgt.		Bradford's	TX.	Cavalry		Magruder		T-MS.	Mexia
Patterson, John	Pvt.	B	10th	TX.	Infantry	Granbury	Cleburne	E. K. Smith	TN.	Kosse
Phillips, J. B.	Pvt.	K	13th	AL.	Infantry	Archer	A. P. Hill	Hardee	N. VA.	Groesbeck
Pool, R. L. P.	2nd Lt.	I	Madison's	TX.	Cavalry	Lane	Green	Jackson	TN.	Armour
Popejoy, N. T.	Pvt.	D	2nd	TN.	Cavalry	Ashby	Wheeler		TN.	Hubbard
Powell, J. G.	Pvt.	K	35th	TX.	Cavalry	Buchel	Green	E. K. Smith	T-MS.	Groesbeck
Powell, Geo. W.	Pvt.	A	34th	TX.	Cavalry	Terrell	Wharton	E. K. Smith	T-MS.	Mexia
Prendergast, A. T.	Pvt.	G	6th	TX.	Cavalry	Ross	Jackson		TN.	Hubbard
Price, J. E.	Pvt.	E	35th	TX.	Cavalry	Terrell	Green	E. K. Smith	T-MS.	Wortham
Prince, J. H.	Pvt.	C	10th	GA.	Infantry	Simms	McLaws	Longstreet	N. VA.	Kosse
Pruit, W. W.	Pvt.	C	15th	TX.	Infantry	Polignac	Mouton	E. K. Smith	T-MS.	Yarbroville
Raborn, Isaac	2nd Sgt.	C	19th	LA.	Infantry	Gibson		Hardee	TN.	Prairie Grove
Rains, J. M.	Capt.	A	4th	VA.	Infantry		A. P. Stewart			Groesbeck
Rambo, J. M.	O. Sgt.	F	9th	MS.	Cavalry	Ferguson	Jackson	Wheeler	TN.	Brewer, Freestone Co.
Rea, S. W.	Pvt.	C	Morgan's	TX.	Cavalry	Parsons	Walker	E. K. Smith	T-MS.	Personville
										Groesbeck

ROSTER OF EX-CONFEDERATE VETERANS OF LIMESTONE COUNTY, TEXAS

Name	Rank	Co.	Regt.	State	Branch	Brigade	Division	Corps	Army	Residence
Reeves, W. J.	Sgt.	F	15th	TX.	Cavalry	Granbury	Cleburne	Hardee	TN.	Personville
Reynolds, M. P.	Pvt.	D	7th	AL.	Cavalry	Rucker	Fitz Lee	Forrest	TN.	Tehuacana
Richardson, W. H.	1st Lt.	F	2nd	MD.	Cavalry	Johnson		Hampton	N. VA.	Austin, Travis Co.
Risien, Sam'l. Sr.	Engineer		Seaman	AL.	Navy					Groesbeck
Roberson, W. D.	Cpl.	C	23rd	GA.	Infantry	Colquitt	Hoke		N. VA.	Groesbeck
Roberts, W. F.	Capt.	G	28th	TX.	Cavalry	Randal	Walker	E. K. Smith	T-MS.	Mexia
Rogers, A. J.	Sgt.	C	20th	TX.	Cavalry	Maxey	Hindman	E. K. Smith	T-MS.	Personville
Ross, G. W.	Pvt.	H	4th	MO.	Cavalry	Cockrell	French	Polk	TN.	Mexia
Sawyer, J. P.	Pvt.	D	12th	MS.	Cavalry	Ferguson	Jackson	Wheeler	TN.	Luther, Howard Co.
Saxon, S. M.	Pvt.	A	15th	TX.	Infantry	Polignac	Mouton	E. K. Smith	T-MS.	Reagan, Falls Co.
Scarborough, S. R.	Pvt.	A	15th	MS.	Infantry	Adams	Loring	Polk	TN.	Mexia
Scruggs, S. K.	Lt.	C	8th	TX.	Cavalry	Wharton	Wheeler		TN.	Mexia
Sexton, A. V.	Pvt.	B	10th	AL.	Cavalry		Jackson	Wheeler	TN.	Armour
Sharp, T. H.	Pvt.	B	10th	TX.	Infantry	Granbury	Cleburne	Hardee	TN.	Groesbeck
Sherrill, B. F.	Pvt.	H	1st	NC	Infantry	Thomas	Breckinridge	Early	N. VA.	Mexia
Shortridge, J. D.	Cpl.	D	23rd	NC	Infantry		Early	A. P. Hill	N. VA.	Groesbeck
Shriver, Adam	Pvt.			LA.	Artillery		Anderson	A. P. Hill	N. VA.	Kirk
Simmons, H. F.	Pvt.	D	Woods'	MS.	Cavalry	Adams	Wheeler		TN.	Kerens, Navarro Co.
Simmons, J. W.	Pvt.	E	27th	MS.	Infantry	Walthall	Johnson	Lee	TN.	Mexia
Skillern, T. W.	Pvt.	C	36th	ARK.	Infantry	Cray	Churchill	Price	T-MS.	Frosa
Skipper, W. M.	Sgt.	E	1st	AL.	Artillery		Maury		TN.	Kosse
Sloan, A. J.	2nd Sgt.	I	20th	MS.	Infantry	Floyd	Loring	Jackson	N. VA.	Mexia
Smith, Jas. L.	Pvt.	C	14th	NC	Infantry	Ramseur	Rodes	Jackson	N. VA.	Mexia
Smyth, E. B.	Pvt.			TX.	Cavalry			E. K. Smith	T-MS.	Mexia
Starley, W. F. [Dr.]	Pvt.	I	2nd	TX.	Par. Ranger	Major	Green	E. K. Smith	T-MS.	Mexia
Steddum, N. B.	Pvt.	F	27th	TX.	Cavalry	Wharton	Mouton	E. K. Smith	T-MS.	Mt. Calm
Steele, J. Warren	Pvt.	G	7th	TX.	Infantry	Granbury	Cleburne	Harcee	TN.	Mexia
Steele, R. E.	1st Lt.	G	7th	TX.	Infantry	Granbury	Cleburne	Hardee	TN.	Mexia
Steele, Rado	Pvt.	B	10th	TX.	Cavalry	Granbury	Cleburne	Hardee	TN.	Mexia
Storey, J. M.	O. Sgt.	H	28th	TX.	Cavalry	Randal	Walker	E. K. Smith	T-MS.	Groesbeck
Stuart, J. W.	Pvt.	B	9th	TX.	Infantry	Wright	Cheatham	Polk	TN.	Mexia
Sturdivant, L. H.	Pvt.	G	38th	TN.	Infantry	Colquitt	Hoke	Longstreet	N. VA.	Mexia
Suttle, J. M.	1st Sgt.	H	23rd	GA.	Infantry	Tappan	Churchill	E. K. Smith	T-MS.	Luther, Howard Co.
Talley, C. H.	2nd Lt.	A	19th	ARK.	Infantry					
Tennison, T. F.	Pvt.									
Therrill, J. D.	Sgt.	C	44th	MS.	Infantry	Tucker	Hindman	Hood	TN.	Mexia
Thomas, J. W.	Cpl.	H	43rd	NC	Infantry	Daniel	Rodes	Ewell	N. VA.	Kirk
Thompson, C. W.	Pvt.	B	20th	TX.	Infantry	Harrison	Walker	E. K. Smith	T-MS.	Tehuacana
Thompson, J. W.	Pvt.	C	4th	AL.	Infantry	Law	Hood	Longstreet	N. VA.	Horn Hill
Thornton, A. N.	O. Sgt.	C	39th	GA.	Infantry	Cumming	Stevenson	Hardee	TN.	Groesbeck
Tucker, M. A.	Sgt. Maj.	F	15th	TX.	Cavalry	Johnson	Cleburne	Hardee	TN.	Tehuacana
Vaughan, H. T.	2nd Sgt.	C	35th	TX.	Cavalry	Buchel	Walker	E. K. Smith	T-MS.	Horn Hill
Walker, G. H.	Pvt.	A	9th	LA.	Infantry	Hays	Ewell	Jackson	N. VA.	Mart, McLennan Co.
Walker, S. S.	Pvt.	I	2nd	TX.	Cavalry	Major	Green	E. K. Smith	T-MS.	Luther, Howard Co.
Waller, N. L.				TX.				Civil Service		Groesbeck Mexia

ROSTER OF EX-CONFEDERATE VETERANS OF LIMESTONE COUNTY, TEXAS

Walling, J. G.	Pvt.	C	15th	TX.	Infantry	Polignac	Mouton	Taylor	T-MS.	Thornton
Ward, R. P.	Pvt.	F	12th	TX.	Cavalry	Parsons	Walker	E. K. Smith	T-MS.	Mexia
Watkins, R. L.	Pvt.	G	12th	TX.	Cavalry	Parsons	Walker	E. K. Smith	T-MS.	Tehuacana
Watson, C. L.	2nd Sgt.	D	10th	TX.	Infantry	Granbury	Cleburne	Hardee	TM	Mexia
Webb, J. C.	Pvt.	K	20th	TX.	Cavalry	Maxey	Hindman	E. K. Smith	T-MS.	Groesbeck
Welch, J. H.	Pvt.	K	20th	TX.	Cavalry	Maxey	Hindman	E. K. Smith	T-MS.	Kosse
Whitfield, James	Cpl.	G	10th	TX.	Cavalry	Ector	Walker	Polk	TM	Mexia
Wickder, J. W.	O. Sgt.	B	7th	FL.	Infantry	Frensley	Breckinridge	Hardee	TM	Mt. Calm
Wilder, W. M.	Pvt.	B	10th	TX.	Infantry	Granbury	Cleburne	Hardee	TM	Cade, Navarro Co.
Wiley, Oscar	1st Sgt.	K	5th	AL.	Infantry	Rodes	Early	Jackson	N. VA.	Groesbeck
Wilie, T. W.	Pvt.	C	8th	TX.	Cavalry	Harrison	Wheeler	Hardee	TN.	Mt. Calm
Williams, E. W.	Pvt.	C	3rd	TX.	Cavalry	Ross	Jackson	Hardee	TN.	Tehuacana
Williams, H. W.	Pvt.	C	36th	NC	H. Arty	Ft. Duty	Fort Fisher		N. VA.	Mexia
Williams, L. H.	Pvt.	I	Phillips'	TX.	Cavalry	Major	Green	E. K. Smith	T-MS.	Mt. Calm
Wood, C. H. F.	3rd Sgt.	F	15th	TX.	Cavalry	Granbury	Cleburne	Hardee	TN.	Mexia
Wood, E. B.	Capt.	B	34th	AL.	Infantry	Manigault	Hindman	Polk	TN.	Hubbard City
Wood, Ira C.	2nd Sgt.	F	15th	TX.	Cavalry	Granbury	Cleburne	Hardee	TN.	Mexia
Woods, D.	Pvt.	F	12th	TN.	Cavalry	Richardson	Buford	Forrest	TN.	Corsicana, Navarro Co.
Wooldridge, C. J.	Pvt.	G	31st	GA.	Infantry					Wortham
Wright, James A.	Pvt.	F	31st	AL.	Infantry	Pettus	Stevenson	Hood	TN.	Prairie Grove
Wright, Jno. A.	Pvt.	C	59th	AL.	Infantry	Gracie	B. Johnson	Gordon	N. VA.	Mexia
Wright, Joel T.	Pvt.	B	20th	TX.	Cavalry	Roane	Steele	E. K. Smith	T-MS.	Mt. Calm
Wyatt, W. W.	Pvt.	G	11th	MS.	Infantry	Davis	Heth	A. P. Hill	N. VA.	Groesbeck
Yankee, J. F.	2nd Lt.	C	13th	TX.	Cavalry	Waul	Walker	E. K. Smith	T-MS.	Ben Hur
Yeldell, J. P.	Pvt.	B	15th	AL.	Cavalry					Mexia

ROSTER OF EX-CONFEDERATE VETERANS OF LIMESTONE COUNTY, TEXAS

1903

NAMES	RANK	CO.	REGT.	STATE	SERVICE	BRIGADE	DIVISION	CORPS	ARMY OF	POST OFFICE
Adams, L. A.	Pvt.	G	11th	TN.	Cavalry	Beale	Jackson	Forrest	TN.	Coolidge
Adams, W. L.	Pvt.	B	10th	TX.	Infantry	Granbury	Cleburne	Hardee	TN.	Mexia
Allen, B. W.	Pvt.	K	20th	TX.	Cavalry	Maxey	Hindman	E. K. Smith	T-MS.	Kosse
Allison, A. B.	Pvt.	C	5th	TX.	Infantry	Hood	Whiting	Longstreet	N. VA.	Groesbeck
Anderson, Boon	Pvt.	A	Timmon's	TX.	Infantry	Waul	Walker	E. K. Smith	T-MS.	Groesbeck
Anderson, W. R.	Capt.	D	22nd	TX.	Infantry	Waul	Walker	E. K. Smith	T-MS.	Tehuacana
Anglin, J. C.	Pvt.	Scout	McNelly	TX.			Green	E. K. Smith	T-MS.	Groesbeck
Archer, Geo. W.	Pvt.	C	8th	TX.	Cavalry	Wharton	Wheeler	Hardee	TN.	Mexia
Archer, J. H.	Cpl.	F	36th	MS.	Infantry	Sears	French	A. P. Stewart	TN.	Mt. Calm
Barrett, J. D.	Pvt.	I	59th	AL.	Infantry	Gracie	B. Johnson	Longstreet	N. VA.	Mexia
Barton, W. M.	Pvt.	E	13th	NC	Lt. Arty				N. VA.	Armour
Batchelor, T. J.	Pvt.	E	62nd	AL.	Infantry	Thomas				Strutman
Beene, R. O.	O. Sgt.	G	45th	MS.	Infantry	Hébert	Maury	Hardee	TN.	Beene, Freestone Co.
Beene, Sam. H.	Pvt.	G	Madison's	TX.	Cavalry	Lane	Major	E. K. Smith	T-MS.	Mexia
Benthall, W. T.	Pvt.	C	3rd	LA.	Cavalry	Harrison	Walker	E. K. Smith	T-MS.	Thornton
Berry, A. J.	Pvt.	D	6th	MS.	Infantry	Lowrey	Loring	Hardee	TN.	Wortham
Bond, S. F.	Pvt.	G	State Troops	TX.				E. K. Smith	T-MS.	Mexia
Bower, C. J.	Pvt.	B	10th	TX.	Infantry	Granbury	Cleburne	Hardee	TN.	Mexia
Boyd, H. A.	1st Lt.	E	35th	TX.	Cavalry	Bee	Cleburne	E. K. Smith	T-MS.	Tehuacana
Bozeman, J. H.	Pvt.	B	2nd	GA.	Infantry	Cumming	Stevenson	Hardee	TN.	Tehuacana
Brady, J. T.	Seaman		Navy							Kosse
Brandon, J. A.	Pvt.	A	14th	ARK.	Cavalry	Cabell	Fagan	Price	T-MS.	Tehuacana
Bridges, J. J.	Cpl.	K	55th	GA.	Infantry	Gracie	Bragg		TN.	Groesbeck
Brooks, C. N.	Pvt.	D	Byrd's Battn		Cavalry			E. K. Smith	T-MS.	Thornton
Browder, W. H.	Pvt.	A	1st	AL.	Cavalry	Allen	Johnson	Wheeler	TN.	Groesbeck
Brown, Geo. T.	Pvt.	K	12th	TX.	Cavalry	Parsons	Walker	E. K. Smith	T-MS.	Thornton
Brown, W. P.	Capt.	K	20th	TX.	Cavalry	Maxey	Hindman	E. K. Smith	T-MS.	Groesbeck
Bryant, R. J.	Sgt.	B		TX.	Infantry	Waul			TN.	Mexia
Burford, A. W.	Pvt.	A	7th	AL.	Cavalry	Chalmers	Maury	Forrest	TN.	Ft. Worth
Burleson, A. J.	Pvt.	K	12th	TX.	Cavalry	Parsons	Walker	E. K. Smith	T-MS.	Kosse
Burney, T. S.	Sgt.	G	4th	GA.	Infantry	Cook	Rodes	Jackson	N. VA.	Thelma
Butler, John	Pvt.	A	5th	AL.	Infantry	Battle	Rodes	A. P. Hill	N. VA.	Mexia
Byers, Wm.	Sgt.	I	1st	TX.	Cavalry	Ross	Price	Bragg	TN.	Mexia
Byrd, T. S.	Pvt.		Turner's Batty	MS.	Artillery	Maney	Cheatham	Hardee	TN.	Mexia
Camp, L. E.	Pvt.		Corfuit's Batty	GA.	Lt. Arty		Stevenson	Hardee	TN.	Mexia
Carroll, J. G.	Pvt.	A	22nd	ARK.	Cavalry	Dockery	Walker	E. K. Smith	T-MS.	Mexia
Carter, Oliver	2nd Lt.	F	53rd	AL.	Cavalry	Hannon	Kelly	Wheeler	TN.	Coolidge
Chandler, S. H.	Pvt.	K	12th	NC	Infantry	Johnson	Pegram	Ewell	N. VA.	Mart, McLennan Co.
Clark, M. H.	Pvt.	E	Willis'	TX.	Lt. Arty	Waul			TN.	Groesbeck
Collier, B. W.	Pvt.	I	7th	AL.	Cavalry	Rucker		Forrest	TN.	Mexia

ROSTER OF EX-CONFEDERATE VETERANS OF LIMESTONE COUNTY, TEXAS

Name	Rank	Co.	Regt.	State	Branch				Location
Collum, Geo.	Pvt.	I	9th	TX.	Cavalry	Ross	Jackson	TN.	Mart, McLennan Co.
Connors, John	Pvt.	G	2nd	TX.	Infantry		Magruder	T-MS.	Hubbard
Cook, J. P. [Dr.]	Pvt.	B	30th	AL.	Infantry	Pettus	Stevenson	TN.	Mexia
Cowart, L. E.	Pvt.	D	12th	GA.	Infantry	Doles	Jackson	N. VA.	Corsicana, Navarro Co.
Cox, A. J.	Pvt.	H	38th	AL.	Infantry	Holtzclaw	Stewart	TN.	Prairie Grove
Cox, M. B.	Pvt.	G	18th	AL.	Infantry	Holtzclaw	Stewart	TN.	Fallon
Currey, A. A.	2nd Lt.		1st	TX.	Cavalry	Ross	Jackson	TN.	Groesbeck
Curry, T. J.	Pvt.	G		TN.	Cavalry	Beale	Jackson	TN.	Kosse
Dailey, W. J.	Cpl.	G	9th	AL.	Cavalry	Allen	Jackson	TN.	Kosse
Davis, R. E.	Col. Br.	H	60th	AL.	Infantry	Gracie	Wheeler	TN.	Coolidge
DeHart, T. A.	Pvt.	G	21st	MS.	Infantry	Barksdale	B. Johnson	N. VA.	Hearne, Robertson Co.
Deis, J. M.	Bugler		1st	MO.	Lt. Arty	Cockrell	Kershaw	N. VA.	Mexia
Dellis, S. F.	Pvt.	B	20th	TX.	Cavalry	Maxey	Price	TN.	Hubbard
Doke, F. Y.	Capt.	F	9th	MO.	Infantry	1st Brigade	Hindman	T-MS.	Corsicana, Navarro Co.
Douglass, N. B.	Cpl.	A	15th	ARK.	Cavalry	Dockery	Parsons	TN.	Mart, McLennan Co.
Douglass, P. O.	Sgt.	A	15th	ARK.	Infantry	Dockery	Walker	T-MS.	Mart, McLennan Co.
Doyle, W. E.	Pvt.	G	7th	SC	Cavalry	Gary	Churchill	T-MS.	Mexia
Durham, C. A.	Pvt.	K	6th	SC	Cavalry	Butler	Field	N. VA.	Coolidge
Durham, M. T.	Sgt.	B	30th	AL.	Infantry	Pettus	Hampton	N. VA.	Odds
Eady, Leander	Pvt.	I	33rd	AL.	Infantry	Lowrey	Stevenson	TN.	Groesbeck
Elzey, F. M.	Pvt.	A	12th	LA.	Infantry	Scott	Cleburne	TN.	Mart, McLennan Co.
English, A. L.	Pvt.	C	62nd	AL.	Infantry		Loring	TN.	Kosse
Ezell, G. M.	Capt.	G	4th	KY.	Infantry	Breckinridge	Liddell		Mart, McLennan Co.
Farrow, R. E.	Lt.	C	28th	LA.	Infantry	Polignac	Mouton	TN.	Mexia
Fife, J. H.	Pvt.	H	31st	MS.	Infantry	Featherston	Loring	T-MS.	Mexia
Fortenberry, J. M.	Pvt.	A	1st	AL.	Infantry	Pettus	Stevenson	TN.	Kirk
Franks, T. L.	Pvt.	F	10th	TX.	Cavalry	Cooper	Gano	T-MS.	Mexia
Frazier, W. D.	Pvt.	I	59th	AL.	Infantry	Gracie	B. Johnson	N. VA.	Coolidge
Frost, W. A.	Pvt.	F	5th	LA.	Cavalry	Harrison	Mouton	T-MS.	Wortham
Gardner, A. E.	Pvt.	E	4th	MS.	Cavalry	Mabry	Chalmers	TN.	Kosse
Gibson, T. J.	Pvt.	B	12th	GA.	Infantry	Doles	Ewell	N. VA.	Mexia
Gilbert, C. T.	Pvt.	C	21st	TX.	Cavalry	Parsons	Walker	T-MS.	Streetman
Gordon, Sandy	Pvt.	I	8th	TX.	Infantry	Young	Walker	T-MS.	Mexia
Gray, H. W.	Pvt.	D	37th	VA.	Infantry	Stuart	Johnson	N. VA.	Mexia
Groover, J. S.	Pvt.	G	Madison's	TX.	Cavalry	Lane	Green	T-MS.	Mexia
Hammond, B. F.	Cpl.	B	20th	TX.	Infantry	Harrison	Walker	T-MS.	Kosse
Hammond, D. P.	Pvt.	D	1st	MS.	Cavalry	Featherston	Loring	TN.	Kosse
Hammond, W. R.	Pvt.	K	12th	TX.	Infantry	Parsons	Walker	T-MS.	Kosse
Harris, C. T.	Sgt.	G	1st	TX.	Det. Cav.	Fagan	Churchill	T-MS.	Mexia
Haskins, T. E.	Pvt.	H	23rd	AL.	Infantry	Pettus	Stevenson	TN.	Waco, McLennan Co.
Hayes, T. H.	Pvt.	B	32nd	TX.	Infantry	Cabell	S. D. Lee	TN.	Groesbeck
Hayes, W. H.	Pvt.	D	33rd	ARK.	Infantry	Tappan	E. K. Smith	T-MS.	Wortham
Herring, W. H.	Sgt.	G	18th	AL.	Infantry	Gladden	Clayton	T-MS.	Prairie Grove
Hickman, J. P.	Pvt.	B	10th	AL.	Infantry	Wilcox	Anderson	N. VA.	Mexia
Hodges, B.	Pvt.	E	17th	AL.	Infantry	Slaughter		TN.	Coolidge

ROSTER OF EX-CONFEDERATE VETERANS OF LIMESTONE COUNTY, TEXAS

Name	Rank	Co.	Regt.	State	Branch	Brigade	Division	Corps/Dept.	Location
Howze, J. W.	Pvt.	K	1st	SC	H. Arty			N. VA.	Navarro, Navarro Co.
Hughes, S.	Pvt.	E	53rd	AL.	Cavalry	Hannon	Wheeler	TN.	Mexia
Humphries, J. W.	Pvt.	C	5th	AL.	Cavalry	Roddey		TN.	Mexia
Ingram, S. C.	Pvt.	G	13th	AL.	Infantry	Archer	A. P. Hill	N. VA.	Mexia
Jackson, J. A.	Pvt.	K	14th	GA.	Infantry	Wilcox	Anderson	N. VA.	Thelma
Jackson, J. G.	Pvt.	G	7th	AL.	Cavalry	Clanton	Jackson	TN.	Mt. Calm
Jackson, John	Pvt.	B	12th	GA.	Infantry	Doles	Ewell	N. VA.	Richland, Navarro Co.
Jayne, A. A.	Qr. Mtr.	G	28th	MS.	Cavalry	Harvey's Scouts	Jackson	TN.	Groesbeck
Jennings, G. L.	Capt.	H	31st	MS.	Infantry	Featherston		TN.	Kirk
Johnson, J. B.	Pvt.	F	6th	MS.	Cavalry		Loring	Polk	TN.	Crockett, Houston Co.
Johnson, T. J.	Pvt.	B	46th	MO.	Cavalry	Merrick		Forrest	TN.	Mexia
Joiner, N. C.	O. Sgt.	E	19th	TX.	Infantry	Scurry	Price	Walker	T-MS.	Groesbeck
Jolley, J. S.	Pvt.	G	3rd	ARK.	Infantry	Hood		Longstreet	N. VA.	Kosse
Jones, Jno A.	Bugler	G	5th	NC	Cavalry	Barringer	W. H. F. Lee	Stuart	N. VA.	Kosse
Jones, Nat. M.	Sgt. Major		1st	NC	Infantry	Armistead	Hoke		N. VA.	Kosse
Justice, Wm.	Pvt.	B	10th	TX.	Infantry	Granbury	Cleburne	Hardee	TN.	Donie, Freestone Co.
Kamsler, Wm.	Pvt.	I	20th	TX.	Infantry	Harrison	Walker	E. K. Smith	T-MS.	Mexia
Keeling, B. D.	Pvt.	I	1st	ARK.	Cavalry	Cabell	Fagan	E. K. Smith	T-MS.	Kosse
Kenney, G. W.	Pvt.	G	6th	AL.	Infantry	Battle	Rodes	Ewell	N. VA.	Hubbard
Keys, J. C. C.	Pvt.	G	34th	TX.	Cavalry	Buchel	Bagby	E. K. Smith	T-MS.	Cotton Gin, Freestone
Kidd, E. Z.	Sgt.	C	28th	LA.	Infantry	Polignac	Mouton	E. K. Smith	T-MS.	Thornton
Kimbell, James	Pvt.	H	1st	ARK.	Cavalry	Cabell	Fagan	E. K. Smith	T-MS.	Groesbeck
Kynerd, A. J.	Pvt.	A	27th	MS.	Infantry	Walthall	Johnson	S. D. Lee	TN.	Dallas, Dallas Co.
LaGrone, D.	Pvt.	I	26th	TX.	Cavalry	Debray	Green	E. K. Smith	T-MS.	Mart, McLennan Co.
Laird, E. E.	Pvt.	D	1st	MS.	Infantry	Featherston	Loring	Polk	TN.	Wortham
Laird, R. S.	Pvt.	A	5th	MS.	Cavalry	Adams	Wheeler	Hardee	TN.	Coolidge
Lanning, W. D.	Pvt.	K	18th	AL.	Infantry	Holtzclaw	Clayton	Hardee	TN.	Mexia
Lee, G. W. [Blind]	Adjt.		Lewis' Battn	AL.	Cavalry		Jackson	Forrest	TN.	Thornton
Leonard, S. R.	Pvt.	A	1st	ARK.	Cavalry	Cabell	Fagan	E. K. Smith	T-MS.	Wortham
Lewis, W. B.	Sgt.	C	2nd	FL.	Cavalry		Finegan		TN.	Coolidge
Lewis, W. G.	Pvt.	C	2nd	FL.	Cavalry		Finegan		TN.	Coolidge
Lindley, J. P.	Pvt.	C	20th	TX.	Infantry	Frost	Hindman	E. K. Smith	T-MS.	Wortham
Livingston, W.	Pvt.	H	20th	ARK.	Cavalry	Brooks	Fagan	E. K. Smith	T-MS.	Wortham
Love, Sam. B.	Pvt.	G	6th	TX.	Cavalry	Ross	Jackson	Hardee	TN.	Richland, Navarro Co.
Mahoney, J. T.	Pvt.	E	1st	AL.	Infantry	Walthall	Johnson	Lee	TN.	Mexia
Mallard, W. L.	Sgt.	A	4th	TN.	Cavalry	Harrison	Wheeler		TN.	Tehuacana
Marshall, C.	Pvt.	B	Byrd's Battn	TX.	Cavalry			E. K. Smith	T-MS.	Mexia
Matthews, F. M.	Pvt.	G	1st	TX.	Infantry	Robertson	Hood	Longstreet	N. VA.	Mart, McLennan Co.
McClintock, J. F.	Pvt.	A	2nd	MS.	Cavalry	Beale	Buford	Forrest	TN.	Hubbard
McCorkle, Jas.	Pvt.	F	15th	TX.	Cavalry	Granbury	Cleburne	Hardee	TN.	Mexia
McDaniel, J. A.	Pvt.		Speight's	TX.	Infantry		Walker	E. K. Smith	T-T-	Mart, McLennan Co.
McDonald, J. C.	Pvt.	K	20th	TX.	Cavalry	Maxey	Hindman	E. K. Smith	T-MS.	Mexia
McDonald, M. L.	Pvt.	D	Woods'	TX.	Cavalry	Adams	Wheeler	Hardee	TN.	Mexia
McKinney, J. W.	Cpl.	H	55th	AL.	Infantry	Buford	Loring	Stewart	TN.	Mt. Calm
McLean, W. F.	Pvt.	E	40th	AL.	Infantry	Pettus	Stevenson	Lee	TN.	Groesbeck

ROSTER OF EX-CONFEDERATE VETERANS OF LIMESTONE COUNTY, TEXAS

Name	Rank	Co.	Regt.	State	Branch	Captain	Brigade	Division	Army	Residence
McNeese, G. W.	2nd Lt.	F	5th	TX.	Cavalry	Green	Taylor	E. K. Smith	T-MS.	Hubbard
Menefee, R. A.	Pvt.	I	28th	TX.	Infantry	Randal	Walker	E. K. Smith	T-MS.	Kirk
Miller, R. S.	Pvt.	I	4th	TX.	Infantry	Hood	Whiting	Longstreet	N. VA.	Hubbard
Mitchell, S. A.	Sgt.	I	2nd	FL.	Infantry	Perry	Anderson	Longstreet	N. VA.	Coolidge
Moore, W. F. [Dr.]	Pvt.	K	15th	MS.	Infantry	Adams	Loring	Stewart	TN.	Mexia
Morrow, M. L.	Pvt.	A	6th	MS.	Cavalry	Mabry	Buford	Forrest	TN.	Wortham
Morton, Z. T.	Pvt.	A	5th	GA.	Infantry	Cumming		Hardee	TN.	Personville
Mulloy, J. W.	Sgt.	B	19th	ARK.	Infantry	Tappan	Churchill	E. K. Smith	T-MS.	Mart, McLennan Co.
Nabors, A. M.	Sgt.	H	49th	AL.	Infantry	Scott	Loring	Polk	TN.	Kosse
Nash, J. W.	Pvt.		Style's Batt.	VA.	H. Arty					
Neill, Geo. A.	Pvt.	McNelly	Scouts	TX.	Cavalry	Det. Service		E. K. Smith	N. VA.	Wortham
Nelson, T. J.	Pvt.	G	20th	AL.	Infantry	Pettus	Stevenson	S. Lee	T-MS.	Groesbeck
Nickles, J.	Pvt.	K	12th	TX.	Cavalry	Parsons	Walker	E. K. Smith	TN.	Frosa
Nobles, J. P.	Cpl.	K	4th	MS.	Infantry	Baldwin	Tilghman	Hardee	TN.	Groesbeck
Ouzts, B. F. [Dr.]	Asst. Surg.	I	2nd	SC	Cavalry	Butler		Hampton	N. VA.	Kosse
Owens, J. M.	Pvt.	I	22nd	GA.	Infantry	Elliott	McLaws	Hardee	TN.	Armour
Parker, J. E.	Pvt.	I	3rd	AL.	Infantry	Battle	Rodes	Ewell	N. VA.	Teague, Freestone Co.
Parson, M. J.	Sgt.		Bradford's	TX.	Cavalry		Magruder	E. K. Smith	T-MS.	Kosse
Parsons, J.	Pvt.	G	4th	GA.	Cavalry	Crew	Martin	Wheeler	TN.	Groesbeck
Patterson, John	Pvt.	B	10th	TX.	Infantry	Granbury	Cleburne	Hardee	TN.	Groesbeck
Perdue, B. F.	Pvt.	A	46th	GA.	Cavalry	Gist	Walker	Hardee	TN.	Mexia
Perkins, J. A.	Pvt.	A	5th	AL.	Infantry			Longstreet	N. VA.	Mexia
Phillips, J. B.	Pvt.	K	13th	AL.	Infantry	Archer	A. P. Hill	Jackson	N. VA.	Armour
Phillips, W. W.	Pvt.	I	6th	MS.	Cavalry	Mabry	Chalmers	Forrest	TN.	Kirk
Plunkett, G. W.	Pvt.	E	6th	ARK.	Infantry	Govan	Cleburne	Hardee	TN.	Wortham
Popejoy, N. T.	Pvt.	D	2nd	TN.	Cavalry	Ashby	Wheeler	Hardee	TN.	Groesbeck
Prather, Edward	Pvt.	F	2nd	TX.	Cavalry	Sibley	Green	E. K. Smith	T-MS.	Mexia
Price, J. E.	Pvt.	E	35th	TX.	Cavalry	Terrell		E. K. Smith	T-MS.	Kosse
Priddy, M. L.	Sgt.	F	31st	MS.	Infantry	Featherston	Loring	Hardee	TN.	Groesbeck
Prince, J. H.	Pvt.	C	10th	GA.	Infantry	Simms	McLaws	Longstreet	N. VA.	Coolidge
Putnam, J. G.	Chaplain									
Rasco, Solon	Pvt.	B	20th	TX.	Cavalry	Maxey	Hindman	E. K. Smith	T-MS.	Groesbeck
Red, W. S. [Rev.]	Chaplain									Mexia
Reynolds, M. P.	Pvt.	D	7th	AL.	Cavalry	Rucker	Chalmers	Forrest	TN.	Tehuacana
Richardson, W. H.	1st Lt.	F	2nd	MD.	Cavalry	Johnson	Fitz Lee	Hampton	N. VA.	Austin, Travis Co.
Richardson, W. R.	Pvt.	H	20th	TX.	Infantry	Harrison	Walker	E. K. Smith	T-MS.	Thelma
Roberts, W. F.	Capt.	G	28th	TN.	Cavalry	Randal	Walker	E. K. Smith	T-MS.	Mexia
Rogers, A. J.	Sgt.	K	20th	TX.	Cavalry	Maxey	Hindman	E. K. Smith	T-MS.	Personville
Ross, Geo. W.	Pvt.	H	4th	MO.	Cavalry	Cockrell	French	Polk	TN.	Mexia
Russell, W. A.	Pvt.	B	J. Davis Legion	MS.	Cavalry	Young	Butler	Hampton	N. VA.	Brownwood, Brown Co.
Sanches, F. M.	Pvt.	H	6th	TX.	Cavalry	Ross	Jackson		TN.	Groesbeck
Satterwhite, J. L.	Pvt.	I	Byrd's Battn	ARK.	Cavalry			E. K. Smith	T-MS.	Wortham
Sawyer, J. P.	Pvt.	D	12th	MS.	Cavalry	Ferguson	Jackson	Wheeler	TN.	Luther
Scruggs, S. K.	Lt.	C	8th	TX.	Cavalry	Wharton	Wheeler	Hardee	TN.	Mexia
Seale, L. B.	Pvt.	C	21st	AL.	Infantry	Gladden	Clayton	A. P. Stewart	TN.	Kosse

ROSTER OF EX-CONFEDERATE VETERANS OF LIMESTONE COUNTY, TEXAS

Name	Rank	Co.	Reg.	State	Branch	Commander	Brigade	Division	Army	Residence
Sellers, F. M.	Pvt.	I	3rd	AL.	Cavalry	Morgan	Allen	Wheeler	TN.	DeLeon, Comanche Co.
Sharp, T. H.	Pvt.	B	10th	TX.	Infantry	Granbury	Cleburne	Hardee	TN.	Mexia
Sherrill, B. F.	Pvt.	H	1st	NC	Infantry	Thomas	Breckinridge	Early	N. VA.	Mexia
Shriver, Adam	Pvt.		Maurin's	LA.	Artillery		Anderson	A. P. Hill	N. VA.	Groesbeck
Simmons, H. F.	Pvt.	D	Wood's	MS.	Cavalry	Adams	Wheeler	Hardee	TN.	Wortham
Simmons, J. W.	Pvt.	C	27th	MS.	Infantry	Walthall	Johnson	S. D. Lee	TN.	Mexia
Skillern, T. W.	Pvt.	C	36th	ARK.	Infantry	Cray	Churchill	Price	T-MS.	Mexia
Skipper, W. M.	Sgt.	E	1st	ARK.	Artillery		Maury		TN.	Kosse
Smith, Jas. L.	Pvt.	C	14th	NC.	Infantry	Ramseur	Rodes	Jackson	N. VA.	Mexia
Smith, L. F.	Pvt.	B	11th	LA.	Infantry	Polignac	Mouton	E. K. Smith	T-MS.	Donie, Freestone Co.
Sowders, J. A.	Pvt.	B	5th	TX.	Cavalry	Sibley	Green	E. K. Smith	T-MS.	Kosse
Speers, B. L.	Pvt.	C	Timmon's	TX.	Infantry	Waul			TN.	Mexia
Stanford, J. T.	Pvt.	G	29th	AL.	Infantry	Shelley	Walthall		TN.	Mexia
Stanford, S. A.	Pvt.			AL.	Infantry			State Troops		Mexia
Starley, W. F. [Dr.]	Pvt.	I	2nd	TX.	Cavalry	Major	Green	E. K. Smith	T-MS.	Mexia
Stedman, Jasper	Pvt.	C	5th	AL.	Infantry	Archer		A. P. Hill	N. VA.	Wortham
Steele, A. L.	Sgt.	F	15th	TX.	Cavalry	Granbury	Cleburne	Hardee	TN.	Mexia
Steele, J. Warren	Pvt.	G	7th	TX.	Infantry	Granbury	Cleburne	Hardee	TN.	Mexia
Steele, R. E.	1st Lt.	G	7th	TX.	Infantry	Granbury	Cleburne	Hardee	TN.	Mexia
Steele, Rado	Pvt.	B	10th	TX.	Infantry	Granbury	Cleburne	Hardee	TN.	Mexia
Steward, F. M.	Pvt.	H	28th	TX.	Cavalry	Randal	Walker	E. K. Smith	T-MS.	Groesbeck
Storey, J. M.	O. Sgt.	H	28th	TX.	Cavalry	Randal	Walker	E. K. Smith	T-MS.	Mexia
Stuart, J. W.	Pvt.	B	9th	TX.	Infantry	Young	Walker	E. K. Smith	T-MS.	Teague, Freestone Co.
Sturdivant, J. H.	Pvt.	G	38th	TN.	Infantry	Wright	Cheatham	Polk	TN.	Mexia
Taylor, John R.	Sgt.	C	25th	TX.	Cavalry	Garland	Holmes	E. K. Smith	T-MS.	Kosse
Taylor, W. H.	Pvt.	K	44th	TN.	Infantry	Johnson	Cheatham	Hardee	TN.	Pursley, Navarro Co.
Terry, T. S.	Pvt.	C		TX.	Cavalry	Sibley	Green	E. K. Smith	T-MS.	Mexia
Tew, C. T. [Rev.]	Chaplain									
Therrill, J. D.	Sgt.	C	44th	MS.	Infantry	Tucker	Hindman	Hood	TN.	Groesbeck
Thomas, J. W.	Cpl.	H	43rd	NC	Infantry	Daniel	Rodes	Ewell	N. VA.	Tehuacana
Thompson, J. W.	Pvt.	C	4th	AL.	Cavalry	Law	Hood	Longstreet	N. VA.	Groesbeck
Tucker, M. A.	Sgt. Major	F	15th	TX.	Cavalry	Granbury	Cleburne	Hardee	TN.	Horn Hill
Tucker, Reuben	Pvt.		Porter's	ARK.	Infantry			E. K. Smith	T-MS.	Teague, Freestone Co.
Vestal, W. A.	Pvt.	I	Sims'	TX.	Cavalry		Walker	E. K. Smith	T-MS.	Marquez, Leon Co.
Walker, G. H.	Pvt.	A	9th	LA.	Infantry	Hays	Ewell	Jackson	N. VA.	Luther
Walker, S. S.	Pvt.	I	2nd	TX.	Cavalry	Major	Green	E. K. Smith	T-MS.	Groesbeck
Wallace, J. D.	Pvt.	F	23rd	MS.	Infantry					Groesbeck
Waller, D. A.	Pvt.	K	20th	TX.	Cavalry	Maxey	Hindman	E. K. Smith	T-MS.	Mexia
Walling, J. G.	Pvt.	C	15th	TX.	Infantry	Polignac	Mouton	E. K. Smith	T-MS.	Thornton
Ward, R. P.	Pvt.	F	12th	TX.	Cavalry	Parsons	Walker	E. K. Smith	T-MS.	Mexia
Watson, C. L.	Sgt.	D	10th	TX.	Infantry	Granbury	Cleburne	Hardee	TN.	Mexia
Welch, J. H.	Pvt.	K	20th	TX.	Cavalry	Maxey	Hindman	E. K. Smith	T-MS.	Kosse
White, H.	1st Lt.	H	15th	TX.	Infantry		Walker	E. K. Smith	T-MS.	Wortham
Wiley, Oscar	Sgt.	K	5th	AL.	Infantry	Rodes	Early	Jackson	N. VA.	Groesbeck
Wilie, T. W.	Pvt.	C	8th	TX.	Cavalry	Harrison	Wheeler	Hardee	TN.	Mt. Calm

ROSTER OF EX-CONFEDERATE VETERANS OF LIMESTONE COUNTY, TEXAS

Williams, E. W.	Pvt.		3rd	TX.	Cavalry	Ross	Jackson	TN.	Mexia
Williams, H. W.	Pvt.	C	36th	NC	H. Arty	Ft. Duty	Ft. Fisher, NC	N. VA.	Mexia
Winfield, W. J.	Pvt.		Mechanic	AL.	Arsenal		Hardee		Kosse
Winters, J. S.	Sgt.	K	2nd	TX.	Cavalry	Sibley	Walker		Buffalo, Leon Co.
Wolverton, Mack	Pvt.	K	20th	TX.	Cavalry	Maxey	Hindman	T-MS.	Mexia
Wood, C. H. F.	Sgt.	F	15th	TX.	Cavalry	Granbury	Cleburne	T-MS.	Mexia
Wood, E. B. [Dr.]	Capt.	B	34th	AL.	Infantry	Manigault	Hindman	TN.	Hubbard
Wood, Ira E.	Sgt.	F	15th	TX.	Cavalry	Granbury	Cleburne	TN.	Waco, McLennan Co.
Wood, Joshua	Pvt.	G	40th	AL.	Infantry	Baker	Clayton	TN.	Groesbeck
Wood, Richard	Pvt.	G	8th	TX.	Infantry	Young	Walker	A. P. Stewart	Wortham
Wooldridge, C. J.	Cpl.	G	31st	GA.	Infantry	Gordon	Early	T-MS.	Wortham
Wright, J. W.	Pvt.	I	19th	TX.	Cavalry	Parsons	Jackson	N. VA.	Groesbeck
Wright, Jas. A.	Lt.	F	31st	AL.	Infantry	Pettus	Stevenson	T-MS.	Fallon
Wright, Z. T.	Pvt.	F	31st	AL.	Infantry	Pettus	Stevenson	TN.	Mexia
Yankie, J. F.	2nd Lt.	C	13th	TX.	Cavalry	Waul	Walker	TN.	Mart, McLennan Co.
Yeldell, J. P.	Pvt.	B	15th	AL.	Cavalry		E. K. Smith	TN.	Mexia

JOE JOHNSTON CAMP NO. 94

Organized the 6th of May 1895 at Mexia, Limestone County, Texas, with 125 members, with membership dues of $12.50 sent to the national United Veterans Camps. The officers elected in July 1894 were as follows:

J. W. Simmons	Captain and Commander
J. M. Suttle	1st Lt. Commander
J. G. Walling	2nd Lt. Commander
J. H. Archer	3rd Lt. Commander
H. W. Williams	Adjutant
R. J. Bryant	Quartermaster
J. P. Cook	Surgeon
L. W. Duke	Chaplain
M. L. McDonald	Treasurer
M. H. Clark	Officer-of-the-Day
W. H. Herring	Color Sergeant [Color Bearer]
W. A. Davis	Bugler

UNITED CONFEDERATE VETERANS
LIMESTONE AND FREESTONE COUNTIES, TEXAS

[Page 5] At a meeting of the Confederates held at the mouth of Jack's Creek in Limestone County, Texas, on the 31st of July and 1st and 2nd days of August 1889 the following constitution was adopted.

ARTICLE 1
Constitution

This association shall be known as the Limestone County Camp Confederate Veterans located in Limestone County, Texas.

ARTICLE 2
Object of Association

The object shall be to perpetuate the memories of our fallen comrades, to administer, as far as practicable, to the wants of those who were permanently disabled in the service, and to aid the indigent widows and orphans of deceased Confederate soldiers and sailors, to preserve and maintain, that sentiment of fraternity born of the Hardships and dangers shared in the march, bivouac and the battlefield. The animosities engendered by the late war shall be buried in one common grave and [Page 6] our late adversaries honored as the brave always honor the brave.

ARTICLE 3
Officers

The officers of this association shall consist of a commander, one 1st, 2nd, and 3rd Lieut. Commanders, Adjutant, Quartermaster, Treasurer, Officer of the Day, Chaplain, Bugler, Color Bearer, and nineteen Trustees, one from each voting precinct in the county and one from the county at large to be elected annually at stated reunions and to hold their office until their successors are elected and qualified.

ARTICLE 4
Election of Officers

Sec. 1: The annual election of officers shall be held at such time and place as may be designated by the camp for the holding of Annual Reunions, vacancies may be filled by appointment by the commander.

Sec. 2: All members of the camp in good standing shall be eligible to any office therein.

[Page 7] Sec. 3: In case of ballot a majority of all the votes cast shall be necessary to a choice.

ARTICLE 5
Meetings

Sec. 1: The meetings of this camp shall be held at such time and place as may be designated by the last preceding meeting of the camp.

Sec. 2: Special call meetings may be had by the commander, upon the application of twenty members, in good standing, setting forth the objects of said meeting.

ARTICLE 6
Duties of Officers

Sec. 1: The Commander shall preside at all meetings, preserve strict order and decorum, and enforce a due observance of the constitution and By laws. Make such details and committees not otherwise provided for; give the casting vote in case of a tie, inspect and announce the result of all ballots or other votes. He shall approve all orders drawn on the Treasurer for the payment of money and shall have power to call special meetings [Page 8] of the Camp in accordance with the provisions of this constitution.

Sec. 2: The Lieutenant Commanders shall assist the Commander in the performance of his duties and in his absence shall take his place in the order of their rank. If neither of them is present the camp shall elect a Commander Pro-tem.

Sec. 3: The Adjutant shall keep an impartial record of the camp and its members, fill up and serve all notices, draw all orders on the Treasurer, receive all money due the camp and hand the same over to the Treasurer, taking his receipt therefor, and assist at the examination of the books. He shall receive such compensation for his services as may be awarded him by the camp.

Sec. 4: It shall be the duty of the Treasurer to take charge of all moneys belonging to the Camp, pay out the same upon orders drawn upon him by the Adjutant, and approved by the Commander, and to keep a fair and regular account in a book, kept for that purpose, of receipts and [Page 9] expenditures. He shall, before entering upon the discharge of his duties, give a bond in such sum as may be required by the Camp payable to the Captains and to be accepted by them.

Sec. 5: The Quartermaster shall have charge of all the property of the Camp and shall superintend all matters of transportation and supplies.

Sec. 6: The Officer of the day shall preserve order, during the meetings, see that the members behave in an orderly and decorous manner, conduct all ballots and render such other service as the commander may require of him.

Sec. 7: It shall be the duty of the Chaplain to open the meetings of the Camp with prayer and attend and officiate at the funerals of its members when possible for him so to do.

ARTICLE 7
Eligibility of Membership

Sec. 1: Any person of good character who served honorably in the confederate States army or Navy may be admitted to active membership in this camp.

[Page 10] Sec. 2: Every application for active membership shall be made by furnishing to the Adjutant the name of the applicant, his Rank, Company, Regt., State, Brigade, Division, Corps, Army and department when possible and also present post office address.

Sec. 3: Any person of good moral character may be eligible to honorable membership in the Camp. the wives, widows & daughters of Confederate soldiers in good standing are honorary members. Such honorary members may attend the meetings of the Camp but shall not be entitled to vote upon any question.

ARTICLE 8
Fees, Dues, and Fines

Sec. 1: The active membership fee shall be fifty cents which shall be paid to the Adjutant at the time of his enrollment or within thirty days thereafter. (Sec. 1 "X" out and Sec. 2, 3, 4 renumbered 1, 2, 3)

[Page 11] Sec. 2: The annual dues of the members of this Camp shall be fifty cents per annum, due and payable at each annual meeting.

Sec. 3: Any member who shall misbehave in the Camp, or shall disobey the commander shall be fined fifty cents.

Sec. 4: Any Officer absenting himself from any meeting of this Camp, without sufficient cause, shall be fined not less than twenty-five cents.[1]

ARTICLE 9
Trustees Duties[2]

Sec. 1: It shall be the duty of the Trustees to report to the Commander any cripple, indigent, or needy member of this Camp who shall have power to take such steps as may be necessary for his relief.

ARTICLE 10
Suspension and Expulsion

Sec. 1: This Camp shall have power to suspend or expel any member upon proper charges, preferred in such manner as may be prescribed by law.

[Page 12]
ARTICLE 11
Cards

Sec. 1: Any member in good standing wishing a traveling card can obtain the same upon application to the adjutant on payment of twenty five cents, provided his dues are paid up to the date of his application, such cards to be countersigned by the Commander.

ARTICLE 12
Badges

Sec. 1: The badges to be worn by the members of this Camp shall consist of a blue ribbon 1-1/4 in. wide by 6 in. long to be worn on left lapel of coat. For Guards a light or sky blue ribbon two in. wide by 8 in. long, upon which shall be printed the word "Guard", to be worn on left lapel.

Sec. 2: The Officer of the day shall in addition to the usual badge wear a red sash round his waist and over his shoulder and upon his right lapel a blue ribbon 2 by 8 inches upon which shall be printed the words Officer of the day.

Sec. 3: Commander shall wear upon his [Page 13] right lapel a red and white rosette 3 inches in diameter and underneath a blue badge upon which shall be printed the word Commander.

---

[1] Sec. 1 had been X out and Sec. 2, 3, 4 have been renumbered 1, 2, and 3 in pencil
[2] Trustees had been crossed out and changed to Captains in pencil

Sec. 4: The 1st, 2nd and 3rd Lieutenant Commanders shall each wear upon the right lapel a 2 by 8 in. blue badge with their rank printed thereon.

Sec. 5: The Adjutant, Quartermaster, and Treasurer shall each wear upon his right lapel a blue badge two by eight inches with their rank printed thereon. The Chaplain's badge shall be a white ribbon two by eight inches worn on right lapel and having printed thereon, Chaplain.

ARTICLE 13
Amendments

These Articles or any part thereof shall not be altered, amended, or annulled unless a written notice of the same be [Page 14] read at a regular meeting after which it shall be referred to a committee and reported upon at same meeting. W. H. Adams, J. W. Storey, W. P. Brown, J. M. Suttle, J. M. Rambo, Committee.

1889

The following Officers were elected to serve for the next ensuing year.

W. H. Richardson	Commander
J. P. Brown	1st. Lt. Commander
Sam B. Love	2nd. Lt. Commander
J. M. Rambo	3rd. Lt. Commander
W. H. Adams	Adjutant
W. P. Brown	Treasurer
C. L. Watson	Quartermaster
H. A. Boyd	Officer-of-the-Day
Rev. G. L. Jennings	Chaplain
W. P. Booth	Color Bearer
W. A. Davis	Bugler

Trustees

J. M. Storey	Mexia
R. W. Payne	Forest Glade
Charles S. Bates	Honest Ridge
James Armour	Armour
J. H. Archer	Mt. Antioch [Mt. Calm P.O.]

[Page 288, Book 2]

No. 1: Confederate Camp Aug. 2nd, 1889 - Rec'd of W. H. Adams, Adj., the sum of thirteen dollars on a/c of membership fee of ex-confederates. W. P. Brown, Treasurer.

No. 3: Rec'd of W. H. Adams, adjutant, five dollars on a/c ex-con. Camp Aug. 15th 1889. W. P. Brown, Treasurer.

J. G. Walling	.50
B. J. Hancock	.50
H. O. Boyd	.50
M. Kaufman	.50
Hop Gray	.50
J. H. Archer	.50
W. M. Wilder	.50
Chris Bower	.50
J. M. Deis	.50
E. B. Smyth	.50
P. O. Douglas	.50
T. J. Gibson	.50
S. B. Love	.50
A. N. Thornton	.50
G. W. Lee	.50
T. M. Havay/Hardin	5.00
L. E. Camp	5.00

[Page 285, Book 2]

11th May 1890
Duties of the Executive Committee

To take cognizance of all matters pertaining to the good of the Camp.

To look after the other committees and their work in other words supervise all work and attend to all the interest of the Camp.

Invite speakers. Let out bids arrange details & programs - and close the Camp - & appoint necessary additional Committees.

"Com. on Grounds" will proceed to lay off grounds, clear land, provide necessary Platform seats etc. and take charge of all matters pertaining to same and Police the grounds. Locating all stands etc. and are empowered to make details for help from the command through the adjt.

"The Finance Com." will collect all moneys necessary to defray expenses - hand over same to Treas., pass upon all bills and draw drafts upon Treas. and adopt such means as they deem be...
[Page 17]

MINUTES OF MEETING OF THE EX-CONFEDERATES VETERANS OF LIMESTONE COUNTY HELD AT THEIR CAMP-GROUNDS ON JACK'S CREEK JULY 30th 1890

July 30th

The Camp was called to order at 10 o'clock by Commander W. H. Richardson who delivered an address of welcome, but the weather being unfavorable, the camp was adjourned until next day.

July 31st

The camp was called to order by the commander at 9 o'clock, when a fine bugle was presented to the Camp by Mr. J. M. Deece [sic Deis] with appropriate remarks; and was received in behalf of the Camp, by an address from Capt. T. J. Gibson.

Gen'l. W. L. Cabell of Sterling Price Camp, Dallas, was introduced and delivered an address, after which, the Camp adjourned until 2 o'clock.

The Camp assembled at the call of the bugle, and the business of the hour being the election of officers, resulted in the following officers being elected for the ensuing year:

W. H. Richardson	Commander
C. L. Watson	1st. Lt. Commander
S. B. Love	2nd. Lt. Commander
J. M. Rambo	3rd. Lt. Commander
J. W. Simmons	Adjutant
J. P. Cook	Quartermaster
W. P. Brown	Treasurer [Page 18]
Rev. J. S. Grooves	Chaplain
J. M. Deece [Deis]	Bugler
C. H. F. Wood	Color Bearer
H. A. Boyd	Officer-of-the-Day

S. D. Walker, J. M. Suttle, Rado Steele, M. W. Kemp, and J. G. Walling were appointed a committee on temporary and permanent location of camp grounds, and recommended the present grounds on Jack's Creek, which was unanimously adopted.

A Resolution was adopted, substituting the word "Captain" in the constitution in place of "Trustee" wherever it appears. A committee was appointed to raise funds for Private Gilmore, a one leg veteran of the camp, which soon reported $42 and the money was turned over to Captain Sellers for his benefit.

The following resolutions of respect were unanimously adopted by the camp: Whereas, Since our last annual reunion it has pleased the God of Battles to call to their final rest to await the resurrection morn, our gallant comrades, Col. J. R. Henry, Capt. W. H. Adams, and A. V. Scott, therefore be it **Resolved**, First, That in their death we mourn the loss of three brave comrades in war and three useful men in peace.

Second, That in their death we realize that our loss is more our country's loss, yet, in our sorrow we bow in submission [Page 19] to the will of Providence, believing that God's dispensations are the best.

Third, That a copy of these resolutions be presented to the Mexia ledger for publication.

Ex-President, Jefferson Davis having died since our last meeting, appropriate resolutions were adopted, and suitable remarks were made by Capt. T. J. Gibson.

T. J. Gibson, B. F. Wallace, H. W. Williams, Mrs. M. W. Kemp and Miss Em Beeson, were appointed a committee to recommend a suitable flag for the next re-union, and reported that the flag be composed of red, white and blue, alternating, with a star for each state, and a large five-pointed star covering the body of the flag, which was adopted.

The following gentlemen were appointed captains of their respective precincts for the next year.

R. W. Payne	Forest Glade	S. D. Walker	Groesbeck
M. W. Kemp	Mexia	O. Wiley	County at large
B. F. Wallace	Hancock	J. M. Suttle	Tehuacana
Wm. Justice	Personville and Farrar	Col. G. B. Vincen [Vinson]	Prairie Grove
J. W. McKinney	Prairie Hill and Kirk	J. H. Archer	Antioch
[Page 20] John Harvey	Shiloh	F. M. Sellers	Thornton
E. D. Polk	Kosse	S. A. Bradley[3]	Pottersville
L. B. Seale[4]	Headsville		

A resolution was adopted authorizing the commander to place this Camp in the general organization of the United Confederate Veterans and take such steps as may be necessary to organize auxiliary camps of the Sons and Daughters of Confederate Soldiers.

---

[3] Not on rosters as member
[4] Not on rosters as member

A resolution to enroll the names of Col. R. Q. Mills and Gen. W. L. Cabell as honorary members of Limestone County's Confederate Veterans was adopted.

The Adjutant reported $50.00 as collected on dues and turned over to the Treasurer.

The Treasurer, W. P. Brown, gave in his report of the financial condition of the camp for the year 1890, which shows a balance of $2.45 in the Treasury.

The camp then adjourned until next day.

August 1st

Camp was called to order at 10 A.M. and the entire day was spent in drilling and speaking by members [Pages 21 and 22 missing]
[Page 23]

MINUTES OF THE REUNION OF THE CONFEDERATES VETERANS OF LIMESTONE COUNTY HELD AT JACK'S CREEK ON JULY 22D, 1891

The Veterans met at their camp grounds for a general reunion by order of their commander.

At 10 A.M. the camp assembled at the call of the bugle and was called to order by the commander.

The chaplain being absent, prayer was offered by Rev. J. S. Tunnell; after which the roll was called and the guards placed on duty.

Commander Richardson then delivered an opening address, welcoming the members and visitors, and outlining the objects of the association.

At 11 A.M. a silken banner, made by the lady friends of the association, was presented by Miss May Watson, with appropriate remarks and was assisted by fourteen young ladies wearing badges to represent each of the Confederate States.

[Page 24] Capt. T. J. Gibson then accepted the banner in behalf of the Veterans with an appropriate address.

A business meeting was then called and a committee was appointed to draft suitable resolutions of respect to our deceased brethren, who have died since our last re-union and submitted the following which was adopted;

Whereas, It has pleased our Heavenly Father to remove from our midst, our true and worthy ex Confederate Veterans: David Stanford, W. B. Kirkpatric, J. R. Montgomery, J. E. Butler, J. L. Johnson, and F. B. Strayhorn, since our last encampment, and who were true and worthy members of the Camp.

Therefore be it resolved 1st, that we bow in humble submission to the Divine Will and deeply mourn the loss of our honored brethren of the Camp.

Resolved 2d., that these resolutions be spread upon the record and made a part of the minutes of the Camp.

Respectfully submitted, R. H. Calhoun, Chm.

[Page 25] The following resolution was submitted and unanimously adopted: Whereas, since our last reunion, it has pleased our Great Creator to remove from among us, our great commander, Jos. E. Johnston, and cross him over the river to rest in the shade with Lee, Jackson, and a host of others who have gone before him.

Therefore, be it resolved 1st. that in the death of Gen'l. Joseph E. Johnston, our country lost the grandest living general, and one that the world has never produced a superior; having been ten times wounded in the defense of his country.

Resolved, 2d, that as a citizen, his life was of the highest type, having filled all the avocations of life with the highest honor to himself and to those whom he represented. Resp't. Submitted, C. L. Watson, Chm.

An auditing committee consisting of S. D. Walker, E. B. Smyth and Ben Wallace was appointed and after examining the Books, [Page 26] made the following report; As far as we have been able to ascertain, the Books of the association have been neatly and correctly kept, and a true and faithful report has been made of all money's received and disbursed. Resp'ct. submitted, Committee.

A committee was appointed on grounds, and reported that 20 acres could be bought for $200.00 and recommended that the same be purchased which was unanimously passed.

The following resolution was introduced and adopted: Resolved that a committee of five be appointed by the Commander with full authority to procure the necessary charter.

Resolved 2d., To open books for sale of stock and to purchase land in the name of said corporation when the same is organized.

Resolved 3d., That same organization shall have authority to adopt by-laws, to lay out these grounds, to sell, and convey lots, and to do all things necessary to be done in [Page 27] order to forward the general purpose of this organization.

The following committee was appointed to procure a charter and to purchase the ground and spring for the Camp, at its earliest convenience. Committee: T. J. Gibson, O. Wiley, J. W. Simmons, Capt. Polk, C. L. Watson.

The camp then adjourned until 2:30 P.M., at which time Mr. J. R. Johnston made an interesting talk on Morgan's Cavalry, C. L. Watson on Granberry's [sic Granbury] Brigade, and Capt's Cashion and Gilbert on the Army of Northern Virginia.

After several speeches by other members; the camp adjourned until next day.

July 23rd 9:30 A.M.

The Camp assembled at the call of the bugle and prayed was offered by Rev. W. L. Lowrance.

Dr. J. I. L. Gray then paid an eloquent tribute to the Tennessee soldiers [Page 28] after which, Col. W. L. Lowrance was introduced and addressed the veterans on the subject of, "The Confederate Soldier in War and in Civil Life, and our Duty to his Memory."

Capt. T. J. Gibson then delivered an address entitled "The Negro before and after the War."

After these speeches, the Camp adjourned until 2 P.M.

2 P.M.

Camp called to order by the Commander, and a business meeting was called.

Col. W. L. Lowrance was elected an honorary member of the association, and was requested to furnish a copy of his speech for publication.

The following officers were elected:

C. L. Watson	Commander
T. J. Gibson	1st. Lt. Commander
Oscar Wiley	2nd. Lt. Commander
E. D. Pope/Polk	3rd. Lt. Commander
H. W. Williams	Adjutant
J. P. Cook	Quartermaster
S. B. Love	Officer-of-the-Day
J. L L. Gray, M.D.	Surgeon
Rev. L. W. Duke	Chaplain
J. M. Deis	Bugler
E. W. Williams[5]	Color Bearer [Page 29]
W. P. Brown	Treasurer

The following resolution was offered by H. W. Williams and adopted: Resolved that the thanks of this association be tendered to Mrs. M. W. Kemp, Miss Em Beeson and the other ladies who helped in making our flag.

A resolution was adopted organizing an adjunct association of the Sons and Daughters of Veterans.

Mr. S. H. Kelley then spoke in behalf of the son's and daughter's of Soldiers and J. I. Moody addressed the Camp in the interest of the soldiers' home at Austin.

After a few other speeches by members, the Camp adjourned until next day.

July 24th 9:30 A.M.

Camp assembled, and another business meeting was [Page 30] called; when the following captains for the various precincts were appointed.

J. B. Tyns[6]	Groesbeck	J. H. Archer	Antioch
L. R. Persons	Personville	J. W. McKinney	Prairie Hill
B. F. Wallace	Hancock	Sam Ingram	Shiloh
J. R. Johnson	Mexia	I. E. Wood	Tehuacana
J. Walling	Thornton	B. W. Allen	Kosse
R. O. Douglas[7]	Kirk	R. W. Payne	Forest Glade
S. D. Walker	County at large	F. M. Trammell[8]	Armour

Judge Gerald of Waco then delivered an eloquent address; and after a few other speeches, the Camp adjourned until after dinner.

2 P.M.

Camp assembled by the Band; after which a business meeting was held; and a motion was made by Capt. W. H Richardson, which was adopted changing the name of the Camp from "Limestone County Camp of Confederate Veterans" to "The Jos. E. Johnston Veteran [Page 31] Association."

The Treasurer's report was read and approved, showing a balance of $48.45 in the Treasury.

The Adjutant reported $27.00 as collected at the present re-union on dues, and turned over to the Treasurer and his receipt taken for the same.

Capt. R. T. Kennedy* was then introduced and delivered and address on "The Suffering, Devotion, and Patriotism of the Ladies of the South."

Judge O. C. Kirven and others made short addresses; after which the Camp was adjourned with appropriate remarks by the Commander, until July, 1892.

[Page 32]

MEETING OF CONFEDERATE VETERANS MARCH 5, 1892

Pursuant to call of Commander Watson, a number of Confederate Veterans met at the Mayor's office in Mexia, on March 5, 1892, for the purpose of organizing to attend the Re-Unions at Dallas and New Orleans.

A motion was offered and carried: That all Confederate Veterans who desired to go to Dallas be appointed delegates to represent this Camp there.

A motion was also offered and carried to appoint a Committee to purchase the Camp Grounds on Jack's Creek, - the price being two hundred ($200) dollars, - with instructions to sell enough lots to pay for it, at five ($5) dollars per lot.

The following Comrades were appointed on the Committee: J. W. Simmons, J. E. Parker, Capt. W. P. Brown, J. M. Suttle, Jno. G. Walling of Thornton and Capt. E. D. Polk of Kosse.

The members of the Committee present raised fifty ($50) dollars of the desired amount in a few minutes.

No further business, the meeting adjourned.

H. W. Williams, Adjutant   C. L. Watson, Commander

[Page 33]

---

[5] R. E. Davis was shown as the Color Bearer on the roster furnished to the Adjt. Gen'l. U.C.V. at New Orleans, Louisiana
[6] Not on rosters as member
[7] Shown on roster as P. O. Douglas
[8] Shown on roster as F. E. Trammell

CONFEDERATES VETERANS' MEETING MAY 28, 1892

Pursuant to call of Commander Watson, a number of Confederate Veterans met at the Mayor's office, in Mexia on 28th of May, for the purpose of arranging for our next Re-Union.

On motion of J. W. Simmons: The time for the Re-Union was set for the 3d, 4th, and 5th of August. - Carried.

On motion of W. E. Doyle: The beer and whiskey privilege was dispensed with for this year. - Carried

On motion: The Commander was instructed to appoint five, or more, Comrades on the following Committees, which was carried out as follows:

Arrangements: Rado Steele, Maj. M. H. Clark[9], S. F. Bond, R. P. Ward, R. J. Bryant,* J. M. Suttle and J. M. Storey.

Privileges: Dr. J. P. Cook, Capt. J. B. Tyns, J. E. Parker, Chas. Bates, M. L. McDonald and C. H. F. Wood.

Invitations: W. E. Doyle, J. W. Simmons, Dr. M. W. Kemp, Maj. L. J. Farrar, John G. Walling and Capt. F. Z. Doak[10].

On motion: All Confederate Veterans who have relics, were requested to bring them to the Re-Union for exhibition. - Carried.

[Page 34] On motion: The picnic, for drawing lots was set for Friday the 17th of June, at the grounds, and all who will have paid for lots by then, will be entitled to first drawing. - Carried.

On motion: The thanks of this Camp was returned to Sterling Price Camp, at Dallas, for their hospitality to some of our Comrades at the Re-Union in April last. - Carried.

No further business, the meeting adjourned.

H. W. Williams, Adjutant					C. L. Watson, Commander

[Page 35]

MINUTES OF JOE JOHNSTON CAMP, NO. 94, CONFEDERATE VETERANS
HELD AT JACK'S CREEK ON 3RD TO 5TH AUG., 1892

Wednesday, August 3rd 10:00 A.M.

Pursuant to adjournment, the Camp was called to order by Commander Watson at 10 o'clock, and was opened with prayer by Rev. G. L. Jennings.

After an address by the Commander, the guard was mounted.

A motion was offered by Capt. Gibson: That fifteen (15) cents of the Camp dues be appropriated to pay the State and United Confederate Veterans' fees, which was adopted.

Rev. G. L. Jennings, being called on, delivered a short address; at the close of which the meeting adjourned till after dinner.

2 o'clock

Camp re-assembled and after music by band, Captain Gibson delivered an instructive and interesting address on "The Army of Northern Virginia."

At 4 o'clock, Capt. S. H. Kelly, of the young Confederates, delivered an eloquent address to the "Sons of Confederate [Page 36] Veterans," followed in like manner by M. Wm. Beeson in an address to the "Daughters of Confederate Veterans;" at the close of which the young Confederates organized themselves into an auxiliary of this Camp, by electing Capt. S. H. Kelly Commander, and all the other necessary officers. - Camp adjourned till next morning.

Thursday, Aug. 4th, - 9:30 A.M.

Camp called to assemble by band. Prayer by Rev. Dr. A. P. Smith of Dallas. A letter was read from Col. Chas. H. Smith (generally known as "Bill Arp") regretting his inability to be present, after which a motion was offered to make "Bill Arp" an honorary member of Joe Johnston Camp, No. 94; which was carried unanimously and with enthusiasm.

Capt. Gibson then addressed the large audience on the importance of improving the grounds, and requested, in an eloquent speech, the contribution of enough money for the purpose.

On motion, a committee from each precinct was appointed to take up a collection for the above purpose.

The committee was appointed as follows: [See list at end of minutes]

At 11 o'clock, Rev. Dr. A. P. Smith [Page 37] addressed the large audience on the subject of "The Soldier Enshrined in the Hearts of his Countrymen."

After the address the Camp adjourned for dinner.

After dinner, Camp reassembled, and Rev. W. L. Lowrance delivered an address on "The Life and Character of Stonewall Jackson," after which Col. Gerald of Waco, delivered an interesting speech which ended the proceedings until the concert and declamations by the young people at 8:30 o'clock, which was well rendered and favorably received by the assembled audience.

Friday, Aug. 5th, - 9:30 A.M.

Camp assembled by band. After reading the Constitution, and minutes of the meeting of 1891, the election of officers took place as follows:

C. L. Watson	Commander
Rado Steele	1st. Lt. Commander
Oscar Wiley	2nd. Lt. Commander
J. G. Walling	3rd. Lt. Commander
H. W. Williams	Adjutant
J. P. Cook	Quartermaster
S. B. Love	Officer-of-the-day

---

[9] Shown on roster as private
[10] Shown on roster as F. J/Y Doke

Rev. W. L. Lowrance	Chaplain
Dr. J. I. L. Gray	Surgeon
Capt. W. P. Brown	Treasurer
C. H. F. Wood	Color Bearer
J. M. Deis	Bugler

[Page 38] On motion, the thanks of this Camp were extended to Camp Sterling Price for their kind invitation to attend the Reunion at Dallas, as the guest of their Camp, on Oct. 24th, 25th, and that ten delegates and ten alternates be elected to represent this Camp. [See list at end of minutes]

The election of delegates and alternates to the grand Reunion to be held at Birmingham, Ala., on the 19th and 29th of July 1893, was then gone into, and resulted as follows: [See list at end of minutes]

A resolution was offered and adopted: That all permanently disabled Confederate Veterans be entitled to the privileges of this Camp without paying dues.

On motion: Rev. Dr. A. P. Smith and Judge G. B. Gerald were elected honorary members of this Camp.

On motion: The thanks of this Camp were unanimously returned to Rev. Dr. A. P. Smith, Rev. W. L. Lowrance and Judge G. B. Gerald for the eloquent addresses delivered by them.

Short addresses were made by Capts. Gilbert, Guynes and Simmons, after which the Camp adjourned for dinner.

At 2 o'clock P.M., the Camp [Page 39] reassembled by band.

The following resolutions were offered by Capt. T. J. Gibson and adopted: Resolved: That the thanks of this Camp are hereby tendered Capt. J. W. Simmons, the ladies and gentlemen, girls and boys, who gave us the benefit of an elegant concert on these grounds last evening, and we request that they repeat the same at such time and places as may suit their convenience. The proceeds to be used for the benefit of this Camp.

Resolved: That the Constitution and By-Laws of this Camp be so amended as to read as follows: Any Confederate soldier or sailor, without reference to his former or present place of residence, is eligible to membership in this Camp.

The following memorial resolutions were offered and adopted: Whereas, It has pleased our Heavenly Father to remove form our midst our true and worthy Confederate Veterans, since our last encampment, who were true and worthy members of the Camp; viz: W. T. Farnsworth, Private, Co. I, 13th Tenn. Infantry, Vaughn's Brigade, Cheatham's Division, Polk's Corps, Army Tenn., and James M. Fitzgerald, Private, Co. A, 2nd Regt. [Page 40] La. Infantry, Hays' Brigade, Jackson's Corps, Army of Virginia; also S. D. Walker, Sergt. Co B, 10th Tex. Infantry, Granbury's Brigade, Cleburne's Division, Hardee's Corps, Army of Tenn.; and also, J. T. Stitt, Private, Co. E, 17th Ala. Infantry, Slaughter's Brigade, Hardee's Corps, Army of Tenn.; Therefore be it.

Resolved 1st: That we bow in humble submission to the Divine Will, and deeply mourn the loss of our honored brethren of the Camp.

Resolved 2nd: That these resolutions be spread upon the record and made a part of the minutes of this Camp.

Respectfully submitted,
G. W. Kenney
R. H. Calhoun   Com.
T. J. Gibson

Short memorial addresses were made by Capt. Gibson, Col. Watson and Rev. Mr. Kirven.

No further business, the Camp was adjourned by a short farewell address by the Comds. and prayer by Rev. Mr. Kirven, to meet during the full moon in July 1893, or, as soon thereafter as convenient.

Our three days meeting passed off pleasantly, without anything serious to mar [Page 41] the enjoyment of the vast assemblage of people.

Following is a list of delegate and alternates to Dallas and Birmingham, and also a list of the committee from each precinct to collect funds for the improvement of the Camp.

Birmingham Delegates: A. J. Burleson, J. W. McKinney, J. M. Rambo, B. F. Wallace, G. W. Kenney, W. M. Barton, J. M. Suttle, J. W. Simmons, Oscar Wiley, and A. J. Cashion. Alternates: S. B. Love, Capt. J. H. Archer, Ira E. Wood, Rado Steele, Chris Bower, Capt. J. S. Gilbert, T. J. Gibson, F. E. Trammell, H. W. Williams and Dr. E. B. Wood.

Dallas Delegates: Capt. W. P. Brown, L. E. Camp, H. C. Joiner, J. M. Deis, J. W. Nash, M. H. Clark, Ira E. Wood, R. J. Bryant, C. S. Bates and J. W. Simmons. Alternates: W. H. Browder, W. A. Buckner, H. A. Boyd, R. H. Calhoun, J. A. T. Richardson, S. A. Stanford, W. E. Durst, J. W. Thomas, Capt. J. H. Archer and B. F. Wallace.

[Page 42] The following is a List of Committees appointed in each Precinct for the purpose of raising funds for the permanent improvement of the Reunion grounds:

Mexia: Dr. M. W. Kemp, Mrs. J. W. Simmons and Mrs. J. W. David.
Groesbeck: Oscar Wiley, Mrs. B. J. Williams and Miss Leila Tyns.
Tehuacana: Sam B. Love, Mrs. Roxie Harris and Miss Lizzie Smith.
Hancock: B. F. Wallace, Miss Grace Davis and Mrs. Geo. Wallace.
Prairie Hill: J. W. McKinney, Miss Mollie Bray and Miss G. W. Lumpkin.
Thornton: W. M. Johnson, Miss Emma Randall and Miss Anna Hawkins. [Page 43]
Kosse: A. J. Burleson, Miss Roark, Mrs. Price.
Big Hill: J. B. Jordan, Mrs. Nora Newman and Miss McDonald.
Oletha [Ferguson's Prairie]: Sam Sadler, Miss Allison, Miss M. Eaton.

Headsville: Sanford Lowery, Mrs. Z. Williams and Mrs. Flint.
Elm Ridge: P. O. Douglas, Mrs. W. B. Carpenter and Miss Kate Douglas.
Kirk: Rev. G. L. Jennings, Mrs. R. H. Swaim and _____.
Forest Glade: Rado Steele, Miss Mary Kenney and Miss T. Stanford.
Honest Ridge: R. P. Ward, Miss Leila Ward and Miss Anna Broadnax. [Page 44]
Armour: James Armour, Mrs. R. E. Farrar and Miss The McCoy.
Personville: Wm. Justice, Mrs. C. C. Shell and Miss Rosa Persons.
Tiger Prairie: John Bishop, _____, _____.
Shiloh: Sam Ingram, Miss Nannie Moody and Miss Eula Eubanks.
Prairie Grove: W. H. Herring, Miss Swaim and Miss Lou Rich.
Antioch: Capt. J. H. Archer, _____, _____.

[Page 45]   Captains of Each Precinct

Mexia	Dr. M. W. Kemp	Thornton	G. W. Lewis*
Kosse	A. J. Burleson	Groesbeck	H. C. Joiner
Headsville		Personville	Wm. Justice
Tehuacana	J. M. Suttle	Oletha	A. B. Allison*
Prairie Grove	Jas. A. Wright*	Forest Glade	G. W. Kenney
Big Hill		Shiloh	Sam C. Ingram
Hancock	B. F. Wallace	Armour	F. E. Trammell
Honest Ridge	R. W. Payne	Elm Ridge	P. O. Douglas
Prairie Hill	J. W. McKinney	Kirk	
Antioch	J. H. Archer	Tiger Prairie	

*Not shown on known rosters

H. W. Williams, Adjutant   C. L. Watson, Commander

[Page 46]   **MEXIA, TEXAS, MARCH 2ND, 1893**

Pursuant to call of Commander Watson, Joe Johnston Camp No. 94, assembled at the Mayor's office in Mexia for the purpose of passing suitable Resolutions on the death of Gen'l. G. T. Beauregard.

A motion was offered and adopted that the Commander appoint a committee of five to draft Resolutions.

The following named Comrades were appointed: Dr. M. W. Kemp, Capt. T. J. Gibson, J. W. Simmons, Dr. J. P. Cook and C. F. Mercer. On motion, the Commander was added to the Committee.

The Committee reported the following: Whereas, It has pleased Almighty God to call from earth to a higher plane our loved Comrade Gen. G. T. Beauregard, who passed over the silent river at his home in New Orleans on Feby. 20th, 1893, therefore be it Resolved 1, That when Gen. Beauregard died death claimed for his own one of the brightest stars in the worlds galaxy of fame, and no name adorns the Pantheon of history with a brighter lustre.

Resolved 2, That we mourn, not as those who have no hope, for we know that our loss is his eternal gain, and we hope to meet him "under the shade of the trees." [Page 47]

Resolved 3, That though in person he is gone from us, yet the hero of Manassas and the defender of Charleston will live in the hearts of a country's grateful people longer than marble monuments and bronze shafts will stand.

Resolved 4, That may the magnolia waft its sweet perfume, and the sturdy Palmetto stand silent guard over the last resting place of the dead Confederacy's great general.

Resolved 5, That may the Father of the orphan bless the children left to mourn with us a country's loss.

> *"There is a page in the book of fame,*
> *On it is written a single name*
> *In letters of gold, on spotless white,*
> *Encircled with stars of quenchless light;*
> *Never a blot that page hath marred,*
> *And the star-wreathed name is Beauregard."*

Resolved 6, That a copy each of these Resolutions be sent to the Dallas News, Houston Post and Fort Worth Gazette for publication and that a copy be placed with the Adjutant for record.

A motion was made and carried that the Resolutions adopted by Camp Sterling Price at Dallas in relation to the Confederate Home at Austin, be endorsed and approved unanimously as our own.

A committee of three was appointed by [Page 48] the Commander on this Resolution consisting of Comrades J. W. Simmons, W. E. Doyle and J. E. Parker, with instructions to use all due diligence for the welfare of the Home.

No further business the meeting adjourned.

H. W. Williams, Adjutant   C. L. Watson, Commander

[Page 49]

RESOLUTIONS ON GEN. E. KIRBY SMITH

At a called meeting of Joe Johnston Camp No. 94, United Confederate Veterans held at Mexia on April 28th, 1893, a committee was appointed by the Commander to which, on motion, he was added, to draft suitable Resolutions on the death of Gen. E. Kirby Smith. The following was submitted:

As it has pleased the Supreme Commander of the Universe to remove from earth, the veteran soldier and knightly gentleman, E. Kirby Smith, the last of the full generals of the Southern Confederacy, Resolved by Joe Johnston Camp No. 94, United Confederate Veterans,

1. That to his sorrowing family we tender the heartfelt sympathies of the entire membership of this Camp, and indulge the hope that they may find consolation in the though that their guardian and protector will be revered so long as men shall admire true chivalry, and so long as courage, patriotism and honor shall be cherished as virtues worthy of commendation.

2. A devoted husband; a kind and indulgent father; a model citizen and great soldier has "crossed over the river to rest under the shade of the trees." Life's battle with him is ended; the bugle's note nor the rattling of drums shall never [Page 50] again fire his soul to deeds of valor, but, as he feared God and loved his neighbor and was always true to duty's call, we fondly hope that "all is well" with him. Peace to noble ashes!

3. That these Resolutions be spread on the minutes of this Camp; that the County papers and Dallas News be requested to publish same, and that a copy be transmitted by the Adjutant to the wife and children of deceased.

Respectfully submitted, J. W. Simmons, T. J. Gibson, M. W. Kemp, C. L. Watson, Committee.

By order of   H. W. Williams, Adjutant   C. L. Watson, Commander

[Page 51]

CALLED MEETING OF JOE JOHNSTON CAMP NO. 94, U. C. V.

Pursuant to call of Commander Watson, Joe Johnston Camp No. 94, United Confederate Veterans, assembled at the Mayor's office in Mexia on May 25th, 1893, for the purpose of arranging for our next Re-Union, and any other business that might come up to be acted on.

On motion, the time set for the Re-Union on Jack's Creek, was the 26th, 27th and 28th of July 1893.

On motion of Capt. Gibson, which was carried, a committee of three was appointed on permanent improvements to report at the meeting in July, as follows: T. J. Gibson, C. T. Harris and J. M. Storey.

On motion of J. E. Parker, the following Comrades were appointed as a committee of arrangements; Rado Steele, J. E. Parker, R. M. Love, W. M. Barton, J. W. Simmons, J. W. Thompson, J. M. Suttle, J. W. Nash, H. C. Joiner, J. W. McKinney and M. L. McDonald.

On motion of Capt. A. J. Burleson, a committee of four was appointed on privileges: Dr. J. P. Cook, R. M. Love, S. S. Walker and R. J. Bryant.

On motion of a Comrade, a committee of three on invitations was appointed as follows: W. E. Doyle, S. B. Love, A. J. Burleson and on motion, Capt. T. J. Gibson and the Commander were added to the committee.

On motion of Comrades Simmons and Gibson, the following Resolution was adopted, and the committee of Ladies appointed: Resolved, That a committee of ten be appointed [Page 52] from the wives and daughters of members of Joe Johnston Camp No. 94, U. C. V., whose duty it shall be to prepare and forward to the committee at New Orleans, La., having in charge the remains of Hon. Jefferson Davis for re-interment at Richmond, Va., a floral design and offering in behalf of said Camp and the wives and daughters of it's members. Com: Madames - J. W. Simmons, M. W. Kemp, J. E. Parker, W. E. Doyle, Dr. J. P. Cook, C. L. Watson, and Misses - Em Beeson, Blanche McCain, Ruby Fay Kelly and Jeanie Smith.

On motion of Commander Watson, a cordial invitation was extended to our former Commander Capt. W. H. Richardson [who was present] to be with us at our next Re-Union.

On motion of Judge Doyle an invitation was tendered Gen'l. Blaine and Staff, to be with us at our next meeting.

On motion of a Comrade, a committee of three was appointed to formulate a Burial Service, to be submitted to the general Re-Union at Birmingham, as follows: H. W. Williams, T. J. Gibson, and J. W. Simmons.

On motion of J. W. Simmons, the following Resolution was adopted: The thanks of this Camp are hereby tendered to the Mexia Silver Cornet Band for the donation of seven ($7) dollars from the proceeds of the Tehuacana Concert. [Davis monument fund][Page 53] Long may they blow to live and live to blow. No further business before it, the Camp adjourned.

H. W. Williams, Adjutant   C. L. Watson, Commander

[Page 54]

MINUTES OF CAMP JOE JOHNSTON HELD AT JACK'S CREEK ON JULY 26TH, 27TH, & 28TH, 1893

Wednesday, July 26th 9:30 A.M.

Camp opened with prayer by Rev. L. W. Duke, after which, Commander Watson delivered an address of welcome. Guard was then mounted. Volunteer speeches being in order, Capt. J. S. Gilbert delivered a short and interesting address followed by Rev. L. W. Duke, Capt. J. M. Rambo and W. H. Herring, who entertained the audience until noon.

Camp then adjourned till Thursday morning 9:30 o'clock. The afternoon was given up to the Sons and Daughters of Confederate Veterans, who used it in a very entertaining manner.

Thursday, July 27th, 9:30

Camp called to assemble by Band.
Chaplain being absent, prayer was dispensed with. Volunteer speeches being called for, Capts. F. M. Sellers, J. S. Gilbert, and A. J. Cashion delivered short addresses, which were highly entertaining.

The hour having arrived for the purpose, Capt. T. J. Gibson delivered an eloquent and instructive address on the Battle of Chancellorsville. Camp then adjourned for dinner.

3 o'clock P.M.

Camp re-assembled, and a committee was appointed by the Commander to name the avenues and streets of the Camp, [Page 55] after which the Hon. Dudley G. Wooten, of Dallas, delivered one of the most eloquent and interesting addresses that we ever listened to, and which was highly appreciated by the large audience.

After the close of the speech, the Camp adjourned until Friday morning. At night the Camp was entertained by the young people with a concert.

Friday, July 28th, 9:30

Camp assembled by Band. After guard mounting, a motion was made and carried, to return the thanks of this Camp to Capt. Gilbert's daughter for delightful music rendered by her and associates.

The time having arrived for the business meeting of the Camp, the minutes of the last Re-Union were read and the election of officers had, which resulted as follows:

J. W. Simmons	Commander
A. J. Burleson	1st. Lt. Commander
H. W. Gray	2nd. Lt. Commander
J. G. Walling	3rd. Lt. Commander
H. W. Williams	Adjutant
R. J. Bryant	Quartermaster
S. B. Love	Officer of the day
L. W. Duke	Chaplain
J. P. Cook	Surgeon
M. L. McDonald	Treasurer
W. H. Herring	Color Bearer
J. M. Deis	Bugler

The following resolution was offered by Capt. J. W. Simmons and Gen'l. W. G. Blaine and adopted; Whereas, It is the wish of Joe Johnston Camp that New Orleans be made the permanent place [Page 56] of the general Re-Union, therefore, be it Resolved, That our delegates be instructed to vote and use their influence towards making the above named place the permanent camping grounds; provided that New Orleans will offer equal inducements to any other city.

Report of Committee on Lots: The committee on lots, begs leave to report as follows: Number of lots sold, 68, at $5.00 each, making a total of $340.00 of which $200.00 has been paid for the purchase of land, leaving a balance of $140.00. the total number of lots laid off is 115, of which 68 lots have been sold leaving 47 lots unsold. Respectfully submitted, J. W. Simmons, Chairman.

Report of Committee on Permanent Improvements. To C. L. Watson, Commander. The undersigned, a majority of your committee appointed to take into consideration and report to this Camp what improvements, if any, should be made on these grounds, make the following report:

1. We recommend that a pavilion be erected on these grounds in time for our next annual Re-Union in accordance with the accompanying plans and specifications, not to exceed in cost the sum of $600.00 and that so much money as is necessary be appropriated for that purpose. [Page 57]

2. That arrangements be made before our next annual Re-Union for having the streets of the Camp well sprinkled during such Re-Union.

3. That a committee of five be appointed to be known as the "Improvement Committee," whose duty it shall be to carry out the recommendations in this report; said committee to consist of the Commander and Quartermaster elected at this meeting, and three discreet members of this Camp. Respectfully submitted. T. J. Gibson, J. M. Storey [Committee].

The following amendment was added: Resolved, That the sum of $500.00 be appropriated and that the "Improvement Committee" be not bound by the plans and specifications of the committee reporting. The report was then adopted.

The Committee on streets - Rado Steele, Chairman, reported the following: That the avenue coming from Mexia be called Lee and the one from Groesbeck be called Jackson.

That the street on the north of Lee Avenue be called Dick Walker and the first street on the south of Lee Avenue be called Adams, and the second one be called McCain. [Page 58]

That the first street on the west of Jackson Avenue be called J. W. Bennett, and that the naming of the second one be postponed until some future time.

For the information of the public, it may be proper to state that the streets were named for dead members of this Camp, except the one named for Capt. J. W. Bennett, who commanded a Limestone County Company in the Army of Tenn., and was killed at Atlanta, Ga. on July 22nd, 1864.

The Auditing committee made the following report:

To the Commander and Comrades of Camp Joe Johnston:

We, your Auditing committee beg leave to make the following report:

Cash received for dues	$ 65.35
Cash paid out of dues	$ 40.70
Balance on hand	$ 24.65
Cash re'c'ed for Privileges	$160.75
Cash paid out of Privileges	$133.00

Balance on hand	$ 27.75
Concert Fund	$109.50
Grand Total on hand	$161.90

We would suggest that in the future, all the funds of the Camp be turned over to the Treasurer, except so much as may be necessary to be expended for cleaning off the grounds. Respectfully submitted, R. M. Love, Chairman. [Page 59]

It was moved and carried, that all members of this Camp who desire to attend the general Re-Union in 1894, be appointed by the Commander as delegates.

After a few farewell remarks by the retiring Commander, the Camp adjourned till near the full moon in July 1894.

Camp Joe Johnston is a *Limestone County organization*, and we would most earnestly request all Confederate Veterans in the County to come and join and help us to maintain the name that we already have of being the "Star Camp" of the State of Texas.

H. W. Williams, Adjutant   C. L. Watson, Commander

[Page 60]   **CALLED MEETING OF CAMP, MARCH 17, 1894**

Pursuant to call of Commander Simmons, Joe Johnston Camp assembled at the Mayor's office in Mexia on March 17, 1894, to elect delegates to Waco and Birmingham and to attend o such other business as might come before it.

On motion of Capt. Gibson, it was ordered that all Comrades of this Camp who wish to attend Waco and Birmingham be appointed as delegates by the Commander.

The following resolution on the death of Gen'l Early was offered by Capt. Gibson and passed:

Whereas, Gen'l. Jubal A. Early, another of the distinguished soldiers who followed the destinies of the "Lost Cause," has been summoned to pass the river and join the immortal hosts who have preceded him,

Resolved by Joe Johnston Camp No. 94 U. C. V.:

1. That in the death of Gen'l. Early the South has lost a good citizen and one of its ablest defenders, and the United Confederate Veterans a Comrade whose name will be a sacred remembrance so long as one of us is left to cherish the memories of the days when together we suffered and battled for a cause ever dear to the heart of the Confederate soldier. [Page 61]

2. That from the close of the war to the hour of his death, Gen'l. Early never faltered in his devotion to his people, and was ever ready to aid and defend them and their cause in peace as he had done in war.

3. That we are again reminded that if we would accomplish the sacred work for which our organization was formed, we must be vigilant in the discharge of duty to the end that the destitute must be cared for; the truth of history vindicated and the pure minds of Southern childhood be kept free from the poison of false teachings issuing from sources venal and mercenary.

4. That to his relations and personal friends we offer our sympathy in their irreparable loss and great affliction.

At our last Re-Union a motion was made and carried that a building committee consisting of the Commander, quartermaster and three Comrades be appointed. At this meeting the Commander appointed the following Comrades: T. J. Gibson, J. M. Storey and R. M. Love.

On motion of a Comrade, a committee to solicit funds to help build the pavilion was appointed consisting of S. S. Walker, J. M. Suttle & Dr. M. W. Kemp.

No further business, on motion, the meeting adjourned.

H. W. Williams, Adjutant   J. W. Simmons, Commander

[Page 62]   **CALLED MEETING OF CAMP, MAY 26, 1894**

By call of Commander Simmons, Camp Joe Johnston assembled at the Mayor's office in Mexia on May 26th, to transact any business that might come before it.

A motion was made and carried that the next Re-Union be held on the 18th, 19th and 20th of July.

The commander was instructed to appoint committees on arrangements, privileges and invitations.

Arrangement committee: Comrades C. L. Watson, J. M. Suttle, M. W. Kemp, J. W. McKinney, & W. H. Browder.

Privilege committee: R. J. Bryant, S. B. Love, J. S. Groover, S. S. Walker and S. F. Bond.

Invitation committee: W. E. Doyle, T. J. Gibson and L. J. Farrar.

It was moved that the privilege of selling beer or whiskey be strictly prohibited, which was unanimously carried. The shooting gallery was also voted out.

After a general conversation about building the Pavilion; no further business, the meeting adjourned.

H. W. Williams, Adjutant   J. W. Simmons, Commander

[Page 63]
MINUTES OF JOE JOHNSTON CAMP NO. 94, UNITED CONFEDERATE VETERANS
HELD AT JACK'S CREEK ON JULY 18TH, 19TH & 20TH 1894
July 18th

Joe Johnston Camp No. 94, U. C. V., was called to order in annual meeting by Commander J. W. Simmons at 10 o'clock A.M. when prayer was offered by Dr. F. T. Mitchell of Waco. Guard for the day was detailed and placed in charge of Comrade S. B. Love, Officer of the day.

The adjutant, Comrade H. W. Williams, being absent on account of sickness, Comrade W. E. Doyle was appointed by the Commander to discharge the duties of that office.

After roll call, Comrades J. W. Simmons and W. E. Doyle delivered addresses of welcome.

Adjourned to 2 o'clock, P.M.

2 o'clock P.M.

The evening was given the "Sons and Daughters" of Joe Johnston Camp for their annual meeting.

July 19th

Camp called to order by Commander Simmons at 9-1/2 o'clock, A. M. Prayer by Dr. Mitchell. Guard Mounting. After brief addresses by several Comrades, Dr. Mitchell of Waco, delivered the address [Page 64] of the day.

Adjourned to 2 o'clock, P.M.

The following by Comrade W. H. Richardson was passed:

Resolved, That Joe Johnston Camp, No. 94, urge upon our National United Confederate Veteran Association the immediate necessity for the completion of a History of our Common country from a Southern stand point.

And to that end, that the Commander appoint a committee of three, whose duty it shall be to take the matter in charge and correspond with the parties in charge of the work, and co-operate with and assist them, and report progress at our next annual encampment.

Committee appointed: J. P. Hickman, L. J. Farrar and T. J. Gibson.

Resolution by Comrade Watson passed: Resolved, That all members of Joe Johnston Camp in good standing be, and they are hereby, elected delegates to the Houston Re-Union in 1895.

The following report by the building committee was read, adopted, and the committee discharged.

To J. W. Simmons, Commander:

Your committee appointed to erect improvements on these grounds beg to report. [Page 65]

That they employed Comrade Boyle to superintend the erection of a Pavilion. This, he, with the assistance of the friends and members of the Camp, proceeded to do, and the structure stands here to speak for itself. The total cost of this improvement, including platform, seats etc. aggregated $399.60.

This amount has been paid in full except a bill for lumber etc. in favor of S. S. Walk and Son, which could not be paid because entitled to a small credit for lumber returned.

From this it will be seen that your committee leaves in the Treasury of the amount appropriated for this purpose a balance of $100.400 with Walker and Son's credit to be added. Itemized accounts of expenditures are herewith filed.

Your committee, therefore, asks to be discharged.

J. W. Simmons
R. J. Bryant
J. M. Storey   Committee
R. M. Love
T. J. Gibson

By Comrade Richardson: A vote of thanks to the Architect Building Committee and Comrades old and young, who worked on, or contributed to the [Page 66] erection of the Pavilion. Passed.

By Comrade M. W. Kemp: To appoint a committee of three to take under consideration the advisability of buying 20 acres of land adjoining the land of the Camp; building thereon a house and put the whole in charge of an old Veteran, whose duty it shall be to care for the property and grounds of the Camp. Adopted.

By Comrade Doyle: To elect officers for the ensuing year. Adopted. Whereupon the following were elected:

J. W. Simmons	Commander
J. M. Suttle	1st. Lt. Commander
J. G. Walling	2nd. Lt. Commander
J. H. Archer	3rd. Lt. Commander
H. W. Williams	Adjutant
R. J. Bryant	Quartermaster
M. H. Clark	Officer of the day
L. W. Duke	Chaplain
J. P. Cook	Surgeon
M. L. McDonald	Treasurer
W. H. Herring	Color Bearer
W. A. Davis	Bugler

July 20th

Camp called to order at 10 o'clock A.M. Prayer by Dr. Mitchell.

Committee on purchase of more land, J. E. Parker, R. M. Love and G. W. Archer.

Vote of thanks tendered Quartermaster [Page 67] R. J. Bryant, for procuring artillery from Oakwood.

By Comrade Deis: That money enough be appropriated to mount the artillery by the next encampment. Adopted.

By Comrade Gibson: Resolution of thanks to Comrade H. W. Williams for efficient services. Adopted.

By Comrade Watson: That the committee on the purchase of land be given 60 days in which to report, and on reporting, the Commander shall, if he deems it advisable, convene the Precinct Captains for advice. Adopted.

Motion by Comrade Watson: That three ladies be appointed a committee on Flag. Adopted. Mrs. W. E. Doyle, Mrs. H. W. Williams and Miss Em Beeson were appointed.

On motion: Comrades T. J. Gibson, W. E. Doyle, C. L. Watson & H. W. Williams be appointed a committee to revise our By-Laws and have 200 copies published. Adopted.

Vote of thanks tendered Rev. F. T. Mitchell, D.D. for his able and eloquent address, and for services and good cheer given the encampment. Adopted.

By Comrade R. M. Love: That we [Page 68] heartily commend the movement now in progress to erect a Monument at Dallas to the memory of our confederate dead, and ask the Sons and Daughters' Society to join us in assisting in the praiseworthy undertaking. Further, that we tender our thanks to Mrs. Kate Cabell Currie for her untiring zeal in this behalf. Adopted.

The auditing committee appointed on the 19th submitted the following report:

We, your committee, appointed to examine the books of the Adjutant and Treasurer, beg leave to report: That from the most accessible data, we believe the books to be correct, showing

balance in the Treasure	$174.55
Held by Adjutant	9.10
Total	$183.65

We suggest that in the future our Adjutant keep separate funds and itemize each account, and that an Auditing Committee be appointed annually to report on the books of the Adjutant and Treasurer. Committee: G. W. Lee, W. P. Brown, J. S. Gilbert.

Comrade W. E. Doyle submitted the following report:

To the Commander, Officers and Comrades of Joe Johnston Camp No. 94, U. C. V.: During the present encampment and [pages 69 to 72 missing].

[Page 73]

MEXIA, APRIL 20TH, 1895

By call of Commander Simmons, Joe Johnston Camp assembled at the Mayor's office in Mexia on April 20th 1895, to transact any business that might come before it.

On motion of Comrade J. P. Cook, the time of holding the next Re-union was set for the 31st of July and 1st and 2nd of August.

On motion, six comrades were appointed on committee of Arrangements and Privileges and three on Invitations and Badges and Flag.

Arrangements: H. A. Boyd, A. J. Burleson, O. Wiley, Rado Steele, J. E. Parker and C. L. Watson.

Privileges: R. J. Bryant, J. G. Carroll, J. P. Hickman, G. W. Lee, J. M. Suttle and Jno. G. Walling.

Invitation: W. E. Doyle, T. J. Gibson, and S. S. Walker.

Badges & Flag: W. H. Herring, Wm. Kamsler & H. F. Simmons.

On motion of Comrade Gibson, the committee on badges were instructed to procure a suitable badge and that $20, or as much as is necessary, be appropriated for that purpose.

On motion of Comrade Doyle, $20 or a sufficiency, was appropriated to repair Flag.

On motion of Comrade Watson, the Adjutant was instructed to make arrangements at Houston to accommodate 50 Comrades with tents and cots free, they to carry their own bedding.

On motion of Comrade Kenney, the sum of $10 was appropriated to pay the Adjutant's expenses to Houston. [Page 74]

On motion of Comrade Gibson, a committee of three was appointed to select a Sponsor and three Maids of Honor to represent our Camp at Houston. Committee: Comrades Doyle, Camp and Kemp.

On motion of Comrade Watson, three were made a quorum on committee of arrangements and privileges.

A resolution was passed that we have a picnic at Re-union grounds on 14th of June to lay off more lots.

No further business, on motion, the Camp adjourned.

H. W. Williams, Adjutant   J. W. Simmons, Commander.

[Page 75]

MINUTES OF JOE JOHNSTON CAMP NO. 94, U. C. V.,
HELD AT JACK'S CREEK ON JULY 31ST AUGUST 1ST & 2ND 1895

July 31st

The Camp was called to order by Commander Simmons at 10 o'clock, and was led in prayer by Gen'l. T. W. Blake, the Chaplain, Rev. L. W. Duke, being absent.

The roll was called and guard mounted. The Commander and Major L. J. Farrar then delivered interesting addresses of welcome; after which Col. T. J. Gibson delivered an excellent impruntu address. The camp then adjourned until next day at 9;30 o'clock.

The afternoon was made use of by the Sons and Daughters of Joe Johnston Camp.

August 1st, 9:30

After prayer and guard mounting a business meeting was called. The committee on Constitution and By-Laws requested further time to make a final report, which was granted. It was made the duty of this committee to report on the first day of our next Re-union.

The committee on the purchase of more land for the camp, reported that they have measured off 20 acres joining our tract on three sides, but have failed to get the land as yet.

A motion was adopted to appoint a committee on resolutions to memorialize the Legislature in the interest of needy widows and orphans of Confederate Veterans. Committee: Jno. G. Walling, E. B. Smyth and S. S. Walker. [Page 76]

At 10 o'clock, Gen'l. H. H. Boone delivered a most interesting and instructive address, after which the Camp adjourned for dinner.

2 o'clock, P. M.

Camp reassembled in a business meeting. The committee on history made their report, which was adopted and the committee continued.

During a short interval in the business proceedings several members of the Camp delivered short and interesting addresses.

Business meeting resumed, and adjourned until next morning at 8 o'clock.

August 2nd, 8 o'clock, A.M.

After prayer by Capt. W. P. Brown, the guard was mounted and the Camp went into the election of officers, which resulted as follows:

R. J. Bryant	Commander
S. S. Walker	1st. Lt. Commander
Jno. G. Walling	2nd. Lt. Commander
Wm. Justice	3rd. Lt. Commander
H. W. Williams	Adjutant
Jno. G. Carroll	Quartermaster
W. H. Herring	Officer of the day
L. W. Duke	Chaplain
J. P. Cook	Surgeon
M. L. McDonald	Treasurer
C. H. F. Wood	Color Bearer
J. M. Deis	Bugler

Comrade L. E. Camp was unanimously elected Captain of the Artillery of the Camp. [Page 77]

Business meeting adjourned till 2 o'clock.

At 10 o'clock, Col. M. D. Herring of Waco delivered an eloquent address, after which Col. Gibson offered the following resolution, which was adopted: Resolved, That the thanks of this Camp be and are extended to Gen'l. H. H. Boone, Col. M. D. Herring and Major L. J. Farrar for their able and patriotic addresses delivered during the present Re-union, and that they are requested to furnish this Camp with copies of their several addresses for publication to be filed among the archives of this Camp as able contributions to the true history of the cause that led to secession; the motives impelling the South, and the facts immediately connected with the civil war.

The committee on Lots made their report and was, on motion, discharged, and the Adjutant was empowered to sell lots in the future.

The Barker Piano Co. of Waco, and Col. Spencer especially, were tendered the thanks of the Camp for the use of their instrument during Re-union. The thanks of the Camp were, also, tendered Mrs. John Jackson for the use of her organ. A motion was carried that the thanks of this Camp be returned to the young people for their very interesting entertainments to the Camp. On motion, the finance committee appointed at our last Re-union was abolished.

[Page 78] The following resolution was adopted, and the committee discharged: To J. W. Simmons, Commander. Your committee appointed to memorialize the Legislature of the State of Texas in the interest of the widows and orphans of Confederate Veterans, beg leave to report the accompanying resolutions and recommend the adoption of the same:

Resolved by Joe Johnston Camp No 94, U. C. V.

1. That our State Legislature be, and the same is hereby memorialized and requested to pass such legislation as may be necessary to relieve the wants of needy widows and orphans of Confederate Veterans, and of such Confederate Veterans who are in needy circumstances, but who are not in a position to accept the benefits of the Confederate Home at Austin.

2. That a copy of these resolution be furnished by the Adjutant of this Camp to our Senator and Representative in the Legislature.

John G. Walling, E. B. Smyth, S. S. Walker, Committee.

Report of Auditing Committee: To J. W. Simmons, Commander, and Comrades: We, your committee appointed to audit the books of this Camp, respectfully submit the following report: We find, after examining [pages 79 to 82 missing] [Page 83] the books of the Quartermaster, Adjutant and Treasurer that they are correct and in good shape.

Total amt. of money received up to July 27th '95	$624.75
Total amt. of money paid out	497.65
Balance to credit of Camp	$127.10

(There has been money received since July 27th, which will be properly reported by the auditing committee for the ensuring year.) W. P. Brown, S. B. Love, J. G. Walling, Committee.

The report was adopted and committee discharged. A motion was carried that the military companies of Mexia and Groesbeck be thanked for their attendance at our Re-union.

On motion, the Comrades in each Precinct were instructed to send to the Adjutant as soon as possible the name of some one of their number as Captain.

A motion was carried that the Adjutant be paid the sum of sixty dollars for the ensuing year.

The business meeting adjourned for a short time and memorial services were held for the dead members of the Camp, conducted by the Chaplain, Rev. L. W. Duke, assisted by Rev. J. S. Grooves and Gen'l. T. W. Blake.

Col. Watson, and Hon. R. E. Steele delivered appropriate eulogies on the death of our late Comrades, Capt. J. S. Gilbert and B. F. Wallace. It was moved and carried that a page of our [Page 84] Camp book be set apart to the memory of each.

A motion prevailed that lot 17 be purchased back from the owner for the use of the Camp.

No further business coming before it, on motion, the Camp adjourned to meet at the call of the Commander in 1896.

Official: H. W. Williams, Adjutant   J. W. Simmons, Commander

According to the Charter it is the duty of the Commander to appoint five Trustees for the Camp, which he did as follows:

J. W. Simmons, Mexia   C. L. Watson, Mexia
S. B. Love, Tehuacana   S. S. Walker, Groesbeck
Jno. G. Walling, Thornton

[Page 85] By a Resolution of Camp Joe Johnston, this page is set apart as Sacred to the Memory of Captain J. S. Gilbert, Company A, 6th Regiment of Louisiana Infantry, Hayes' Brigade, Ewell's Division, Jackson's Corps, Army of Northern Virginia, who died at his home near Cade, Navarro County, Texas, on the 19th day of March, 1895. He was a good and faithful Confederate soldier to the end, and has crossed the river to "rest under the shade of the trees" with his old Commander, Stonewall Jackson. May our Camp ever keep his memory green!

[Page 86 blank] [Page 87] By a Resolution of Camp Joe Johnston, this page is set apart as Sacred to the Memory of B. F. Wallace, Company F, 15th Regiment of Texas Cavalry, Granbury's Brigade, Cleburn's Division, Hardee's Corps, Army of Tennessee, who died at his home at Hancock, Limestone County, Texas, on the ___ day of June, 1895. He was a good and faithful Confederate soldier during the war, and after its close, made one of our best and most useful citizens. May his comrades ever revere his memory!

[Page 88]

CALLED MEETING OF JOE JOHNSTON CAMP

By call of Commander Bryant, Joe Johnston Camp No. 94, assembled at Mexia on April 18th, 1896, to fix the time for holding the Re-union. On motion, the 22nd, 23rd and 24th of July was set as the time.

The next business was to elect delegates to the General Re-union at Richmond. On motion, all Comrades who intend to go were made delegates. It was also decided that the same rule apply to the State Re-union at Dallas on 24th & 25 of June. On motion, the Commander was instructed to appoint the various Camp Committees.

Privilege Com.: J. G. Carroll, J. M. Suttle, J. M. Storey, H. F. Simmons, W. H. Browder and A. J. Burleson.

Arrangement Com.: Rado Steele, M. P. Fuqua, C. L. Watson, E. B. Smyth, H. C. Joiner, W. M. Barton, J. W. Thompson and J. W. Nash.

Invitation Com.: T. J. Gibson, W. E. Doyle, F. Y. Doke, J. G. Walling and W. W. Wyatt.

Spring Com.: I. E. Wood, G. W. Kenney, G. C. Boyle, J. W. McKinney and S. F. Bond.

Concert Com.: J. W. Simmons, J. P. Hickman with the privilege of adding more Comrades to the committee.

On motion, all military and five companies of the County were invited to attend the Re-union in a body.

[Page 89] It was decided that the 1st day of May be appointed for a general basket picnic at the Re-union grounds, and every body invited to come.

On motion, all old Texans were especially invited to our next Re-union.

No further business, the Camp adjourned.

Official: H. W. Williams, Adjutant   R. J. Bryant, Commander

[Pages 90-99 blank] [Pages 100-233 Camp Rosters]
[Page 284]

ROSTER OF EX-CONFEDERATES OF LIMESTONE COUNTY, TEXAS

Symbols for year on rosters:
a = Roster from 31st July – 2nd August 1889
b = Roster of 1890
c = Roster of 1891
d = Roster of 1892
e = Roster of 1895
f = Roster of 1896
No letter is listed every year
(Editor has added additional information on the veteran in italics)

Samuel M. Adair, Co. C, 10th Alabama. Residence - Big Hill. [a]*[Buried Big Hill Cemetery 7/26/1847 – 6/19/1923]*

L. A. Adams, Pvt., Co. G, 11th Tennessee Cavalry, Beall's Brigade, W. H. Jackson's Division, Forrest's Corp. Residence - Armour. [a] *[Buried Armour Cemetery, South Section 10/11/1845 – 6/9/1912]*

M. Adams, 1st Lt., Co. D, 20th Texas Infantry, Harrison's Brigade, Army of the Trans-Mississippi. Residence – Mexia. [a] *[Buried Mexia City Cemetery, 4/29/1827-11/19/1892]*

W. H. Adams, Capt., Co. F, 33rd Tennessee Infantry, Strahl's Brigade, Cheatham Division, Polk and Hardee's Corps, Army of the Tennessee. Residence – Mexia. [a] *[Buried Mexia City Cemetery, 1840-1886 "This death date is probably wrong or misread]*

T. H. Adkinson, Pvt., Co. E, 38th Alabama Infantry, Holtzclaw's Brigade, Clayton's Division, Stuart's Corp. [a] Hood's Corp, Army of the Tennessee. Residence – Mexia. [a] [b] *{name maybe T. N. Atkisson}*

N. W. Alford, Pvt., Co. K, 20th Texas Cavalry, Maxey's Brigade, Hindman's Division, Army of the Trans-Mississippi. Residence - Groesbeck. [a]

B. W. Allen, Pvt., Co. K, 20th Texas Cavalry. Residence - Kosse. [a][f]

James H. Allen, Co. F, 9th Alabama Infantry. [a] *[Buried Kosse Cemetery ND]*

Wilie B. Allen, Sgt., Co. K, Bass' Infantry, Cooper's Brigade, Steel's Division, Trans-Mississippi. [c] *[Buried Kosse Cemetery, 1834-1907]*

C. A. Anderson, Bledsmiss Battery, French's Division, Pope's Corp, Army of the Tennessee. Residence – Shiloh. [a]

F. M. Anderson, Musician, Co. I, 82nd Texas Cavalry, Hindman's Division, Army of the Tennessee. [b] *[Buried Mexia City Cemetery, 10/17/1844-1/29/1900]*

E. W. Anglin, [McNally's Company under General Horton]. Residence - Groesbeck. [a] *[Buried Faulkenberry Cemetery 2/24/1845 – 4/26/1891]*

J. C. Anglin, Pvt., Texas Cavalry Indian Scout, [McNally's Company Independent Scouts under General Horton] Greene's Brigade, Army of the Trans-Mississippi. Residence - Groesbeck. [a][b][d][e] *[Faulkenberry Cemetery 7/18/1847 Limestone Co., TX - 5/21/1905]*

John T. Anglin, Pvt., Johnson's Battalion, Texas Cavalry Indian Scout, [McNally's Company under General Horton] Greene's Brigade, Army of the Trans-Mississippi. Residence - Groesbeck. [a][b][d][e] *[Faulkenberry Cemetery 3/23/1823 Clay Co., Ill. – ND, 10th TX Infantry CSA]*

Geo. W. "Gus" Archer, Pvt., Co. C, 8th Texas Cavalry, Wharton's Brigade, Wheeler's Division and Corp, Army of the Tennessee. Residence – Mexia. [a]

J. H. Archer, Pvt., Co. F, 36th Mississippi Infantry, Sear's Brigade. Residence - Mt. Calm. [a][d][e][f] *[Old Town Cemetery, Mt. Calm, 8/2/1830 – 11/13/1914]*

Elmer Leroy Archibald, Pvt., Co. B, Rucker's Mississippi Cavalry, Chalmer's Brigade, Outlaw's Division, Forrest's Corp, Army of the Tennessee. Residence - Groesbeck. [b] *[Blair-Stubbs Funeral Home Records, 11/28/1840 Mississippi – 3/27/1923 4 miles south Mexia, father Jim Archibald, burial Oletha, Texas]*

James Armour, Pvt., Co. C, Bradford's Texas Cavalry Regiment. [a][d] *[Buried Armour Cemetery, South Section 8/10/1825 Jackson Co., GA – 4/25/1896 Masonic][Member of A.F. & A.M. and I.O.O.F.]*

S. Thomas Arnett, Pvt., Co. I, 21st Texas Cavalry, Parson's Brigade, Greene's Division, Wharton's Corp. [a][f] *[Buried Kosse Cemetery, 1844-1909]*

James A. Arvin, 9th Regiment Virginia Infantry, Corse's Brigade, Pickett's Division, Longstreet's Corp, Army of Northern Virginia. Residence – Mexia. [a] *[Buried Mexia City Cemetery, 11/5/1838-4/17/1910]*

James H. Athey[11], Pvt., Co. F, 6th Alabama Cavalry, Clanton's Brigade, Johnson's Division. Residence – Armour. [a]

David H. Bailey, 2nd Sgt., Co. F, 32nd Georgia Infantry, Harrison's Brigade, McLaws' Division, Stewarts' Corp, Army of the Tennessee. Residence - Honest Ridge Precinct No. 2. [a]

Ed Bailey, Pvt., Co. A, 11th Texas Cavalry. Residence - Prairie Hill. [c]

G. C. Baisden, Co. B, 10th Mississippi Cavalry, Goleton's Brigade, Forrest's Division, Trans-Mississippi. Residence – Groesbeck. [c]

W. A. Ball, Loring's Scout. Residence - Kosse. [a]

A. H. Banks, Co. I, Arkansas, Cabell's Brigade. Residence - Big Hill. [a]

A. G. Barnard, Pvt., Co. B, 22nd Arkansas Infantry, Fagan's Brigade, Army of the Trans-Mississippi. Residence - Honest Ridge Precinct No. 2. [a]

---

[11] Listed as James H. Athery on the rolls of the 6th AL Cavalry

Marcellus E. Barkwell, Pvt., Co. B, Anderson's Georgia Battery, Brackenridge's Division, Hardee's Corp, Army of the Tennessee. Residence - Kirk. [c] *[Buried Kirk Cemetery 7/11/1835 – 3/7/1908]*

J. M. Barrey, Co. D, Bob Willis' Regiment, Waul's Texas Legion. Residence – Mexia. [a]

W. M. Barton, Pvt., Co. E, 13th North Carolina Artillery, Dixon's Brigade, Army of Northern Virginia. Residence – Mexia. [a][b][d][f] *[Buried Armour Cemetery, North Section 9/28/1837 – 4/12/1907]*

T. J. Bachelor/Batchelor, Pvt., Co. E, 62nd Alabama Infantry, Thomas' Brigade, Army of the Trans-Mississippi. [b][d]

Charles Seth Bates, 1st Sgt., Co. K, 20th Texas Cavalry, Maxey's Brigade, Hindman's Division, E. K. Smith's Corp, Army of the Trans-Mississippi. Residence – Honest Ridge Precinct No. 2. [a][b][d][e][f] *[Ft. Parker Memorial Park 5/10/1833 Coles Co., Ill. – 6/30/1890]*

James F. Beaty, Co. F, Texas Cavalry Scout, Burnett's Regiment. Residence – Kosse. [a][1847 Jasper Co., TX. - ?]

Samuel Houston Beene, Pvt., Co. G, Madison's Texas Cavalry. [f]

J. M. Bell[12], 1st Lt., Co. A, 6th Alabama Infantry, Rode's Brigade, A. P. Hill's Division, Jackson's Corp. Residence – Honest Ridge Precinct No. 2. [a]

James M. Bell, Pvt., Co. A, 6th Alabama Infantry, Battle's Brigade, Rode's Division, Ewell's Corp, Army of Northern Virginia. [b] Gordon's Corp, Army of Northern Virginia. Residence – Horn Hill. [c] *[Buried Horn Hill Cemetery 8/26/1824 – 1/11/1899]*

J. N. Bell, Waul's Battalion, Green's Brigade, Army of the Trans-Mississippi.

J. W. Bell, Co. H, 20th Texas, Cooper's Brigade, Marmaduke's Division. Residence – Tehuacana. [a]

W. N. Bell, Capt., Co. A, Hindman's Legion.

Elson G. Bennett, 15th Texas Infantry, Trans-Mississippi Department[d] *[Buried Faulkenberry Cemetery 1/28/1832 Jackson Co., AL – 6/23/1916]*

Frank Berry, Co. H, 1st Mississippi. Residence – Honest Ridge Precinct No. 2. [a]

J. W. Berry, Co. H, 31st Mississippi, Featherson's Brigade, Loring's Division, Hardee's Corp, Army of the Tennessee. Residence – Honest Ridge Precinct No. 2. [a]

Warren Berry, Co. H, 1st Mississippi. Residence – Honest Ridge Precinct No. 2. [a]

Henry G. Berryman, Pvt., Co. H, 20th Texas Infantry, Ellmore's Brigade, Trans-Mississippi. [b][d][e][f] *[Buried Prairie Grove Cemetery 1/27/1843 – 3/6/1908]*

John Bishop, Co. A, 33rd Alabama. Residence – Farrar. [a] *[Buried Lost Prairie 1843 – 1918]*

B. F. Black, Co. C, 3rd Louisiana Infantry, Thomas' Brigade, Mouton's Division, Army of the Trans-Mississippi. Residence – Elem Ridge. [a]

H. C. Blackmon, Co. D, 8th Alabama Cavalry. Residence – Kosse. [a] *[Buried Faulkenberry Cemetery 8/14/1844 – 11/14/1929]*

D. H. Bolton, Pvt., Co. H, 10th Virginia Infantry, Taliaferro's Brigade, Jackson's Division, Ewell's Corp, Army of Northern Virginia. Residence – Prairie Hill. [c]

Stephen Finley Bond, Pvt., Co. G, Texas Cavalry, State Troops. [e][f] *[Buried Mexia City Cemetery, 7/10/1834-6/14/1913, TX. Frontier Regt. Under Capt. McCune]]*

S. Booth. Residence – Armour [a] *[Wife buried in Armour Cemetery, South Section]*

W. P. Booth, Color Bearer, Co. E, 36th Arkansas Infantry, McRae's Brigade, Churchill's Division, Army of the Trans-Mississippi. Residence – Armour. [a]

---

[12] Listed as J. M. Bell, Jr. on rolls of the 6th AL Infantry.

Christopher J. Bower, Pvt., Co. C, 8th Texas Infantry, McCullough's Brigade, Walker's Division.[10] Residence – Mexia. [a] Young's Brigade, Walker's Division, E. K. Smith's Corp, Army of the Trans-Mississippi. [b][d] *[Buried Point Enterprise Cemetery 2/17/1839 – 8/22/1920 Mason]*

J. R. Boyd, Co. C, 7th Infantry, Elmon's Brigade. Residence – Mt. Calm. [a]

Horace A. Boyd, 1st Lt., Co. E, 35th Texas Cavalry, Bee's Brigade, Walker's Division, E. K. Smith's Corp, Army of the Trans-Mississippi. [b][d][f] *[Buried Tehuacana Cemetery 7/7/1823 – 2/4/1906]*

W. P. Boykin, Pvt., Co. K, 1st [Cookes'] Texas Artillery, Magruder's Division, E. K. Smith's Corp, Army of the Trans-Mississippi. Residence – Mexia. [a][b] *[Buried Prairie Hill Cemetery 10/12/1843 – 2/16/1899]*

G. C. Boyle, Pvt., Co. C, 2nd Mississippi Infantry, McGowan's Brigade, Johnson's Division, Lee's Corp, Army of Northern Virginia. Residence – Tehuacana. [f]

C. M. Bradford, Pvt., Co. D, 20th Texas Infantry, Harrison's Brigade, Magruder's Division, Army of the Trans-Mississippi. Residence - Groesbeck. [a][b]

John Bradshaw, Pvt., Co. A, 33rd Alabama Infantry, Wood's Brigade, Hardee's Corp, Army of the Tennessee. Residence – Personsville. [b] *[Buried Lost Prairie Cemetery 1/10/1829 – 2/24/1901]*

J. J. Bridges, Co. J, 55th Georgia Infantry. Residence - Kosse. [a] *[Buried Kirk Cemetery 11/29/1841 – 1/10/1910]*

L. M. Briggs, Co. B, 15th Texas Infantry. Residence – Kosse. [a]

F. Brooks, Co. K, Swets' Brigade. Residence – Heads Prairie. [a]
James H. Brooks, Co. E, 19th Texas Infantry. Residence – Heads Prairie. [a] *[Buried Ebenezer Cemetery 1/29/1845 – 5/19/1908]*

Thomas W. Brooks, Co. E, 19th Texas Infantry. Residence – Heads Prairie. [a] *[Buried King Cemetery 8/25/1847 – 8/11/1922]*

W. F. Brooks, Co. K, 1st Texas Infantry, Hood's Brigade, Field's Division, Longstreet's Corp, Army of Northern Virginia.

W. T. Brooks, Capt., Co. I, 22nd Missouri Infantry, Early's Brigade, Banks' Division, Army of the Tennessee. Residence – Prairie Hill. [c]

W. H. Browder, Co. A, 1st Alabama Cavalry. Residence – Groesbeck. [a][e][f] *[Buried Faulkenberry Cemetery 5/25/1849 – 5/5/1923]*

E. J. Brown, Pvt., Co. C, 8th Texas Cavalry. [f]

J. M. Brown, Pvt., Co. E, 3rd Texas Cavalry, Greene's Brigade, Army of the Trans-Mississippi. Residence – Mexia. [a][b] *[Buried Shead Cemetery 10/19/1841 – 12/1/1906]* OR *[John Marsh Brown buried Lost Prairie 7/12/1846 – 1/26/1915]*

James P. Brown, Capt., Co. K [Limestone Mounted], 12th Texas Cavalry, Parson's Brigade, Green's Division, Wharton's Corp. Residence – Kosse. [a][e][f] *[Buried Brown Cemetery 3/5/1829 – 7/23/1897][Served in TX House of Representatives 1879-1880]*

Mc N. Brown, 3rd Louisiana Cavalry, Cabell's Brigade. Residence – Mt. Calm. [a] *[Buried Mt. Antioch Cemetery, 11/2/1827 – 2/14/1912]*

Wiley P. Brown, 1st Lt./Capt., Co. K, 20th Texas Dismounted Cavalry, Maxey's Brigade, Hindman's Division, Army of the Trans-Mississippi. Residence – Groesbeck. [a][b][e][f] *[Buried Faulkenberry Cemetery 12/12/1837 – 2/7/1918]*

Elbert Bryan, Co. C, Gurley's Texas Cavalry, Laws' Brigade, Army of the Trans-Mississippi. Residence – Mt. Calm. [a] *[Buried Mt. Antioch Cemetery, 11/3/1840 – 5/20/1921]*

E. R. Bryan, Pvt., Co. G [Travis Rifles], 6th Texas Cavalry, Ross' Brigade, Hood's Division, Army of the Tennessee. Residence - Prairie Hill. [c]

Riley Jackson Bryant, Sgt., Co. B, Texas Infantry, Waul's Legion. Residence – Mexia. [a][b][d][f] *[Buried Mexia City Cemetery, 1839-1923]*

Thomas Bryant, Sgt., Co. H, Spaight's Texas Infantry, Nelson's Brigade, Walker's Division, Army of the Trans-Mississippi. Residence – Honest Ridge Precinct No. 2. [a] 2nd Sgt., Co. B, Spaight's Texas Infantry, Walker's Brigade, Army of the Trans-Mississippi. [b]

---

[10] Shown as 9th Texas Infantry

W. M. C. Bryan, Co. A, 60th Alabama, Gracie's Brigade, Army of the Tennessee. Residence – Point Enterprise. [a] *[Buried Point Enterprise Cemetery 1/16/1844 – 11/20/1898]*

William Alette Buckner, 2nd Lt., Co. B, 9th Virginia Cavalry, W. H. F. Lee's Brigade, See's Division, Stewart's Corp, Army of Northern Virginia. Residence – Mexia. [a][b][d][f] *[Buried Mexia City Cemetery, 11/11/1847-12/23/1902]*

J. R. Bugg, Co. C, 11th Tennessee Cavalry, Forrest's Brigade. Residence – Mt. Calm. [a]

W. R. Burditt, Co. H, 18th Texas. Residence – Big Hill. [a]

John Burleson, Pvt., Co. K, 12th Texas Cavalry. [e] *[Buried Eutaw Cemetery with no first name or dates – Confederate Soldier]*

Thomas S. Burney, Pvt., Co. C, 8th Texas Cavalry, Harrison's Brigade, Wharton's Division, Wheeler's Corp. Residence – Honest Ridge Precinct No. 2. [a] *[Buried Honest Ridge Cemetery 5/28/1842 – 3/23/1885]*

W. A. Burney, Co. F, 15th Texas Cavalry, Holmes Division. Residence – Armour. [a] *[Buried Honest Ridge Cemetery 11/8/1835 – 7/8/1903]*

John Burns[13], Pvt., Co. H, 6th Texas Infantry, Granberry's Brigade, Cleburne's Division, Hardee's Corp, Army of the Tennessee. Residence – Groesbeck. [c]

J. E. Butler, Owens' Battery, Arkansas Detached Service. Residence – Mt. Calm. [a] *[Mt. Antioch Cemetery 11/2/1824 SC – 12/2/1890]*

T. E. Buttrell, Co. K, McNally's Scout, 12th Texas Cavalry. Residence – Heads Prairie. [a]

T. W. Byars, 2nd Lt., Co. A, Steven's Arkansas Cavalry, Pike's Brigade, Holmes' Division, Army of the Trans-Mississippi. [b]

R. H. Calhoun, Pvt., Co. C, Floyd's Rifle Regiment, 2nd Georgia Battalion, Wright's Brigade, Mahone's Division, Longstreet's Corp, Army of Northern Virginia. [a][b]

Lafayette Emerson Camp, Pvt., Georgia Light Artillery, Confuit's Battery, Cherokee Brigade, Stevenson's Division, Hood's Corp, Army of the Tennessee. [a] Hardee's Corp, Army of the Tennessee. [b][d][f] *[Buried Mexia City Cemetery, 7/18/1845-3/13/1920]*

W. L. Carleton, Surgeon, 2nd Arkansas Infantry. [e] *[Buried as Rev. in Armour Cemetery, South Section 3/8/1825 – 1/10/1889]* DD probably 1898

G. M. Carpenter, Co. D, 8th Mississippi Cavalry. Residence – Farrar. [a]

W. L. Carpenter Residence – Tehuacana. [a]

J. G. Carroll, Pvt., Co. A, 22nd Arkansas Cavalry. [e][f] *[Buried Mexia City Cemetery, 6/11/1847 – 4/21/1907]*

W. A. Carruth, Pvt., Co. F, 11th Mississippi Infantry. [e][f]

Andrew Jackson Cashion, Capt., Co. H, 1st Tennessee Infantry, Archer and Bee's Brigade, Hill and Johnson's Divisions, Jackson's Corp, Army of Northern Virginia. [a][b][d][f] *[Buried Lindley Cemetery 2/18/1840 – 7/9/1898]*

C. A. Castellow, Co. C, 9th Texas. Residence – Honest Ridge Precinct No. 2. [a]

Edward C. Chambers, Pvt., Lewis' Company, Elmore's Regiment, Texas Infantry. [e] *[Buried Thornton Cemetery, 1831-1912]*

H. J. Chandler, Co. I, 17th Texas Cavalry. Residence – Farrar. [a]

J. R. Chatham, Co. E, Texas Cavalry, Baylor's Brigade. [a]

D. N. Chisholm, 4th Mississippi, Clark's Brigade, Marmaduke's Division.

James Clanahan, Pvt., Co. I, 21st Mississippi Infantry, Humphreys' Brigade, McLaw's Division, Longstreet's Corp, Army of Northern Virginia. [a][b][d][f]

---

[13] Shown on rolls as John Bums

M. H. Clark, Pvt., Co. E, Willis' Battalion, Texas Artillery, Waul's Legion, Army of the Tennessee. Residence – Groesbeck. [a][e][f] *[Buried Faulkenberry Cemetery 1830 – 1919]*

J. Cline, Co. D, 5th South Carolina Infantry, Jenkins' Brigade. Residence – Mt. Calm. [a]

A. M. Clinton, Pvt., Co. A, 38th Tennessee Infantry, Wright's Brigade, Cheatham's Division, Polk's Corp, Army of the Tennessee. [a] Bragg's Corp, Army of the Tennessee. [b]

J. W. Cockran, Co. E, 6th Mississippi Cavalry. Residence – Kosse. [a]

W. M. Coker, Texas Taylor's Regiment. Residence – Kosse. [a] *[Buried Sansom/Wedgeman Cemetery – No Marker]*

T. J. Collins, Pvt., Co. A, 7th Louisiana Infantry, Peck's Brigade, Jackson's Division, Army of Northern Virginia. Residence – Honest Ridge Precinct No. 2. [a]

George Collom, Pvt., Co. I, 9th Texas Cavalry, Ross' Brigade, Jackson's Division, Army of the Tennessee. [a][b][d][f] *[Buried Armour Cemetery, East Section 1854-1916]*

J. B. Conley, Pvt., Co. I, 12th Tennessee Cavalry. [e]

John P. Cook, Pvt., Co. B, 30th Alabama Infantry, Pettus' Brigade, Stevenson's Division, Lee's Corp, Army of the Tennessee. [b][f] *[Buried Mexia City Cemetery, 12/31/1844-10/1/1910][Dr.]*

W. R. Cooper, Pvt., 47th Tennessee Infantry, Manley's Brigade, Cheatham's Division, Bragg's Corp, Army of the Tennessee. [b]

S. M. Cotton, Pvt., Co. C/E, 19th Arkansas Infantry, Tappan's Brigade, Churchill's Division, Price's Corp, Army of the Trans-Mississippi. Residence – Honest Ridge Precinct No. 2. [a][b][d] *[Buried Honest Ridge Cemetery 7/18/1842 – 3/25/1922]*

L. E. Cowart, Pvt., Co. D, 12th Georgia Infantry. [f]

A. J. Cox, Pvt., Co. H, 38th Alabama Infantry, Holtzclaw's Brigade, Stewart's Corp, Army of the Tennessee. [b][e] *[Buried Waller Cemetery, 8/9/1840 – ND]*

Milton Burwell Cox, Co. G, 18th Alabama. Residence – Prairie Grove. [a] *[Born Jefferson Co., Ala.][Buried Prairie Grove Cemetery 1838 - ?]*

F. M. Crawford, Pvt., Co. E, 32nd Alabama Infantry, Holtzclaw's Brigade, Steward's Division. Residence - Armour. [a] *[Buried Armour Cemetery, South Section 2/8/1836 – 4/10/1901]*

W. E. Curry, Pvt., Co. F, Baylor's Texas Cavalry, Lane's Brigade, Hunt's Division. [a] Greene's Division, Army of the Trans-Mississippi. [b]

J. M. Davidson, Pvt., Co. B, 30th Mississippi Infantry, Walthall's Brigade, Anderson's Division, Polk's Corp, Army of the Tennessee. [a][b][d]

J. I. Davis, Pvt., Co. E, Baylor's Texas Cavalry, Stone's Brigade, Greene's Division, Wharton's Corp, Army of the Trans-Mississippi. [a][b]

J. W. Davis, Pvt., Co. K, 2nd Texas Cavalry [Partisan Rangers], Cooper's Brigade, Laws' Division, Army of the Trans-Mississippi. Residence – Forest Glade. [b]

R. E. Davis, Pvt., Co. C, 1st Alabama Legion, Gracie's Brigade, B. R. Johnson's Division, Longstreet's Corp. [Transferred to 60th Alabama, Co. H] Residence – Armour. [a] *[Buried at Armour Cemetery, South Section 3/8/1837 – NDD]*

Samuel A. Davis, Co. A, Arkansas, Cabell's Brigade. Residence – Big Hill. [a] *[Buried Big Hill Cemetery 10/6/1844 – 4/29/1936]*

W. A. Davis, Bugler, Pvt., Co. A, 33rd Arkansas Infantry, Tappan's Brigade, Churchill's Division, Stile's Corp. Residence – Armour. [a] Musician, Co. H, 33rd Arkansas Infantry, Tappan's Brigade, Churchill's Division, E. K. Smith's Corp, Army of the Trans-Mississippi. [b] *[Buried Old Town Cemetery, Mt. Calm, 3/21/1847 – 12/13/1913]*

Robert M. Day, Pvt., Co. F, 55th Georgia Infantry, Army of the Tennessee. [b] *[Buried Horn Hill Cemetery 11/14/1828 – 4/1/1914]*

John M. Deis, Pvt., Sanders' Battery, 1st Missouri Artillery, Price's Division, Polk's Corp, Army of the Tennessee. [a] Hardee's Corp, Army of the Tennessee. [b][f] ['93 and '96 Bugler] *[Buried Spillers Cemetery 3/31/1841 – 11/10/1918]*

F. J/Y. Doke, Capt., Co. F, 9th Missouri Infantry. Residence - Kosse. [a][f]

P. O. Douglas, Pvt., Co. A, 15th Arkansas Infantry, T. P. Dockery's Brigade, Churchill's Division, E. K. Smith's Corp, Army of the Trans-Mississippi. Residence – Elem Ridge. [a][f]

William Elliott Doyle, Pvt., Co. G, 7th South Carolina Cavalry, Gray's Brigade, Field's Division, Longstreet's Corp, Army of Northern Virginia. [a][b][d][f] *[Buried Mexia City Cemetery, 4/26/1846 Oconee Co., SC – 9/9/1934][Mason and Knights of Pythias][Democrat][Attorney, Mayor of Mexia, editor of Banner Democrat]*

Allen M. Drinkard, Pvt., Co. I, 7th Texas Cavalry, Sibley's Brigade, Trans-Mississippi. Residence – Kirk. [c] *[5/5/1837 AL - ?][Mason, Royal Arch][Methodist]*

L. W. Duke, Cpl., Co. C, 5th Alabama Infantry. [e][f]

W. H. Duke, Pvt., Co. C, Louisiana Infantry, Gray's Brigade, Polinac's Division, Buckner's Corp, Trans-Mississippi. Residence – Prairie Hill. [c]

R. W. Dumis, Pvt., Co. A, 15th Mississippi Infantry, Ferguson's Brigade, Loring's Division, Stewarts Corp, Army of the Tennessee. Residence – Prairie Hill. [c]

Nathaniel Young Duncan, Pvt., Co. G, 10th Mississippi Infantry. [a][f] *[Buried Prairie Grove Cemetery 1/6/1844 – 3/31/1887]*

C. A. Durham, Pvt., Co. K, 6th South Carolina Cavalry, Hampton's Brigade. Residence – Armour. [a] *[Buried Armour Cemetery, East Section 2/8/1844 – 8/10/1922 Masonic]*

F. M. Durham, Pvt., Co. K, 20th Texas Dismounted Cavalry, Maxey's Brigade, Hindman's Division, Trans-Mississippi. [b]

W. E. Durst, Pvt., Co. A, 5th Texas Infantry. Residence – Prairie Grove. [a] Young's Brigade, Walker's Division, E. K. Smith's Corp, Army of the Trans-Mississippi. [b][d] Co. A, 13th Texas Infantry. Residence – Mexia. [c]

J. G. Dyer, Artillery, Tappan's Brigade. Residence – Prairie Hill. [a]

L. Eady, 1st Lt., Co. I, 33rd Alabama Infantry, Lowry's Brigade, Cleburne's Division, Hardee's Corp, Army of the Tennessee. Residence – Honest Ridge Precinct No. 2. [a][b] *[Buried Bennett-LeNoir Cemetery 5/15/1836 – 9/13/1927]*

Elias E. East, Pvt., Co. I, 13th Alabama Infantry. [e] *[Buried at Armour Cemetery, South Section ND]*

Samuel Ellison, Pvt., Co. C, 25th Alabama Infantry, Deas' Brigade. [a] Gordon's Brigade, Wither's Division, Hardee's Corp, Army of the Tennessee. Residence – Prairie Hill. [c] *[Buried Mt. Antioch Cemetery 2/28/1845 – 5/17/1904]*

F. M. Elzy, Pvt., Co. A, 12th Louisiana Infantry, Scott's Brigade, Loring's Division, Hood's Corp, Army of the Tennessee. Lived at Honest Ridge Precinct No. 2. [a] Residence - Horn Hill. [c][d]

J. C. Erwin, Pvt., Co. K, 48th Alabama Infantry, Taliaferro's Brigade, Jackson's Division, Longstreet's Corp. Residence - Elem Ridge. [a]

B. R. Ethridge, Co. B, 7th Infantry, Maxey's Brigade. Residence - Mt. Calm. [a] *[Buried Old Town Cemetery, Mt. Calm, 2/3/1828 – 4/22/1906]*

John Eubanks, Pvt., Co. B, 9th Mississippi Cavalry, Ferguson's Brigade, Jackson's Division, Army of the Tennessee. [b][d] *[Buried Mexia City Cemetery 5/7/1823-12/19/1907]*

G. M. T. Evans, Sgt., Co. B, Louisiana Infantry, Trans-Mississippi. Residence – Prairie Hill. [c]

W. L. Farmer, Co. D, 34th Regiment, Anderson's Brigade. [a] *[Son buried Mexia Cemetery]*

W. T. Farnsworth, Pvt., Co. J, 13th Tennessee Infantry, Vaughn's Brigade, Cheatham's Division, Polk's Corp, Army of the Tennessee. Residence – Tehuacana. [a][b]

Locklin Johnson Farrar, Major, 12th Texas Cavalry, Parson's Brigade, Army of the Trans-Mississippi. Residence – Groesbeck. [a][e][f] *[Buried Faulkenberry Cemetery 12/27/1837 – 7/16/1901]*

W. O. Farrington, Co. C, 15th Arkansas, Beall's Brigade, Army of the Tennessee. [a]

R. E. Farrow, Co. C, 28th Louisiana, Mouton's Brigade, Polignac's Division. Residence – Armour. [a] *[Buried Mexia City Cemetery, 1837-1917]*

James M. Fife, Pvt., Co. H, 31st Mississippi Infantry. [e] *[Buried Kirk Cemetery 10/5/1843 – 9/24/1935]*

James M. Fitzgerald, Pvt., Co. A, 2nd Louisiana Infantry, Hay's Brigade, Jackson's Division, Army of Northern Virginia. [a][b]

J. C. Flanekin, Pvt., Co. E, 9th Tennessee Infantry, Mana's Brigade, Cheatham's Division, Polk's Corp, Army of the Tennessee. Residence – Tehuacana. [a][b][d]

John D. Flannagan, Co. E, 7th Alabama Cavalry. [a] *[Buried Kosse Cemetery, 1840 AL – 1895][Member of I.O.O.F. #1504, and K. of H., Kosse Lodge #2315]*

E. T. Fontinott, Pvt., Co. G, 8th Louisiana Cavalry, Brint's Brigade, Trans-Mississippi. Residence – Prairie Hill. [c]

Moses W. Foster, Co. G, Hardiman's Cavalry. Residence – Groesbeck. [a] Pvt., Co. G, 22nd Texas Cavalry, Gano's Brigade, Indian Territory. Residence – Kirk. [c]

T. C. Foster, Pvt., Co. D, 7th Mississippi Cavalry, Chalmer's Brigade, Forrest's Division, Army of the Tennessee. [a][b]

T. L. Franks, Pvt., Co. F, 10th Texas Cavalry, Cooper's Brigade, Army of the Trans-Mississippi. [a][d][f] *[Buried Point Enterprise Cemetery 12/3/1844 – 1/11/1929]*

W. D. Frazier, Pvt., Co. I, 59th Alabama Infantry, Gracie's Brigade, Longstreet's Corp, Army of Northern Virginia. [a][b][d][f] *[Buried Armour Cemetery, West Section 4/29/1843 – 11/1/1911 Masonic]*

E. Fullinwider, Pvt., Co. J, Texas Mounted Infantry, Hardeman's Brigade, Magruder's Corp, Trans-Mississippi. [b]

M. P. Fuqua, Pvt., Co. B, 22nd Arkansas Infantry, Fagan's Brigade, Churchill's Division, Magruder's Corp, Army of Northern Virginia. Residence – Tehuacana. [a] Hawthorne's Brigade, Churchill's Division, E. K. Smith's Corp, Army of the Trans-Mississippi. Residence - Tehuacana. [b][d][f]

W. H. Furguson, Co. D, Elmon's Texas Infantry. Residence – Kosse. [a]

H. J. Gardner, Co. I, 24th Mississippi. [a] *[Buried Old Bethel Cemetery 1/25/1825 – 11/13/1894]*

F. M. Garner, Pvt., Co. B, 1st Mississippi Artillery, Army of the Tennessee. Residence – Prairie Hill. [c]

Thomas S. Gatlin, Co. A, 33rd Arkansas, Tappan's Brigade, Army of the Tennessee. [a] *[Buried Point Enterprise Cemetery 10/9/1830 Green Co., GA – 6/11/1909]*

T. George, Co. E, 10th Texas Cavalry, Parson's Brigade, Army of the Trans-Mississippi. Residence – Tehuacana. [a]

H. Gibson, Pvt., Co. A, 9th Mississippi Cavalry, Ferguson's Brigade, Army of the Tennessee. Residence – Mexia. [c]

Hiram Gibson, Pvt., Co. A, 1st/5th Mississippi. [e]

Thomas Jefferson Gibson, Pvt., Co. B[14], 12th Georgia Infantry, Doles' Brigade, Rode's Division, Jackson's Corp, Army of Northern Virginia. [a] Ewell's Division, Jackson's Corp, Army of Northern Virginia. [b][f] *[Buried Mexia City Cemetery, 4/23/1848 Boulding Co., GA – 2/14/1914]*

B. F. Gilbert, Pvt., Co. A, 17th Texas Cavalry, Dashler's Brigade, Churchill's Division, E. Kirby Smith's Corp, Army of the Trans-Mississippi. [a] Polignac's Brigade, Walker's Division, E. K. Smith's Corp, Army of the Trans-Mississippi. [b]

Capt. Gilbert. [d]

---

[14] ED. Note: Tombstone shows Co. J but there were NO company J's during the Civil War.

C. T. Gilbert, Co. C, 21st Texas Cavalry. [f]

R. D. Gilmore, Pvt., Co. B, 4th Texas Infantry, Hood's Brigade, Ewell's Division, Jackson's Corp, Army of Northern Virginia. [b]

Absalom Pratt Glass, Co. G, 1st Mississippi Cavalry. Residence – Kosse. [a] *[Buried Faulkenberry Cemetery 1843 – 1911]*

W. S. Glass, Co. B, 20th Georgia.

J. H. Goodman, Pvt., 4th Texas Infantry. [e]

James Gorden, Co. A, 38th Tennessee, Wright's Brigade, Cheatham's Division. Residence – Armour. [a]

W. A. Graham, Pvt., Co. I, 31st Mississippi Infantry, Bradford's Regiment, Featherson's Brigade, Loring's Division, Stewart's Corp, Army of the Tennessee. Residence – Tehuacana. [a] Residence – Kirk. [c]

W. A. Grasse. Residence – Kosse. [a]

N. Gravs, Co. G, 15th Arkansas Infantry. [f]

H. W. Gray, Pvt., Co. D, 37th Virginia Infantry, 3rd "Stewart's" Brigade, Johnston's Division, Jackson's Corp, Army of Northern Virginia. [a][b][d][f] *[Buried Mexia City Cemetery, 2/12/1842 Scott Co., VA – ½/1909]*

J. I. L. Gray, Pvt., Co. A, 33rd Tennessee Infantry, Stradol's Brigade, Cheatham's Division, Hardee's Corp, Army of the Tennessee. [b]

Jacob Grice, Co. J, 15th Scouts. Residence – Mt. Calm or Mt. Antioch. [a]

T. H. Griffen, Pvt., Co. B, Mississippi Cavalry, Armstrong's Brigade, Trans-Mississippi. Residence – Kirk. [c]

John L. Griffis, Pvt., Co. C, 24th Mississippi Infantry, Walthall's Brigade, Nethers' Division, Polk's Corp, Army of the Tennessee. Residence – Elem Ridge. [a] Johnson's Division, Lee's Corp, Army of the Tennessee. Residence - Kirk. [c] *[Buried Kirk Cemetery 3/7/1842 Chickasaw Co., MS – 8/31/1897]*

John S. Groover, Pvt., Co. G, Texas Cavalry. [d][e][f] *[Buried Mexia City Cemetery, 1/28/1845-2/28/1918 W.O.W.]*

J. S. Grooves [Rev.], Pvt., Co. E, 15th Texas Infantry. [a]   Co. G, Madison's Texas Cavalry, Lane's Brigade, Green's Division, Trans-Mississippi. [c][f] [This may be same man as above]

J. R. Groves, Co. C, 15th Arkansas. Residence – Honest Ridge Precinct No. 2. [a]

Noble Groves, Pvt., Co. G, 15th Arkansas Infantry, Army of the Tennessee. [a][b][d]

W. J. Guy, Pvt., Co. E, 16th Mississippi Infantry, Harris' Brigade, Anderson's Division, Hill's Corp, Army of Northern Virginia. Residence – Groesbeck. [c][d]

John F. Guynes, Pvt., Co. F, 6th Mississippi Infantry. [a][d] *[Buried Mexia City Cemetery, 1841-1893]*

Joseph C. Hall, Co. B, 40th Alabama, Days' Battalion. [a] *[Buried Mexia City Cemetery, ND]*

B. F. Hammond, Co. D, 20th Texas Infantry. Residence – Kosse. [a] *[Buried Eutaw Cemetery 1833 – 1922]*

D. P. Hammond, Co. D, 1st Mississippi Battalion/Battery. [a] *[Buried Kosse Cemetery, 1842-1922]*

William Rayform Hammond, Co. K, 12th Texas Cavalry. [a] *[Buried Kosse Cemetery, 1840-1928]*

Bluford Jordan Hancock, Pvt., Co. I, 19th Texas Cavalry, Parson's Brigade, Marmaduke's Division, Army of the Trans-Mississippi. [a][b][f] *[Buried Hancock Cemetery 2/17/1833 Cannon Co., TN – 11/11/1898]*

Lewis Ross Hancock, Sr., Pvt., Co. B, 12th Texas Cavalry, Parson's Brigade, Couples' Division. Residence - Mexia. [c][d] *[Buried Hancock Cemetery 5/25/1829 – 5/21/1893]*

J. W. Hanica, Pvt., Co. F, 22nd Texas Infantry, Waul's Legion, Walker's Division, Army of the Trans-Mississippi. Residence – Elem Ridge. [a]

S. H. Hannah, Pvt., Co. K, 14th Mississippi Infantry, Adam's Brigade, Loring's Division, Stewart's Corp, Army of the Tennessee. [b]

David Hardy, Capt., Co. G, 28th Louisiana Infantry, Mouton/Gray's Brigade, Polignac/Mouton's Division, Taylor's Corp, Army of the Trans-Mississippi. Residence – Prairie Hill. [a][c] *[Buried Delia Cemetery ND]*

Moses M. Harper, Co. G, Infantry, Spieght's Scouts. Residence – Mt. Calm or Mt. Antioch. [a] *[Buried Mt. Antioch Cemetery, 1/8/1834 – 2/20/1913]*

Robert Harrington, Co. H, 20th Texas Infantry. Residence – Farrar. [a] *[Buried New Hope Cemetery 12/24/1845 – 5/23/1918]*

C. T. Harris, Pvt., Co. G, 1st MS Infantry, Fagan's Brigade, Churchill's Division, Army of the Trans-Mississippi. [At end of war in charge of a brigade] Residence - Mexia. [c] Sgt. [e][f] *[1/29/1846 Pickens Co., AL - ?]*

John Louis Harthcock, Pvt., Co. C, 15th Mississippi, Adams' Brigade, Loring's Division, Stewart's Corp, Army of the Tennessee. [a] *[Buried Point Enterprise Cemetery 7/31/1842 – 7/29/1900 Regt. MS Inf. CSA]*

J. W. Harvey, Pvt., Co. F, 38th Alabama Infantry, Holtzclaw's Brigade, Cheatham's Division, Hood's Corp, Army of the Tennessee. [b][d]

J. Hayes, Co. F, 56th Georgia, Cumming's Brigade. Residence – Armour. [a]

N. G. Henderson, Co. F, 1st Texas, Willis' Battalion, McCulloch's Brigade, Waul's Legion

J. R. Henry [a] *[Buried Mexia City Cemetery, 4/16/1815-10/6/1889]*

William Henry, Pvt., Benivides Texas Cavalry, Trans-Mississippi. Residence – Mexia. [c][d] *[Buried Forest Glade Cemetery, 1840-1919]*

William S. Henson, Co. D, Wood's Mississippi, Adams' Brigade. [a] *[Buried Mexia City Cemetery, 8/21/1826-12/5/1896]*

J. H. Herbert, Pvt., 4th Texas Infantry. [d][e][f]

E. Herring, Sgt., Co. G/K, 36th Alabama Infantry, Clayton's Brigade, Cheatham's Division, Hardee's Corp. [a][b] *[Buried Prairie Grove Cemetery 6/12/1834 – 8/30/1912]*

Ewin R. Herring, Pvt., 2nd Lt., Co. F, 15th Texas., Trans-Mississippi, Regimental Quartermaster. Residence – Prairie Hill. [a] *[3/10/1834 Montgomery Co., TN - ?][Member of I.O.O.F.]*

M. Herring, Co. A, 1st Alabama Infantry, Days' Battalion, Johnson's Division, Hood's Corp, Army of the Tennessee. [a] *[Buried Mexia City Cemetery, 12/14/1833-4/3/1904]*

W. H. Herring, 1st Sgt./2nd Sgt., Co. G, 18th Alabama Infantry, Holtzclaw's Brigade, Clayton's Division, Hardee's Corp, Army of the Tennessee. [a][b][e][f] *[Buried Prairie Grove Cemetery 5/31/1838 Tuscaloosa Co., AL – 10/22/1904]*

J. P. Hickman, Pvt., Alabama Infantry. [e][f] *[Buried Mexia City Cemetery, 1/18/1842-3/7/1904]*

_____ Hicks, Pvt., Co. F, 20th Texas. Residence - Honest Ridge Precinct No. 2. [a]

William S. Hillyer, Co. B, 27th Louisiana, Shoup's Brigade. Residence - Mt. Calm. [a] *[Buried Mt. Antioch Cemetery, 1833 – 1913]*

David Hinch, Pvt., Co. F, 16th Georgia Battery. Residence - Shiloh. [a]

J. H. Hines, Pvt., Co. E, 31st Louisiana Infantry, Baldwin's Brigade, Johnson's Division, Hardee's Corp, Army of the Tennessee. [a]

Bennett Hodges, Co. E, 17th Alabama, Holtzclaw's Brigade, Steward's Division. [a] *[Buried Armour Cemetery, South Section 6/18/1839 – 3/17/1926]*

G. W. Hollaway, Pvt., Co. E, 8th Texas Infantry, Young's Brigade, Walker's Division, Army of the Trans-Mississippi. Residence - Prairie Hill. [a][c]

J. W. Holladay, Pvt., Co. B, Texas Cavalry, Hardee's Brigade, Independent Scouts. Residence – Prairie Hill. [c]

J. V. Holloway, Co. A, 7th Texas, Gregg's Brigade. Residence - Mt. Calm. [a] *[Buried Mt. Antioch Cemetery, 11/27/1841 – 7/20/1916]*

R. T. Holt [a]

C. B. Hood, Pvt., Co. E, 51st Alabama Cavalry. [f]

W. F. Hood, Sgt., Co. B, 1st Arkansas Infantry. [e][f]

Robert Hooker, Pvt., Co. E, Captain McCordle's Texas Infantry, Elmores' Brigade, MaGruder's Division, Trans-Mississippi. Residence - Hubbard. [c]

T. A. Hord [a]

F. M. Howard, O. Sgt., Co. A, 1st Tennessee Infantry. [e][f]

Robert Howell, Co. H, 5th Tennessee Infantry, Featherson's Brigade. Residence - Mt. Calm. [a] *[Buried Ruyle Cemetery 7/15/1838 – 6/27/1895]*

J. G. Howze, Pvt., Co. H, 4th South Carolina Cavalry, Butler's Brigade, Hampton's Division, Longstreet's Corp. Residence - Groesbeck. [a][e]

David Franklin Hughes [a] *[Buried Mexia City Cemetery, 4/14/1846-6/12/1924]*

E. C. Hughes, Pvt. Co. A, 30th Texas Cavalry. Residence - Prairie Hill. [c]

S. Hughes, Co. E, 53rd Alabama Cavalry, Roddy's Brigade, Army of the Tennessee. [a] *[Buried Mexia City Cemetery, 1838-2/18/1922][Blair-Stubbs Funeral Records: born 10/16/1837]*

W. J. Hughes, Pvt., Co. G, 28th Texas Cavalry, King's Brigade, Walker's Division, Army of the Trans-Mississippi. Residence - Elem Ridge. [a]

W. P. Hughes, Co. G, Texas Cavalry. Residence - Mt. Calm. [a]

David A. Hunt, Pvt., Co. F, 16th Georgia Infantry Battalion. *[Buried Prairie Grove Cemetery 2/14/1831 – 3/22/1908]*

Bennett Hunt, Pvt., Co. H., 38th Alabama Infantry, Clayton's Brigade. [a] Holtzclaw's Brigade, Stewart's Division, Hood's Corp, Army of the Tennessee. Residence - Mexia. [c][d]

T. B. Hunter, Co. G, 12th Texas Cavalry. Residence - Big Hill. [a]

T. R. Hunter, Color Bearer, Pvt., Co. G, 12th Texas Cavalry Parson's Brigade. Residence - Groesbeck. [a]

J. H. Hutford, Mississippi Service. Residence - Honest Ridge Precinct No. 2. [a]

John Ingram, Pvt., Co. G, 13th Alabama Infantry, Colquitt's Brigade, Hill's Division, Longstreet's Corp, Army of Northern Virginia. [b]

Samuel C. Ingram, Pvt., Co. G, 6th Alabama Cavalry, Clanton's Brigade, Army of the Tennessee. Co. B, 13th Alabama Infantry, Magruder's Brigade, Johnston's Corp, Army of Northern Virginia. [b][d][f] *[Buried Old Bethel Cemetery 4/8/1839 – 12/4/1908]*

J. C. Irwin, Pvt., Co. A, 48th Alabama Infantry, Taliaferro's Brigade, Hood's Division, Longstreet's Corp, Army of Northern Virginia. [b]

F. M. Jackson, Pvt., Co. G, 6th Texas Cavalry, Ross' Brigade, Trans-Mississippi. [b]

James Gordon Jackson, Pvt., Co. G, 7th Alabama Cavalry, Farris' Brigade, Army of the Trans-Mississippi. Residence - Kirk. [c] *[Buried Prairie Hill Cemetery 10/13/1845 AL – 7/1/1916 CSA]*

N. H. Jackson, 13th Texas, Walker's Division, Detailed in Government. Residence - Groesbeck. [a] *[Buried Faulkenberry Cemetery 7/4/1827 Wilson Co., TN - 1916]*

Thomas Edison Jackson, Co. I, 7th Texas Cavalry, Green's Brigade, Army of the Trans-Mississippi. Residence - Groesbeck. [a] *[Buried Faulkenberry Cemetery 6/28/1844 – 2/21/1884]*

A. Jayne, Pvt., Co. G, 28th MS Infantry and in 1862 Harvey's Scouts. [c] *[12/13/1838 Simpson Co. MS - ?][Mason][Single]*

G. L. Jennings, [Rev] Capt., Co. H, 31st Mississippi Infantry, Featherson's Brigade, Loring's Division, Army of the Tennessee. Residence - Honest Ridge Precinct No. 2. [a] Residence - Kirk. [c][d][f] *[Buried Kirk Cemetery 9/9/1830 – 11/23/1911]*

D. C. Johnson, Pvt., Co. H, Alexander's Texas Infantry, Polignac's Brigade, Mouton's Division, Army of the Trans-Mississippi.

J. B. Johnson, Pvt., Co. F, 6th Mississippi Cavalry. [e]

J. C. Johnson, Pvt., Co. A, 4th Georgia Cavalry, Morgan's Brigade, Allen's Division, Wheeler's Corp, Army of the Tennessee. [a][b]

Joe G. Johnson, Co. C, Hubard's Texas Infantry, Waul's Legion, Walker's Division, Army of the Trans-Mississippi. [a] *[Buried Prairie Hill Cemetery 1835 – 1912]*

Jas. R. Johnson, Co. D, 2nd Kentucky, Morgan's Brigade. [a]

W. M. Johnson, Pvt., Co. A, 32nd Texas Cavalry, Brachelle's Brigade, Dagley's Division, Army of the Trans-Mississippi. [b][d][f]

C. W. Johnston, 3d Sgt., Co. H, 11th Texas Infantry, Runnel's Brigade, Walker's Division, Army of the Trans-Mississippi. Residence - Buena Vista. [c]

Henry C. Joiner, O. Sgt., Co. E, 19th Texas Infantry, Scurry's Brigade, Walker's Division, E. K. Smith's Corp, Army of the Trans-Mississippi. Residence - Groesbeck. [a][b][c][e][f] *[Buried Faulkenberry Cemetery ND]*

James Saulsbury Jolly, Pvt., Co. G, 2nd Arkansas Infantry. [f] *[Buried Kosse Cemetery, 1842-1929]*

Jno. Alston Jones, Pvt., Co. G, 5th North Carolina Cavalry, Barringer's Brigade, W. H. F. Lee's Division, Humphreys' Corp, Army of Northern Virginia. Residence - Thornton. Residence - Kosse. [a] Bugler, Co. K, Stewart's Division, Hampton's Corp. [b][e][f] *[Buried Eutaw Cemetery 7/31/1844 Chatham Co., NC – 7/18/1907]*

Nat. M. Jones, Sgt. Major, Co. H, 1st/7th North Carolina Infantry, Armistead's Brigade, Hoke's Division, Army of Northern Virginia. Residence - Kosse. Residence - Thornton. [a][b][e][f] *[Buried Eutaw Cemetery 11/20/1846 Chatham Co., NC – 11/29/1917]*

E. J. Jordan, Co. C, 22nd Texas Infantry. Residence - Farrar. [a]

G. L. Jordan, Co. B, 12th Texas, Parson's Brigade, Green's Division, Wharton's Corp.

J. B. Jordan, Capt., Co. G, 36th Alabama Infantry. [e] *[Buried Ft. Parker Memorial Park 3/13/1838 – 11/11/1924]*

William Justice, Pvt., Co. B, 10th Texas Infantry, Granberry's Brigade, Cleburne's Division, Harelus' Corp, Army of the Tennessee. [c][d][f] *[Buried at Oakes Cemetery ND]*

William Kamsler, Pvt., Co. I, 25th Texas Infantry, Harrison's Brigade, Walker's Division, Jackson's Corp. [a][d][f]

M. Kaufman, Capt., Co. B, 45th Georgia Infantry, Lowry's Brigade, Cleburne's Division, Hardee's Corp, Army of the Tennessee. [a][b][d][f]

B. D. Keeling, Co. I, 1st Arkansas Cavalry. [f] *[Buried Kosse Cemetery, 1846-1922]*

William Henry Kierbow, 2nd Georgia Cavalry. [a] *[Buried Prairie Grove Cemetery 1847 – 1922]*

Mark Wiley Kemp, 1st Lt., Co. D, 13th Alabama Infantry, Archer's Brigade, A. P. Hill's Division, Jackson's Corp, Army of Northern Virginia. Residence – Mexia.[21] [a][b][d][f]*[Buried Mexia City Cemetery, 11/23/1832-1/5/1898]*

P. H. Kemper, Pvt., Co. B, 8th Tennessee Cavalry, Morgan's Brigade, Army of the Tennessee. Residence - Prairie Hill. [[c]

P. L. Kendall, Co. C, 8th Texas. Residence - Armour. [a]

A. W. Kennedy, Co. F, Bradford's Brigade. Residence - Honest Ridge Precinct # 2. [a] *[Buried Faulkenberry Cemetery 1845 – 1918]*

James Kenner, Co. E, 19th Infantry, W. R. Scurrys Brigade, Walker's Division. Residence - Groesbeck. [a]

---

[21] Ledger showed Army of the Trans-Mississippi

G. W. Kenney, Pvt., Co. G, 6th Alabama Infantry, Battle's Brigade, Rode's Division, Ewell's Corp, Army of Northern Virginia. Residence - Tehuacana. [a][b][d][e][f] *[Buried Point Enterprise Cemetery 9/22/1837 – 5/27/1909]*

D. C. Kincaid, Quarter-Master, Texas, Trans-Mississippi. [b] *[Buried Tehuacana Cemetery 1/2/1828 Madison Co., AL – 10/1/1902 Rev.]*

V. R. Kirkpatrick, Major of Engineers, Department of Mississippi. Residence - Prairie Hill. [c]

W. R. Kirkpatrick, Chief Engineer, Van Dam's Division. Residence - Prairie Hill. [Dead] [a]

J. R. Knowls, Co. D, 12th Louisiana Infantry. [f]

J. M. Langston, Pvt., Co. A, 1st Florida Cavalry, Longstreet's Corp, Army of Northern Virginia. [a] *[Buried Mexia City Cemetery, Section V, 2/23/1832-4/28/1904]*

S. R. Lanning, Co. K, 1st Tennessee Cavalry. [a]

W. D. Lanning, Pvt., Co. K, 18th Alabama Infantry, Holtzclaw's Brigade. [a][f] *[Wife buried in Mexia City Cemetery]*

G. W. Lansford, 10th Mississippi Infantry. Residence - Farrar. [a]

J. Y. LeNoir, Pvt., Co. B, 1st South Carolina Battery, State Service. [b] *[Buried Bennett-LeNoir Cemetery 1849 – 3/18/1908]*

H. A. Leach, Co. B, 62nd Alabama Infantry. Residence - Big Hill. [a] *[Buried Big Hill Cemetery 9/7/1848 – 8/4/1922]*

G. W. Lee, 1st Lt., Alabama, Forrest's Cavalry. Residence - Groesbeck. [a][e][f]

Isaac Lee, Co. I, 9th Texas.

H. E. Lester, Arkansas Artillery, Tappan's Brigade. Residence - Mt. Calm. [a]

H. M. Lewis, Pvt., Co. G, 24th Texas Cavalry, Granberry's Brigade, Cleburne's Division, Hood's Corp, Army of the Tennessee. [b] *[Buried Mexia City Cemetery, 12/7/1841-4/13/1915][Blair-Stubbs Funeral Records: born 12/17/1842]*

W. C. Linday, 2nd Florida Artillery. Residence - Mt. Calm. [a]

J. P. Lindley, Pvt., Co. C, 20th Texas Infantry, Frost's Brigade, Hindman's Division, Army of the Trans-Mississippi. Residence - Tehuacana. [a][b][d][f]

W. H. H. Lindsay, Pvt., Co. K, 23rd Alabama Infantry, Pettus' Brigade, Stevenson's Division, Lee's Corp, Army of the Tennessee. [a][b][d]

J. T. Lindsley. Residence - Tehuacana. [a]

J. M. Linebarger, Pvt., Co. A, 34th Arkansas Infantry, Feggin's Brigade, Army of the Trans-Mississippi. [b]

W. H. H. Little, Pvt., Co. E, Texas Artillery, Army of the Trans-Mississippi. Residence - Kirk. [c] *[Buried Kirk Cemetery 8/17/1842 – 1/29/1913]*

Robert Marshall Love, Pvt., Co. G, 6th Texas Cavalry, Ross's Brigade, Jackson's Division, Army of the Tennessee. [b][d][e][f] *[Buried Tehuacana Cemetery 1847 - mortally shot by Wm. G. Hill at his office (State Controller of Public Accounts) in Austin on 30th June 1903]*

Samuel Braden Love, Pvt., Co. G, 6th Texas Cavalry, Ross' Brigade, Jackson's Division, Polk's Corp, Army of the Tennessee. Residence - Tehuacana. [a][b][f] *[Buried Tehuacana Cemetery 6/20/1838 – No Marker]*

R. N. Loventte, 2nd Lt., Co. A, 1st Richmond H.C. Newty's Brigade, McLaw's Division, Longstreet's Corp, Army of Northern Virginia. [a]

D. H. Loving, Pvt., Co. A, 52nd Virginia Infantry, Pegram's Brigade, Early's Division, Jackson's Corp, Army of Northern Virginia. Residence - Prairie Hill. [c][d]

M. S. P. Lowery, Co. K, Cavalry, Parson's Brigade. Residence - Mt. Calm or Mt. Antioch. [a]

J. B. Lumpkin, Pvt., Co. E, 8th Texas Infantry, Young's Brigade, Walter's Division, Trans-Mississippi. Residence - Kirk. [c] *[Royal Arch Mason]*

J. Macom, Georgia, Cobb's Brigade, W. D. Wooten's Corp. [c]

Samuel Benton Maffett, Co. E, 2nd Texas Infantry, Cavalry Division. Residence - Big Hill. [a] *[Buried Big Hill Cemetery 12/7/1835 – 3/27/1896]*

D. A. Mahoney, Co. A, 60th Alabama, Gracie's Brigade, Army of the Tennessee. [a]

Isaac T. Mahoney, Pvt., Co. E, 1st Alabama Infantry, Walthall's Brigade, Army of the Tennessee. [b] *[Buried Point Enterprise Cemetery 1842 – 1904 Confederate Veteran of Pike Co., AL CSA]*

L. H. Martin, Pvt., Co. E, 3rd Louisiana Infantry. [f]

G. W. McAnelly, Co. I, 4th Texas Cavalry. Residence - Farrar. [a]

J. N. McCain, Capt., Co. B, 30th Alabama Infantry, Pettus' Brigade, Stevenson's Division, Lee's Corp, Army of Northern Virginia. [a]

Jas. McCorkle, Pvt., Co. F, 15th Texas Cavalry. [f]

Ben McCullough, Pvt., Co. D, Col. Perrin's Mississippi Cavalry, Ferguson's Brigade, Army of the Tennessee. Residence - Armour. [a][c][d]

J. C. McDonald, 20th Texas.

J. E. McDonald, Pvt., Co. A, 2nd Alabama Cavalry, Ferguson's Brigade, Wheeler's Division, Jackson's Corp, Army of the Tennessee. [b] Residence - Prairie Hill. [c][d][e] *[Buried Mexia City Cemetery, 4/17/1840-1/17/1901]*

M. L. McDonald, Pvt., Co. D, Wood's Mississippi Cavalry, Adam's Brigade, Wheeler's Division, Army of the Tennessee. [b][d][f] *[Buried Mexia City Cemetery, 9/24/1838-7/20/1910]*

Charles W. McElroy, Pvt., Sheldon's Alabama Artillery. Residence - Kirk. [c] *[Buried Kirk Cemetery 11/4/1844 – 1/3/1914]*

J. W. McKinney, Cpl./Capt., Co. H, 55th Alabama Infantry, Buford's Brigade, Loring's Division, Stuart's Corp, Army of the Trans-Mississippi. [b] Residence - Prairie Hill. [c][d][e][f]

G. W. McNeese, 2nd Lt., Co. F, 5th Texas Cavalry. [f]

Joseph McPherson, Co. B, 3rd Alabama Cavalry. Residence - Groesbeck. [a]

T. M. Meeks, Co. D, New Orleans Confederate Scouts. Residence - Kosse. [a]

R. T. Merrie, Co. C, Speight's Regiment.

J. S. Michard, Cpl., Co. A, 1st Virginia Infantry, Huger's Brigade, Army of Northern Virginia. [a]

W. D. Michum, Pvt., Co. E, 28th Texas Infantry, Ferguson's Brigade, Loring's Division, Stewart's Corp, Army of the Tennessee. Residence - Prairie Hill. [c] *[Buried Prairie Hill Cemetery 1846 – 1/16/1922]*

J. L. Miller, Co. D, Texas Infantry, Waterson's Brigade. Residence - Mt. Calm or Mt. Antioch. [a]

J. M. Miller, Co. I, 23rd Mississippi. [a]

Sutherland S. Monroe, Co. A, 1st North Carolina Battery, Heavy Artillery. [a] *[Buried Kosse Cemetery, 1845-1901]*

Joseph R. Montgomery, Pvt., Co. F, 4th Louisiana Cavalry, Harrison's Brigade, Trans-Mississippi. [b] *[Buried Point Enterprise Cemetery 1845 – 1891 CSA]*

John Nelson Moody, Co. G, 13th Alabama Infantry [Buried Old Bethel Cemetery, 1840-1914]

N. R. Moody, Pvt., Co. C, 37th Mississippi Infantry, Parksdale and Martin's Brigade, Maury's Division, Longstreet's Corp, Army of Northern Virginia. [a] Price's Corp, Army of the Tennessee. [b]

P. Moody, Co. B, Infantry. Residence - Groesbeck. [a]

Theophilus Moody, 3rd Battalion, Hellian's Legion; Pvt. Co. C, 60th AL Infantry CSA *[Buried Prairie Hill Cemetery 1/15/1835 – 7/2/1909]*

Jas. Moon, Pvt., Co. K, Green's Texas Cavalry, Walker's Division, Army of the Trans-Mississippi.

J. Morgan, Pvt., Co. A, Texas Cavalry, Whitfield's Legion, Price's Corp, Army of the Tennessee. [b]

G. W. Morris, Pvt., Co. E, 4th Arkansas Infantry, Runnel's Brigade, McNair's Division, Army of the Tennessee. Residence - Prairie Hill. [c]

H. T. Morris, Co. E, 20th Infantry. Residence - Groesbeck. [a]

G. M. Morrow, Co. K, 36th Alabama.

Zackey T. Morton, Pvt., Co. A, 5th Georgia Infantry, Cumming's Brigade, Army of the Tennessee. *[Buried Lost Prairie Cemetery 7/8/1846 – 4/15/1924]*

John W. Moss, Co. K, 12th Texas Cavalry. Residence - Kosse. [a] *[Buried Moss Cemetery – ND]*

John H. Mullens, Co. H, 26th Alabama, Days' Battalion, Withers' Division, Polk's Corp. *[Buried Mexia City Cemetery, 1843-1936]*

R. E. Myers, Co. H, 11th Georgia Infantry. Residence - Kosse. [a] *[Buried Eutaw Cemetery 2/11/1841 – 11/14/1922]*

J. W. Nash, Pvt., Styles' Virginia Battalion Heavy Artillery. [f] *[Buried Mexia City Cemetery, 5/24/1844-4/9/1918]*

J. Nelson, Co. E, 29th Alabama Infantry, Cantey's Brigade, Stewart's Division. Residence - Tehuacana. [a][f]

T. J. Nelson, Pvt., Co. G, 20th Alabama Infantry. [f]

William W. Newberry, Co. D, 23rd North Carolina, Army of Northern Virginia. Residence - Armour. [a] *[Buried Tehuacana Cemetery 1/25/1844 – 6/9/1893]*

E. T. Newcomb, Co. I, 7th Cavalry, Stewart's Brigade. Residence - Mt. Calm or Mt. Antioch. [a]

J. S. Newton, Co. C, 41st Mississippi Infantry. Residence - Kosse. [a]

J. M. Nickels, Co. C, 10th Texas Cavalry, Parson's Brigade. Residence - Mt. Calm or Mt. Antioch. [a] *[Buried Honest Ridge Cemetery 7/4/1840 – 12/3/1908]*

T. A. Norwood, Co. A, 14th Louisiana.

R. O'Neal, Co. E, 35th Texas Cavalry. Residence - Kosse. [a]

G. W. Oakes, Co. K, 8th Alabama Infantry. *[Buried Oakes Cemetery 1843 – 11/22/1917]*

John Dennis Oakes, Co. A, 62nd Alabama. *[Buried Oakes Cemetery 10/9/1847 – 9/19/1907 Thomas Brigade of Confederate Volunteers of America]*

J. M. Oakes, Pvt., Co. K, 8th Alabama Infantry. [d][f] *[Buried Oakes Cemetery 10/27/1841 – 3/20/1919]*

B. F. Ouzts, Asst. Surgeon, Co. I, 2nd South Carolina, Hampton's Legion. [a][f]*[Buried Kosse Cemetery, 1838-1907, Dr.]*

Sam Owens, Co. H, 67th Alabama, Scott's Brigade, Loring's Division, Stewart's Corp. Residence - Groesbeck. [a]

John M. Palmer, Co. B, 60th Georgia Infantry, Gordon's Brigade, Ewell's Division, Jackson's Corp. *[Buried Honest Ridge Cemetery 5/3/1842 – 11/19/1915]*

D. H. Parker, Co. K, 50th Alabama Cavalry. Residence - Kosse. [a]

J. E. Parker, Pvt., Co. I, 3rd Alabama Infantry, Battle's Brigade, Rode's Division, Jackson's Corp, Army of Northern Virginia. [a] Ewell's Corp, Army of Northern Virginia. [b][d][f]

J. F. Parker, Co. B, 3rd Louisiana Cavalry. Residence - Honest Ridge Precinct No. 2. [Reported dead in August 1889]. [a]

J. G. Parten, Co. E, 20th Georgia Infantry. Residence - Kosse. [a]

John Patterson, Pvt., Co. B, 10th Texas Infantry, Granberry's Brigade, Cleburne's Division, Hardee's Corp, Army of the Tennessee. [b] *[Buried Faulkenberry Cemetery 12/25/1835 – 10/6/1908]*

R. W. Payne, Pvt., Co. H, 12th Mississippi Cavalry, Ferguson's Brigade, Jackson's Division, Wheeler's Corp, Army of the Tennessee. [b][d]

J. S. Payne, Co. A, 1st Alabama Battalion [Mexican War, 1847/48], Co. A, 16th Texas Infantry, Walker's Division. [a]

S. P. Perkins. Residence - Armour. [a]

L. R. Persons, Co. F, 15th Texas. *[Buried Lost Prairie Cemetery 12/8/1844 – 2/25/1904]*

J. B. Phillips, Pvt., Co. K, 13th Alabama Infantry. [e]

R. E. Pitt, Co. H, 3rd Kentucky Infantry. Residence - Kosse. [a]

J. L. Pleasant, Co. H, 2nd Texas Infantry. Residence - Groesbeck. [a]

J. K. P. Poindexter, Co. H, 9th Texas Cavalry. [a] *[Buried Kosse Cemetery, 1841-1924, Dr.]*

E. D. Polk, Capt., Co. B, 4th Tennessee Infantry, Maxey's Brigade, Cheatham's Division, Polk's Corp, Army of the Tennessee. [b]

E. D. Pope, Co. B, 21st Tennessee Cavalry. Residence - Kosse. [a]

J. G. Powell, Pvt., Co. K, 35th Texas Cavalry, Buchelle's Brigade, Greene's Division, Army of the Trans-Mississippi. [b][d]

W. L. Powell, Pvt., Co. F, 9th Louisiana Infantry, Hays' Brigade, Gordon's Division, 2nd Corp T. J. "Stonewall" Jackson. Residence - Armour. [a] Residence - Mt. Calm or Mt. Antioch. [a] J. Early's Corp, Army of Northern Virginia. [b][d]

W. A. Powers, Pvt., Georgia Infantry, McCoy's Brigade, Army of the Tennessee. [c]

B. P. Price, Pvt., Co. E, 8th Louisiana State Troops, Trans-Mississippi. Residence - Kirk. [c]

James E. Price, Co. E, 35th Texas Cavalry, Terrill's Rangers, Bagby's Division, Horton's Corp, Army of the Trans-Mississippi. [a] *[Buried Kosse Cemetery, 1845-1937]*

G. M. D. Prichard, Co. G, 9th Texas.

J. H. Prince, Pvt., Co. C, 10th Georgia Infantry, Simm's Brigade, McLaw's Division, Longstreet's Corp, Army of Northern Virginia. [a][b][d] *[Buried at Armour Cemetery, Northeast Section 11/19/1840 – 7/24/1915]*

J. K. Pringle, Co. I, 37th Mississippi Infantry. Residence - Kosse. [a]

Issac Raborn, 2nd Sgt., Co. C, 19th Louisiana Infantry. [e] *[Buried Faulkenberry Cemetery 7/13/1844 – 11/14/1896]*

J. M. Rambo, O. Sgt., Co. F, 9th Mississippi Cavalry, Ferguson's Brigade, Wheeler's Division, Jackson's Corp. Jackson's Division, Wheeler's Corp, Army of the Tennessee. [b][d][1893 – Infantry] [f]

W. L. Rambo, Co. E, 8th Mississippi Infantry. Residence - Farrar. [a]

J. B. Ramsey, Co. A, 1st North Carolina Cavalry, Hill's Brigade. Residence - Mt. Calm or Mt. Antioch. [a]

Jason Rasco, Pvt., Co. B, 20th Texas Cavalry, Cooper's Brigade, Trans-Mississippi. [b] *[Buried Cobb Cemetery under John Rasco ND]*

Cull C. Ratliff, Pvt., Co. L, Whitfield's Legion and Sgt., Co. A, 19th Texas Cavalry, Parsons' Brigade. Residence - Honest Ridge No. 2. [a] *[Buried Ft. Parker Memorial Park 10/3/1838 TN – 10/23/1913]*

Joel B. Reed, Pvt., Co. E, 8th Louisiana State Troops, Trans-Mississippi. Residence - Kirk. [c] *[Buried Kirk Cemetery 1843 – 1920]*

J. M. Reed, Co. F, 5th Louisiana, Harrison's Brigade. [c]

T. L. Reed, Co. F, 3rd Missouri Cavalry. [f]

M. P. Reynolds, Pvt., Co. D, 7th Alabama Cavalry. [e][f]

J. A. T. Richardson, Pvt., Co. H, 1st Tennessee Infantry, Maney's Brigade, Cheatham's Division, Polk's Corp, Army of the Tennessee. Residence - Tehuacana. [a][b][d]

S. H. Richardson, Co. I, 1st Confederate Battalion. [a] *[Buried Kosse Cemetery, 1837-1909]*

Wm. H. Richardson, 1st Lt., Co. F, 2nd Mounted Virginia Cavalry, Johnson and Rosser's Brigade, Fitz Lee's Division, Hampton's Corp, Army of Northern Virginia. [a][b][c][d][f][Past Commander]

J. E. Riddle, Pvt., Co. B/I, 36th Alabama, Clayton's Brigade, Cheatham's Division, Hardee's Corp. Residence - Elem Ridge. [a] Residence - Kirk. [c][d] *[Buried Kirk Cemetery 5/1/1833 – 11/1/1914]*

W. P. Rivers, Co. B, 3rd Mississippi.

H. M. Roberts, Co. L, 16th Alabama Infantry, Johnson's Brigade, Walker's Division. Lived at Mt. Calm or Mt. Antioch. [a] *[Buried Mexia City Cemetery, 12/11/1822-1/29/1914]*

J. J. Roberts, Co. A, 42nd Alabama. Residence - Armour. [a] *[Possibly James N. Roberts buried Armour Cemetery, South Section 10/28/1845 – 3/21/1921]*

W. F. Roberts, Capt., Co. G, 28th Texas Cavalry. [f]

W. G. Roberts, Co. F, 7th Texas Cavalry, Green's Brigade. Residence - Mt. Calm or Mt. Antioch. [a]

M. C. Rodgers, Co. K, 20th Texas. Residence - Prairie Grove. [a]

Allen Jefferson Rogers, Sgt., Co. K, 20th Texas Dismounted Cavalry, Bass' Regiment, Maxey's Brigade, Hindman's Division, Trans-Mississippi Department *[Buried Lost Prairie Cemetery 6/18/1831 Perry Co., AL - ND]*

M. C. Rogers, Pvt., Co. K, 20th Texas. Co. F, 10th Texas Infantry, Granberry's Brigade, Cleburne's Division, Hardee's Corp, Army of the Tennessee. [b]

M. L. Rogers, Pvt., Co. K, 22nd Texas Infantry, Forney's Brigade, Walker's Division. [b]

R. Rogers, Pvt., Co. I, 9th Texas Infantry, Ector's Brigade, Cheatham's Division, Polk's Corp, Army of the Tennessee. [b]

W. M. Roper, Co. I, 4th Texas. Residence - Honest Ridge Precinct No. 2. [a]

George Washington Ross, Pvt., Co. H, 5th Missouri Cavalry, Cockrell's Brigade, French's Division, Polk's Corp, Army of the Tennessee. [a][b][d][f] *[Buried Tehuacana Valley Cemetery 1826 – 1912 No Marker]*

M. L. Royen, Co. K, 22nd Texas Infantry, Hawes' Brigade, Walker's Division, Army of the Trans-Mississippi. Residence - Tehuacana. [a]

H. P. Rucker, Pvt., Co. D, 12th Kentucky Cavalry, Forrest's Brigade, Wheeler's Division, Army of the Tennessee. [a][b][d]

J. W. Ruff, Sgt., Co. G, 36th Mississippi Infantry, Anderson's Brigade, French's Division, Stewart's Corp. [a] *[Buried Mexia City Cemetery, 11/7/1837-10/12/1892]*

Reuben Ewing Sanders, Capt., Co. E, 19th Texas Cavalry. *[Buried Tehuacana Cemetery 3/17/1822 – 11/20/1894]*

T. A. Sanders, Co. A, Arkansas, McLenay's Regiment. Residence - Honest Ridge Precinct No. 2. [a]

W. M. Sanders, Co. E, 27th Louisiana. Residence - Honest Ridge Precinct No. 2. [a]

J. Z. Sandifer, Co. H, 1st Arkansas. *[Buried Lost Prairie Cemetery 4/27/1843 – 6/5/1916]*

James Polk Sawyer, Pvt., Co. D, 12th Mississippi Cavalry, Ferguson's Brigade, Wheeler's Division, Georgia Army. Army of the Tennessee. [b][d][f] *[Buried Prairie Grove Cemetery 2/14/1846 – 4/23/1922]*

S. R. Scarborough, Co. K, 40th Mississippi Infantry, Featherson's Brigade, Loring's Division, Polk's Corp, Army of the Tennessee. [b] Pvt., Co. A, 15th Mississippi Infantry, Adams' Brigade, Loring's Division, Stewart's Corp. [f]

V. Scott, Co. C, 44th Alabama Infantry, McLaw's Brigade, Field's Division, Longstreet's Corp, Army of Northern Virginia. [a]

M. Scroggin, Co. E, 46th Georgia. Co. K, 40th Mississippi Infantry, Featherson's Brigade, Loring's Division, Polk's Corp, Army of the Tennessee. [b]Honest Ridge Precinct No. 2. [Reported dead in August 1889]. [a]

F. M. Sellers, Pvt., Co. I, 3rd Alabama Cavalry, Morgan's Brigade, Allen's Division, Wheeler's Corp, Army of the Tennessee. [b][e]

G. H. Shaffer, Co. K, 36th Alabama Cavalry, Ferguson's Brigade. Residence – Mt. Calm or Mt. Antioch. [a]

Charles B. Shead, Co. A, 7th Texas Infantry, Grigg's Brigade. Residence – Mt. Calm or Mt. Antioch. [a][Buried Mt. Antioch Cemetery 1839 – 1925]

C. C. Shell, Co. G, 8th Alabama.

W. A. Shelton, Pvt., Co. A, Texas Cavalry. Residence – Prairie Hill. [c] *[Buried Antioch Cemetery, 6/6/1843 – 9/4/1891]*

C. T. Shilling, Co. I, Louisiana. Residence – Mt. Calm or Mt. Antioch. [a]*[Buried Antioch Cemetery, 2/9/1846 – 11/3/1925]*

Adan H. Shriver, Pvt., Richmond Battery, Louisiana Artillery, Anderson's Division, Hill's Corp, Army of Northern Virginia. Residence – Elem Ridge. [a] *[Buried Faulkenberry Cemetery ND, Landry's Co. A, Artillery, CSA]*

H. F. Simmons, Pvt., Co. D, Wood's Mississippi Cavalry, Adams' Brigade, Johnson's Division, Lee's Corp, Army of Northern Virginia. [a][d][f]

John W. Simmons, Pvt., Co. E, 27th Mississippi Infantry, Walthall's Brigade, Johnson's Division, Lee's Corp, Army of Tennessee. [b][d][f] Army of the Tennessee. [a] [Past Commander] *[Buried Mexia City Cemetery, 10/1/1838 Winston Co., MS –4/12/1912][Member of A.F. & A.M. of Springfield #74 and R.A.M. of Mexia #131][Democrat]*

B. R. Sims, Co. A, 40th Mississippi.

James R/B. Sims, 2nd Lt., Co. E, 8th Mississippi Infantry, Lowry's Brigade, Cleburne's Division, Hardee's Corp, Army of the Tennessee. [b] *[Buried Lost Prairie 11/28/1836 – 7/24/1898 Mason]*

T. W. Skillern, Pvt., Co. C, 36th Arkansas Infantry, McRae's Brigade, Churchill's Division, Price's Corp, Army of the Trans-Mississippi. Residence – Honest Ridge Precinct No. 2. [a][b][f]

S. K. Skruggs, Co. C, 8th Regiment. [a]

J. J. Sloan, 2nd Sgt., Co. I, 20th Mississippi Infantry. [e][f]

Alexander Smith, Co. I, Young's Texas, Walker's Division. [Dead]

J. B. Smith, Co. I, 30th Alabama. Residence – Big Hill. [a] *[Buried Big Hill Cemetery 12/1/1833 – 11/11/1893 Dr.]*

Elias Brooks Smyth, Pvt., Captain Sanders' Co., Col. Bates Texas Cavalry Regiment, stationed on Texas coast and Colonel Bradford's Regiment. [a][d][f] *[Buried Mexia City Cemetery, Section III,1/9/1832 Abbeville District, SC – 5/15/1899][1876 – State Legislature; 1891 appointed as Commissioner of the State Penitentiary]*

J. A. Spruill, Pvt., Co. H, Whitfield's Texas Cavalry. [e]

A. S. Squyres, Pvt., Co. I, 7th Texas Cavalry, Sibley's Brigade [a] *[Buried Tidwell Cemetery 4/8/1840 -3/12/1906]*

G. F. Stafford. Residence – Armour. [a]

J. T. Stanford, Co. G, 27th Alabama, Shelby's Brigade, Army of the Tennessee. [a] *[Buried Point Enterprise Cemetery 11/19/1841 – 2/15/1919]*

David Stanford, Pvt., Alabama Infantry, Home Guards. [b] *[Buried Mexia City Cemetery, 8/25/1815-3/18/1891]*

Simon Allen Stanford, Pvt., Alabama Infantry, Home Guards. [b][d] *[Buried Mexia City Cemetery, 1846-1924]*

J. Starkey, Arkansas. Residence – Kosse. [a]

O. Statesman/Stutesman, Co. E, 5th Arkansas Infantry, McRea's Brigade, Hindman's Division, Trans-Mississippi. Residence – Mexia. [c][d]

N. B. Steeddum, Pvt., Co. F, 22nd Texas Cavalry. [e][f]

L. Steele, Sgt., Co. F, 15th Texas Infantry, Granberry's Brigade, Cleburne's Division, Hardee's Corp, Army of the Tennessee. Residence – Groesbeck. [c]

James Warren Steele, Pvt., Co. G, 7th Texas Infantry. [e][f] *[Buried Oak Island Cemetery 1844 – 1929]*

Avarado "Rado" Steele, Pvt., Co. B, 10th Texas Infantry, Granberry's Brigade, Cleburne's Division, Hardee's Corp, Army of the Tennessee. [b][d][f] *[Buried Steele Cemetery 7/23/1843 – 5/17/1933]*

B. C. Stephens, Co. A, 4th Tennessee.

William M. Stephens, Co. D, 51st Alabama Cavalry. [a] *[Buried Kosse Cemetery, 1839 – 1915 Ala. Partisan Rangers – CSA][Odd Fellow and Knight of Pythias]*

F. M. Stewart, Co. H, 28th Texas. Residence – Honest Ridge Precinct No. 2. [a]

W. O. Stewart.

John T. Stitt, Pvt., Co. E, 17th Alabama Infantry, Slaughter's Brigade, Hardee's Corp, Army of the Tennessee. [b] *[Buried Mexia City Cemetery, 1839-1892]*

J. M. Storey, Orderly Sgt., Co. H, 28th Texas Infantry, Randall's Brigade, Walker's Division, Army of the Trans-Mississippi. [a][b][d][e][f] *[Buried Point Enterprise Cemetery 6/17/1829 – 5/4/1912]*

T. B. Strayhorn, Co. D, 3rd Arkansas, Cabell's Brigade, Fagan's Division, E. K. Smith's Corp. Residence – Groesbeck. [a] *[Buried Faulkenberry Cemetery 8/5/1833 – 12/9/1890]*

Isaac H. Sturdivant, Pvt., Co. G, 38th Tennessee Infantry, Cheatham's Division, Army of the Tennessee. [b][f] *[Buried New Hope Cemetery 8/10/1837 – 10/28/1919]*

Joseph M. Suttle, 1st Sgt., Co. H, 23rd Georgia Infantry, Colquitt's Brigade, Hoke's Division, Longstreet's Corp, Army of Northern Virginia. Residence – Tehuacana. [a][b][d][f] *[Buried Mexia City Cemetery, 2/2/18??-11/5/1898]*

J. Swain, Co. I, 43rd Mississippi Infantry. [f]

R. H. Swaim, Pvt., Co. F [Capt. Tyus], 15th Texas [Col. G. H. Sweet] Cavalry, Granberry's Brigade, Cleburne's Division, Hardee's Corp, Army of the Tennessee. Residence – Kirk. [c] *[9/20/1843 Clay Co., MO - ?][Mason]*

William Burt Swinney, Pvt., Co. A, 12th Mississippi Cavalry, Farris' Brigade, Army of the Trans-Mississippi. Residence – Prairie Hill. [c] *[1824 – after 1910 probably Palo Pinto Co., TX]*

E. V. Tackett, Pvt. Co. C, 3rd Louisiana Cavalry. Residence – Honest Ridge Precinct No. 2. [a]

J. L. Taylor, Pvt., Co. A, 7th Texas Infantry, Granberry's Brigade, Cleburne's Division, Hood's Corp, Army of the Tennessee. [b] *[Tidwell Cemetery, west of Thornton, marked with rock marker far left side of cemetery]*

J. S. Teakell, Co. G, 2nd Alabama Cavalry, Ferguson's Brigade. Residence – Mt. Calm or Mt. Antioch. [a]

G. I. Thomas, Co. G, 42nd Tennessee Infantry. Residence – Farrar. [a] *[Buried Lost Prairie Cemetery 3/22/1846 – 7/8/1916]*

J. W. Thomas, Cpl., Co. H, 43rd North Carolina Infantry, Daniel's Brigade, Rode's Division, Ewell's Corp, Army of Northern Virginia. [b][d][e][f]

J. B. Thompson, Co. I, 18th Alabama. [a] *[Buried Faulkenberry Cemetery 1/25/1837 – 10/16/1916]*

J. W. Thompson, Co. C, 4th Alabama, Law's Brigade, Hood's Division, Longstreet's Corp. Residence – Groesbeck. [a]

L. E. Thompson, Pvt., Co. B, 3rd Missouri Cavalry, Marmaduke's Brigade, Marmaduke's Division, Price's Corp, Trans-Mississippi. [b]

J. N. Thornton, O. Sgt., Co. C, 39th Georgia Infantry. [e][f]

D. K. Tidwell, Pvt., Co. A, 11th Alabama Cavalry, Roddy's Brigade, Forest's Division, Army of the Tennessee. [b]

C. E. Tiles, 20th Texas Infantry. Residence – Farrar. [a]

S. H. Tipton, Pvt., Co. F, 15th Texas Cavalry, Granberry's Brigade, Cleburne's Division, Harelus' Corp, Army of the Tennessee. Residence – Mexia. [c]

Frank E. Trammell, Capt., Co. B, 17th Arkansas Infantry, Herbert's Brigade, Little's Division, Price's Corp, Army of the Tennessee. Residence – Armour. [a][c][d] *[Buried Trammell Family Cemetery 1/27/1839 – 2/20/1900]*

B. F. Tribble, Texas Cavalry. Residence – Kosse. [a]

C. G. Tubb, Pvt., Co. G, 12th Texas Cavalry, Smith's Brigade, Magruder's Corp, Army of the Trans-Mississippi. [b][d]

M. A. Tucker, Sgt. Major, Co. F, 15th Texas Infantry, Granberry's Brigade, Cleburne's Division, Hardee's Corp, Army of the Tennessee. Residence – Honest Ridge Precinct No. 2. [a][b][f]['93 and '96-Cavalry]

M. T. Tucker, Pvt., Co. G, 8th Texas Infantry, Waul's Legion, Walker's Division, Taylor's Corp. Residence – Thornton. [a]

B. W. Turner, Co. E, 30th Alabama, Pettus' Brigade, Stevenson's Division, Hardee's Corp.

G. W. Turner, Sgt., Co. I, 28th Texas, Randall's Brigade, Walker's Division.

Ushe. Residence – Groesbeck. [a]

B. M. F. Usry, 15th ____ Cavalry, Deshler's Brigade, Army of the Trans-Mississippi. Residence – Groesbeck. [a] *[Buried Ft. Parker Memorial Park 1/13/1838 – 5/31/1902]*

John H. Vickers, Cpl., Co. E, 9th Georgia Infantry, Smith's Division, Army of Georgia. [b][d] *[Buried Mexia City Cemetery, 4/12/1848 Troup Co., GA – 1899]*

G. B. Vinson, Col., Co. A, 2nd Louisiana Infantry, Moore's Brigade, Jackson's Division, Army of Northern Virginia. [b]

G. W. Wacaster, Pvt., Co. H, 24th Georgia Infantry, Wofford's Brigade, McLaw's Division, Longstreet's Corp, Army of Northern Virginia. Residence – Thornton. [a]

T. W. Wade, 20th Texas Infantry. Residence – Tehuacana. [a] *[Buried Tehuacana Cemetery 1/3/1833 – 11/5/1895]*

R. L. Wadkins, Pvt., Co. G, 12th Texas Cavalry, Parson's Brigade. [c]

G. D. Wait, Wood's Cavalry, Bee's Division, E. K. Smith's Corp, Army of the Trans-Mississippi. Residence – Groesbeck. [a]

L. D. Walker, Pvt., Co. B, 10th Texas Infantry, Granberry's Brigade, Cleburne's Division, Hardee's Corp, Army of the Tennessee. [b]

S. D. Walker, Co. B, 10th Texas Infantry. Residence – Groesbeck. [a]

S. S. Walker, Pvt., Co. I, 2nd Texas Cavalry, B. W. Stone's Brigade, Major's Division, Green/Gaylor's Corp, Army of the Trans-Mississippi. Residence – Groesbeck. [a][b][e][f]

B. F. Wallace, Pvt., Co. F, 15th Texas Cavalry, Granberry's Brigade, Cleburne's Division, Hardee's Corp, Army of the Tennessee. Residence – Armour. [a][b][d]

J. D. Wallace, Co. F, 23rd Mississippi Infantry. Residence – Kosse. [a]

N. L. Waller [a] *[Buried Mexia City Cemetery, 8/5/1840-12/2/1900]*

J. G. Walling, Pvt., Co. C, 15th Texas Infantry, Polignac's Brigade, Mouton's Division, Taylor's Corp, Army of the Trans-Mississippi. [b][e][f]

J. J. Ward, Co. K, Terry's Texas Cavalry. [a]

Richard "Dick" P. Ward, Pvt., Co. F, 12th Texas Cavalry, Parson's Brigade, Trans-Mississippi Department. Residence – Honest Ridge Precinct No. 2. [b][d][f] *[Buried Mexia City Cemetery, 7/3/1848 Henry Co., GA –8/23/1912]*

W. J. Ward, Pvt., Co. D, 7th South Carolina Cavalry, Gary's Brigade, Lee's Corp, Army of Northern Virginia. Residence – Tehuacana. [a][b]

M. L. Washam, Pvt., Co. G, 5th Texas Cavalry, Greene's Brigade, Army of the Trans-Mississippi. Residence – Farrar. [a]

R. L. Watkins, Co. G, 12th Texas Cavalry, Parsons' Brigade, Walker's Division, Army of the Trans-Mississippi. Residence – Tehuacana. [a]

Charles Lewis Watson, 2nd Sgt., Co. D, 10th Texas Infantry, Granberry's Brigade, Cleburne's Division, Hardee's Corp, Army of the Tennessee. [a][b][f][Past Commander] *[Buried Mexia City Cemetery, 1841-1926]*

William A. Watson, Pvt., Co. H, 4th Texas Infantry, Hood's Brigade, Field's Division, Longstreet's Corp, Army of Northern Virginia. Residence – Groesbeck. Residence – Thornton. [a] *[Buried Thornton City Cemetery, 7/21/1835 AL – 1/11/1908 Mason]*

M. B. Watty, Pvt., Co. D, Clanton's Alabama Cavalry, Hanson's Brigade, Forest's Division, Army of the Tennessee. [b]

J. C. Webb, Sgt., Co. K, 20th Texas Infantry, Maxey's Brigade, Hindman's Division. Residence – Honest Ridge Precinct No. 2. [a]

Jacob Webb, Pvt., Co. B, 10th Texas Infantry, Granberry's Brigade, Cleburne's Division, Hardee's Corp, Army of the Tennessee. Residence – Groesbeck. Residence – Thornton. [a] *[Buried Faulkenberry Cemetery 1842 – 1/20/1906]*

W. B. Whattley, Pvt., Co. B, 7th Alabama Cavalry, Farris' Brigade, Army of the Trans-Mississippi. Residence – Kirk. [c]

J. B. White, Pvt., Co. A, Johnson's Texas Cavalry, Army of the Trans-Mississippi. [b]

Joseph L. Wilder, 2nd Sgt., Co. K, 2nd Louisiana Infantry, Stafford's Brigade, Walker's Division, Jackson's Corp, Army of the Trans-Mississippi. [a] *[Buried Mexia City Cemetery, 5/4/1841-2/10/1896]*

V. S. Wilder, Pvt., Co. E, 29th Alabama Infantry, Johnson's Corp, Army of the Tennessee. Residence – Groesbeck. [a]

W. M. Wilder, Pvt., Co. B, 10th Texas Infantry, Granberry's Brigade, Cleburne's Division, Hardee's Corp, Army of the Tennessee. [b][d][e][f]

Oscar Wiley, 1st Sgt., Co. K, 5th Alabama Infantry, Rhode's Brigade, Early's Division, Jackson's Corp, Army of Northern Virginia. [b][e] Residence – Groesbeck. [a] *[1839 Dallas Co., AL - ?][JP and County Treasurer]*

D. C. Williams, Pvt., Co. C, 16th Texas Infantry, Gibson's Brigade, Hardee's Corp, Army of the Tennessee. [a]

E. W. Williams, Pvt., Co. C, 3rd Texas Cavalry, Ross' Brigade, Jackson's Division, Hardee's Corp, and Co. G, 4th Mississippi, Army of the Tennessee. Residence – Tehuacana. [a][b][d][f] *[Buried Mexia City Cemetery, 6i/13/1845-10/27/1916]*

Henry Walter Williams, Pvt., Co. C, 36th North Carolina Heavy Artillery, Post Duty at Ft. Fisher, North Carolina. Captured there in January 1865. [a][b][f] *[Buried Mexia City Cemetery, 1845 NC – 1928]*

David Wilson, Co. C, Parson's Brigade. Residence – Mt. Calm or Mt. Antioch. [a] *[Buried Ebenezer Cemetery 10/5/1828 – 10/29/1900]*

T. M. Wilson, Co. A, 16th North Carolina and Co. K, 39th North Carolina. Residence – Kosse. [a]

Christopher H. F. Wood, 3rd Sgt., Co. F, 15th Texas Cavalry, Granberry's Brigade, Cleburne's Division, Hardee's Corp, Army of the Tennessee. [a][b][d][f] *[Buried Mexia City Cemetery, 1844-1907]*

E. B. Wood, Capt., Co. B, 34th Alabama Infantry. [e][f]

Ira E. Wood, 2nd Sgt., Co. F, 15th Texas Dismounted Cavalry, Granberry's Brigade, Cleburne's Division, Hardee's Corp, Army of the Tennessee. Residence – Tehuacana. [a][b][d][f] *[6/22/1836 Weakley Co., TN - ?][Lost an arm during GA campaign]*

J. H. Wood, Co. C, Lewis' Battalion, Wheeler's Brigade. [a] *[Buried Kosse Cemetery, 1835-1914]*

W. O. Wood, Pvt., Arkansas' Reserved Corp, E. Kirby Smith Corp. Residence – Armour. [a]

Arthur Woods, Co. D, 20th Texas Infantry. [a] *[Buried Kosse Cemetery, 1827-1914]*

William Spencer Wooten, Co. G, Georgia, Cobb's Division. [a] *[Buried Mexia City Cemetery, 12/25/1841-5/4/1906]*

G. M. Word, Pvt., McAnally's Scouts. [a]

G. H. Wright, Pvt., Co. I, 2nd Arkansas Infantry, Govan's Brigade, Cleburne's Division, Hardee's Corp, Army of the Tennessee. [b][d]

Joel T Wright, Co. B, 20th Texas Cavalry, Spieght's Brigade. Residence – Mt. Calm or Mt. Antioch. [a] *[Buried Mt. Antioch Cemetery NBD – 1906, Pvt. TX 13th Infantry CSA]*

W. Z. Wright, Co. D, 8th Arkansas Cavalry, McRae's Brigade. Residence – Mt. Calm or Mt. Antioch. [a]

Z. T. Wright, Pvt., Co. F, 31st Alabama Infantry, Pettus's Brigade, Stevenson's Division, Hood's Corp, Army of the Tennessee. [a][b][d]

M. D. Yates, Co. F, 49th Tennessee. Residence – Honest Ridge Precinct No. 2. [a] *[Buried Armour Cemetery, North Section 4/1/1838 – 8/17/1899]*

1893 Officers [paid dues $13.60, 136 members]

C. L. Watson	Commander
Rado Steele	1st. Lt. Commander
Oscar Wiley	2nd. Lt. Commander
J. G. Walling	3rd. Lt. Commander
H. W. Williams	Adjutant
J. P. Cook	Quartermaster
S. B. Love	Officer of the Day
W. L. Lowrance	Chaplain
J. I. L. Gray	Surgeon
W. P. Brown	Treasurer
C. H. F. Wood	Color Bearer
J. M. Deis	Bugler

1895 Officers

J. G. Walling
J. H. Archer
M. H. Clark
L. W. Duke
W. H. Herring

1896 Officers [paid dues $11.50, 115 members]

R. J. Bryant	Commander
S. S. Walker	1st Lt. Commander
J. G. Walling	2nd Lt. Commander
Wm. Justice	3rd Lt. Commander
H. W. Williams	Adjutant
J. G. Carroll	Quartermaster
W. H. Herring	Officer of the Day
L. W. Duke	Chaplain
J. P. Cook	Surgeon
M. L. McDonald	Treasurer
C. H. F. Wood	Color Bearer
J. M. Deis	Bugler

Book 2
Active Roster of Joe Johnston Camp No. 94

[Page 1] The new Constitution of Joe Johnston Camp No. 94, adopted at the 8th annual Reunion held at Jack's Creek on July 22nd, 23rd, 24th 1896.

ARTICLE 1

This association shall be known as Joe Johnston Camp No. 94, United Confederate Veterans located in Limestone County, Texas.

ARTICLE 2
Object of Association

The object of this association shall be to perpetuate the memories of our fallen Comrades; to administer, as far as practicable, to the wants of those who were permanently disabled in the service, and to aid the indigent widows and orphans of deceased Confederate soldiers and sailors; to preserve and maintain that sentiment of fraternity born of the hardships and dangers shared in the march, the bivouac and the battle field. The animosities engendered by the war between the States shall be buried in one common grave, and our former adversaries honored as the brave always honor the brave.

ARTICLE 3
Officers

The officers of this association shall consist of a Commander, one 1st, 2nd and 3rd Lieutenant Commanders, Adjutant, quartermaster, Surgeon, Chaplain, Treasurer, Officer of the day, Color Bearer, Bugler, Captain of Artillery, and one Captain from each voting precinct in the County, to be elected annually at stated Reunions, and to hold their office until their successors are elected and qualified.
[Page 2]

ARTICLE 4
Election of Officers

Section 1: The election of officers shall be held at the Camp grounds at annual Reunions. Vacancies may be filled by appointment by the Commander.

Section 2: All members of the Camp in good standing shall be eligible to any office therein.

Section 3: In case of ballot, a majority of all the votes cast shall be necessary to a choice.

ARTICLE 5
Meetings

Section 1: The annual meetings shall be held at the Camp grounds at such time as the Camp may designate.

Section 2: Special call meetings may be had by the Commander upon the application of twenty members in good standing, setting forth the objects of said meeting.

ARTICLE 6
Duties of Officers

Section 1: The Commander shall preside at all meetings, preserve strict order and decorum, and enforce a due observance of the Charter, Constitution and By Laws; make such details and committees not otherwise provided for; give the casting vote in case of a tie; inspect and announce the result of all ballots or other votes. He shall approve all orders drawn on the Treasurer for the payment of money, and shall have power to call special meetings of the Camp in accordance with the provisions of this Constitution.

Section 2: The Lieutenant Commanders shall assist the Commander in the performance of his duties, and in his absence, shall take [Page 3] his place in the order of their rank. If neither of them is present, the Camp shall elect a Commander pro tem.

Section 3: the Adjutant shall keep an impartial record of the Camp and its members; fill out and serve all notices; draw all orders on the Treasurer; receive all money due the Camp and pay the same over to the Treasurer, taking his receipt therefor and assist at the examination of the books.

Section 4: It shall be the duty of the Treasurer to take charge of all money belonging to the Camp, pay out the same upon orders drawn upon him by the Adjutant and approved by the Commander, and to keep a fair and regular account, in a book kept for that purpose, of receipts and expenditures. He shall, before entering upon the discharge of his duties, give a bond in such sum as may be required by the Camp, payable to the Commander and to be accepted by him.

Section 5: The Quartermaster shall have charge of all the property belonging to the Camp, and shall superintend all matters of transportation and supplies.

Section 6: The Officer of the day shall preserve order during the meetings, see that the members behave in an orderly and decorous manner, conduct all ballots and render such other service as the Commander may require of him.

Section 7: It shall be the duty of the Chaplain to open the meeting of the Camp with prayer, and attend and officiate at the funerals of its members, when possible for him so to do.
[Page 4]

ARTICLE 7
Eligibility of Membership

Section 1: Any person of good character, who served honorably in the Confederate States Army or Navy, may be admitted to active membership in this Camp.

Section 2: Every application for active membership shall be made by furnishing to the Adjutant the name of the applicant, his rank, Company, Regiment, State, Brigade, Division, Corps, Army and Department, when possible, and also present post office address.

Section 3: Any person of good moral character may be eligible to honorary membership in the Camp. The wives, widows and daughters of Confederate soldiers in good standing are honorary members. Such honorary members may attend the meetings of the Camp, but shall not be entitled to vote upon any question.

ARTICLE 8
Dues and Fines

Section 1: The annual dues of the members of this Camp shall be fifty cents per annum, due and payable to the Adjutant at each annual Reunion, or thirty days thereafter.

Section 2: Any member who shall misbehave in the Camp, or shall disobey the Commander, shall be fined fifty cents.

Section 3: Any officer absenting himself from any meeting of this Camp, without sufficient cause, shall be fined not more than one dollar, nor less than twenty five cents.

ARTICLE 9
Captains Duties

It shall be the duty of the Captains to report to the Commander any cripple, [Page 5] indigent or needy member of this Camp, who shall have power to take such steps as may be necessary for his relief.

ARTICLE 10
Suspension and Expulsion

This Camp shall have power to suspend or expel any member, upon proper charges, preferred in such manner as may be prescribed by law.

ARTICLE 11
Travelling Cards

Any member in good standing wishing a travelling card, can obtain the same upon application to the Adjutant, on payment of twenty five cents, provided his dues are paid up to the date of his application. Such cards to be countersigned by the Commander.

ARTICLE 12
Badges

Section 1: The badges to be worn by the members of this Camp, shall consist of a blue ribbon one and one fourth [1¼] inches wide by six [6] inches long, to be worn on left lapel of coat. For guards, a deep red ribbon, two inches wide by eight inches long, upon which shall be printed the word "Guard," to be worn on left lapel.

Section 2: The Officer of the day shall wear a red sash around his waist and over his shoulder, and upon his right lapel a blue ribbon two by eight inches, upon which shall be printed the words "Officer of the Day."

Section 3: The Commander shall wear upon his left [Page 6] lapel a red and white rosette, three inches in diameter and underneath, a blue badge two by eight inches, upon which shall be printed the word "Commander."

Section 4: The 1st, 2nd and 3rd Lieutenant Commanders shall each wear upon the left lapel a two by eight inch badge with their rank printed thereon.

Section 5: The Adjutant, quartermaster, Surgeon, Treasurer, Color Bearer and Bugler shall each wear upon his left lapel a blue badge two by eight inches with their rank printed thereon. The Chaplain's badge shall be a white ribbon two by eight inches, worn on left lapel and having printed thereon the word "Chaplain."

Section 6: Past Commanders shall wear solid gray badges of the same size and design as Commander's badge, with the words "Past Commander" printed thereon.

ARTICLE 13
Amendments

These articles, or any part thereof, shall not be altered, amended, or annuled, unless a written notice of the same be read at a regular meeting; after which it shall be referred to a committee and reported upon at the next regular meeting.
[Page 7 – 11] Blank [Page 12]

MINUTES OF THE 8TH ANNUAL REUNION AT JACK'S CREEK HELD ON JULY 22ND, 23RD, & 24TH, 1896
July 22nd

The Camp assembled on call of bugle at 9:30 o'clock and after prayer by Rev. T. W. Blake, - a Chaplain being absent – roll was called, the minutes of last Reunion were read and a detail of twenty Sons of Confederate Veterans was made for guard duty. An auditing committee was appointed – S. B. Love, J. G. Walling and C. T. Gilbert, - to examine the books of the Adjutant and Treasurer. The hour having arrived for the purpose, Genl. T. W. Blake, on behalf of Commander Bryant, extended the people a cordial welcome to the Reunion, - after which the Camp adjourned until 9 o'clock July 23rd.

The afternoon was used by the Sons and Daughters of Confederate Veterans.

July 23rd: 9 o'clock

Prayer by Chaplain L. W. Duke. Guard mounting; after which Col. C. L. Watson being called for, delivered an interesting talk, showing and explaining some of the objects of our meeting here annually. Col. Gibson being requested to address the audience, did so in a thirty minutes impromptu speech. Among other things, he counseled Southern women to hold to the traditions of Southern womanhood, and to reject all innovations, no matter from what source they may come. That their happiness would be best subserved by following in the footsteps of their mothers and grandmothers, and keeping the place intended by nature and natures God. Adjourned to 2 o'clock P.M.

2 o'clock

The new Constitution was read and, with a slight change, adopted, and the County papers were requested to publish it, if they could conveniently do so. The question of getting up a Camp sketch book was brought out, and on motion, a committee of five was appointed on it, consisting of Comrades Watson, Gilbert, Walling, J. W. Simmons and Kenney, who made a report recommending that the Camp buy a substantially bound blank book in which to preserve the record and sketch of any Confederate Veteran who wished to contribute them, and that they be sent in to the Adjutant. The resolution was adopted and the committee discharged. The Camp then went into the election of officers, which resulted as follows:

R. J. Bryant	Commander
F. Y. Doke	1st Lieutenant
E. B. Wood	2nd Lieutenant
C. T. Gilbert	3rd Lieutenant
H. W. Williams	Adjutant
J. G. Carroll	Quartermaster
J. P. Cook	Surgeon
L. W. Duke	Chaplain
M. L. McDonald	Treasurer
J. M. Suttle	Officer of Day
Rado Steele	Color Bearer
J. M. Deis	Bugler

W. M. Barton was elected Chief of Artillery. The following resolution by J. W. Simmons was adopted:

Resolved, That this Camp recommend the adoption and use in our public and private schools the histories recommended by our Comrades in Reunion at Richmond. On motion, a committee of three was appointed [Page 14] by the Commander in relation to enclosing the grounds, Comrades G. W. Archer, S. S. Walker, and S. B. Love, - Camp adjourned to 9 o'clock July 24th.

July 24th

Camp assembled at 9 o'clock. After prayer and guard mounting, Hon. R. E. Steele was called upon and delivered an interesting address. Among other things, requesting the Sons and Daughters never to forget nor be ashamed of the record of their fathers, and to always keep their memories green. Col. Steele was followed by Rev. G. L. Jennings, who spoke mostly about Spiritual matters of the war.

He was followed by Col. J. W. Simmons, who spoke about the exploits and death of Samuel Davis, who was unjustly hung as a spy at Pulaski, Tennessee during the war. On motion of Comrade Watson, the Commander and Quartermaster were empowered to have the grounds sprinkled at the next Reunion.

A motion was carried that the Adjutant be authorized to have enough badges made for all the wives, mothers and widows of the camp.

An invitation being received from the Hill County Camp on motion, thanks were returned to it. On motion of Comrade Simmons, the young people were cordially thanked for their services at the concerts.

The committee on fencing the grounds reported against fencing. The report was received and committee discharged. Camp adjourned to 2 o'clock P.M.

2 o'clock

Comrade Doyle submitted the following amendment to the Constitution, and resoliction:

Article – Section --. No Comrade shall [Page 15] be eligible to the office of Commander for more than one year in succession. This amendment to be effective on its adoption at our annual Reunion in 1897.

Resolved, That the companies composing Joe Johnston Camp No. 94, shall be lettered, [this means the different precincts in the County]. A committee of three consisting of Comrades Doyle, Camp and J. W. Simmons was appointed to report on above at our next Reunion. The hour having arrived for holding memorial services, they were conducted by Chaplain Duke.

The first address was delivered by Rev. G. L. Jennings, followed by Rev. J. L. Jennings and finished by Chaplain Duke.

The comrades who have died since our last meeting are James Armour, Charles S. Bates, T. L. Reed and J. L. Wilder.

Business being resumed, the auditing committee submitted the following report, which was adopted:

We, your auditing committee, beg leave to report that we have examined the books of the Adjutant and Treasurer and find them neatly and correctly kept. We find the total amount of money collected for 1895 to be:

	$514.85
Amount paid out	497.34
Cash on hand July 24th 1896	$ 17.51

All of which is mostly respectfully submitted, this 24th of July 1896. S. B. Love, J. G. Walling, C. T. Gilbert (Com.)
No further business being before it, the Camp adjourned until called together by the Commander.

        H. W. Williams, Adjutant   R. J. Bryant, Commander

[Page 16]

Trustees of Joe Johnston Camp

J. W. Simmons, Mexia	C. L. Watson, Mexia	S. B. Love, Tehuacana
S. S. Walker, Groesbeck	Jno. G. Walling, Thornton	

Captains of Precincts

W. D. Frazier, Amour	J. W. Wickder, Mt. Calm	S. F. Dillis, Hancock
S. C. Ingram, Shiloh	G. L. Jennings, Kirk	W. H. Browder, Groesbeck
P. O. Douglass, Mart	A. J. Burleson, Kosse	W. E. Doyle, Mexia
Wm. Justice, Personville	W. H. Herring, Pr. Grove	C. N. Brooks, Thornton
	J. W. McKinney, Pr. Hill & Frosa	

CALLED MEETING OF JOE JOHNSTON CAMP

Pursuant to call of Commander Bryant, Joe Johnston Camp assembled in Mexia on September 19th 1896, for the purpose of discussing the advisability of purchasing more land for the Camp, and to attend to any other business for the welfare of the Camp. On motion of Comrade Boyd, the Camp was empowered to buy 20 acres more land for Camp purposes, which was carried unanimously.

No further business coming before the meeting, on motion, the Camp adjourned to call of commander.

        H. W. Williams, Adjutant   R. J. Bryant, Commander

[Page 17]

CALLED MEETING OF JOE JOHNSTON CAMP NO. 94

By call of Commander Bryant, Joe Johnston Camp assembled in Mexia on the 20th of March 1897. The first order of business was to fix the time for our next Reunion, which, on motion, was set for the 14th, 15th and 16th of July, 1897.

The next business was to elect seven delegates and seven alternates to go to Nashville, Tennessee, to the General Reunion.

The following named Comrades were elected: Dr. Jno. P. Cook, W. E. Doyle, G. W. Archer, R. J. Bryant, J. W. Simmons, M. H. Clark and J. W. Thompson.

On motion, it was decided to elect any Comrade as alternate who desired to attend. On motion, all Comrades who wished to attend the State Reunion at San Antonio in June, were elected as delegates.

A motion was made by Col. C. L. Watson, and carried, that Friday, the 7th of May, be set as the time for our annual picnic at the Reunion grounds, and that all the schools in the County, which desired to do so, give their pupils holiday, and, as for as possible, be with us at that time. Also, that all persons who wished to look at or purchase lots, would come, as the lot committee, with the new map of the Camp, would be on hand.

On motion, it was decided that anyone wishing to purchase the privilege to sell anything at the picnic should apply to the privilege committee of the Camp.

Moved by Col. Watson, that Col. Lowrance of Dallas be most cordially invited to visit us during our next Reunion and enjoy all of its hospitalities. Carried. Moved by same, that Comrade J. W. Simmons be appointed a committee of one to manage the [Page 18] concerts of our next Reunion, and also, that hereafter, it shall be decided by vote at each Reunion upon which nights the different communities shall have their respective concerts, and that Col. Simmons be chairman of any committee that may be appointed to manage same. Moved by Comrade Simmons and carried, that a committee of three, be appointed to draft proper resolutions on the death of General Joe Shelby of Missouri: -- Committee, J. W. Simmons, J. M. Deis and F. Y. Doke.

The Commander was empowered to make arrangements for the purchase of any additional lands near the Camp grounds if he saw fit to do so. It was moved, and carried, that the Camp refund the sum of Fourteen [$14.00] Dollars overdrawn at the bank on the memorial fund.

A motion carried, that the Commander appoint the various Camp committees, which he did, as follows:

    Privilege Com. – J. G. Carroll, J. M. Suttle, W. H. Browder, A. J. Burleson, J. M. Storey and H. F. Simmons.
    Invitation Com. – W. E. Doyle, T. Y. Doke, S. S. Walker and R. E. Steele.
    Arrangement Com. -- C. L. Watson, Rado Steele, O. Wiley, J. A. Arvin, G. W. Kenney, Capt. W. R. Anderson, Jno. G. Walling, W. D. Frazier, A. J. Cashion, W. M. Barton, Jno. E. Parker, H. C. Joiner, C. J. Bower, M. L. McDonald and B. J. Hancock.
    Spring Com. – S. F. Bond, W. H. Herring, R. W. Payne and J. M. Deis.
    Locating Com. – S. B. Love, J. W. McKinney, M. P. Fuqua, E. W. Williams and R. P. Ward.

There being no further business, the Camp adjourned.

Official: H. W. Williams, Adjutant   R. J. Bryant, Commander
[Page 19]

MINUTES OF THE 9TH ANNUAL REUNION AT JACK'S CREEK HELD ON THE 14TH, 15TH AND 16TH OF JULY 1897

July 14th

On July 14th Joe Johnston Camp No. 94 assembled at 9:30 A.M. After prayer by the Rev. H. M. Haynie, the Chaplain, Rev. L. W. Duke, being absent, the roll was called and the minutes of the last regular Reunion were read and approved. After guard mounting the Camp went into a short business meeting.

The first order of business was concerning the adoption of an amendment to the Constitution limiting the term of the office of future Commanders to one year, and also, to letter each precinct in the County as a Company.

The committee appointed on the above matter, Comrades Doyle, Camp and J. W. Simmons, asked further time in which to make their report. An auditing committee was appointed. The hour having arrived for the address of welcome to all, on behalf of Commander Bryant, Col. R. E. Steele delivered an interesting address inviting all comers to participate in the pleasures of our Reunion, after which the Camp adjourned to 9 o'clock next morning.

The balance of the day was used by the Sons and Daughters of the Camp.

July 15th, 9 o'clock

After prayer and guard mounting, the committee on resolutions about electing future Commanders for one year and lettering the precincts reported as follows; "We, your committee, on the resolution relating to electing all future Commanders for one [Page 20] year, have to report that we cannot assume the responsibility of reporting on same and it is, therefore, referred back for the decision of the Camp." On motion of Dr. J. P. Cook, the resolution was tabled.

"We, your committee, on resolution about lettering the precincts of the County, beg to recommend that the Camp do not adopt the resolution." On motion, this report was adopted by the Camp, and the committee discharged. The Constitution remains as it was before.

The following resolution was offered by Comrade Doyle and unanimously carried:

Whereas, Comrade M. W. Kemp has been confined to his bed by sickness for three long months, and whereas, since the organization of this Camp, he has been an active member and has contributed much to its success, therefore be it, Resolved, that in his suffering, Comrade Kemp has the sympathy of all the members of Joe Johnston Camp No. 94, and it is their prayer that he be blessed with a speedy recovery and permitted to meet his Comrades in many future Reunions. Resolution adopted.

On motion of Comrade J. P. Cook, a committee was appointed to petition the next Legislature to amend our Charter so as to prevent the giving away or selling any spirituous liquors within two miles of our Camp grounds. Carried unanimously and with great enthusiasm. Committee appointed, Comrades Watson, Doyle and R. E. Steele.

On motion of Comrade Watson, the Camp instructed the Quartermaster to collect, in the future, 25 per cent of all gross [Page 21] proceeds of privileges let by the Camp on this ground, except Reunion privileges.

The hour having arrived for the purpose, General R. H. Phelps, Commander of the Texas Division, delivered an interesting and instructive address to the vast assembly present, after which the Camp adjourned to 2 o'clock P.M.

2 o'clock P.M.

Camp reassembled, and the Auditing committee made their report as follows: To R. J. Bryant, Commander, We, your committee, appointed to examine the books of the Adjutant and Treasurer, beg leave to report: We have checked up the Treasurer and find that he has vouchers for all money paid out by him, leaving balance in his hands of 4134.7, and his books correctly kept. We find the books of the Adjutant correctly kept and that he has paid over all money coming into his hands to the Treasurer and holds his receipts for same. Respectfully Submitted, Rado Steele, L. E. Camp, T. J. Gibson [Com.]

The report was adopted and committee discharged. The survivors of the siege of Vicksburg present were invited to come on the stand, which they proceeded to do, and held a "young reunion" among themselves that was very much enjoyed by onlookers as well as the "pea bread and mule eaters" themselves.

The next business before the Camp was the annual election of officers, which, on motion, was gone into, and resulted as follows:

[Page 22]

Rado Steele	Commander
W. H. Herring	1st Lieutenant Commander
J. M. Storey	2nd Lieutenant Commander
A. J. Cashion	3rd Lieutenant Commander
H. W. Williams	Adjutant
H. F. Simmons	Quartermaster
J. P. Cook	Surgeon
G. L. Jennings	Chaplain
M. L. McDonald	Treasurer
W. H. Browder	Officer of the Day
C. J. Bower	Color Bearer
J. M. Deis	Bugler
W. M. Barton	Chief of Artillery

On motion, the Camp adjourned to 9 o'clock next morning.

July 16th 9 o'clock

Camp assembled and was opened with prayer by Rev. W. L. Lowrance. After guard mounting, a short business session was held. The following resolution by Comrade Gibson carried unanimously:

Resolved, That General L. S. Ross and General R. H. Phelps be, and they are hereby, elected Honorary Members of Joe Johnston Camp No. 94, U.C.V.'s.

On motion of Comrade Watson, all of the land of the Camp on the East side of Jackson Avenue and north of the two tiers of lots first laid off by the Camp north of Lee Avenue, be perpetually held as a reservation. Carried.

Comrade T. J. Gibson offered the following resolution, which was adopted:

Resolved, That all reservations be reserved, and that the Quartermaster and his associates are directed to keep intruders off of all reserved land.

The time arriving, General L. S. Ross entertained the large audience by an [Page 23] amusing and interesting address, after which, the Camp adjourned to 4 o'clock P.M.

4 o'clock

On the reassembling of the Camp, Colonel W. L. Lowrance of Dallas, delivered a stirring address to the members of the Camp, also, to the mothers, sons and daughters, urging them all to assembly here annually and the young people never to forget what their fathers and mothers had passed through and when they were all gone to still keep their memory green, and at the proper time to erect a marble shaft in their honor.

Two of our Comrades having died since our last meeting, Isaac Raborn and W. M. Wilder, a short memorial service was held, conducted by the Rev. W. L. Lowrance. The band first played, "Nearer my God to Thee," after which the audience was requested to stand and sing the first stanza of that beautiful hymn. After the close of the service the Commander asked all the members of the Camp to come up and shake hands with Colonel Lowrance, who is an honorary member of our Camp, before his departure. During the time the band was playing "God be with you till we meet again." It was an affecting scene and will be long remembered by all who participated in it.

At a short business meeting, a resolution was passed thanking the young people of Groesbeck, Hubbard, Mexia and the country generally, for their aid in entertaining the vast crowds that assembled on the grounds each day.

A resolution also, was carried thanking the Thomas Goggan Piano Company for the use of their instrument.

There were on the grounds daily from [Page 24] seven to ten thousand people, and if there was anything to mar the pleasure of any one we have failed to hear of it, and on behalf of the Camp, the Commander here by returns, sincere thanks to all for the good behavior observed, and hopes that all may return next year to enjoy themselves again.

He wishes to say to any one who desires to purchase a lot to let the Adjutant know as early as possible, as the time is rapidly approaching when to own a lot at Joe Johnston Camp will be a privilege indeed. Camp adjourned.

Official: H. W. Williams, Adjutant   R. J. Bryant, Commander

CALLED MEETING OF JOE JOHNSTON CAMP

A called meeting of Joe Johnston Camp No. 94, was held in Mexia on 31st of July 1897. On motion of Comrade J. W. Simmons, the Commander was authorized to get some one to live on and take care of the Reunion grounds. Motion carried. On motion of Comrade Watson, a committee of three was appointed by the Commander to investigate the cost and the way of getting a water supply for sprinkling the Camp grounds next year. Committee: Watson, Bryant, C. H. T. Wood and J. W. Simmons.

By Comrade Watson: Resolved, That any member of the Camp, or any visitor, seeing or knowing any violation of the law at our last Reunion, be requested to inform the grand jury of County Attorney of same. Carried.

After some promiscuous talk about various matters, it was decided to meet on the 1st Saturday in each month at 3 o'clock P.M. Adjourned to the 1st Saturday in Sept.

H. W. Williams, Adjutant   Rado Steele, Commander

[Page 25]

CALLED MEETING OF JOE JOHNSTON CAMP NO. 94, MARCH 26th 1898

Pursuant to call of Commander Rado Steele, Joe Johnston Camp No. 94, assembled in Mexia on the 26th of March, 1898, for the purpose of fixing the time of holding the next Reunion, and to transact any other business necessary for the welfare of the Camp. On motion, the 13th, 14th and 15th of July was chosen as the time.

The election of delegates to the General Reunion at Atlanta was postponed to the meeting in July. By motion, the various committees were appointed by the Commander as follows:

Privilege Committee: Comrades H. F. Simmons, Jno. G. Carroll, J. M. Suttle, W. H. Browder and R. P. Ward.
Invitation Committee: Comrades T. J. Gibson, L. J. Farrar, R. E. Steele, W. P. Brown, John G. Walling and B. F. Ouzts.
Arrangement Committee: Comrades Rado Steele, C. L. Watson, J. W. Simmons, R. J. Bryant, M. Kaufman, S. S. Walker, Geo. W. Archer, Ira E. Wood, Wm. Justice and B. D. Keeling.
Spring Committee: Comrades W. E. Doyle, S. F. Bond, D. A. Murphy, Jno. M. Deis, Taylor Wright and H. C. Joiner.
Locating Committee: Comrades E. W. Williams, J. W. McKinney, M. P. Fuqua, W. A. Buckner and W. D. Frazier.
Concert Committee: Comrade J. W. Simmons, with full power to select his assistants.
Reception Committee: All Past Commanders of the Camp.

A motion prevailed that Friday, the 6th of May, be set for the annual picnic of the Camp, and that all the schools in the County be invited, with the request that, if possible, some of them would get up a suitable entertainment for the occasion.

Resolution by Comrade C. L. Watson in relation to the Confederate Veteran pension amendment was adopted, urging all Camps in Texas [Page 26] to aid in passing same at November election. Comrades C. L. Watson, J. W. Simmons and T. J. Gibson were appointed to draft suitable resolutions on the death of General Phelps, Past Commander of the Texas Division U. C. V.'s.

There being no further business, the Camp adjourned.

Official: H. W. Williams, Adjutant   Rado Steele, Commander

[Page 27]

MINUTES OF THE 10TH ANNUAL REUNION AT JACK'S CREEK HELD ON THE 13TH, 14TH AND 15TH OF JULY 1898

July 13th

Joe Johnston Camp No. 94, United Confederate Veterans, assembled, according to call of Commander Rado Steele, at 10 o'clock, A.M. on the 13th of July, 1898.

After prayer by the Chaplain Rev. G. L. Jennings, the roll was called and the minutes of the last Reunion were read and approved.

On motion, Guard mounting for the day was dispensed with by the U.C.V.'s and the guard duty of the Camp was turned over to the Sons and Daughters of Confederate Veterans.

The Commander delivered an address of welcome to all to participate with us in our Reunion.

A beautiful Flag was presented to the Camp by the ladies of Mexia, represented by Miss Lela Kennedy in an appropriate address, and responded to by Comrade T. J. Gibson, in behalf of the Camp, in his pleasant style.

A resolution by Comrade Watson was carried calling upon all the voters of Limestone County to support the amendment to the Constitution in relation to the Confederate Veterans.

The Camp adjourned to 9:30 o'clock, a.m. July 14th. The afternoon was used by the Sons and Daughters of the Camp.

July 14th

Camp reassembled at 9:30 o'clock. Prayer by Chaplain Jennings. Roll was called and guard mounted.

General W. T. Merriwether, Commander of the Texas Division, who was expected to address the Camp at this hour, failing, by reason of misconnection, to be present, Ex-Governor Hubbard, by special request, delivered a very instructive and amusing lecture on Japan, [Page 28] to the great pleasure of the vast audience who heard it. Camp adjourned for dinner.

3 o'clock, P. M.

Camp reassembled. The auditing committee, which had been previously appointed by the Commander, reported as follows:

"We, your committee, beg leave to report that we have examined and compared the books of the Adjutant and Treasurer and find them correct. We find balance in Treasury of $110.62.

Respectfully submitted, C. L. Watson, M. H. Clark, A. J. Burleson [Com.]"

Resolution by Comrade J. W. Simmons: Resolved, That this Camp meet at City Hall in Mexia, on the first Saturday in each month at 3 o'clock P. M. Carried.

The time having arrived for the address of Judge Polley, who could not be present, an interesting letter from him to the Camp, was read by Comrade Gibson.

After the reading of the letter, on motion of Comrade Gibson, the thanks of the Camp were extended to Judge Polley, and he was elected an Honorary member.

The time arriving for the annual election of officers, the following named Comrades were elected:

Commander	C. L. Watson
1st Lieutenant Commander	W. H. Herring
2nd Lieutenant Commander	B. F. Ouzts
3rd Lieutenant Commander	J. M. Storey
Adjutant	H. W. Williams
Quartermaster	C. H. F. Wood
Surgeon	J. P. Cook
Chaplain	G. L. Jennings
Treasurer	M. L. McDonald
Officer of the Day	H. C. Joiner
Color Bearer	C. J. Bower
Bugler	Jno. M. Deis
Chief of Artillery	W. M. Barton

[Page 29]

Camp adjourned to 9 o'clock A.M. July 15th.

July 15th

Camp assembled at 9 o'clock. Prayer by Chaplain Jennings. Guard mounting. The following resolution by Comrade Gibson was read and adopted:

Whereas, Misses Em Beeson, Sallie Smith, Sallie F. Smith, Emma Smith, Lela Kennedy, Jennie A. Kirby and Mrs. Mary Long, assisted by Mr. Henry Philpott, have made and presented to this Camp a beautiful and attractive Flag, designed for the use of this Camp, Resolved, That Joe Johnston Camp No. 94, U.C.V.'s extends to Miss Beeson and her associates the thanks of the veterans belonging to this Camp for this Flag with the assurance that the kindness and sympathy prompting its presentation will ever be gratefully remembered and appreciated by us.

Resolution by Comrade Simmons was carried thanking the young people for their kindness in helping the Camp in the Concerts.

The following named Comrades were elected Delegates and Alternates to Atlanta:

Delegates: A. J. Burleson, J. S. Jolley, J. W. Simmons, M. H. Clark, Geo. W. McNeese, R. J. Bryant and H. W. Williams.
Alternates: L. E. Camp, J. W. Thompson, P. O. Douglass, J. P. Hickman, J. W. Thomas, M. L. McDonald and E. B. Wood.

General Merriwether, Ex-Governor Hubbard, and Colonel John Karnes and Alphonso Steele were elected Honorary members of this Camp. The last two are Texas Veterans.

The time arriving for the purpose, Ex-Governor Hubbard entertained the vast concourse of people by an interesting and instructive [Page 30] address on "The South, Past, Present and Future." Camp adjourned for dinner.

3 o'clock P.M.

Camp reassembled. A resolution was passed, That all Comrades of this Camp who wished to attend the State Reunion at Galveston on August 5th, 1898, be declared delegates to same.

General Merriwether, being present, delivered an interesting address, after which, there being no further business, the Camp adjourned subject to the call of the Commander.

Official: H. W. Williams, Adjutant   Rado Steele, Commander
[Page 31]

MINUTES OF CALLED MEETING HELD MARCH 25th, 1899

By call of Commander, C. L. Watson, Joe Johnston Camp No. 94, assembled at Mexia on the 25th of March, 1899, and was called to order by the Commander.

On motion of Comrade Bryant, the Reunion was set for the 19th, 20th and 21st of July 1899.

The following named Comrades were elected to represent the Camp at the State Reunion at Austin on the 3rd and 4th of May: J. P. Hickman, C. L. Watson, G. W. Archer, Wm. Justice, J. M. Storey, W. H. Browder, Dr. J. P. Cook, Jno. G. Walling, R. M. Love, W. H. Herring, Rado Steele, C. J. Bower, Jno. W. Simmons, A. J. Kynerd and any others who desire to attend can get credentials by applying to the Adjutant.

Delegates to General Reunion at Charleston, South Carolina: Comrades H. W. Williams, W. E. Doyle, J. H. Archer, Dr. E. B. Wood, J. W. Thompson, Rev. W. C. Friley, Jno. S. Grooves, Jas. L. Smith, and all others who wish to go can get credentials on applying to the Adjutant.

Privilege Committee: Comrades C. H. F. Wood, W. H. Browder, C. T. Harris, R. M. Love and S. F. Bond.
Invitation Committee: Comrades T. J. Gibson, R. E. Steele, Jno. G. Walling, B. F. Ouzts and W. P. Brown.
Locating Committee: Comrades E. W. Williams, J. W. McKinney, W. A. Buckner, W. D. Frazier and J. W. Thompson.

On motion, the Quartermaster was empowered to have the grounds and spring properly prepared for the use of the Camp.

A motion prevailed that the Commander appoint Comrades W. F. Roberts, N. A. Boyd and J. P. Hickman as a Concert committee with full power to impress any one into service to help them.

[Page 32] The delegates to the State Reunion were instructed to vote against the Per Capita Tax of 10 cents and let it remain at 5 cents per member.

By motion, the Commander appointed Comrades R. J. Bryant, L. E. Camp and John W. Simmons as a sprinkling committee.

The annual Confederate picnic was set for Friday the 5th of May, and the schools in the County were cordially invited to be present and, if any of them could do so, to furnish some kind of an entertainment for the occasion.

There being no further business the Camp adjourned.

Official: H. W. Williams, Adjutant   C. L. Watson, Commander
[Page 33]

MINUTES OF THE 11TH ANNUAL REUNION HELD ON THE 19TH, 20TH AND 21ST OF JULY 1899
July 19th

Joe Johnston Camp, No. 94, U.C.V.'s assembled at the Camp ground on the 19th of July, 1899, to hold a three days Reunion.

The Camp was called to order by the Commander, C. L. Watson. Prayer was offered by the Chaplain, Rev. G. L. Jennings. The roll was called and the minutes of the last Reunion read and approved.

On motion of the Chaplain, a committee of five was appointed by the Commander to draft suitable resolutions of the death of Comrades who have died since the last Reunion. The following named Comrades were appointed: E. B. Wood, M. B. Cox, R. M. Love, Jno. W. Simmons and W. P. Brown. On motion, the committee was continued for the ensuing year. It was decided to hold memorial services as the first business for Friday afternoon, the 21st of July.

The Commander appointed Comrades S. S. Walker, L. E. Camp, and S. B. Love as an auditing committee.

The afternoon was given up to the Sons and Daughters of Confederate Veterans.

July 20th

Camp called to order by the Commander. Prayer by the Chaplain.

A motion was carried that a committee be appointed to consider the advisability of enlarging the Pavilion. Committee appointed: Comrades G. C. Boyle, A. E. Steele, W. H. Herring, W. R. Anderson and John W. Simmons.

A letter was read from Governor Sayers, who had promised to be present, stating that official duties, because of the recent heavy freshets, prevented his attendance and expressing regrets for not meeting with the Camp. Impromptu addresses were made by Comrades W. H. Herring and G. L. Jennings.

The Commander of the Sons of Confederate Veterans [Gen'l. B. H. Kirk of Waco] for the Trans-Mississippi Department, being present delivered an interesting address to the young people.

Camp was adjourned to 2 o'clock.

2 o'clock, P.M.

Camp reassembled and proceeded to elect officers for the ensuing term with the following results:

J. M. Storey	Commander
S. S. Walker	1st Lieutenant Commander
A. J. Burleson	2nd Lieutenant Commander
P. O. Douglass	3rd Lieutenant Commander
H. W. Williams	Adjutant
C. H. F. Wood	Quartermaster
Dr. J. P. Cook	Surgeon
Rev. G. L. Jennings	Chaplain
J. W. Simmons	Treasurer
J. G. Walling	Officer of the Day
C. J. Bower	Color Bearer
Jno. M. Deis	Bugler
H. W. Gray	Captain of Artillery

A short impromptu speech was made by Capt. W. R. Davie of Mexia. Camp was adjourned to 9:30 Friday, 21st of July.

July 21st

Camp assembled by bugle call. A very interesting address was delivered by G. W. McDaniel, a son of a veteran, on the needs of educating the young people of the South in Southern schools and colleges.

At the appointed time, General J. B. Polley, Commander of the Texas Division, delivered an interesting address to the Camp.

The committee on enlarging the Pavilion reported as follows: "We, your committee, recommend that an addition be built to the Pavilion of 100 feet in length by 12 feet in width, which will [Page 35] cost about $100.00 with level seats, and with elevated seats – which we recommend – will cost about $125.00. Respectfully submitted, G. C. Doyle, Chairman."

The report was adopted, and a motion prevailed that the same committee be continued to carry on the improvements recommended by it.

A motion was carried that the Camp donate to the Adjutant $20.00 for his invoices.

Camp adjourned to 2:30 P.M.

2:30 o'clock P.M.

Camp reassembled and the committee on memorial resolutions made a suitable report on the death of Comrades J. M. Suttle, B. J. Hancock and E. B. Smyth, which was adopted and committee continued to next Reunion. Memorial services were then conducted by Chaplain, G. L. Jennings.

The auditing committee reported as follows: "We, your committee, beg to report that we have examined the books, checks and receipts of the Adjutant and Treasurer of the Camp, and are pleased to report that both are in good shape and nicely kept, and that they tally out correctly and show the same result, and that there is a balance of $35.07 cash to the credit of the Treasurer. S. B. Love, L. E. Camp, S. S. Walker [Com.]."

After a short talk by Comrade R. E. Steele, a resolution was carried that the thanks of the Camp be tendered to all the young people of the surrounding towns and country for assisting us in entertaining the vast concourse of people.

There being no further business, the Commander, in a nice little speech, proceeded to thank the people for their good behavior while present and invited them [Page 36] to meet with us next year, after which the Camp adjourned.

The three days encampment were greatly enjoyed, and, so far as we know, there was nothing to mar the pleasure of those present.

Official: H. W. Williams, Adjutant   C. L. Watson, Commander

[Page 37]

CALLED MEETING OF JOE JOHNSTON CAMP, MARCH 24th, 1900

By call of Commander James M. Storey, Joe Johnston Camp No. 94, assembled at Mexia on the 24th day of March, 1900, and was called to order by the Commander.

On motion of Comrade Watson the Reunion was set for the 11th, 12th and 13th of July 1900.

The following named Comrades were selected to attend the State Reunion at Ft. Worth on May 22nd: E. B. Wood, A. J. Burleson, S. S. Walker, W. H. Browder, Rado Steele, R. M. Love, J. W. Simmons and W. H. Herring.

Delegates to General Reunion at Louisville, Kentucky, from May 30th to June 3rd: O. Wiley, M. L. McDonald, J. W. Thompson, W. E. Doyle, M. H. Clark, C. L. Watson, W. H. Browder, M. Kaufman, Sam Risien, J. G. Walling and P. O. Douglass.

By motion, the Commander was instructed to appoint the various committees, which he proceeded to do as follows:

> Privilege Committee: Comrades C. H. F. Wood, J. L. Smith, W. H. Browder, R. J. Bryant and Geo. A. Neill.
> Invitation Committee: Comrades C. L. Watson, R. E. Steele, J. G. Walling, W. P. Brown and B. F. Ouzts.
> Locating Committee: Comrades E. W. Williams, J. W. McKinney, W. A. Buckner, W. D. Frazier and J. W. Thompson.

The Concert business was turned over to the Sons and Daughters of the Camp, [W. A. Keeling, Commander] with the request that they get up an entertainment for each night.

A communication was received from the Kennesaw Chapter U.D.C. of Marietta, Georgia, asking for a small contribution "to help erect a Monument to the memory of 3,000 of [Page 38] our boys who wore the gray" that lie buried there. On motion of Comrade Simmons $2.00 was donated.

The Quartermaster was empowered to spend as much as $10.00 towards decorating the pavilion with bunting and flags of Confederate colors. The quartermaster was instructed to prepare the grounds for the next Reunion.

On motion, the letting of the melon and peach privilege was left to the discretion of the Privilege Committee.

The annual Confederate basket picnic was set for Friday, May 4th, to which everybody is cordially invited.

On motion of Comrade Watson $20.00 was added to the building committee fund.

Comrade R. J. Bryant was requested to make arrangements for having the programs printed.

There being no further business, on motion, the Camp adjourned.

Official: H. W. Williams, Adjutant   J. M. Storey, Commander
[Page 39]

MINUTES OF THE 12TH ANNUAL REUNION HELD ON THE 11TH, 12TH AND 13TH OF JULY, 1900
Written by Major N. P. Houx, Secretary of Adjutant, First Day, Wednesday the 11th

The members were assembled by Bugler Deis at 9 o'clock A.M. and at 9:30 o'clock Commander Jas. M. Storey called the Camp to order and, after a fervent prayer by Chaplain G. L. Jennings, the minutes of the last annual meeting were read and approved.

It was requested that names of deceased members be handed in.

Commander Storey then delivered the annual address in which he welcomed all to the Reunion and hoped they would enjoy themselves.

Comrade Watson, by request of the Commander, then made some announcements and stated some of the rules of the organization. He said there was a "beer joint" adjoining the grounds and appealed to all to let it alone and force it to close up and move. The Adjutant announced that there were guards and deputy sheriffs on the grounds to keep peace and order.

Comrade Gibson asked that all Confederates register in a book provided for that purpose, and invited all visitors to do likewise. All Confederates present registered. The Camp was then turned over to the Sons and Daughters for their annual meeting.

Second day, Thursday the 12th, Morning Session

Camp was called to order at 9:30 A.M. by the Commander and prayer was offered by Comrade Duke.

The Commander announced the appointment of Comrades R. M. Love, L. E. Camp and John E. Parker as an Auditing Committee. [Page 40] Past Commander, John W. Simmons, then presented a Gavel to the Camp, making the following presentation speech:

"Commander and Comrades: I have a Gavel that I wish to present to this Camp. It is made from the limb of a tree that stood on the bloody plains of Chickamauga battlefield. It has imbedded in it one of the missiles of death that caused such destruction in our ranks on that fearful day.

The battle of Chickamauga, as many of you are well aware, was the hardest contested field, and greatest destruction of life, according to the numbers engaged, of any battle of the entire war; there having fallen on that day about Thirty Four Thousand [34,000] American soldiers.

Commander, I hope you will receive this Gavel and you and your successors use it to call and control this Camp until we have all answered to the last roll call and crossed over the river and rest under the shade.

And when there are none of us left to meet together and obey its summons, I hope the last surviving member will turn it over to the Sons of Confederate Veterans so that they may keep it in remembrance of the fact that their ancestors were Confederate soldiers, and had the courage to obey their country's call and bare their breasts to the leaden hail and face death in all its hideous forms in defense of the Constitution of the United States, as they understood it, and what they then believed to be right, and what they now know was right."

Comrade T. J. Gibson, for the Camp, accepted the Gavel in an eloquent impromptu speech that could not be furnished the Adjutant. [Page 41]

The Camp was then turned over to the Sons and Daughters, and Congressman Joe W. bailey delivered a splendid address on the winds of the war, that was listened to by an immense crowd.

Afternoon Session

The Camp was called to order by the Commander at 2:30 P.M.

General John C. Moore, of Mexia, was introduced and delivered an address especially to the members of the Camp.

The building committee reported work done on the Pavilion to the amount of $120.00. Report received, bill approved, and committee thanked and discharged.

The program was changed so as to elect officers this afternoon. Comrade Sam Love in a neat speech nominated Comrade T. J. Gibson and he was unanimously elected. The officers elected are as follows:

T. J. Gibson	Commander
W. H. Browder	1st Lieutenant Commander
W. R. Anderson	2nd Lieutenant Commander
J. H. Archer	3rd Lieutenant Commander
H. W. Williams	Adjutant
R. J. Bryant	Quartermaster
J. P. Cook	Surgeon
G. L. Jennings	Chaplain
J. W. Simmons	Treasurer
E. W. Williams	Officer of the Day
G. W. Kenney	Color Bearer
J. M. Deis	Bugler & Captain of Artillery

The committee appointed in 1897 to have a special law passed by the Legislature prohibiting the sale of spirituous liquors within two miles of the grounds was called on for a report. The committee [Page 42] reported that it was an oversight that the matter had not already been attended to, and promised to have a more satisfactory report at the next annual meeting. Report received and the committee granted one more year and the Camp officially requested the Legislature to pass the desired law.

It was suggested that, in the future, upon the death of a member of the Camp, the Adjutant write a short obituary and send it to the "Confederate Veteran" at Nashville for publication.

A motion by a Comrade was carried, That a reward be offered of from Ten [$10] to Twenty Five [$25] Dollars for evidence sufficient to convict any one depredating on the property of the Camp.

By request, Comrade Gibson read a letter from Madison, Wisconsin, concerning the graves of Confederate soldiers in that city, and the devotion of Mrs. Waterman, a Southern born lady, also of that city, in caring for said graves. After some remarks, the letter was referred to a committee composed of Comrades T. J. Gibson, W. H. Herring and W. H. Browder.

After some announcements, the Camp adjourned until Friday morning.

Third Day – Friday the 13th, Morning Session

The Camp was called to order by the Commander, and the Chaplain offered prayer. Comrade Gibson, for the committee to whom was referred the Madison, Wisconsin letter, submitted the following report: "To J. M. Storey, Commander: Your committee appointed to consider the letter written from Madison, Wisconsin to Comrade W. H. Herring by T. J. Davis, a Federal soldier and member of the G.A.R., beg leave to recommend the adoption of the following resolutions:

1st: We extend to Mr. Davis our sincere thanks for his interest in the matters referred to in his kind and appreciated letter, touching the graves of Confederate dead buried in his city, and through him, we extend the thanks of this Camp, individually and collectively, to his Comrades who wore the blue and fought for their convictions in the unhappy strife of 186-65, for the attention given the graves of our dead Comrades whose ashes repose in that far away land. We reciprocate their kindly feelings, and with them we join in thanks to an all wise Providence that we have lived to see the time when peace reigns over our once distracted land, and when the brave men of the Northland and the Southland can unite, in a tribute such as brave men alone can understand, to the valor of American soldiers who fought and suffered and gave their lives in defense of their convictions.

2nd: We join in a tribute to Mrs. Waterman, whose life was devoted to the cause of humanity, and we recommend that our Comrades contribute to a fund to place a monument over her grave.

3rd: That a copy of these resolutions be sent by the Adjutant to Mr. Davis."

The resolutions were unanimously adopted and several dollars were contributed to the fund.

Comrade Gibson then introduced Governor Jas. D. Sayers, who delivered a splendid speech to the Camp and the audience, after which, he received many congratulations. [Page 44] The Governor was made an honorary member of the Camp. State Treasurer Robbins also made a short speech.

Camp adjourned for dinner.

Afternoon Session

Camp called to order at 2:30 P.M. by the Commander.

On motion of Comrade Jennings, the committee on the Madison, Wisconsin letter was continued and Comrade P. O. Douglass added to it, and an invitation extended to all who felt inclined to contribute to the monument fund.

This being the hour for memorial services, Chaplain Jennings said it was the first time in the history of the Camp that one or more members had not died during the year, and, instead of a memorial service, he held a short thanks giving service, and prayed that the members of the Camp might continue to be spared.

Comrade Simmons moved a vote of thanks be tendered the young people of Tehuacana, Hubbard City, the old fiddlers, the Wortham Band, and the Mexia Minute Men for entertainments furnished.

The auditing committee reported as follows:

"To Camp Joe Johnston No. 94: We, the committee, auditing the books of your Adjutant and Treasurer by leave to report that we find receipts and disbursements properly made and checked, leaving $2.90 in General Fund in hands of your Adjutant and $77.33 of the General Fund in hands of Treasurer at the beginning [Page 45] of the present Reunion. Respectfully Submitted, R. M. Love, J. E. Parker, L. E. Camp [Com.]"

The report was adopted and committee discharged. The adjutant was allowed $25.00 and a ticket to the next Reunion at Memphis, Tennessee for his services.

Will A. Watkin's Music Co. of Dallas was thanks for loan of the Piano used during the Reunion.

The members of the Artillery Company in the Camp were tendered a vote of thanks for dressing up "Old Val Verde."

Comrade Gibson extended an invitation to all Confederates to join the Camp and several joined.

Nick Blaine, "the colored Confederate soldier" of Fairfield Camp was introduced and made a short speech to the Camp that was full of devotion to the "Loved Cause."

There being no further business, the Camp adjourned to meet at call of the Commander.

Official: H. W. Williams, Adjutant   J. M. Storey, Commander

[Page 46] **CALLED MEETING OF JOE JOHNSTON CAMP AUGUST 11th 1900**

By call of Commander T. J. Gibson, Joe Johnston Camp No. 94 assembled at the City Hall in Mexia on August 11th, 1900.

The purpose of the meeting was to wind up the business of the last Reunion year and to transact any other business that would be necessary for the welfare of the Camp.

The annual report of the Adjutant was read and, on motion, adopted, with instructions to have same published if the County papers would do so without charge to the Camp.

A motion carried that Comrade S. F. Bond be paid Three [$3.00] Dollars for work done on road from Mexia to Reunion grounds and Fifteen [$15.00] Dollars be paid to the Sons of Confederate Veterans for expenses incurred during Reunion.

On motion a committee was appointed to confer with Joe Echols and others owning land joining Camp grounds about leasing their land for a certain period. Committee: W. E. Doyle, H. W. Williams, T. J. Gibson.

There being no further business, the Camp adjourned subject to call of Commander.

Official: H. W. Williams, Adjutant   T. J. Gibson, Commander
[Page 47]

CALLED MEETING OF JOE JOHNSTON CAMP, MARCH 30th, 1901

By call of Commander Gibson, Camp Joe Johnston No. 94, assembled in Mexia on March 30th, 1901, and was called to order by the Commander.

The first business was appointing the time for the annual Reunion at Jack's Creek.

On motion, it was decided to hold the Reunion our days, commencing on Tuesday, July 30th, and ending Friday, August 2nd, 1901.

The following named Comrades were chosen as delegates to the State Reunion at Waco on May 8th and 9th, 1901: R. J. Bryant, H. A. Boyd, C. J. Bower, M. H. Clark, L. E. Camp, W. E. Doyle, H. W. Gray, T. J. Gibson, G. L. Jennings, B. D. Keeling, J. C. C. Keys, M. Kaufman, S. B. Love, M. L. McDonald, R. E. Steele, J. W. Thompson, E. B. Wood, C. L. Watson, R. P. Ward, H. W. Williams and as many more as wish to attend will be given certificates as delegates. The delegates and alternates to the Memphis Reunion on May 28th, 29th and 30th, are as follows: Delegates: J. C. Anglin, W. M. Barton, M. H. Clark, G. L. Jennings, J. W. Thompson, O. Wiley and H. W. Williams. Alternates: B. W. Allen, W. E. Doyle, T. J. Gibson, J. S. Jolley, M. L. McDonald, J. D. Therrell, and J. W. Thomas.

The various other committees were appointed as follows:

> Privilege Committee: R. J. Bryant, H. A. Boyd, J. S. Groover, J. M. Deis, Rado Steele, W. H. Browder and A. J. Burleson.
> Invitation Committee: R. E. Steele, C. L. Watson, W. E. Doyle, B. F. Ouzts and W. P. Brown.
> Locating Committee: J. W. Thompson, J. W. McKinney, H. C. Joiner, W. A. Buckner, J. W. Nash and W. D. Frazier.
> Concert Committee: Jno. W. Simmons.

On motion, the Quartermaster was instructed to prepare the grounds and spring for the coming Reunion.

A communication from the Corresponding Secretary [Rev. J. M. Newburn] of the [Page 48] Baptist Missionary Association of Texas was received, requesting the use of the Reunion grounds about the first part of August to hold its annual meeting. The request was readily granted.

The annual Confederate picnic was set for Friday, May 3rd, to which everybody was invited. There being no further business the Camp adjourned.

Official: H. W. Williams, Adjutant   T. J. Gibson, Commander
[Page 49]

MINUTES OF THE 13TH ANNUAL REUNION OF JOE JOHNSTON CAMP NO. 94, U.C.V.'S HELD ON JULY 30TH AND 31ST AND AUGUST 1ST AND 2ND 1901
Written by Major N. P. Houx, Secretary of Adjutant
First Day – Tuesday July 30th

At 9:30 A.M. assistant bugler, G. Howard Fields, assembled the Camp by bugle call, and, after music by the Hubbard City Band and a general hand shaking, at 9:45 o'clock Commander T. J. Gibson called the Camp to order, and Chaplain G. L. Jennings offered prayer.

The Adjutant then called the roll and quite a large number answered "Here." On motion of Comrade C. L. Watson, the reading of the Minutes of the last meeting was dispensed with.

The Adjutant reappointed Major N. P. Houx as Secretary to assist in keeping the records of the meeting.

Commander Gibson then delivered the annual address of welcome, and asked everyone present to have a good time. Col. Matt. Pearson of McKinney was then introduced and made a short talk to the Camp, after which the Camp adjourned for dinner.

There was no session in the afternoon, as the Sons and Daughters occupied the stage.

Second Day – Wednesday July 31st

The Camp was called to order by the Commander at 9 o'clock, A.M.

The Commander announced as the Auditing Committee, Comrades W. P. Brown, Sam B. Love, and P. O. Douglass. Motion by Comrade J. W. Simmons, that a committee be appointed to wait on keepers [Page 50] of stands and see that they give good service. Carried, and Commander appointed as said committee Comrades L. E. Camp, Rado Steele and S. B. Love.

Comrade Simmons suggested that the Camp parade Friday morning at 8 o'clock, and the suggestion was adopted.

The Commander stated that General Van Zandt could not be with us on account of sickness in his family, but had Col. Goodman, Inspector General on his Staff, who made a business talk to the Camp concerning the next General Reunion to be held at Dallas next My and the adoption of a uniform.

Congressman S. W. T. Lannam was then introduced and entertained the Camp and a large audience for about two hours, - making a splendid speech.

Adjourned for dinner.

Afternoon

In the afternoon there was an address by Col. Burton, but no business was transacted.

Third Day – Thursday, August 1st

Camp was called to order at 9 o'clock by the Commander and prayer was offered by the Chaplain.

Comrade W. H. Herring moved to appoint a committee to have retreats built for Ladies, which motion prevailed, and Comrades Herring, C. H. F. Wood and Rado Steele were appointed as said committee. It was decided to reserve the jungles along the river west of the spring for said retreats. Comrade W. H. Browder suggested that the Camp build its own water works, and moved that a [Page 51] committee be appointed to consider it. Carried. Committee: Bryant, Browder and Simmons. Comrade Browder in the chair.

Commander T. J. Gibson brought up the matter of uniforms for the Camp, and the matter was discussed at considerable length. Commander in the chair. Comrade Browder moved that the Camp adopt a gray uniform, but, after more discussion and several amendments, the matter was tabled.

Comrade Camp's little daughter was introduced and sang a pretty Confederate song. Comrade Ouzts brought up the question of rendering financial aid to Dallas in entertaining the General Reunion next spring, and Comrade Strother, of Dallas, made a few remarks that any aid that might be offered would be gratefully received. After some discussion and several motions, it was finally decided to defer the matter until the next business meeting at Mexia.

The Commander announced that Gen'l. Roller had not arrived and introduced Major Dillard, of Meridian, who made a short talk. Adjourned for dinner.

Afternoon

Camp was called to order by the Commander at 2 o'clock, and Comrade Anderson was called to the chair. Commander Gibson then received the work performed by the Adjutant and the Quartermaster in the interest of this Reunion and recommended that those officers be compensated for their services. Comrade S. B. Love moved [Page 52] to pay each the sum of Twenty Five [$25.00] Dollars. An amendment was offered to pay each Fifty [$50.00] Dollars, which was carried.

Mr. Alphonso Steele, a veteran of the battle of San Jacinto, was present and had a seat on the platform.

Comrade S. B. Love moved that the Camp attend the next General Reunion in a body, and that the Commander appoint a committee to make the necessary arrangements. Motion was adopted, and the Commander appointed the Quartermaster, the Adjutant and W. H. Browder as said committee.

The Auditing Committee made the following report, which was adopted: "To the Commander of Joe Johnston Camp No. 94, U.C.V.'s: We, your committee, appointed to audit the books of the Adjutant and Treasurer, beg leave to submit the following report: We have carefully examined said books and find them correct in every particular; showing a balance on hand in Treasurer's office of Seventy Eight and 97/100 Dollars. We further state, that the officer's books are kept in a neat and businesslike manner. W. P. Brown, P. O. Douglass, S. B. Love [Com.]"

The uniform question was again taken up and Comrade Simmons moved to recommend the Five [$5.00] Dollar gray uniform and that all who desire to buy the uniform can do so, and those who do not, need not do so. Motion to table the question was last. [Page 53] Original motion was then carried.

Comrade Carroll suggested that some old soldier be employed to live on the grounds and take care of the Camp property, and made a motion to that effect. Comrade W. P. Brown in the chair. Comrade C. L. Watson offered a substitute that the matter be left to a committee of three, with the Quartermaster as chairman and they report to the Camp with recommendations. Carried, and the Commander appointed as said committee Comrades R. J. Bryant, J. M. Storey and C. L. Watson. Adjourned.

Fourth Day – Friday, August 2nd

Parade at 8 o'clock, after which the Camp was called to order, and Nick Blaine, the colored Confederate soldier, of Fairfield was introduced and made a talk.

The Commander extended thanks to the unknown donor of a pretty bouquet placed on the Commander's table. The Chaplain asked that the Program be changed so as to elect officers at the morning session, and hold memorial services at 2 o'clock, P.M. On motion of Comrade Watson, the change was made.

Comrade H. A. Boyd moved that a committee of three be appointed to look after the grave of Comrade W. H. Adams, the first Adjutant of this Camp, and report to the Commander the amount of money necessary to put the grave in repair. Carried, and Comrades C. L. Watson, H. A. Boyd and H. W. Williams appointed as said committee.

On motion of Comrade Simmons, a vote [Page 54] of thanks was tendered the young people of Thornton, Tehuacana, Groesbeck and Mexia for the entertainments given during this Reunion.

Comrade Gibson moved that a vote of thanks be tendered Major N. P. Houx for the able manner in which he had reported the proceedings of this Reunion, and, through him, the Dallas News for publishing said reports, which motion prevailed.

The Camp then proceeded to the election of officers.

Commander Gibson placed the name of Comrade W. P. Brown before the Camp for Commander, which was seconded by Comrade C. L. Watson, and he was elected by acclamation. The officers for the ensuing year are as follows:

W. P. Brown	Commander
S. B. Love	1st Lieutenant Commander
R. E. Steele	2nd Lieutenant Commander
P. O. Douglass	3rd Lieutenant Commander
H. W. Williams	Adjutant
R. J. Bryant	Quartermaster
Dr. J. P. Cook	Surgeon
Rev. G. L. Jennings	Chaplain
J. W. Simmons	Treasurer
E. W. Williams	Officer of the Day
G. W. Kenney	Color Bearer
J. M. Deis	Bugler and Captain of Artillery

Commander Gibson then introduced the newly elected Commander, who thanked the Camp for the honor.

The Commander then thanked the members for the support they had given him during his term of office and, also, thanked the members of the "Mexia Minute Men" for their kindness in acting as guards and assisting in keeping order in the Camp. Comrade R. E. Steele moved to appoint a committee of three to approve all bills before they are paid. The motion was adopted, and Comrade C. L. Watson, J. S. Groover and L. E. Camp were appointed on said committee, after which the Camp adjourned for dinner.

Afternoon

Camp was called to order at 2 o'clock and turned over to Chaplain G. L. Jennings, who conducted Memorial Services, reporting seven deaths since the last Reunion as follows: Comrades N. L. Waller, John Thomas, Wm. Henry, J. E. McDonald, T. A. Germany, T. M. Crawford and L. J. Farrar. Appropriate remarks were made by the Chaplain and Comrades Gibson, Watson, Douglass and Lewis, and a page in the Minute Book on ____ set apart for each of the dead Comrades. Then, after a general hand shaking, while a duet was being played on the Piano by the blind wife and little daughter of a Comrade, the Camp adjourned sine die.

Official: H. W. Williams, Adjutant   T. J. Gibson, Commander
[Page 56]

CALLED MEETING OF JOE JOHNSTON CAMP NO. 94, AUGUST 31st, 1901

By call of Commander Gibson Joe Johnston Camp No. 94 met at the City Hall in Mexia on Saturday, August 31st, 1901, for the purpose of winding up the business of the Reunion held in 1901, and for anything else that might be for the welfare of the Camp.

The Adjutant, Quartermaster and Treasurer's reports were read and adopted. The Financial report showed $1173.47 collected from all sources and $724.49 expended for all purposes to date, leaving a balance on hand of $448.98.

The Quartermaster report showed the property in his hands to be worth $76.90. On motion, the bill of $17.00 for decorating the Car that went to Memphis was allowed. A motion was carried that a committee of three be appointed to look after the Deed to the last 26 acres of land purchased from the Mexia Estate. Committee: T. J. Gibson, H. W. Williams and J. W. Simmons.

The committee on getting some one to take charge of the Reunion grounds made the following report: "We, the committee, on getting some body to live on the Reunion grounds would respectfully report that we find that the Camp has some $400.00 on hand. That we recommend that none but a Confederate be given the place, and would recommend that the Camp do not expend more than $150.00 for that purpose. R. J. Bryant, J. M. Storey, C. L. Watson [Com.]"

The committee to look after the grave of Capt. W. H. Adams recommended that it be put in good repair with the view, in the near future, of raising a suitable shaft to his memory.

Commander Gibson, in appropriate remarks, turned over the management of the Camp to the new Commander W. P. Brown.

There being no further business, the Camp adjourned until called together by the Commander.

Official: H. W. Williams, Adjutant   W. P. Brown, Commander
[Page 58]

CALLED MEETING OF JOE JOHNSTON CAMP NO. 94, FEBRUARY 22nd, 1902

By call of Commander W. P. Brown, Joe Johnston Camp No. 94, U.C.V.'s, assembled at Mexia on Saturday, February 22nd, 1902. The Camp was called to order by the Commander and the first order of business was appointing the time for the next Reunion.

The time was set for four days, beginning Tuesday, July 15th and ending Friday, July 18th, 1902.

The Commander appointed the various committees as follows:

Privilege Committee: R. J. Bryant, Rado Steele, J. S. Groover, W. H. Browder, A. J. Burleson and H. A. Boyd.
Invitation Committee: T. J. Gibson, W. E. Doyle, C. L. Watson, S. S. Walker, J. W. Thompson, R. E. Steele and Dr. B. F. Ouzts.
Locating Committee: H. C. Joiner, J. W. McKinney, W. A. Buckner and W. D. Frazier.
Concert Committee: John W. Simmons.

Delegates to the General Reunion at Dallas: W. P. Brown, J. M. Storey, C. L. Watson, H. A. Boyd, J. W. Thompson, R. J. Bryant and J. W. McKinney. Alternates: Rado Steele, H. C. Joiner, C. H. F. Wood, S. S. Walker, W. L. Mallard, T. J. Gibson and Dr. E. B. Wood.

Various subjects were discussed for the good of the Camp, after which a motion prevailed to adjourn.

Official: H. W. Williams, Adjutant   W. P. Brown, Major Commanding

[Page 59]

MINUTES OF THE 14TH ANNUAL REUNION OF JOE JOHNSTON CAMP NO. 97, U.C.V.'S HELD ON JULY 15TH TO 18TH 1902

First Day – Tuesday, July 15th

The Camp was called to order by Commander W. P. Brown at 10 o'clock, and the Chaplain being absent, divine blessing was invoked by the Commander.

On motion, the roll call and reading of the minutes of the last Reunion was dispensed with until Wednesday morning, on account of the inclemency of the weather.

The Commander delivered a short address of welcome and requested Comrade C. L. Watson to deliver the main address, which he did in a very interesting manner.

By request, Miss Beulah Reagan Stewart, daughter of Comrade W. L. Stewart, recited a beautiful piece of welcome, after which several members of the Camp made short talks.

Miss Kate Daffan, State Sponsor, being present was heartily welcomed by the members of the Camp, especially by our Bachelor Comrade Sam B. Love, who was detailed by the Commander to see that she had a good time while at the Reunion, which he proceeded to do with great pleasure to himself, and, we hope, to the entire satisfaction of the fair recipient of his attentions.

Camp adjourned to 2 o'clock.

Afternoon – 2 o'clock

Camp called to order by the Commander, and adjourned to 9 o'clock Wednesday morning, and the afternoon was used by the Sons and Daughters of Veterans.

[Page 60]

Wednesday Morning, July 16th

Camp called to order by Commander Brown at 9 o'clock. The Chaplain being absent, divine blessing was invoked by Mr. W. F. Batchelor of Groesbeck. The roll was called and the minutes of the last Reunion read and adopted.

On motion of Comrade J. W. Simmons, a committee was appointed to see that the several privilege men render good service to customers. Committee: Rado Steele, L. E. Camp and C. H. F. Wood.

The Commander appointed as Auditing committee, Comrades T. J. Gibson, S. S. Walker and B. W. Allen.

Judge John W. Stevens, of Hillsboro, made a very interesting talk to the ladies on the trials and hardships they endured during the war, and requesting the young people to see that a true history of those times be written, and to keep the memory of their sires green.

The Division Commander, General Van Zandt, was expected to be present and address the Camp, but, on account of serious sickness in his family, he could not be with us, but wrote the Camp a very nice letter of regrets, and sent it by Mr. W. P. Lane, a devoted young Confederate, who made the Camp, and especially the young people, an exceedingly interesting talk on the causes of the war between the States. Rev. E. P. West, of Waco, made a short and pleasant talk, mostly to the young folks, about the necessity of being educated on the above mentioned lines. Mr. Thomas P. Stone, of Waco, Commander in Chief of the Sons [Page 61] of Confederate Veterans, made a fine talk to the young men, urging them to organize a Camp here and stating that such organization would not interfere with the local order of Sons and Daughters of Veterans. A Camp was organized, and it is the sincere wish of every member of Joe Johnston Camp, that, when we all pass away, the Sons will keep up the organization of their fathers.

On motion of Comrade Gibson, the thanks of this Camp were returned to Miss Daffan and Messrs. Stone, Lane and West for their several talks.

Miss Daffan, replying, stated that they thought the thanks should be on their side.

Camp adjourned for dinner.

Afternoon 2 o'clock

Camp, reassembled. There being no business to transact, the Camp adjourned to 9 o'clock Thursday morning.

Thursday Morning, July 17th

Camp assembled at 9 o'clock, and the Chaplain being absent, prayer was offered by Judge J. W. Stevens of Hillsboro. The building committee reported that they had built a small stone house on the grounds, and, also, had bought an additional tract of land for the purpose of the keeper of the Camp making a living on. Report adopted, committee continued, and, on motion, a further appropriation of $150.00 was made to build a small residence for the occupant of the grounds.

The committee appointed to look after the grave of Capt. Adams, our first Adjutant, reported progress and the report was adopted and committee continued. [Page 62] The same investigating committee on payment of bills by the Camp was continued.

At 10 o'clock Capt. James D. Shaw, of Waco, delivered a very interesting address and was followed by Gen'l. Felix Robertson, also of Waco, by one equally interesting. Both speeches were heard with great pleasure by a large audience.

Adjourned to 2 o'clock.

Afternoon

Camp reassembled at 2 o'clock.

The Daughters of the Confederacy held a short meeting and listened to an admirable address by Miss A. A. Dunavan, the head of the order in Texas, which was full of deep thought and eloquent words, after which, Comrade Gibson delivered an address to the ladies on the hardships they and their mothers endured during war times, which was rendered in his usual eloquent manner.

The Camp elected officers for the ensuing term as follows:

W. H. Browder	Commander
P. O. Douglass	1st Lieutenant Commander
R. E. Steele	2nd Lieutenant Commander
Jno. E. Parker	3rd Lieutenant Commander
H. W. Williams	Adjutant
R. J. Bryant	Quartermaster
Dr. W. F. Starley	Surgeon
Rev. G. L. Jennings	Chaplain
J. W. Simmons	Treasurer
E. W. Williams	Officer of the Day
L. E. Camp	Color Bearer
J. M. Deis	Bugler
H. W. Gray	Chief of Artillery

On motion, all Comrades who wished to attend the State Reunion at Dallas on July 30th was elected as delegates. [Page 63]By motion, the Camp voted $50.00 each to the Adjutant and Quartermaster for their services.

The auditing committee reported as follows: "To W. P. Brown, Commander. We, your committee appointed to examine the books and accounts of the officers of this Camp, make the following report: We have carefully examined the accounts of the Adjutant, Quartermaster and Treasurer and have compared same with the vouchers required to be produced and we find the accounts of these officers show the following balances: In Bank to credit of J. W. Simmons, Treasurer $118.28; In hands of Adjutant not paid over $6.95; July 17th, 1902 To credit of Camp $125.23. We further report that we find the books of these officers neatly and correctly kept. Respectfully Submitted, Thos. J. Gibson, B. W. Allen, S. S. Walker [Com.]"

The report was adopted and committee discharged. Camp adjourned to 9 o'clock Friday morning.

Friday Morning, July 18th

Camp assembled at 9 o'clock and was called to order by the Commander. Prayer by Chaplain Jennings, after which there was a parade by "the old boys" up and down the avenues led by the Band and followed by "Young America" in full bloom.

After the parade Camp reassembled. A motion prevailed ordering the development of water on the grounds at any reasonable cost, and a committee of five Comrades was appointed to carry out the order. Committee: C. T. Harris, S. B. Love, [Page 64] Rado Steele, C. H. F. Wood and J. W. Simmons. The committee was instructed to report at the first called meeting in Mexia.

The water committee of the last Reunion rendered its report on the contract made with the parties to furnish water to the Camp. The report was adopted with the distinct understanding that the water company's contract would not interfere with watering horses in the Navasota river or digging wells or buying water any where in Camp for family use.

A bill for $36.80 for additional water pipes was allowed. Camp adjourned to 2:30 o'clock.

Afternoon, 2:30 o'clock

Camp reassembled. On motion of Comrade Simmons, the thanks of the Camp were extended to all the young folks who assisted in entertaining the crowd. Thanks of the Camp were returned to Harry Steen for the donation of a beautiful Confederate flag. Misses A. A. Dunavant and Kate Daffan were made honorary members of the Camp. On motion of our gallant Comrade S. B. Love, all Daughters of the Confederacy within the jurisdiction of this Camp were made members of it. The electric light bill of $50.00 was allowed. At 3:30 o'clock memorial services were held by Chaplain Jennings. Comrade J. W. Moss, of Kosse, was the only member of the Camp reported dead since our last meeting. The thanks of the Camp were returned to the Hubbard Band, and also to Misses Dunavant and Daffan. There being no further business to transact, the Camp adjourned, after which a cordial hand shaking took place among the Comrades and the audience.

Official: H. W. Williams, Adjutant   W. P. Brown, Major Commanding
[Page 65]

CALLED MEETING OF JOE JOHNSTON CAMP NO. 94, AUGUST 16th, 1902

By call of Commander W. P. Brown, Joe Johnston Camp No. 94, U.C.V. assembled at the City Hall in Mexia on August 16th, 1902, for the purpose of winding up the business of the past Reunion and turning over the Camp to the new officers.

The Commander and Lieutenant Commanders being absent, on motion, Comrade C. L. Watson was called on to preside. The report of the investigating committee on bills payable was adopted.

The building and water committees reports were received and committees continued. Building Committee: R. J. Bryant, J. M. Storey and C. L. Watson. Water Committee: C. T. Harris, S. B. Love, Rado Steele, C. H. F. Wood and J. W. Simmons. The new Commander, W. H. Browder, being present the Camp was turned over to him and, there being no further business, on motion, the Camp adjourned to the call of the new Commander.

Official: H. W. Williams, Adjutant W. H. Browder, Major Commanding

[Page 66] **CALLED MEETING OF JOE JOHNSTON CAMP NO. 94, FEBRUARY 28TH, 1903**

By call of Commander W. H. Browder, Joe Johnston Camp No. 94, U.C.W., met in Mexia on Saturday, February 28th, 1903 On motion, the time for holding the annual Reunion was set for August 4th to 7th, 1903. All members of the Camp who desired to attend, were elected as delegates to the State Reunion to be held at Sherman. [Date not named yet]

The following named Comrades were elected as delegates and alternates to the General Reunion at New Orleans on May 19th to 22nd, 1903. Delegates: W. H. Browder, S. S. Walker, Rado Steele, Dr. W. F. Moore, M. H. Clark, J. M. Deis, J. W. Thompson and P. O. Douglass. Alternates: Rev. G. L. Jennings, S. B. Love, Dr. J. P. Cook, J. C. C. Keys, J. W. McKinney, A. B. Allison, J. G. Carroll and M. L. McDonald.

The various committees were appointed as follows:

Privilege: R. J. Bryant, H. C. Joiner, C. L. Watson, Rado Steele, M. L. McDonald, J. M. Storey, J. C. C. Keys, H. A. Boyd and Dr. W. F. Moore.
Invitation: T. J. Gibson, S. S. Walker, R. E. Steele, W. F. Roberts and Dr. J. P. Cook.
Locating: N. T. Popejoy, C. J. Bower, A. W. Burford, S. C. Ingram and W. D. Frazier.
Concert: John W. Simmons.

On motion, Miss Nina Watson was elected Camp Sponsor to go to New Orleans, with expenses paid by the Camp. A motion carried, that the program and advertising privilege be controlled exclusively by the Camp and Comrade Bryant be appointed to attend to it and make his report at the Reunion.

A motion prevailed, also, that the watermelon privilege be controlled exclusively [Page 67] by the Camp, and all parties who wish to sell melons will apply to the Quartermaster for permits to do so.

There being no further business, on motion, the Camp adjourned.

Official: H. W. Williams, Adjutant W. H. Browder, Major Commanding
[Page 68]

MINUTES OF THE 15TH ANNUAL REUNION OF JOE JOHNSTON CAMP NO. 94, U.C.V.'S HELD ON AUGUST 4TH TO 7TH, 1903

First Day – Tuesday August 4th

The Camp opened by the Band playing "Nearer my God to Thee," and prayer by Comrade W. D. Frazier, the Chaplain being absent.

On motion, calling the roll and reading the minutes was postponed till Wednesday morning.

On behalf of Commander Browder, Comrade Gibson delivered a most eloquent address of welcome.

Several Comrades made short impromptu speeches which was enjoyed by all present. The following resolution by Comrades Gibson and Simmons was offered and adopted:

Resolved, That this Camp endorses Judge Rodgers' speech at the New Orleans Reunion as being true history, and recommend its careful study by all who seek the truth. Resolved further, That we endorse the action of the State Division U.C.V.'s, in recommending that it be appended to the school history of Texas and taught in the public schools.

On motion of Comrade Watson, all Confederate Veterans on the grounds were made aids to the Officer of the Day. Camp adjourned for dinner.

Afternoon 2:30 o'clock

Camp reassembled. Comrades L. E. Camp, H. C. Joiner and W. D. Frazier were appointed Auditing Committee.

The water committee appointed at [Page 69] the Reunion in 1902 reported as follows: "We, your committee, appointed at last Reunion, beg leave to report that we have a well of good water at a cost complete of $107.55. Rado Steele, S. B. Love, C. H. F. Wood, J. W. Simmons [Com.]"

The Camp adjourned to 9 o'clock Wednesday morning.

Second Day. Wednesday August 5th

Camp opened by Band playing "Nearer my God to Thee." Invocation by Comrade W. D. Frazier. The roll was called and minutes of last Reunion read and adopted.

On motion of Comrade Simmons, a committee was appointed by the Commander to prepare a burial service for the Camp. Committee: J. W. Simmons, Rado Steele and T. J. Gibson.

At 11 o'clock, Col. J. Q. Chenoweth, Superintendent of the Confederate Home at Austin, delivered an eloquent address, after which the Camp adjourned for dinner.

Afternoon 2 o'clock

Camp reassembled, and Hon. L. S. Schluter addressed the audience, after which the United Daughters of the Confederacy bestowed crosses of honor on several of the Veterans.

Capt. W. H. Richardson of Austin, the first Commander of the Camp, being present, was called on and made his old Comrades a short talk.

Camp adjourned to Thursday, 9 o'clock.

[Page 70] **Third Day. Thursday, August 6th**

Camp assembled at 9 o'clock and was opened with prayer by Chaplain.

The following resolution was adopted: Resolved, That the quartermaster be requested to state to all parties concerned that any camper, or other person, has the right to get water from any source they see fit and that Joe Johnston Camp assumes all responsibility.

A motion was adopted that no privileges be located on the South side of Lee Avenue between the pavilion and Bennett street.

The election of officers for the ensuing year resulted as follows:

H. A. Boyd	Commander
W. D. Frazier	1st Lieutenant Commander
J. S. Groover	2nd Lieutenant Commander
J. W. McKinney	3rd Lieutenant Commander
H. W. Williams	Adjutant
Rado Steele	Quartermaster
Dr. W. F. Starley	Surgeon
Rev. G. L. Jennings	Chaplain
J. W. Simmons	Treasurer
H. C. Joiner	Officer of the Day
L. E. Camp	Color Bearer
J. M. Deis	Bugler
W. M. Barton	Chief of Artillery

A motion to pay the Adjutant and Quartermaster $50.00 each was carried. An invitation to the members of the Camp and their wives by Best and Stevens to a treat of lemonade was accepted with thanks.

At 11 o'clock, Gen'l. Jno. E. Roller of Virginia delivered a very interesting address on "Stonewall Jackson and his men," [Page 71] after which the Camp adjourned to Friday morning 9 o'clock.

Fourth Day. Friday, August 7th

Camp assembled at 9 o'clock, and was called to order by the Commander, and all the Veterans in Camp paraded up and down Lee Avenue, lead by the Kirk band and Sponsor and Maids of Honor and followed by the Prairie Grove band with appropriate music by each band.

After the parade a business meeting was held. The following resolution was offered and carried: Resolved 1st, That $25, or so much there of as may be necessary, be appropriated for the purpose of digging a pit for barbecuing meats. Resolved 2nd, That this pit is to be used by Confederate Veterans only, and they are not to barbecue meats for sale, but for their own private use. Resolved 3rd, That any Confederate Veteran who wishes to, can, by paying for it, have his own meat barbecued at this pit.

The Commander appointed a committee consisting of Comrades Watson, Camp and Groover to investigate all bills to be paid by the Camp. Camp adjourned to 2 o'clock. [Page 72]

Afternoon 2 o'clock

The following resolution was offered by Comrades Gibson and Simmons and carried: Resolved, that the thanks of this Camp are extended to Col. J. Q. Chenoweth, Hon. L. S. Schluter and Gen'l. Jno. E. Roller for the excellent addresses delivered by them during this Reunion and they each be elected honorary members of this Camp.

The auditing committee made the following report: "We, your auditing committee, appointed to examine the books and accounts of the Adjutant and Treasurer, beg leave to submit the following report: We have carefully investigated each department and find the books of each carefully and correctly kept. We further find the following, to wit: Balance in hands of Adjutant $6.20; Amount overdrawn at Bank $29.25. Respectfully submitted by L. E. Camp, H. C. Joiner, W. D. Frazier [Com.]"

On motion of Comrade Gibson, the thanks of the Camp were returned to the U.D.C.'s for their interest in, and bestowing of crosses of honor on, several Veterans. By motion, the Camp thanked the Sponsor and Maids of Honor for participating in the parade, the young people of the County for their concerts, W. D. Pittman for the phonograph exhibition, Best and Stevens for treating the Veterans to cold drinks, the Kirk and Prairie Grove bands for their services, and the people in general for their good behavior while on the grounds. [Page 73]

The dead Comrades reported since the last Reunion were: W. A. Buckner, M. Kaufman, R. M. Love and J. M. Rambo. Appropriate remarks in memory of each were made by the Chaplain and Comrades Bryant, Simmons, Gibson and Watson.

After memorial services, there being no further business, the Camp adjourned, and was closed with prayer by the Chaplain.

Official: H. W. Williams, Adjutant   W. H. Browder, Major Commanding
[Page 74]

CALLED MEETING OF JOE JOHNSTON CAMP NO. 94, AUGUST 29TH, 1903

By call of Commander Browder, Joe Johnston Camp No. 94 assembled at the City Hall in Mexia, on August 29th, 1903, for the purpose of winding up the business of the last Reunion year. Commander Browder being absent, Comrade A. E. Steele, the next in command, presided. The report of the quartermaster on advertising the Program was adopted. By his report, after all the expenses were deducted there remained a balance of $90.90, and, on motion, the Camp donated $45.45 to the Quartermaster as his salary for doing the work.

The Treasurer reported $801.05 as received, and $522.66 as paid out, leaving a balance in the Treasury at date of $278.39.

The committee on burial service, appointed at the last Reunion, made their report, which was adopted. The committee was instructed to have 200 copies printed and send one copy to each active member of the Camp.

On motion, Comrade Bryant was added to the building committee.

The time of the present occupant of the Reunion grounds being about to expire, the camp requested that all applicants for the position see the building committee, consisting of Comrades Rado Steele, C. L. Watson, J. M. Storey and R. J. Bryant.

There being no further business, Comrade R. E. Steele turned the Camp over to the new Commander, Major H. A. Boyd, who, on motion, adjourned the meeting subject to future call of the Commander.

Official: H. W. Williams, Adjutant   H. A. Boyd, Major Commanding
[Page 75]

CALLED MEETING OF JOE JOHNSTON CAMP NO. 94, FEBRUARY 27TH, 1904

By call of Commander Boyd, Joe Johnston Camp No. 94 assembled in Mexia on February 27th, 1904.

On motion, the time set for the Reunion was July 26th to 29th, 1904. All Comrades who wished to attend the State and General Reunions to be held at Temple, Texas and Nashville, Tennessee respectively, were elected as delegates.

The Commander appointed the various committees as follows:

> Privilege Committee: Rado Steele, J. M. Deis, W. B. Lewis, W. H. Browder, C. L. Watson, W. P. Brown, J. S. Groover and I. T. Mahoney.
> Invitation Committee: R. E. Steele, T. J. Gibson, W. H. Herring, W. E. Doyle, J. W. Thompson and A. J. Burleson.
> Locating Committee: E. W. Williams and H. C. Joiner, with power to select their assistants.
> Concert Committee: J. W. Simmons.
> Flag Committee: L. E. Camp, R. J. Bryant, J. W. Simmons and H. A. Boyd. On motion, the Camp appropriated the sum of $25.00 and instructed the committee to buy the material and have the flag made at home.
> Cannon Committee: J. M. Deis, L. E. Camp, W. M. Barton and H. W. Gray.

There being no further business the Camp adjourned.

Official: H. W. Williams, Adjutant   H. A. Boyd, Major Commanding
[Page 76]

MINUTES OF THE 16TH ANNUAL REUNION OF JOE JOHNSTON CAMP NO. 94, U.C.V'S HELD ON JULY 26TH TO 29TH, 1904

First Day – Tuesday, July 26th

The Camp assembled at 10 o'clock and was opened with prayer by Comrade Frazier.

On behalf of Commander Boyd, Comrade Gibson delivered an eloquent address of welcome.

The roll call and reading of the minutes of the last Reunion was postponed until Wednesday morning.

There being no further business to transact, the Camp took recess till 2 o'clock.

Afternoon 2 o'clock

Camp reassembled at 2 o'clock, and there being no business, adjourned to 9:30 o'clock Wednesday morning. The afternoon was turned over to the young people.

Second Day – Wednesday, July 27th

Camp assembled at 9:30 o'clock, and was opened with prayer by Comrade Frazier. The roll was called and the minutes of last Reunion read and adopted.

At 10:30 o'clock, Colonel Frank Rainey of Fort Worth delivered an interesting address and was followed by Judge Cummings of the same city by an equally interesting one.

After the addresses, Camp adjourned to Thursday morning.

Third Day – Thursday, July 28th

Camp opened at 9 o'clock. Comrades S. B. Love, Dr. B. F Ouzts and James A. Wright were appointed auditing committee.

Comrade J. W. Simmons offered the following: [Page 77] Resolved, That Joe Johnston Camp No. 94, Mexia, Texas, is in full sympathy with, commend and approve the action of the Daughters of the Confederacy, Texas Division, in their efforts to have the birthday, June 3rd, of Jefferson Davis, made a legal holiday.

A motion carried that the Adjutant and Quartermaster be allowed $50.00 each for their services.

A motion by Comrade Watson prevailed, that the sum of $3.00 per month, until further ordered, be appropriated for the benefit of Mrs. Stewart, widow of Uncle Billy Stewart, who made the last successful fight of the Confederate war and destroyed the opposing forces.

The Camp went into the election of officers which resulted as follows:

S. B. Love	Commander
R. E. Steele	1st Lieutenant Commander
W. B. Lewis	2nd Lieutenant Commander
G. W. Lee	3rd Lieutenant Commander
H. W. Williams	Adjutant
Rado Steele	Quartermaster
Dr. J. P. Cook	Surgeon
Rev. G. L. Jennings	Chaplain

J. W. Simmons	Treasurer
H. C. Joiner	Officer of the Day
L. E. Camp	Color Bearer
J. M. Deis	Bugler
Adam Shriver	Captain of Artillery

There being no further business, Camp adjourned to Friday morning.

Fourth Day – Friday, July 29th

Camp assembled at 9 o'clock and was opened with prayer by Comrade Frazier, after which there was a parade by the Confederate Veterans and the [Page 78] United Daughters of the Confederacy. After the parade the Camp went into a business meeting.

The auditing committee reported as follows: "To the Commander and Comrades of Joe Johnston Camp No. 94: We, your auditing committee, beg leave to report that we have made a careful examination of the Adjutant's and Treasurer's books and find them neatly and correctly kept, and that the finances of the Camp are in good condition, and that there is a balance in the Treasury of $101.39 and in the hands of the Adjutant $11.90, making a total of $113.29. S. B. Love, Jas. A. Wright, B. F. Ouzts [Com.]"

The report was adopted and committee discharged.

A motion by Comrade Watson was carried, that the Privilege committee to be appointed in the future be empowered to take into consideration the advisability of making any improvements that may be necessary for the good of the Camp.

A motion by Comrade Gibson was carried that $10.00 be appropriated to set out shade trees just East of the pavilion. Camp took recess at 3:30 o'clock.

Afternoon 3:30 o'clock

Camp reassembled at 3:30 o'clock. Memorial services were held for Comrades J. P. Hickman, Dr. W. F. Moore, Melvin Herring, A. A. Jayne and Dr. J. S. Michard.

The thanks of the Camp were [Page 79] extended to the U.D.C. for the beautiful flag presented to the Camp, the crosses of honor bestowed and for their general assistance to the U.C.V.'s, with the hope that they may continue to meet with us and cheer us by their presence.

The thanks of the Camp were, also, extended W. D. Pitman for graphaphone, J. B. Best for treats, Goggan Piano Co. for use of instrument, Prairie Grove Band for its excellent music, Company G 3rd Regiment for their drill and the people generally for the good behavior while on the grounds.

There being no further business, the Camp adjourned to meet again at call of the Commander.

Official: H. W. Williams, Adjutant   H. A. Boyd, Major Commanding
[Page 80]

CALLED MEETING OF JOE JOHNSTON CAMP NO. 94, FEBRUARY 25TH, 1905

By call of Commander Love, Joe Johnston Camp No. 94, assembled at Mexia on February 25th, 1905. The commander being absent on account of sickness, Lieutenant Commander, R. E. Steele, presided.

The time fixed for the next Reunion was July 18th to 21st, 1905.

The following committees were appointed:

Privilege: Rado Steele, C. L. Watson, J. M. Deis, J. S. Groover, W. H. Browder, W. P. Brown, W. B. Lewis, W. R. Anderson, S. C. Ingram and J. W. Thompson.

Invitation: T. J. Gibson, R. E. Steele, W. E. Doyle, Dr. C. J. Wooldridge, Dr. B. F. Ouzts and S. S. Walker.

Locating: E. W. Williams, H. C. Joiner, A. W. Burford, and J. T. Stanford; with the privilege of adding more, if necessary.

Concert: John Whitsell Simmons

All Comrades who desire to attend, were elected delegates to the State and General Reunions. The monthly donation to Mrs. Stuart was, on request of recipient, discontinued. The Quartermaster was authorized by the Camp to furnish wood for the Confederate pit at the Reunion grounds for the benefit of any Comrades who wish to have their own meat barbecued.

There being no further business, on motion, the Camp adjourned.

Official: H. W. Williams, Adjutant   R. E. Steele, Lieut. Commander
[Page 81]

MINUTES OF THE 17TH ANNUAL REUNION OF JOE JOHNSTON CAMP NO. 94
HELD ON JULY 18TH TO 21ST, 1905

First Day – Tuesday, July 18th

Camp assembled at 10 o'clock and was opened with prayer by Chaplain Jennings. On motion, the roll call and reading of minutes of the last Reunion was postponed until Wednesday morning.

The Commander S. B. Love, being absent on account of sickness, First Lieutenant Commander R. E. Steele assumed command and delivered an address of welcome. Comrade Gibson was called on by the Commander and made a short address of welcome in addition to his own.

On motion of Comrade Watson, three Comrades were appointed an advisory committee to assist the officer of the day and deputy sheriffs to keep order. Committee: Watson, Thompson and Dr. E. B. Wood.

Short impromptu talks were made by several Comrades, after which the Camp adjourned to 9 o'clock Wednesday morning. The afternoon was used by the young people.

Second Day – Wednesday, July 19th

Camp assembled at 9:30 o'clock. Prayer by Comrade Frazier. An auditing committee was appointed consisting of Comrades L. E. Camp, Clark and Frazier. By resolution, the Camp opposed the employment of any one at the Confederate Home but a Confederate Veteran.

The hour having arrived for same, Col. T. M. Campbell of Palestine delivered an address, after which the Camp took [Page 82] recess until 2 o'clock.

Camp reassembled at 2 o'clock. A motion prevailed that Thursday, the third day of each Reunion, be set apart for the Sons and Daughters of the Camp.

A resolution was adopted that the Improvement Committee be empowered to make any improvements on the grounds that it may deem necessary for the welfare of the Camp.

Camp adjourned to 9 o'clock Thursday morning. Judge Rufus Hardy of Corsicana addressed the audience on Wednesday night.

Third Day – Thursday, July 20th

Camp assembled at 9:30 o'clock and was opened with prayer by Rev. Robert E. Lee Stutts, of Horn Hill. The Camp proceeded to the election of officers for the ensuing year, as follows:

W. E. Doyle	Commander
C. J. Wooldridge	1st Lieutenant Commander
S. C. Ingram	2nd Lieutenant Commander
L. E. Camp	3rd Lieutenant Commander
H. W. Williams	Adjutant
R. J. Bryant	Quartermaster
Dr. J. P. Cook	Surgeon
Rev. G. L. Jennings	Chaplain
J. W. Simmons	Treasurer
E. W. Williams	Officer of the Day
W. D. Frazier	Color Bearer
J. M. Deis	Bugler
L. E. Camp	Captain of Artillery

On motion, the left south side of the platform was assigned to the wives of Confederate Veterans, and the Quartermaster was instructed to provide plenty of seats for same.

The Adjutant and Quartermaster, [Page 83] each, was allowed $50.00 for their services to the Camp.

The hour arriving, Hon. M. M. Brooks delivered an address. He was followed by Hon. Scott Field, of Calvert, after which the Camp took recess until 2 o'clock.

Camp reassembled at 2:30 o'clock, but then being no business before it, adjourned to 9 o'clock Friday morning.

Fourth Day – Friday, July 21st

Camp assembled at 9 o'clock. Opened with prayer by Comrade Frazier. After a short parade, Camp went into a business meeting. On motion, it was decided to have badges for the wives of the members of the Camp.

The report of the building committee was received and the committee continued. Mr. John Perkins, of Honest Ridge, was selected to take care of the grounds.

Hon. C. K. Bell, of Fort Worth, delivered an address, and was followed by Hon. Richard Mayes of Corsicana.

Camp took recess to 2 o'clock.

Camp reassembled at 2:30 o'clock. The auditing committee made the following report: "We, in auditing the books of the Adjutant and Treasurer find the orders issued by the Adjutant to agree with the amount the Treasurer's books show to have been paid out. Also, receipts given by Treasurer to agree with receipts on his books. We find the books of the Adjutant and Treasurer to agree in all respects and to have been kept in a neat and plain manner. We also find the amounts turned over to the Treasurer by the Adjutant to agree with the several accounts of receipts [Page 84] on his books, and hereby affirm the accounts of each as correct. We find the Treasurer has in his hand $187.74, we find the Adjutant has in his hands $12.75, total amount $200.49. Respectfully submitted, L. E. Camp, W. D. Frazier, C. T. Harris for Nat. Clark [Com.]"

The future invitation committee was instructed to invite a speaker to address the ladies on the Womanhood of the South from 1861 to 1865.

A motion was carried thanking the ladies for their fine dinner given to the Camp on the grounds today.

It was ordered by the Camp that the building of a lodging place be referred to the Improvement Committee.

Memorial services were held for the following Comrades: J. C. Anglin, W. H. Herring, J. P. Lindley, I. T. Mahoney, Dr. J. T. Sloan, R. L. Watkins and C. H. F. Wood.

Mr. H. F. Marr, of Corsicana, recited a poem entitled "Echoes of the Confederacy" by H. L. Piner.

There being no further business, the Camp adjourned.

Official: H. W. Williams, Adjutant   R. E. Steele, Acting Commander
[Page 85]

CALLED MEETING OF JOE JOHNSTON CAMP NO. 94, AUGUAT 19TH, 1905

By call of the Commander, Joe Johnston Camp No. 94, met at Mexia on Saturday, August 19th, 1905.

The Commander, Sam B. Love, being absent, First Lieutenant Commander, R. E. Steele, presided. The business of the last Reunion was wound up, and the amount in the Treasury was $421.49.

A committee was appointed, consisting of Quartermaster Bryant and Comrades Watson, Grooves and Deis, to see about buying the Light Plant from Mr. Houx, with the understanding that the Commander, Adjutant and Treasurer were to be added if necessary.

The Quartermaster was authorized to set aside as much ground below the bluff as he saw fit for a Base Ball ground.

After the business was transacted, the Camp was turned over to the new officers.

Official: H. W. Williams, Adjutant R. E. Steele, Lieut. Commander

[Page 86]

CALLED MEETING OF JOE JOHNSTON CAMP NO. 94, FEBRUARY 24TH, 1906

By call of Commander Doyle, Joe Johnston Camp assembled in Mexia on February 24th, 1906. The time for the next Reunion was set for July 31st and August 1st, 2nd and 3rd, 1906.

The election of delegates to the State Reunion to be held at Dallas in October was postponed until the meeting in July. All Comrades who wished to attend, were elected delegates to the General Reunion in New Orleans on April 25th to 27th. The following committees were appointed:

Privilege: Comrades Bryant, Camp, Joiner, Deis, Groover, Wooldridge, Gardner, Rado Steele and Watson.
Improvement: Comrades Bryant, Watson, Storey and Browder.
Invitation: Comrades Gibson, R. E. Steele, Harris, Ingram and Ouzts.
Concert: Comrade J. W. Simmons, Chairman. The United Daughters of the Confederacy of Mexia for one night; Mrs. W. W. Brown and the other ladies of Groesbeck for one night, and the ladies of Tehuacana, Coolidge and Hubbard for one or two nights.

A motion was unanimously carried that, hereafter, no amusements would be allowed practiced on the Camp and surrounding grounds, between the hours of 9 o'clock, A.M. and 1 o'clock, P. M., such as shooting, dancing, flying jinny running, base and foot ball games, and the Privilege Committee and Officer of the Day were instructed to see that these orders be strictly conformed with.

Comrade Robert Jackson, formerly of Palestine, presented the Camp with a Roster of John H. Reagan Camp of that place and the thanks of this Camp were extended to him for same. [Page 87]

A resolution was passed sympathizing with Comrades W. M. Barton, Dr. J. P. Cook and S. S. Walker in their afflictions.

A donation of Five [$5.00] Dollars from this Camp for the monument to General Granbury was ordered sent to the ladies of Granbury.

At our last Reunion in 1905, by resolution, Thursday, the third day of future Reunions, was turned over to the Sons and Daughters, and it is the earnest desire of this Camp that they will properly utilize it.

Official: H. W. Williams, Adjutant W. E. Doyle, Commander

[Page 88]

MINUTES OF THE 18TH ANNUAL REUNION OF JOE JOHNSTON CAMP NO. 94
HELD ON JULY 31ST AND AUGUST 1ST, 2ND AND 3RD, 1906

First Day – Tuesday, July 31st

Camp was called to order by Commander Doyle at 10 o'clock and was opened with prayer by Comrade Frazier, after which the Commander delivered an address of welcome. Comrade Watson was called on and, in a short speech, urged the young people to keep up the Camp organization when all the old Confederates would be no more.

Comrade Gibson gave some of his war experiences, and was followed by Comrades P. O. Douglass, J. W. Simmons, R. E. Steele, Hayes and Harris, after which, the Camp took recess to 3:15 o'clock.

Afternoon

Camp reassembled at 3:30. An auditing committee consisting of Comrades Love, Joiner and Rado Steele was appointed. There being no further business to transact, the Camp adjourned to 9 o'clock Wednesday morning.

Second Day – Wednesday, August 1st

Camp was called to order by the Commander at 9:30 o'clock and was opened with prayer by Comrade Frazier. The roll was called and the minutes of the last Reunion read and approved. Camp took recess to 3 o'clock.

Afternoon

Camp reassembled at 3 o'clock and proceeded to the election of officers, which resulted as follows:

H. C. Joiner	Commander
C. L. Watson	1st Lieutenant Commander
John A. Jones	2nd Lieutenant Commander
Geo. W. McNeece	3rd Lieutenant Commander
H. W. Williams	Adjutant
R. J. Bryant	Quartermaster
Dr. C. J. Wooldridge	Surgeon
Rev. G. L. Jennings	Chaplain

[Page 89]

W. D. Frazier	Assistant Chaplain
J. W. Simmons	Treasurer
E. W. Williams	Officer of the Day
P. O. Douglass	Color Bearer
J. M. Deis	Bugler
H. W. Gray	Captain of Artillery
Miss Gary Doyle	Sponsor

On motion, the Adjutant and Quartermaster were allowed fifty [$50.00] Dollars each for their services. The sum of Twenty Five [$25.00] Dollars was donated to Comrade Barton, who is in feeble health. The lease of the dance hall having expired, the Quartermaster was directed to take charge of same as any other property of the Camp.

The contract for furnishing water and sprinkling being out, the Commander appointed a committee consisting of Comrades Browder, Gibson and P. O. Douglass, to which the Quartermaster was added, to confer with the contractor about continuing the lease.

No further business, the Camp took a recess to 4 o'clock Thursday afternoon.

Third Day – Thursday, August 2nd

This day was used mostly by Sons of Confederate Veterans, who elected their officers for the ensuing year, and in the forenoon were favored with a most eloquent and instructive address by Judge Yancey Lewis, of Dallas.

At 4 o'clock the Camp reassembled and heard the report of the water committee. The report was, that the contractor agreed [Page 90]to renew the contract for Five Years at Seventy five [$75.00] Dollars annually, and promised to extend the sprinkling somewhat further than at present. The report was adopted and the committee continued with instructions to draw up the contract.

On motion, the Camp adjourned to 9 o'clock Friday morning.

Fourth Day – Friday, August 3rd

Camp was called to order by the Commander at 9 o'clock, and was opened with prayer by Comrade Frazier.

Most of the Veterans present were formed in ranks by the Officer of the Day and marched up and down the Avenues for a short while, and after breaking ranks, the Camp went into a business meeting.

The auditing committee reported as follows: "To the Commander and Comrades of Joe Johnston Camp No. 94: We, your auditing committee, beg to report that after checking all the orders and receipts, as well as the books of the Adjutant and Treasurer, find that they balance to one cent, and that the collections amounted to $971.54, and that the disbursements are $908.50 showing a balance in the Treasurer's hands of $63.04. We also find the amount of $9.30 in the Adjutant's hands, making the total of the Camp Funds $72.34. Respectfully submitted, S. B. Love, H. C. Joiner, Rado Steele [Com.]"

Report adopted and committee discharged. Camp took recess to 3 o'clock.

At 12 o'clock, all Confederates present fell into ranks, and, lead by the Bank and the Sponsor and her Maids of Honor, marched [Page 91] to, and surrounded tables loaded with a sumptuous dinner provided by the Ladies for their benefit. It is needless to say that every one enjoyed himself and "fell back" in better condition than when he made "the attack."

Afternoon

Camp reassembled at 3 o'clock. The following Resolutions, offered by Comrade T. J. Gibson, were passed: Resolved: That the thanks of the Veterans of this Camp be and are hereby, tendered the Ladies for the excellent dinner given us on the grounds today. Resolved: That the thanks of this Camp are extended to the Dallas News for the courtesies shown us and for the very full and satisfactory reports made of our proceedings from day to day by its representative, Mr. Baldwin, alias "Dick Naylor."

On motion, the Improvement committee composed of Comrades Bryant, Browder, Storey and Watson was continued another year. A committee consisting of Comrades Groover, Harris and Watson to examine all bills was appointed.

Memorial services were held for the following named Comrades: Geo. W. Archer, H. A. Boyd, L. E. Camp, J. W. Ferrell, Sandy Gordon, R. W. Payne, J. L. Smith and Jno. A. Wright. Revs. A. A. Davis of Tehuacana, and W. F. Kearby, of Mexia, assisted in the Services. The Chaplain, Rev. G. L. Jennings, was absent on account of sickness.

After close of the Services, there being no further business, on motion, the Camp adjourned.

Official: H. W. Williams, Adjutant   W. E. Doyle, Commander

[Page 92]

CALLED MEETING OF JOE JOHNSTON CAMP NO. 94, FEBRUARY 23RD, 1907

By call of Commander Joiner, Joe Johnston Camp No. 94 met at Mexia on February 23rd, 1907. The first order of business was fixing the time of the next Reunion, which will occur on July 23rd – 26th, 1907. All Comrades who desire to attend the State Reunion at Bowie, Texas [time not set] and the General Reunion at Richmond, Virginia, [May 30th to June 3rd] were appointed delegates to same.

The Privilege Committee was appointed as follows: Comrades Bryant, Rado Steele, Watson, Thompson, Groover, Keeling, Gardner, Wooldridge, Deis, Frazier, Beene and Stanford. On motion, as many as four were to be present on opening of bids.

Invitation Committee: Comrades Gibson, Doyle, R. E. Steele, Ingram and Love.

A. B. Reynolds, commander of the Sons of Confederate Veterans, with the assistance of U.D.C.'s, was appointed to arrange for the Concerts on the four nights at the Reunion. Motion by Comrade Gibson: If by the 1st of May the concerts have not been arranged for, the Privilege committee is authorized to engage a Theatrical Troupe to perform under the Pavilion. On motion, no base nor foot ball playing was to be allowed between the hours of nine and twelve o'clock, a.m.

The Privilege committee was instructed most emphatically not to allow any rubber return balls nor confetti "on the grounds." By a standing rule, Thursday, the third day, and the several nights, being set apart for the Sons and Daughters of Confederate Veterans, they are earnestly urged and requested to see that the time is properly utilized.

No further business, Camp adjourned.

Official: H. W. Williams, Adjutant   H. C. Joiner, Commander

[Page 93]

MINUTES OF THE 19TH ANNUAL REUNION OF JOE JOHNSTON CAMP NO. 94
HELD ON JULY 23RD TO 26TH, 1907

First Day – Tuesday, July 23rd

Camp was called to order by Commander Joiner at 10 o'clock a.m., on Tuesday, July 23rd, and was opened with prayer by Rev. John K. Lippard, of Blooming Grove, acting for the Chaplain.

On motion, the roll call and reading of the minutes was set for Wednesday, the second day of each Reunion, on account of a fuller attendance. The Commander delivered an appropriate address of welcome to all. Several Comrades made short talks.

Comrade Gibson gave the Camp a very interesting account of his visit to the Shenandoah Valley of Virginia and the Reunion at Richmond. Camp took recess to 2:30 o'clock.

Afternoon

Camp reassembled at 2:30 o'clock. There being no immediate business to transact, it adjourned to Wednesday morning.

Second Day – Wednesday, July 24th

Camp assembled at 9 o'clock. Was opened with prayer by Comrade Frazier. The roll was called and minutes of last Reunion read. A resolution was offered by Comrade Bryant to abolish the fifty cents dues, which was amended by Comrade R. E. Steele to change the by-laws so as to reduce the dues to fifteen cents, which was adopted. A motion was carried that there be no badges issued for three years from this meeting.

At 10 o'clock, Private J. M. Long, of Paris, delivered a most interesting address. An auditing committee consisting of Comrades Gibson, Gardner and Lewis, was appointed. Camp took recess to 2:30 o'clock. [Page 94]

Afternoon

Camp met at 2:30 o'clock. On motion of Comrade Watson, the sum of Fifty [$50.00] Dollars was donated to Comrade Barrett, and Fifty [$50.00] Dollars to the United Daughters of the Confederacy. Camp adjourned to 5 o'clock p.m. Thursday.

Third Day – Thursday, July 25th

This day was set apart to the Sons and Daughters of Confederate Veterans. Camp assembled at 5 o'clock, p.m. and proceeded to elect officers for the ensuing year, with the following results:

Geo. W. McNeese	Commander
J. W. Nash	1st Lieutenant Commander
Wm. Justice	2nd Lieutenant Commander
J. P. Yeldell	3rd Lieutenant Commander
H. W. Williams	Adjutant
R. J. Bryant	Quartermaster
C. J. Wooldridge	Surgeon
G. L. Jennings	Chaplain
W. D. Frazier	Assistant Chaplain
J. W. Simmons	Treasurer
E. W. Williams	Officer of the Day
P. O. Douglass	Color Bearer
J. M. Deis	Bugler
H. W. Gray	Captain of Artillery
Miss Mattie Watson	Sponsor

Comrades Doyle, Gibson and Bond were appointed on the Finance Committee to pass upon bills that may be presented to the Camp for payment. The report of the Improvement Committee, Comrades Watson, Storey and Browder, was adopted and committee continued. The sum of Ten [$10.00] Dollars was appropriated to Comrade Lee. Fifty [$50.00] Dollars each was allowed the Adjutant and Quartermaster for their services to the Camp.

Camp adjourned to 9 o'clock Friday morning. [Page 95]

Fourth Day – Friday, July 26th

Camp assembled at 9 o'clock and led by the Coolidge band, the Officer of the Day, E. W. Williams, on his prancing steed, marched up and down the avenues for a short time. A short business meeting was held. Private J. M. Long, of Paris and Capt. W. E. Barry of Navasota, were elected honorary members of the Camp.

At 10:30 o'clock, Senator Chas. A. Culberson delivered a most eloquent and instructive address, at the end of which the Camp took recess to attend a sumptuous dinner prepared by the Ladies for all Confederate Veterans on the grounds.

Camp reassembled at 3 o'clock. The auditing committee made the following report, which was adopted: "To H. C. Joiner, Commander: Your committee, appointed to examine the books of the Adjutant, Quartermaster and Treasurer, beg to report: That we find the books of these several officers neatly and correctly kept and that the Camp is due the Quartermaster $5.00. Thos. J. Gibson, W. B. Lewis, A. E. Gardner [Com.]

On motion, the thanks of the Camp were extended to the Coolidge Band for the excellent music; to the Ladies for the elegant dinner, and to Senator Culberson and Comrade Long for the eloquent addresses.

Memorial services were held for the following named Comrades: W. M. Barton, John G. Carroll, John A. Jones, B. F. Ouzts, W. J. Reeves, J. C. Webb, J. H. Welch and W. W. Wyatt.

There being no further business, the Camp adjourned.

Official: H. W. Williams, Adjutant   H. C. Joiner, Commander

CALLED MEETING OF JOE JOHNSTON CAMP NO. 94, AUGUST 24TH, 1907

By call of Commander Joiner, Joe Johnston Camp met at Mexia on August 24th, 1907; for the purpose of winding up the Camp business for 1906 and turning over the Camp to the new officers for the ensuing year.

Commander Joiner being absent, First Lieutenant Commander Watson presided. The Treasurer, J. W. Simmons, reported the amount of $672.29 in the Treasury.

On motion, the sum of $10.00 was donated to Comrade E. W. Williams, the Officer of the Day, for his services at the Reunion.

After some miscellaneous discussion about the good of the Camp, Lieutenant Commander Watson turned it over to the new Commander, Geo. W. McNeese.

There being no further business, on motion, the Camp adjourned to call of Commander.

Official: H. W. Williams, Adjutant   Geo. W. McNeese, Commander

CALLED MEETING OF JOE JOHNSTON CAMP NO. 94, FEBRUARY 29TH, 1908

By call of Commander Geo. W. McNeese, Joe Johnston Camp No. 94, met at Mexia on February 29th, 1908. The Commander being absent on account of sickness, First Lieutenant Commander J. W. Nash presided.

The time set for the next Reunion was July 14th to 17th, 1908.

The following committees were appointed:

Privileges: Comrades R. J. Bryant, W. D. Frazier, P. O. Douglass, S. H. Beene, A. J. Burleson, A. W. Burford, W. H. Browder, J. W. Thompson, R. E. Farrow, A. E. Gardner, T. E. Haskins, Wm. Justice, A. M. Nabors, J. E. Parker, T. W. Wilie, A. J. Cox, J. P. Yeldell, J. S. Groover, C. L. Watson and Rado Steele.
On motion: Five [5] of this committee constitutes a quorum.
Invitation: Comrades W. E. Doyle and T. J. Gibson.
Locating: Comrades H. C. Joiner and J. W. McKinney.

A motion was adopted that the Program business be left to the Privilege Committee.

The following resolution was passed: Resolved, That a committee of five [5] be appointed by the Commander to confer with the T. and B. V. R. R. Co. and obtain from it a clear and distinct proposition as to what it wants and what it proposes to do and to pay for the privilege of using part of the Camp grounds for any purpose, and to report to this Camp at a special meeting to be called by the commander, or at our Reunion in July. Committee: Comrades T. J. Gibson, C. L. Watson, W. E. Doyle, R. E. Steele and Rado Steele. No further business, on motion, Camp adjourned.

Official: H. W. Williams, Adjutant   J. W. Nash, 1st Lieutenant Commander

[Carried to Page 158]

MINUTES OF THE 20TH ANNUAL REUNION OF JOE JOHNSTON CAMP NO. 94 HELD ON JULY 14TH – 17TH, 1908
First Day – Tuesday, July 14th

Camp assembled at 10 o'clock and was called to order by Commander McNeese, and Assistant Chaplain W. D. Frazier offered prayer. The Commander called on Comrade Watson to welcome the people to enjoy themselves during the four days meeting, which he did in a neat little talk.

The reading of the minutes of last Reunion and roll call was postponed to Wednesday morning.

Comrade Gibson was requested to make a talk, and he complied with his customary eloquence. Good talks were, also, made by Comrades Sellers, R. E. Steele and E. W. Williams

A committee was appointed consisting of Comrades J. W. Simmons, H. C. Joiner and J. P. Yeldell to see that the different Privilege men charge reasonable prices.

Camp took recess till 2:30 o'clock.

Afternoon

Camp reassembled at 2:30. Rev. Jake Hodges being present, was called on and made a good speech. Camp adjourned to Wednesday morning 10 o'clock.

Second Day – Wednesday, July 15th

Camp was called to order by the Commander at 10 o'clock. Opened with prayer by Comrade Sellers. The roll was called and minutes read of last Reunion, after which the Maccabee Ladies of Groesbeck extended an invitation to the Veterans of the Camp to attend a lecture by Hon. Bob Taylor at "Doyle's Coliseum" which was accepted and a vote of thanks returned to the Ladies. Camp took recess to 2:30.

Afternoon

Camp reassembled at 2:30. Judge Norman Kittrell, of Houston, delivered a most eloquent address. Comrades J. P. Yeldell, H. C. Joiner and F. M. Sellers were appointed on the Auditing Committee. The United Daughters of the Confederacy bestowed Crosses of Honor on several Comrades after which the Camp adjourned to 5 o'clock Thursday afternoon.

Third Day – Thursday, July 16th

This day is set apart to the Sons of Confederate Veterans. Their business being finished, at 5 o'clock, p.m., our Camp held a short business meeting. The sum of $25.00 was donated to Comrade T. S. Boyd. $50.00 each was appropriated to the Adjutant and Quartermaster. $25.00 apiece was given to U.D.C. and Sons of Confederate Veterans. $15.00 was allowed Comrade Joiner for guard duty, to be paid to several parties, and $10.00 to Comrade E. W. Williams, Officer of the Day. The thanks of the Camp were extended Mrs. Lowe for her excellent recitation, and Judges Kittrell and Hardy for their good speeches. Camp adjourned to 10 o'clock Friday morning.

Fourth Day – Friday, July 17th

Camp met at 10 o'clock and was called to order by the Commander and opened with prayer by Comrade Frazier. After a short parade, the Camp proceeded to the election of officers, which resulted as follows:

P. O. Douglass	Commander
J. W. Nash	1st Lieutenant Commander
C. J. Brown	2nd Lieutenant Commander
James McCorkle	3rd Lieutenant Commander
H. W. Williams	Adjutant
R. J. Bryant	Quartermaster
C. J. Wooldridge	Surgeon
G. L. Jennings	Chaplain
W. D. Frazier	Assistant Chaplain
J. S. Groover	Treasurer
E. W. Williams	Officer of the Day
H. C. Joiner	Color Bearer
J. M. Deis	Bugler
H. W. Gray	Captain of Artillery

[Page 160]

On motion, a committee composed of Comrades J. M. Deis, E. W. Williams and C. L. Watson was appointed to look after the grave of our first Adjutant, Captain W. H. Adams, and report at our next Reunion. The sum of $50.00 or as much thereof as necessary, was set apart for policing the Camp at future Reunions.

The auditing committee made the following report, which was adopted: "To Capt. G. W. McNeese, Commander: We, your auditing committee, beg leave to submit the following report: We have carefully examined the books of the Adjutant, Treasurer and Quartermaster and report the following facts: Amount in hands of Treasurer $582.94; amount in hands of Adjutant $3.00; total amount cash on hand $585.94. We further find that the books of the above named officers are neatly and correctly kept and tally to a cent. Respectfully submitted, J. P. Yeldell, H. C. Joiner, F. M. Sellers [Com.]"

J. K. P. Hanna made a short talk in favor of raising a monument to Hood Brigade at Austin.

Camp took recess to 3 o'clock.

[Page 161]

Afternoon

Camp reassembled at 3 o'clock.

The thanks of the Camp were extended the Ladies for the bountiful dinner prepared for the members.

Memorial services were held for the following deceased Comrades: B. W. Allen, H. C. Berryman, J. W. Humphries, W. G. Lewis, T. W. Wilie, E. B. Wood and Jesus Flores [Mexican, called "Val Verde"]

There being no further business, Camp adjourned.

Official: H. W. Williams, Adjutant   Geo. W. McNeese, Commander

[Page 162]

CALLED MEETING OF JOE JOHNSTON CAMP NO. 94, FEBRUARY 27TH, 1909

By call of Commander Douglass, Joe Johnston Camp No. 94 met at Mexia on February 27th 1909. The coming Reunion was set for July 27th to 30th, 1909. The following committees were appointed by the Commander:

Privilege Committee: Comrades R. J. Bryant, J. P. Yeldell, J. A. Wright, W. D. Frazier, T. E. Haskins, A. M. Nabors, A. J. Cox, Wm. Justice, H. C. Joiner, Rado Steele, S. H. Beene, A. E. Gardner, M. P. Reynolds, N. T. Popejoy, S. F. Bond, B. W. Collier and C. L. Watson.

Invitation Committee: Comrades Gibson, Doyle and R. E. Steele.

Locating Committee: Comrade J. W. McKinney, with right to select his assistants.

Concert Committee: Comrade W. H. Browder, who may appoint his staff, male or female.

On motion of Comrade Doyle, a committee consisting of Comrades Gibson, R. E. Steele, Mrs. Bryant and Miss Mattie Watson was appointed to entertain the invited speakers.

All Comrades, who wished to attend, were elected delegates to the State and General Reunions. The sum of Twenty Five [$25.00] Dollars was appropriated to each of three places for expenses in getting up a suitable concert for three nights at the Reunion. A motion was carried requesting our Representatives in the Legislature to vote for the Constitutional Amendment in relation to indigent wives and widows of Confederate soldiers.

The business being finished, Camp adjourned to July 27th, 1909.

Official: H. W. Williams, Adjutant   P. O. Douglass, Commander

[Page 163]

MINUTES OF THE 21ST ANNUAL REUNION OF JOE JOHNSTON CAMP NO. 94, HELD ON JULY 27TH, 28TH, 29TH AND 30TH, 1909

First Day – Tuesday, July 27th

Joe Johnston Camp No. 94 held the 21st annual reunion commencing at 10 o'clock on July 27th, 1909, and was called to order by Commander, P. O. Douglass, and was opened with prayer by Comrade Nash, the Chaplain being absent.

The Commander delivered a short address of welcome, which was responded to by Comrade Gibson.

Short impromptu speeches were made by Comrades E. W. Williams, C. L. Watson, S. B. Love, R. E. Steele, J. W. Nash, W. B. Lewis and J. C. McDonald.

On motion of Comrade Gibson, the policing the Camp and compensating the guards was left to the Commander, Officer of the Day, and four Comrades to be appointed by the Commander. Camp took recess to 3 o'clock.

Afternoon

Camp reassembled at 3 o'clock. There being no business to transact it adjourned to 10 o'clock Wednesday morning.

Second Day – Wednesday, July 28th

Camp assembled at 10 o'clock and was opened with prayer by Comrade Frazier. Comrades S. B. Love, H. C. Joiner and R. E. Steele were appointed as an auditing committee. On motion, Camp took recess to 2:30 o'clock.

Afternoon

Camp reassembled at 2:30 o'clock. The roll was called and Minutes of last Reunion were read and adopted. Comrade Gibson made a talk in relation [Page 164] to the career of General Pat Cleburne. On motion of Comrade Gibson, a committee of three was appointed to draft resolutions of condolence on the death of Mrs. Hayes, daughter of Jefferson Davis, who died recently in Colorado. The committee was composed of Comrades Gibson, Wooldridge and Browder. Camp adjourned to 9:30 o'clock Friday morning.

Third Day – Thursday, July 29th

By standing rule, this day is given to the Sons of Confederate Veterans.

Fourth Day – Friday, July 30th

Camp assembled at 9:30 o'clock and was opened with prayer by Comrade Frazier. The first business was the election of officers, which resulted as follows:

A. E. Gardner	Commander
J. P. Yeldell	1st Lieutenant Commander
N. T. Popejoy	2nd Lieutenant Commander
A. J. Burleson	3rd Lieutenant Commander
H. W. Williams	Adjutant
R. J. Bryant	Quartermaster
C. J. Wooldridge	Surgeon
G. L. Jennings	Chaplain
W. D. Frazier	Assistant Chaplain
J. S. Groover	Treasurer
E. W. Williams	Officer of the Day
Rado Steele	Color Bearer
J. M. Deis	Bugler
J. M. Deis	Captain of Artillery

The auditing committee made the following report, which was adopted: "Commander and Comrades: We, your auditing committee, beg to report that we have made a careful examination of the books of the Adjutant and Treasurer and find the books are correct and that [Page 165] they tally with each other, and that the amount that has been collected for 1908 is $1944.84, and that the amount paid out is $959.05, leaving a balance in the Treasury of $985.79. Respectfully submitted, S. B. Love, R. E. Steele, H. C. Joiner [Com.]"

The memorial committee on the death of Mrs. Hayes submitted a suitable report, which was adopted.

On motion of Comrade Gibson, the Adjutant and Quartermaster were allowed $50.00 each and the Officer of the Day $10.00 for their services to the Camp. Camp took recess to 3 o'clock.

Afternoon

Camp reassembled at 3 o'clock. On motion of Comrade R. E. Steele, the sum of $25.00 was donated to the Sons of Confederate Veterans with the understanding that they would hold a suitable Reunion in the year 1910. With regret, the Camp realizes the fact that they are sadly neglecting their duty in this matter.

Memorial services were conducted by Rev. J. Stuart Pearce on request of the Chaplain, Rev. G. L. Jennings, who could not be present on account of sickness. The following named Comrades have died since our last Reunion: R. O. Beene, T. S. Byrd, T. S. Gatlin, H. W. Gray, S. C. Ingram, G. W. Kinney, G. W. McNeese, John Patterson, S. K. Scruggs and B. F. Sherrill.

There being no further business, Camp adjourned.

Official: H. W. Williams, Adjutant   P. O. Douglass, Commander

[Page 166]

CALLED MEETING OF JOE JOHNSTON CAMP

Joe Johnston Camp No. 94 met in called session at Mexia on Saturday August 14th, 1909, to wind up the Reunion business for the Camp year 1908, and to turn over the Camp to the new officers elected for 1909.

In the absence of the Commander, P. O. Douglass, 1st Lieutenant Commander J. W. Nash presided.

On motion, the Fifty [$50.00] Dollars to be paid to the Camp for the year 1908 for the Theatre by Comrade W. E. Doyle was remitted, with the distinct understanding that this is not to be a precedent for the Camp in the future.

There being no further business to transact, the Camp was duly turned over to the new Commander, A. E. Gardner, and adjourned.

Official: H. W. Williams, Adjutant   J. W. Nash, 1st Lieutenant Commander
[Page 167]

CALLED MEETING OF JOE JOHNSTON CAMP, FEBRUARY 26TH, 1910

By call of Commander Gardner, Joe Johnston Camp No. 94 assembled at Mexia on February 26th, 1910, to make arrangements for the meeting of the 22nd Reunion.

The time set for the Reunion this year was July 19th – 22nd. The following committees were appointed:

    Privilege: R. J. Bryant, S. H. Beene, S. F. Bond, Geo. T. Brown, A. J. Burleson, B. W. Collier, A. J. Cox, M. B. Cox, J. M. Deis, P. O. Douglass, C. A. Durham, R. E. Farrow, W. D. Frazier, T. E. Haskins, S. Hughes, H. C. Joiner, J. S. Jolley, Wm. Justice, J. C. McDonald, A. M. Nabors, J. W. Nash, M. P. Reynolds, F. M. Sellers, W. M. Skipper, Rado Steele, C. L. Watson, Joshua Wood, C. J. Wooldridge, Jas. A. Wright and J. P. Yeldell.
    Invitation: T. J. Gibson, W. P. Brown, W. E. Doyle, S. B. Love and R. E. Steele.
    Locating: J. W. McKinney. To select his assistants.
    Concert: W. H. Browder. To appoint his staff.

All comrades who desire to attend the State and General Reunions were elected as delegates to same. The sum of $75.00 was appropriated to assist in getting up concerts for three nights at the Reunion. The following preamble and resolutions were unanimously adopted by the Camp.

"At a meeting of Joe Johnston Camp No. 94 U.C.V., held in the City of Mexia, Texas, on February 26th, 1910, the following preamble and resolutions were unanimously adopted: Whereas, it has been brought to our notice through the columns of the '*Confederate Veteran*' that the Daughters of the Confederacy at Dalton, Georgia have formed an organization to raise funds to erect at that historic City a monument to the memory of General Joseph E. Johnston, for whom this Camp was named: Be it resolved: First: That we heartily endorse this patriotic movement of the U. D. C. at Dalton, Georgia [Page 168] and commend same to all Camps wherever located and to all the survivors of the Confederate Armies and Navies. No more appropriate place than the one named could be found at which to erect a monument that shall perpetuate the name and fame of one of the greatest Commanders of modern times.

It was at Dalton, Georgia, that General Johnston assumed the command of the Western Army. He found it disorganized and its efficiency greatly impaired by reason of the disastrous retreat from Missionary Ridge. In a few weeks General Johnston had, through his intelligence and untiring effort, brought the Army to a very high standard of efficiency. In the Spring of 1864 the Federal Army under General Sherman advanced in greatly superior numbers and then began a series of battles and retrograde movements on the part of the Confederate Army that has rarely ever been equaled in the annals of war.

Step by step the Federal advance was contested when the Army reached the vicinity of Atlanta in July, more Federal Soldiers had been killed and wounded than the Confederates had at any one time in their ranks.

Their confidence in their Commanding General was unlimited, and the efficiency of the army unimpaired. These brave and gallant men were still ready to do what ever their beloved Commander should desire.

Second: that the sum of $50.00 is hereby appropriated for the purpose named and we promise to supplement this by an additional amount when this Camp meets in annual Reunion in July next.

Third: The adjutant is directed to forward to the chairman of the Monument association the amount above named, together with these [Page 169] resolutions. That a copy of the same be sent to the *Veteran*, and other copies be furnished the local and County papers with the request that they be published. Thos. J. Gibson, C. L. Watson, W. E. Doyle [Com.]"

There being no further business, on motion, the Camp adjourned.

Official: H. W. Williams, Adjutant   A. E. Gardner, Commander
[Page 170]

MINUTES OF THE 22ND ANNUAL REUNION OF JOE JOHNSTON CAMP NO. 94
HELD ON JULY 19TH, 29TH, 21ST & 22ND, 1910
First Day – Tuesday, July 19th

The Camp assembled at 10 o'clock.

The Commander, Comrade A. E. Gardner, being sick, and the Lieutenant Commanders being absent, the Camp elected Comrade T. J. Gibson to preside as temporary commander.

The Chaplain being absent, the Assistant Chaplain, W. D. Frazier, requested Rev. L. D. Bass to open the Camp with prayer.

The commander pro. tem. delivered an address of welcome; after which, short speeches were made by Comrades C. L. Watson, J. W. Simmons, E. W. Williams & P. O. Douglass. Camp took recess to 3 o'clock.

Afternoon

Camp reassembled at 3 o'clock. First Lieutenant Commander, J. P. Yeldell presiding. An auditing committee was appointed, composed of Comrades Rado Steele, M. H. Clark and C. A. Durham.

The resignation of Comrade J. M. Storey of the Improvement Committee was accepted and Comrade Rado Steele was appointed to fill the place. Adjourned to 10 o'clock Wednesday.

Second Day – Wednesday, July 20th

Camp assembled at 10 o'clock and was opened with prayer by Chaplain Jennings. The roll was called and minutes of last Reunion read and adopted.

The following resolution was passed: Be it resolved, That a committee of three be appointed by the Commander whose duty it shall be to prepare and present at this meeting a plan for the erection of a monument on these grounds to the memory of the Veterans, members of this Camp. Offered by: [Page 171] P. O. Douglass, T. J. Gibson and W. D. Frazier.

At 11 o'clock Rev. L. D. Bass delivered an address on "Love, Courtship and Marriage," in which he gave some exceeding good advice to the young people on that subject.

Camp took recess to 2:30 o'clock.

Afternoon

Camp reassembled at 2:30 o'clock.

The Commander appointed Comrades T. J. Gibson, P. O. Douglass and W. D. Frazier on the monument committee.

On motion, the sum of $50 was donated to the Adjutant and Quartermaster and $20 to the Officer of the Day for their services to the Camp.

Thanks of the Camp were tendered Rev. Dr. L. D. Bass for his excellent address this morning. Adjourned to Thursday 9 o'clock.

Third Day – Thursday, July 21st

Camp assembled at 9 o'clock and was opened with prayer by Rev. C. C. Castles of Palestine. There was no special business transacted, but several Comrades made short talks for the good of the Camp. This day being set apart for the Sons of Confederate Veterans, the Camp adjourned to 9 o'clock Friday.

Fourth Day – Friday, July 22nd

Camp assembled at 9 o'clock and was opened with prayer by assistant Chaplain W. d. Frazier. A motion was carried to rescind the rule concerning the election of Commander. The auditing committee made the following report: "We, your Auditing committee beg to submit the following report: We have checked up the books of the Adjutant and Treasurer and find them correct. We find the following amounts: [Page 172] In the hands of the Adjutant $5.35; In the hands of the Treasurer $1182.74; Making a total of $1188.09. M. H. Clark, Rado Steele, C. A. Durham [Com.]"

Report was adopted. The Camp proceeded to the election of officers, which resulted as follows:

J. P. Yeldell	Commander
C. L. Watson	1st Lieutenant Commander
A. J. Cox	2nd Lieutenant Commander
P. O. Douglass	3rd Lieutenant Commander
H. W. Williams	Adjutant
R. J. Bryant	Quartermaster
C. J. Wooldridge	Surgeon
G. L. Jennings	Chaplain
W. D. Frazier	Assistant Chaplain
J. S. Groover	Treasurer
E. W. Williams	Officer of the Day
Rado Steele	Color Bearer
J. M. Deis	Bugler
J. M. Deis	Captain of Artillery

The sum of $25 was appropriated to the Sons of Confederate Veterans.

The monument committee brought in the following report: To Major J. P. Yeldell, acting Commander: Your committee appointed to draft a plan for raising the necessary funds to erect a monument on these grounds to the memory of the Veterans composing this Camp report as follows:

First: That a committee of seven members of this Camp, four of whom shall constitute a quorum, be appointed by the Commander to be known as the monument committee, whose duty it shall be to take all necessary steps to raise the money necessary to erect a monument on these grounds to the [Page 173] memory of the veterans who have been members of this Camp. Said committee shall meet at such times and places as it may deem proper, and at its first meeting shall elect a Chairman, Secretary and Treasurer.

Said committee shall have the right to adopt such By-Laws and regulations as it may deem proper.

Second: Said committee is authorized to appoint auxiliary committees from the Sons and Daughters of Confederate Veterans to aid them in raising the money aforesaid.

Third: The members of the committee shall serve without compensation. Provided, that they may use enough of the funds raised by it to purchase books and stationery and to pay the actual expenses of its members while actually engaged in the business of the committee. Said committee shall make an annual report to this Camp while in annual Reunion, showing the amount of money raised, where deposited and the exact condition of its finances.

Fourth: The Headquarters of said committee shall be at Mexia and its officers shall reside there. And it is made the duty of the committee to place all money received by it in some good and solvent Bank at interest.

Fifth: That the sum of Five Hundred [$500] Dollars be, and the same is hereby, set apart out of the money in the Treasury of this Camp and put in the hands of said committee for the purpose aforesaid. Provided, that said $500, nor any part thereof, shall ever be used for any other purpose except that above named. All of which is respectfully submitted, P. O. Douglass, W. D. Frazier, T. J. Gibson [Com.] [Page 174] An amendment was offered, and accepted by the committee, that the sum of One Thousand [$1000.00] Dollars should first be raised by private subscription. The report was then adopted.

On motion, the usual memorial service was dispensed with at this Reunion on account of the acting Chaplain having to attend a funeral, and on account of the death of Comrade M. L. McDonald, who died Friday morning while in Camp. Suitable resolutions were passed expressing heartfelt sympathy and condolences with his family in their sad affliction.

At 11 o'clock, Judge Hardy, of Corsicana, delivered an able address on Confederate subjects, after which, Camp took recess to 3 o'clock.

Afternoon

Camp reassembled at 3 o'clock.

The thanks of the Camp were tendered Prof. Lumpkins and the Mart Band for the good music, Judge Hardy for his speech to the Veterans and Mrs. Robt. C. Ledford, of San Angelo, for her splendid address to the Sons and Daughters of Veterans.

The Commander appointed the following named Comrades on the monument committee: T. J. Gibson, P. O. Douglass, W. D. Frazier, H. W. Williams, Rado Steele, W. H. Browder, J. S. Groover, and, on motion, the Commander, J. P. Yeldell, was added to the committee. The following Comrades have died since our last Reunion: A. B. Allison, S. T. Arnett, J. A. Arvin, Thos. Burney, M. L. McDonald, N. T. Popejoy, J. D. Therrell, J. W. Thompson and J. D. Wallace.

No further business, on motion, Camp adjourned.

Official: H. W. Williams, Adjutant   J. P. Yeldell, 1st Lieut. Commander

[Page 175]

CALLED MEETING OF JOE JOHNSTON CAMP, FEBRUARY 25TH, 1911

By call of Commander J. P. Yeldell, Joe Johnston Camp assembled in Mexia on Saturday, February 25th, 1911. The time set for the coming Reunion was August 1st to 4th, 1911. All comrades who desire to attend the General Reunion at Little Rock, Arkansas, on May 16th to 18th were elected as delegates. The H. & T. C. R. R. was chosen as the official route of this Camp.

The Transportation Committee is Comrades W. H. Browder, T. J. Gibson and W. E. Doyle.

Privilege Committee: Comrades R. J. Bryant, W. H. Browder, Rado Steele, Wm. Justice, A. J. Cox, C. L. Watson and S. H. Beene.

Invitation Committee: Comrades T. J. Gibson, W. E. Doyle, R. E. Steele and F. M. Sellers.

Locating Committee: Comrades H. C. Joiner and J. W. McKinney.

Comrade T. J. Gibson was appointed to draw up suitable resolutions on the death of Gen'l. W. L. Cabell.

A motion was carried unanimously that the sum of $75.00 be appropriated to Miss Mamie Kennedy for the purpose of rendering three Concerts at the Reunion.

Business being finished, on motion, Camp adjourned.

Official: H. W. Williams, Adjutant   J. P. Yeldell, Commander

[Page 176]

MINUTES OF THE 23RD ANNUAL REUNION OF JOE JOHNSTON CAMP NO. 94
HELD ON AUGUST 1ST, 2ND, 3RD & 4TH, 1911

First Day – Tuesday, August 1st

Joe Johnston Camp No. 94 was called to order at 10 o'clock by Commander J. P. Yeldell. By request of assistant Chaplain Frazier, Comrade Sellers offered prayer. The Commander requested Comrade Gibson to make the address of welcome, which he did in a very appropriate manner. Comrades Sellers, E. W. Williams, Watson and P. O. Douglass made short impromptu speeches, after which the Camp took recess to 3 o'clock p.m.

Afternoon

Camp assembled at 3 o'clock. On motion of Comrade Gibson, the sum of $15.00 was appropriated for the purpose of setting out shade trees on the grounds, and a committee of three, consisting of Comrades Rado Steele, C. L. Watson and T. J. Gibson was appointed, with the Quartermaster, to attend to that business. Camp adjourned to 9:30 o'clock Wednesday.

Second Day – Wednesday, August 2nd

Camp was called to order by the Commander at 9:30. Prayer by Comrade Sellers. The roll was called and the minutes of the last Reunion read and adopted. At 10 o'clock, Rev. Dr. W. L. Lowrance delivered an eloquent address on the subject "Our Hero and his Chieftain." Camp took recess to 2:30.

Afternoon

Camp reassembled at 2:30. The following named comrades were appointed as an auditing committee: F. M. Sellers, S. H. Beene and Wm. Justice. Col. Harper of Mississippi [Page 177] delivered a pleasing address, after which the Camp adjourned to 9 o'clock Friday morning.

Third Day – Thursday, August 3rd

This day was turned over to the Sons of Confederate Veterans.

Fourth Day – Friday, August 4th

Camp was called to order by Commander. Prayer by Comrade Sellers.

A resolution was offered and carried that the Camp recommend the building of a dam, by the Camp, across the Navasota river at the lower land line. The Camp to pay one half of the amount of cost, provided it cost not more that $900.00. The said dam to be not less than thirty [30] feet wide and to be used as a public road. A committee composed of Comrades Ward, Sellers, Bryant, Watson and Rado Steele was appointed to attend to this matter. The monument committee appointed at last Reunion, reported progress and asked for extension of time. A motion was carried that the Camp build a Calaboose. A resolution was passed that the sleeping apartments at Headquarters be reserved strictly for the invited guests of the Camp. The auditing committee made the following report: "To Commander J. P. Yeldell: We, your committee appointed to audit the books of the Adjutant and Treasurer, beg leave to report that we have examined said books, and find cash in hands of the Adjutant the sum of $7.75; In the Treasury the sum of $447.09; Total amount $454.84. We are glad to state that these books have been neatly kept, and congratulate the Camp in having such efficient officers. Respectfully submitted. Wm. Justice, F. M. Sellers, S. H. Beene [Com.]" [Page 178]

The Improvement committee reported the building of the new Pavilion and some improvements on the dance Pavilion, [the contractor rendering an itemized statement for same] at the total amount of $1110.26.

A resolution of sympathy was passed for Comrades Rev. G. L. Jennings, W. F. Roberts and J. M. Storey in their afflictions.

A motion prevailed that the Camp give the children a suitable treat for the beautiful drill rendered by them at the Concert on Thursday night. The sum of $50.00 was donated to the Adjutant and Quartermaster and $20.00 to the Officer of the Day for their services to the Camp. The Camp proceeded to the election of officers for the ensuring year, which resulted as follows:

F. M. Sellers	Commander
J. W. Nash	1st Lieutenant Commander
R. E. Davis	2nd Lieutenant Commander
Rado Steele	3rd Lieutenant Commander
H. W. Williams	Adjutant
R. J. Bryant	Quartermaster
C. J. Wooldridge	Surgeon
G. L. Jennings	Chaplain
W. D. Frazier	Assistant Chaplain
J. S. Groover	Treasurer
E. W. Williams	Officer of the Day
S. H. Beene	Color Bearer
J. M. Deis	Bugler
J. M. Deis	Captain of Artillery

Col. O. P. LeVert, of Atlanta, Georgia, delivered an eloquent address on Confederate matters which was highly appreciated by the Camp and the audience. Camp took recess to 2:30 p.m.

Afternoon

Camp reassembled at 3 o'clock and held services in memory of Comrades J. J. Bridges, [Page 179] J. P. Cook, J. M. Fortenberry, T. J. Johnson and M. J. Parsons, - they having died since last Reunion. Services were conducted by Rev. Dr. Red of Mexia.

No further business, Camp adjourned.

Official: H. W. Williams, Adjutant   J. P. Yeldell, Commander

CALLED MEETING OF JOE JOHNSTON CAMP FEBRUARY 24TH, 1912

By call of Commander F. M. Sellers, Joe Johnston Camp No. 94 assembled at Mexia on February 24th for the purpose of fixing the time of the Reunion of 1912, and for transacting any other business for the welfare of the Camp.

On motion, July 25th, 1912, was chosen as the time for holding the Reunion. The various committees were appointed as follows:

Privilege Committee: Comrades R. J. Bryant, Rado Steele, J. S. Groover, J. P. Yeldell, C. L. Watson, W. H. Browder, B. D. Keeling, Dr. C. J. Wooldridge, R. E. Davis, Wm. Justice, W. L. Mallard, J. A. Wright and J. W. Nash.

Invitation Committee: Comrades T. J. Gibson, W. E. Doyle and L. B. Seale.

Locating Committee: Comrade J. W. McKinney, he to appoint his assistants.

All members of the Camp who wished to attend the State Reunion at Cleburne [date not fixed] and the General Reunion at Macon, Georgia, on May 7th to 9th, 1912 were elected as delegates to same. A motion was carried that the Improvement Committee be instructed to prepare a suitable place to be let out to someone for the accommodation of transient visitors at a reasonable price for lodgings.

The H. & T.C.R.R. was chosen as the official route of this camp to Macon, Georgia to General Reunion. There will be a Chair Car placed on the track at Mexia which will leave at about 10 o'clock on May 5th attached to the Hustler and will arrive at Macon on morning of May 7th. The round trip will be about $17.65 with lay over privileges. Business being finished, on motion, Camp adjourned.

Official: H. W. Williams, Adjutant   F. M. Sellers, Commander

[Page 180]

MINUTES OF THE 24TH ANNUAL REUNION OF JOE JOHNSTON CAMP NO. 94
HELD ON JULY 23RD TO 26TH, 1912
First Day – Tuesday, July 23rd

The Camp was called to order by Commander F. M. Sellers at 10 o'clock a.m. the Chaplain and assistant Chaplain both being dead, the Commander offered prayer. An address of welcome was made by the Commander to all present, after which, short speeches were made by Comrades E. W. Williams, T. J. Gibson, C. L. Watson and W. B. Lewis. A resolution of sympathy for Comrade, Rev. W. L.

Lowrance, D.D., on account of the death of his daughter by rail road and automobile collision was passed, and the Adjutant instructed to notify him of same. Camp recessed to 2:30 p.m.

Afternoon

Camp reassembled at 2:30 p.m. Comrades R. E. Steele, P. O. Douglass, F. M. Sellers, T. J. Gibson and George A. Bell [a Confederate Son] made short speeches. Comrades J. P. Yeldell, P. O. Douglass and A. E. Gardner were appointed on the auditing committee. On motion, the Quartermaster was instructed to purchase some chairs for the platform. Camp adjourned to 9:30 Wednesday morning.

Second Day – Wednesday, July 24th

Camp was called to order at 9:30 a.m. by the Commander, who opened the Camp with prayer. The roll was called and the minutes of the last Reunion read and adopted. Short impromptu talks were made by Comrades Browder, Sellers, Gibson, Lewis and T. H. Hayes. Camp took recess to 2:30 p.m.

Afternoon

Camp reassembled at 2:30. Judge D. E. Garrett of Houston delivered a very suitable address to the Veterans. At 4 o'clock memorial services, conducted by Rev. John A. Williams of Mt. Pleasant, were held for deceased Comrades: L. A. Adams, W. D. Frazier, Rev. G. L. Jennings, G. L. Jordan, [Pages 181-182 missing]

[Page 183]

MINUTES OF THE 25TH ANNUAL REUNION OF JOE JOHNSTON CAMP NO. 94
HELD ON JULY 22ND TO 25TH, 1913

First Day – Tuesday, July 22nd

The Commander, J. W. Nash, and the Lieutenant Commanders being absent, Comrade C. L. Watson was elected Temporary Commander. The Camp was opened with prayer by Comrade T. J. Gibson, the Chaplain being absent. The Commander made a very appropriate address of welcome. A very nice letter was read, by Comrade Gibson, from Miss Pearl Hearne, of Bryan, who was made Honorary Sponsor of the Camp. An impromptu speech was made by Comrade E. W. Williams, Officer of the Day. No business to transact, Camp recessed to 3 o'clock.

Afternoon

Camp met at 3 o'clock. On motion, the Camp dues were abolished, and the present Roster was declared to be the active membership of the Camp. The adjutant was instructed to enroll any bona fide Confederate Veteran who could show proper credentials.

The Improvement Committee was instructed to have shade trees planted around the Pavilion. Camp adjourned to 9:30 Wednesday morning.

Second Day – Wednesday, July 23rd

Camp assembled at 9:30. Opened with prayer by Comrade F. M. Sellers. The roll was called and the minutes of the last Reunion read and adopted. Comrades J. P. Yeldell, R. E. Steele and P. O. Douglass were appointed on the Auditing committee, and T. J. Gibson, R. E. Steele and J. P. Yeldell on the Finance Committee.

Comrade T. J. Gibson delivered an address suitable to the occasion. At 11 o'clock, Joe Johnston Farrow, of Groesbeck, delivered a most eloquent address on the "Private Confederate Soldier." Camp took recess to 4 o'clock.

Afternoon

Camp reassembled at 4 o'clock, and held memorial services for the following Comrades: S. F. Bond, [Page 184] John Butler, J. Y. Doke, H. C. Joiner, Jacob Parsons, Geo. W. Ross, Jasper Stedman and R. P. Ward. The Adjutant was instructed to enroll the name of each deceased Comrade.

Camp adjourned to 9 o'clock Friday morning.

Third Day – Thursday, July 24th

This day was used by the Sons of Confederate Veterans.

Fourth Day – Friday, July 25th

Camp assembled at 9 o'clock and was opened with prayer by the Chaplain, Dr. W. S. Red. Camp proceeded to elect officers for the ensuing year as follows:

R. E. Steele	Commander
C. L. Watson	1st Lieutenant Commander
J. G. Jackson	2nd Lieutenant Commander
T. H. Hayes	3rd Lieutenant Commander
H. W. Williams	Adjutant
R. J. Bryant	Quartermaster
C. J. Wooldridge	Surgeon
Rev. W. S. Red	Chaplain
J. S. Groover	Treasurer
E. W. Williams	Officer of the Day
S. H. Beene	Color Bearer
J. M. Deis	Captain of Artillery
Geo. Deis	Bugler

The following resolution was carried:

Whereas, We have heard with sorrow that our commander, J. W. Nash, is confined to his bed with sickness and could not meet with us on this occasion as usual: Therefore, be it Resolved, that the sympathy of this Camp be extended to him in his affliction, with the hope that he may soon be restored to health and strength. On motion, the sum of $50 each to the Adjutant and Quartermaster and $20 to the Officer of the Day was donated for their services to the Camp. The Camp decided that hereafter the election of officers be held on Wednesday afternoon, the second day of [Page 185] each Reunion. The Camp requested the Ladies to aid the Improvement Committee to beautify the grounds.

The auditing committee made the following report, which was adopted: "To the Commander of Joe Johnston Camp No. 94: We, your committee appointed to audit the books of the Adjutant and Treasurer, beg to say that we have examined the same and find that they have been kept correctly and balanced. We find in the Treasurer's hands $388.36; We find in the Adjutant's hands $6.80; Making a total of $395.16; All of which we beg to submit to you as our report. J. P. Yeldell, R. E. Steele, P.O. Douglass [Com.]"

Camp took recess to 3 o'clock.

Afternoon

Camp reassembled at 3 o'clock. On motion, the Camp thanked the Coolidge Band for its good music and behavior and the Show people for courtesies to the Veterans.

All business being finished, on motion, the Camp adjourned.

Official: H. W. Williams, Adjutant   C. L. Watson, Commander Pro. Tem.

[Page 186]

CALLED MEETING OF CAMP FEBRUARY 28TH, 1914

By order of Commander, R. E. Steele, Joe Johnston Camp No. 94 met in Mexia on February 28th, 1914. The first order of business was to set the time for the Reunion of 1914. Time set, 4th, 5th, 6th, & 7th of August.

The Privilege Committee consists of the following named Comrades: R. J. Bryant, W. H. Browder, R. E. Davis, J. M. Deis, P. O. Douglass, A. E. Gardner, Wm. Justice, J. W. Nash, W. A. Russell, Rado Steele, C. L. Watson, Dr. C. J. Wooldridge, J. A. Wright and J. P. Yeldell. Five members will be a quorum.

Invitation Committee: F. M. Sellers, C. L. Watson and J. P. Yeldell.

The sum of $75.00 was appropriated to the Concerts and the management of same was turned over to the Sons and Daughters of Confederate Veterans.

All comrades who wished to attend, were elected delegates to the State and General Reunions. On motion, the Camp adjourned.

Official: H. W. Williams, Adjutant   R. E. Steele, Commander

[Page 187]

MINUTES OF THE 26TH ANNUAL REUNION OF JOE JOHNSTON CAMP NO. 94
HELD ON AUGUST 4TH TO 7TH, 1914

First Day – Tuesday, August 4th

Camp was called to order by Commander R. E. Steele at 10 o'clock. Prayer by Chaplain, Dr. W. S. Red. The Commander made appropriate remarks for the occasion. Comrades Watson and E. W. Williams made short talks, after which the Camp took recess to 2:30 p.m.

Afternoon

Camp called to order at 2:30 o'clock. There being no business to transact, Camp adjourned to 9:30 Wednesday morning.

Second Day – Wednesday, August 5th

Camp assembled at 9:30. Called to order by Commander, opened with prayer by the Chaplain. The Roll was called and minutes of last Reunion read and adopted. Comrade Rado Steele was appointed on the Finance committee and Comrades J. P. Yeldell, E. Prather and Rado Steele on the auditing committee. Several Comrades gave reminiscences of their army life, after which Camp took recess to 2:30 p.m.

Afternoon

Camp reassembled at 2:30. The first order of business was the election of officers, which resulted as follows:

Dr. C. J. Wooldridge	Commander
W. A. Russell	1st Lieutenant Commander
John Jackson	2nd Lieutenant Commander
T. W. Skillern	3rd Lieutenant Commander
H. W. Williams	Adjutant
R. J. Bryant	Quartermaster
Dr. C. J. Wooldridge	Surgeon
Dr. W. S. Red	Chaplain
J. S. Groover	Treasurer
E. W. Williams	Officer of the Day
S. H. Beene	Color Bearer
J. M. Deis	Captain of Artillery
George Deis	Bugler

At 4 p.m. Memorial services were held for the following named deceased Comrades: [Page 188] M. Adams, W. L. Adams, A. W. Burford, T. J. Gibson, A. M. Nabors, and M. L. Priddy, after which the Camp adjourned to 9:30 Friday morning.

Third DayError! Bookmark not defined. – Thursday, August 6th

This day was used by Sons and Daughters of Confederate Veterans.

Fourth Day – Friday, August 7th

Camp called to order by Commander at 10 o'clock. The report of the auditing committee follows: "We, your Auditing committee appointed to audit the books of Adjutant H. W. Williams and Treasurer J. S. Groover have examined the same and found them kept correctly. We find that there is $251.76 in the hands of the Treasurer. J. P. Yeldell, Edwr. Prather, Rado Steele [Com.]"

According to the Charter, a Board of Five Directors was appointed as the legal managers of the Corporation of the Camp as follows: C. L. Watson, J. P. Yeldell, Rado Steele, W. H. Browder and W. E. Doyle.

The following resolution was offered and carried unanimously: Whereas, It is the purpose of our organization to provide reunions and social gatherings for the families and friends of our membership, and to aid in perpetuating such facts as will give to posterity a correct understanding of the causes that led up to the war of 1861-65, the environments of the Confederate States, and the privations endured and the valor displayed by her armies and navies; And whereas, during the past twenty six years we have carried on those purposes to our satisfaction, and now, as we look into the western horizon of life, we feel [Page 189]the necessity of providing means and ways for the perpetuation of our reunions and the caring for our grounds, And whereas, we have confidence in the valor, and patriotism of our sons and daughters and faith in their organizations as auxiliaries of our Camp, Now therefore, Be it Resolved 1st That it is the wish of this Camp to turn the management and control of our reunion grounds over to our sons and daughters as organizations; Resolved 2nd That the Board of Directors be fully empowered, and they are hereby fully authorized to make such transfer as to them may seem best and under such conditions as they may name; Resolved 3rd That when such transfer has been made by said Board of Directors, then it shall only be necessary for the controlling Board to make written acceptance of said trust and file same with the Adjutant of Joseph E. Johnston Camp No. 94 of Confederate Veterans to make same binding and complete.

On motion, a donation of $50.00 each to the Adjutant and Quartermaster and $20.00 to the Officer of the Day was made. Motions carried thanking the Mexia Band for good music and behavior while in Camp, to the Ladies and Mr. Anderson for ice cream and cake and to Priddy Bros. for barbecued goats. Notwithstanding all the drawbacks of the occasion, we had a pleasant Reunion much enjoyed by all present. Let it be stated right here, that our Reunions are never postponed under any circumstances.

Official: H. W. Williams, Adjutant   R. E. Steele, Commander
[Page 190]

CALLED MEETING OF CAMP FEBRUARY 27TH, 1915

By call of Commander C. J. Wooldridge, Joe Johnston Camp assembled in Mexia on February 27th, 1915. The commander being absent, First Lieutenant Commander W. A. Russell presided. The first order of business was to fix the time of the next Reunion, which was set for July 27th to 30th, 1915. The next business was appointing the committees.

Privilege Committee: R. J. Bryant, W. H. Browder, A. J. Burleson, R. E. Davis, J. M. Deis, P. O. Douglass, S. Hughes, Wm. Justice, W. Livingston, J. W. Nash, Rado Steele, C. L. Watson and J. P. Yeldell.

Invitation Committee: R. E. Steele, W. A. Russell and F. M. Sellers.

A motion carried that three members of the Privilege Committee will constitute a quorum in cases of emergency. From some cause best known to themselves, the Sons of Confederate Veterans failed to appear. They are again invited to meet with the Privilege Committee on Saturday, June 26th, at which time the bids will be opened. All Comrades who may attend the General Reunion at Richmond, Va. On June 1st to 3rd, were elected delegates. They are requested to apply to the Adjutant for credentials.

A motion prevailed that the Camp again assume the management of the Program. Comrades Watson and Deis were appointed a committee on same, and a donation of $25.00 was made to each for services to be rendered in getting up the program.

The Methodist Brethren of the Horn Hill Circuit were cheerfully granted the privilege of holding a Camp Meeting on the Reunion grounds about July 1st, 1915.

Business being ended, on motion, the Camp adjourned.

Official: H. W. Williams, Adjutant   W. A. Russell, 1st Lieutenant Commander
[Page 191]

MINUTES OF THE 27TH ANNUAL REUNION OF JOE JOHNSTON CAMP NO. 94
HELD ON JULY 27TH TO 30TH, 1915

First Day – Tuesday, July 27th

At 10 o'clock the Camp was called to order by the Commander, Dr. C. J. Wooldridge. Prayer by Chaplain, Dr. W. S. Red. By request of the Commander, Comrade C. L. Watson made an address of welcome. Talks were made by Comrades F. M. Sellers, J. W. Nash, T. H. Hayes, C. J. Wooldridge and Dr. W. S. Red. Camp took recess for Dinner.

Afternoon

Camp reassembled at 2:30 p.m. Comrade Russell made a talk about his trip to the Richmond Reunion and Comrade Watson and Sellers, also, made interesting talks on Confederate matters. There being no business to transact, Camp adjourned to 9:30 o'clock Wednesday morning.

Second Day – Wednesday, July 28th

Camp was called to order at 9:30 by Commander. Opened with prayer by Comrade Boon Anderson. The roll was called and minutes of last Reunion read and adopted. Comrades Yeldell, Watson and Davis were appointed to audit the books of the Adjutant and Treasurer. A short talk was made by Comrade Boon Anderson. There being no more business to attend to, the Camp took recess to 2:30 o'clock.

Afternoon

Camp reassembled at 2:30. The election of officers for the ensuing year was held, which resulted as follows:

Wm. Justice	Commander
J. C. McDonald	1st Lieutenant Commander

T. H. Hayes	2nd Lieutenant Commander
J. P. Yeldell	3rd Lieutenant Commander
H. W. Williams	Adjutant
Rado Steele	Quartermaster
Dr. C. J. Wooldridge	Surgeon
W. S. Red, D. D.	Chaplain
J. S. Groover	Treasurer
E. W. Williams	Officer of the Day
J. P. Sawyer	Color Bearer
J. M. Deis	Captain of Artillery

[Page 192]

Memorial services were held for the following deceased Comrades: J. H. Archer, W. H. Hayes, J. H. Prince and J. W. Thomas. Camp adjourned to 9:30 Friday morning.

Third Day – Thursday, July 29th

This day was used by the Sons of Confederate Veterans.

Fourth Day – Friday, July 30th

Camp met at 9:30. The Commander and Lieutenant Commanders being absent, on motion, Comrade C. L. Watson was called to preside. The auditing committee made the following report, which was adopted: "To the Commander and Comrades of Joe Johnston Camp: We, your committee appointed to audit the books of the Adjutant and Treasurer beg leave to report that we have examined the same and find that they have been kept neat and correct, and find that there is $21.02 in the treasurer's hands. C. L. Watson, R. E. Davis, J. P. Yeldell [Com.]"

The following communication was received from the Sons of Confederate Veterans: "To Joe Johnston No. 94 U.C.V. Greeting: I am directed by the organization of the Sons of Confederate Veterans to inform your Honorable body that we have accepted, under your resolution, the offer to take charge of the Reunion for the year 1916, and in accordance with said resolution and your action thereon, we have adopted the following plan: By the election of four committees composed each of our organization and that the chairman of each committee compose the Executive Board for the control and carrying on of the Reunion and that the Commander of our organization be the chairman of said Executive Board and the Adjutant of our Camp be the Secretary of said Executive Board. That said four committees be named as follows: First, Committee on Privileges; Second, Committee on Entertainment and Speakers; Third, Committee on Improvements, Camping and Grounds; Fourth, Committee on Membership, Publicity and Finance. Without further detail we respectfully offer our organization in the undertaking of taking charge [Page 193] and carrying on the Reunion for 1916, having in view your pleasure and entertainment and the perpetuation of Joe Johnston Camp. Respectfully submitted, W. J. Bryant, Commander Sons of Confederate Veterans."

The usual amounts were donated to the Adjutant, Quartermaster and Officer of the Day for their services to the Camp. The Band was thanked for its good behavior and music, and the general public was, also, thanked for the good behavior while on the grounds. All business being ended, on motion, Camp adjourned.

Official: H. W. Williams   C. L. Watson, Commander Pro Tem

[Page 194]

MINUTES OF THE 28TH ANNUAL REUNION OF JOE JOHNSTON CAMP NO. 94
HELD ON JULY 18TH TO 21ST, 1916
Under the Management of the Sons of Confederate Veterans

Wednesday, the second day was assigned to the Confederate Veterans.

The Camp was called to order by the Commander, Wm. Justice, and opened with prayer by Rev. W. T. Cochran of Groesbeck. On request of the Commander, Comrade C. L. Watson delivered the address of welcome. The roll was called and minutes of last Reunion read and adopted. Camp took recess to 3:00 o'clock p.m.

Afternoon

Camp reassembled at 3:00 o'clock. The first order of business was election of officers, which resulted as follows:

C. L. Watson	Commander
J. C. McDonald	1st Lieutenant Commander
F. M. Sellers	2nd Lieutenant Commander
Y. W. Plunkett	3rd Lieutenant Commander
H. W. Williams	Adjutant
Rado Steele	Quartermaster
C. J. Wooldridge, M.D.	Surgeon
W. S. Red, D.D.	Chaplain
J. S. Groover	Treasurer
E. W. Williams	Officer of the Day
J. P. Sawyer	Color Bearer
J. M. Deis	Captain of Artillery

Comrade C. J. Wooldridge offered the following Resolution, which was adopted: Whereas, at the last Reunion held at Birmingham, Alabama, Washington, D.C. was selected as the place for holding the Reunion of 1917; Therefore, be it resolved by Joe Johnston Camp No. 94, that we condemn the act of selecting said place, from the fact, that it is too far, and it was never intended by those who founded the different encampments in the South, that any of our Reunions should ever be held in any State or Territory that did not furnish Troops to the Southern Confederacy, and hereby instruct our delegates to the next Reunion [Page 195] to vote to carry a Resolution to confine the location of our Reunions to some Southern State.

The Sons of Veterans were heartily thanked for their good management of the Reunion of 1916.

Memorial services were held for Comrade J. S. Burney, M.D., after which, on motion, the Camp adjourned.

Official: H. W. Williams, Adjutant   Wm. Justice, Commander

MINUTES OF THE 29TH ANNUAL REUNION OF JOE JOHNSTON CAMP NO. 94 U.C.V.
HELD ON JULY 31ST TO AUGUST 3RD, 1917
Under the Management of the Sons of Confederate Veterans.

Wednesday, the second day, August 1st, 1917, being set apart as Veterans' Day, the Camp was called to order by Commander C. L. Watson and opened with prayer by Comrade J. W. Nash. The Commander delivered an address of welcome. An eloquent address was delivered by Comrade James Kimbell on Confederate matters in general; after which the Camp recessed for dinner.

Afternoon

Camp reassembled at 2:30. The calling of the Roll was dispensed with and the minutes of the last Reunion read and adopted. The election of officers for ensuing year was held, which resulted as follows:

C. L. Watson	Commander
James Kimbell	1st Lieutenant Commander
Rado Steele	2nd Lieutenant Commander
Geo. Plunkett	3rd Lieutenant Commander
H. W. Williams	Adjutant
Rado Steele	Quartermaster
Dr. C. J. Wooldridge	Surgeon
W. S. Red, D.D.	Chaplain
J. S. Groover	Treasurer
W. H. Browder	Officer of the Day
J. P. Sawyer	Color Bearer
J. M. Deis	Captain of Artillery

Inasmuch, as the Legislature had passed a bill so that each County, by action of the Commissioner's Court, could have a Public Park at some convenient [Page 196] location, it was suggested by the Commander of the Sons, W. J. Bryant, that this Camp ground be offered to the County for that purpose, with the distinct understanding that all rights to individual Lots be not disturbed thereby; and that a committee of five be appointed from the Veterans and Sons and Daughters of Veterans to confer with the County authorities in relation to same. The suggestion was accepted and the following committee appointed: C. L. Watson, James Kimbell, P. O. Douglass, J. W. Nash and H. W. Williams.

Memorial services were held for the following Comrades deceased since last Reunion: George Collum, R. E. Farrow, C. T. Gilbert, David LaGrone, F. M. Sellers, T. H. Sharp and M. A. Tucker.

The thanks of the Veterans were rendered to the Ladies for the excellent dinner, to the Sons for the successful management of the Reunion and to the crowd in general for its good behavior. No further business, Camp adjourned.

Official: H. W. Williams, Adjutant   C. L. Watson, Commander

MINUTES OF THE 30TH ANNUAL REUNION OF JOE JOHNSTON CAMP NO. 94 U.C.V.
HELD ON JULY 24TH, 1918

On account of the war with Germany and the failure to procure supplies for the Privilege Stands the Camp met only one day. On motion, all of the old officers were re-elected for the ensuing year.

The Camp extended thanks to the Sons and Daughters for their good work in carrying on the business of the Reunion. No other business, on motion, Camp adjourned.

Official: H. W. Williams, Adjutant   C. L. Watson, Commander

[Page 197]

MINUTES OF THE 31ST ANNUAL REUNION OF JOE JOHNSTON CAMP NO. 94 U.C.V.
HELD ON AUGUST 6TH, 1919

Camp assembled at 11 o'clock on Wednesday August 6th, 1919 – Confederate Veteran's Day – and was called to order by Commander C. L. Watson and opened with prayer by Rev. C. T. Tew, of Mexia. Roll call and reading of minutes of last Reunion was dispensed with. An address suitable to the occasion was delivered by D. Leon Harp. Comrade Boone Anderson was called on and made an interesting talk to the Camp. Camp recessed to 3 o'clock.

Afternoon

Camp reassembled at 3 o'clock. The election of officers was the first order of business which resulted as follows:

C. L. Watson	Commander
Rado Steele	1st Lieutenant Commander

James Kimbell	2nd Lieutenant Commander
G. W. Plunkett	3rd Lieutenant Commander
H. W. Williams	Adjutant
Rado Steele	Quartermaster
Dr. C. J. Wooldridge	Surgeon
Rev. C. T. Tew	Chaplain
Rado Steele	Treasurer
W. H. Browder	Officer of the Day
J. P. Sawyer	Color Bearer
Adam Shriver	Captain of Artillery

At 4 o'clock Memorial Services were held for the following named deceased Comrades: For 1918: Comrades Capt. W. P. Brown, Geo. T. Brown, R. E. Davis, Jno. S. Groover, W. D. Lanning, J. W. Nash and J. W. Stuart. For 1919: Jno. M. Deis, P. O. Douglass, R. S. Laird, James McCorkle, J. T. Stanford and Ira E. Wood. Suitable remarks on the memory of the above named Comrades were made by Rev. C. T. Tew of Mexia and Rev. John A. Williams of Mt. Pleasant. The Camp was highly gratified on the management of the Reunion by the Sons of Veterans. No further business, Camp adjourned.

Official: H. W. Williams, Adjutant   C. L. Watson, Commander

[Page 198]

MINUTES OF THE 32ND ANNUAL REUNION OF JOE JOHNSTON CAMP NO. 94 U.C.V.
HELD ON JULY 21ST, 1920

Camp met at 10 o'clock and was opened with prayer by Rev. J. G. Putnam of Mexia. The Commander, C. L. Watson, then made a speech of welcome to all, requesting them to enjoy themselves to the fullest extent.

Roll was called and minutes of last Reunion read and adopted. Impromptu speeches were made by comrades James Kimbell and W. H. Browder. On motion, the Camp authorized the Commander to sell to Wm. Kimbell a small portion of the land on the East side of the Camp. Judge W. C. Davis of Bryan delivered a very interesting address to the Veterans. Camp took recess to 2:30 o'clock.

Afternoon

Camp reassembled at 2:30. The election of officers was gone into which resulted as follows:

C. L. Watson	Commander
Rado Steele	1st Lieutenant Commander
James Kimbell	2nd Lieutenant Commander
G. W. Plunkett	3rd Lieutenant Commander
H. W. Williams	Adjutant
Rado Steele	Quartermaster
Dr. C. J. Wooldridge	Surgeon
Rev. J. G. Putnam	Chaplain
Rado Steele	Treasurer
W. H. Browder	Officer of the Day
J. P. Sawyer	Color Bearer
Adam Shriver	Captain of Artillery

After election of officers a recess was taken until 4 o'clock when memorial services were held for the following deceased Comrades: J. T. Brady, M. H. Clark, A. E. Gardner, Nat M. Jones, W. M. Skipper, J. A. Sowders and J. G. Jackson. No further business, on motion, Camp adjourned.

Official: H. W. Williams, Adjutant   C. L. Watson, Commander

[Page 199]

CALLED MEETING OF JOE JOHNSTON CAMP MARCH 25TH, 1921

At a called meeting of Joe Johnston Camp No. 94 held on March 25th, 1921, the following resolution was unanimously passed: We wish to extend our thanks to Col. A. E. Humphreys for the magnificent work he is having done on the Reunion Grounds towards preserving and beautifying them. As a further token of our appreciation we have made him an Honorary Member of said Camp. It is our sincerest wish that his every effort shall be crowned with success for the good deeds he has so kindly bestowed on our community. This resolution shall be spread on the minutes of the Camp and a copy sent to him.

Official: C. L. Watson, Commander; H. W. Williams, Adjutant; Rado Steele, Quartermaster [Executive Com.]

MINUTES OF THE 33RD ANNUAL REUNION OF JOE JOHNSTON CAMP NO. 94
HELD ON JULY 20TH, 1921

Camp was called to order by Commander C. L. Watson. Opened with prayer by Chaplain J. G. Putnam. The commander made an address of welcome to all to enjoy themselves to the extent of their abilities. The roll was called and minutes of last Reunion read and adopted.

The resolution of the called meeting of the Camp making Col. A. E. Humphreys an Honorary member of the Camp was adopted by a rising vote.

Capt. W. H. Richardson, of Austin, the first regular Commander of the Camp was introduced and made an interesting talk about the past history of the Camp. A delegation of Confederate Veterans of Waco was welcomed by the Commander whose address wad responded to by Genl. Felix Robertson, Col. Bradford Hancock and Russell Kingsberry who, also, made short talks to the Camp. Camp took recess to 2:30.

Afternoon

Camp reassembled at 2:30. The Contract [Page 200] with Col. A. E. Humphreys in relation to turning over the improvement of the Camp to him was read and adopted. Col. Humphreys made a very interesting and instructive address about improving the grounds.

The Camp proceeded to elect officers for the ensuing year. On motion, the rules were suspended and all officers of 1920 were re-elected for 1921, as follows: Comrades C. L. Watson, Commander; Rado Steele, 1st Lieut. Commander; James Kimbell, 2nd Lieut. Commander; G. W. Plunkett, 3rd Lieut. Commander; H. W. Williams, Adjutant; Rado Steele, Quartermaster; Dr. C. J. Wooldridge, Surgeon; Rev. J. G. Putnam, Chaplain; Rado Steele, Treasurer; W. H. Browder, Officer of the Day; J. P. Sawyer, Color Bearer; Adam Shriver, Captain of Artillery.

At 4 o'clock memorial services were held for the following deceased members: C. J. Bower, J. A. Brandon, Wm. Justice, W. L. Mallard, T. J. Nelson, M. P. Reynolds, R. E. Steele, F. M. Steward, E. W. Williams and Z. T. Wright.

The thanks of the Camp were extended to the Ladies for the nice dinner for the Veterans. No further business, Camp adjourned.

Official: H. W. Williams, Adjutant   C. L. Watson, Commander

[Page 13 – additional pages glued to page 200 not in consecutive order]

MINUTES OF THE 34TH ANNUAL REUNION OF JOE JOHNSTON CAMP NO. 94
HELD JULY 18TH TO 21ST, 1922

First Day – Tuesday, July 18th

Camp was opened at 10 o'clock by Commander, C. L. Watson. Chaplain was absent. He explained the contract which was made with Col. A. E. Humphreys in relation to the management of the Reunion Grounds. After which the Camp took recess to 3 o'clock.

Tuesday Afternoon

Camp reassembled at 3:30 o'clock. There being no business to transact, Camp adjourned to 9:30 o'clock Wednesday.

Second Day – Wednesday, July 19th

Camp assembled at 9:30 o'clock. Chaplain absent. Commander Watson made a short speech welcoming the people to enjoy themselves to the extent of their ability. The Contract between the Camp and Col. Humphreys in relation to the management of the Camp Grounds was read by Comrade Rado Steele. The roll was called and minutes of last Reunion read and adopted. Several impromptu talks were made by Comrades, after which the Camp took recess to 3 o'clock.

Wednesday Afternoon

Camp met at 3 o'clock. The election of officers for ensuing year was gone into, which resulted as follows:

J. P. Yeldell	Commander
C. L. Watson	1st Lieutenant Commander
T. H. Hayes	2nd Lieutenant Commander
G. W. Plunkett	3rd Lieutenant Commander
H. W. Williams	Adjutant
Rado Steele	Quartermaster
Dr. C. J. Wooldridge	Surgeon
Rev. J. G. Putnam	Chaplain
Rado Steele	Treasurer
W. H. Browder	Officer of the Day
J. W. Wright	Color Bearer
Adam Shriver	Captain of Artillery

The names of comrades who have died since last Reunion were read as follows: S. Hughes, B. D. Keeling, G. W. Lee, J. F. McClintock, J. A. McDaniel, J. P. Sawyer and L. B. Seale. The Camp extended hearty thanks to the ladies for the good dinner donated to the Veterans. No further business, Camp adjourned to Thursday morning.

Third Day – Thursday, July 20th

At 9:30, in absence of Commander, Camp was called to order by Comrade Rado Steele. Comrade Boon Anderson made a short talk. At 11 o'clock Hon. Luther Johnson of Corsicana delivered an interesting address to the Veterans and young people on Confederate matters, [Page 14] after which Camp adjourned to Friday morning.

Fourth Day – Friday, July 21st

Camp called to order by Commander Watson. County Judge Kirby, Commander of the Groesbeck organization of National Sons of Confederate Veterans, made a talk urging all Sons of Veterans to join the order and work with the Daughters of Veterans for the welfare of the Camp.

The following resolution was adopted by the Camp: Be It Resolved, by Joe Johnston Camp No. 94, that our Reunion has been a most enjoyable one with all comforts and conveniences provided to a large extent by Col. Humphreys and his efficient employees, Messrs. Kahle, Erschel and Birmingham, who have worked with our Officer of the Day, W. H. Browder. We extend to them a vote of thanks to express our appreciation for the courtesies shown us; that a copy of these resolutions be spread on the minutes, published in the papers of the County, and a copy be sent to Col. Humphreys at Wagon Wheel Gap, Colorado.

No further business to be transacted, Camp adjourned.

Official: H. W. Williams, Adjutant   C. L. Watson, Commander

[Back cover – given here by date]

MINUTES OF THE 35TH ANNUAL REUNION OF JOE JOHNSTON CAMP NO. 94
HELD JULY 24TH, 1923
Tuesday, July 24th, 1923

Camp called to order by Commander J. P. Yeldell. Minutes read by Adjutant and adopted. Talk by C. L. Watson. Letter read from Col. A. E. Humphreys. The old soldiers – Officer of Day – Hon. John Jackson appointed to take the place of our departed Brother Browder. Dr. Red called to stand by Commander Yeldell and made a splendid talk telling the Comrades of their Comrade Richardson bringing a message of love to his friends saying that Adams and Capt. Richardson made the Reunion grounds possible. Moved and seconded, we adjourn subject to call of Commander.

[Page 11]

[A list of names with no indication for what purpose]

Mattie B. Watson	Mamie Kennedy	Rado Steele Jr.	May Bessling Eulah Shultz	Doyle Harris
Frank Steele	Mrs. Joe Vaiden nee Steele	Walter Steele	Mrs. Sam McCleskey nee Steele	Ernest Watson
Chas. Watson	Mrs. L. C. Wells nee Watson	Clay Watson	Mrs. J. W. David nee Watson	Jim Cannon
Jaz Watson	Lizzie Harris	Alma Harris	Mr. Sam Fishburn – Gaston Bldg.	Charles Harris
Mrs. Blossom Seventt	Mrs. Ella Steele Bonner	Mrs. Young?	Margaret Clark Ruth Clark	Zuma Steel
Mr. Bates				

[Page 12 – blank]
[Page 9]

A resolution was introduced by C. L. Watson thanking the officers of Pure Oil Co. for their excellent care of the grounds and their many courtesies shown the old soldiers during this reunion. Joe Johnston Camp No. 94 extends to them their best wishes for continued prosperity. Resolution carried.

[Pages 10, 7, 8, 5, 6 blank]
[Page 4]

July 1924

In the absence of Commander J. P. Yeldell, Camp was called to order by 1st Lt. Commander C. L Watson. Minutes read and adopted. Short address made by Commander. After a short business meeting, a motion to elect the old officers with the exception of Commander. Comrade Watson was unanimously elected to that place and Comrade John Jackson, Officer of the Day.

At 11 o'clock Hon. Luther Johnson of Corsicana made a very interesting address. Dinner for the Confederates was announced for 12:30. Camp adjourned to meet at 8:00 – club – for dinner.

[Page 3]

By request of Commander, Dr. Jackson opened the 1925th reunion by a very inspiring speech by urging the young people, Sons and Daughters to carry on.

[END of Active Roster of Joe Johnston Camp No. 94 except for rolls which will be found at end of the minutes, etc.]
[Page 274]   **July 27, 1926**

Camp called to order by Com. Judge Jas. E. Kimbell. Eleven answered to roll call:

Dr. Wooldridge*	Wortham
H. C. Blackmon	Groesbeck
Judge Jas. E. Kimbell*	Groesbeck
T. H. Hayes*	Groesbeck
M. L. Morrow*	Wortham
J. C. C. Keyes*	Cotton Gin
Adam Shriver*	Groesbeck
N. B. Douglas*	Mart
W. A. Frost*	Wortham
J. Neill*	Wortham
J. A. Wright*	Mexia

*Not shown on known rosters

After music by the band an inspiring address on "Love" was made by Commander Judge Jas. E. Kimbell. The business of the camp was then taken up and following committees appointed:

To draft resolutions of respect to our late adj. Miss Mattie Watson: Scott Reed - Groesbeck, Ed Allen - Groesbeck, W. J. Bryant - Wortham. [Page 275] To draft resolution of respect to our late Comrade J. P. Yeldell the following were appointed: T. H. Hayes, J. M. Wright, Dr. Wooldridge.
[Page 282]

Whereas the great General over all has called to his eternal rest our Comrade J. P. Yeldell to rest under, the shade of the trees with his former Gen. Joe E. Johnston it is resolved:

1: That the Camp is deprived of one of its best & most untiring members.
2: That the Executive board will miss his affable presence.
3: That he wore the gray with honor even to the grave. That not only the Camp but all Sons & Daughters of the Camp offer sympathies to his bereaved.

        Committee: Rado Steele, Dr. Wooldridge, J. M. Doyle

The following resolutions were offered and carried unanimously: 1st - Rado Steele motion: Whereas by reason of death of J. P. Yeldell a vacancy is left on our execution committee, who has active charge and control of the business affairs of the camp; that the name of W. E. Doyle be added to our execution committee to fill the vacancy. 2nd motion - T. H. Hayes: Whereas, by reason of the depleted ranks of our membership, it is necessary to add to our membership the Sons & Daughters organization of this Camp in order to perpetuate the ideals for which our camp has stood and to continue the organization [Page 276] for time immemorial. Therefore be it resolved - that all Sons & Daughters and their descendants, who are now enrolled as honorary members of this Camp, or members of any Sons & Daughters organization, that care to be enrolled as members at any time; shall automatically become members of this Camp and be entitled to all the privileges of said Camp, to vote to do and perform any and all duties of such members.

Motion asks that it be further resolved that a supernumerary committee of three members be created to be elected from Sons & Daughters belonging to this Camp to act with the executive committee and have all the rights and privileges of said committee and be entitled to vote in the same manner as said executive committee.

Motion carried unanimously. The following committee was elected as new members on Executive Committee: E. Watson - Mexia, D. H. Gibson - Mexia, W. J. Bryant - Wortham. [Page 277] Camp adjourned to meet at 2 p.m. for election of officers.

    Mamie Kennedy, Adj. (pro tem)   Judge Jas. E. Kimbell, Commander

2 P.M. July 27, 1926

Camp called to order by Commander Kimbell and election of officers was announced as order of business. By motion all former officers were elected by acclimation. The office of Adjutant being declared vacant - Miss Mamie Kennedy was elected to fill office of same.

The following motion was made by E. Watson: That the Executive Committee be instructed to see that all lot owners on these grounds be notified that they are violating (over 2nd page) [page 262] the deed to their lots when they are used for business purposes; namely renting or making permanent living quarters of them. Also that their deeds are for camping purposes only and when they violate their deed they violate our charter also which makes our grounds free from taxation. Motion carried.

The following resolution was offered by W. J. Bryant: That this camp goes on record as opposed to any live stock being grazed on these grounds and to all other depredations on our property. That the Executive Committee be instructed to employ legal assistance if necessary, to see that these resolutions are enforced. Motion carried.

After a report from committees in resolutions of respect their reports were adopted. A resolution was offered and adopted to thank the author of all resolutions offered for the [page 243] betterment of the camp.

Resolution adopted to thank all who helped in making the Reunion a success by contributing music – good behavior – clean grounds – lights, etc an assuring them that the remaining few original members are grateful to all who assisted.

Telegram of greeting read from Lon. A. Sweth State Com. of Sons and Daughters by W. S. Banks.

Camp adjourned to meet summer of 1927.

    Mamie Kennedy, Adjutant   Judge Jas. E. Kimbell, Commander

[Page 234]

LIST OF CONFEDERATE VETERANS LIVING JULY 27, 1926

Name	Location	
H. C. Blackmon	Groesbeck	
Frank Wilson*	Groesbeck	
L. Eady	Mexia, Route 5	(Died)
J. C. McDonald	Mexia	
Rado Steele	Mexia	
Warren Steele	Mexia	(Died)
J. F. Gilbert*	Groesbeck	
J. A. Wright*	Groesbeck	
Berl Cox	Fallon	
Hampton Steele*	Kosse	
Abb Waller*	Mexia	
Joshua Wood*	Groesbeck	
Jno. Machon*	Groesbeck	
A. J. Burleson	Kosse	
Ralph Hammond*	Kosse	
W. E. Doyle	Teague	
Judge Jas. E. Kimbell*	Groesbeck	
Wm. T. H. Hays*	Groesbeck	

M. L. Morrow*	Wortham
J. C. C. Keys*	Cotton Gin
Adam Shriver*	Groesbeck
M. B. Douglas*	Mart
I. K. Harris*	Thornton
W. A. Frost	Wortham
J. Neill	Wortham

Not shown on known rosters

[Page 269]

LIST OF CONFEDERATE WIDOWS LIVING JULY 27, 1926

Mrs. G. W. Neill	no address	Mrs. Boone Anderson	Groesbeck
Mrs. Jno. S. Groover	Mexia	Mrs. Joe Steele	Mexia
Mrs. Geo. Means	Mexia	Mrs. C. L. Watson	Mexia
Mrs. S. A. Stitt	Mexia	Mrs. J. F. Gilbert	[?]
Mrs. A. J. Rogers	[?]	Mrs. Cora Tyns	Groesbeck
Mrs. J. M. Brown	Groesbeck	Mrs. Jack T. Morton	[?]
Mrs. W. H. Browder	Groesbeck	Mrs. Warren Steele	Mexia
Mrs. J. W. Thompson	Groesbeck		

LIST OF SONS & DAUGHTERS

Honorary members of Joe Johnston Camp, U. C. V., No. 94, as revised of July 21, 1926.

T. W. Arnett	Groesbeck	pd.
I. R. Rasco	Thornton	pd.
A. M. Henderson	Groesbeck	pd.
R. A. Ferrill	Groesbeck	pd.
Mr. & Mrs. Hamp Gibson	Mexia	pd.
Mr. & Mrs. S. T. Yowell	Mexia	pd.
Mr. & Mrs. D. Oliver	Groesbeck	pd.
Mr. & Mrs. Jack Womack	Mexia	pd.
Mr. & Mrs. H. L. Spikes		pd.
M. W. Turner	Webster	pd.
Mr. & Mrs. C. A. Kennedy	Mexia	pd.
Mr. & Mrs. A. C. Prendergast	Dallas	pd.
Al Prendergast	Dallas	pd.
Mrs. Ona Young	Wortham	pd.
Mrs. Ella Bonner	Mexia	pd.
Mr. & Mrs. Emmett Wright	Mexia	pd.
Mr. & Mrs. J. W. Elliott	Mexia	pd.
Mr. & Mrs. Wyatt Priddy	Mexia	pd.
Mr. & Mrs. Walter Beaver	Mexia	pd.
Miss Zuma Steele	Mexia	pd.
Mrs. J. L. Sinclair	Mexia	pd.
Miss Bird Storey	Dallas	pd.
Mrs. Cora Ferguson	Groesbeck	pd.
E. L. Harris	Thornton	pd.
Miss Mamie Kennedy	Mexia	pd.
Mrs. Wiley Pierce	Mexia	pd.
Mrs. S. J. Moody	Mexia	pd.
Mr. & Mrs. Howard Wright	Mexia	pd.
Miss Sudie Wright	Mexia	pd.
Miss Mabel Hall	Mexia	pd.
Dr. Chas. Watson	Waco	pd.
Dr. Clay Watson	Waco	pd.
Alfred Kelley	Wortham	pd.
Leonard Hastons	Wortham	pd.
Geo. Leverett	Wortham	pd.
W. J. Bryant	Wortham	pd.

Mr. & Mrs. Jno. Monroe	Wortham	pd.
Mr. & Mrs. Henry Meador	Wortham	pd.
Mr. & Mrs. Oscar Manning	Wortham	pd.
Mr. & Mrs. W. K. Boyd	Wortham	pd.
Mr. & Mrs. Scott Reed	Groesbeck	pd.
Mr. & Mrs. Fountain Kirby	Groesbeck	pd.
Mr. & Mrs. Lewis Seay	Groesbeck	pd.
Mr. & Mrs. Jno. Cox	Groesbeck	pd.
Mr. & Mrs. E. A. Allen	Groesbeck	pd.
Miss Mabel Hall	Groesbeck	pd. [duplicate]
Mrs. R. L. Capell	Waco	pd.
Mrs. Zeno King	Mexia	pd.
Mrs. J. W. David	Corsicana	pd.
Mrs. Ralph Stitt	Corsicana	pd.
Mrs. Mina Wells	Hubbard	pd.
Miss Ruth Wells	Hubbard	pd.
Joe Wells	Hubbard	pd.
L. C. Wells	Hubbard	pd.
Mrs. Roger Adamson	Mexia	pd.
Roger Mac Adamson	Mexia	pd.
Mr. & Mrs. Geo. Perkins	Mexia	pd.
Mr. & Mrs. Jess McLendon	Mexia	pd.
Misses Ione & Inez McSwane	Mexia	pd.
Mrs. Jno Neece	Mexia	pd.
Mrs. Sam Cox	Mexia	pd.
Mrs. Tracy McKenzie	Mexia	pd.
Mr. & Mrs. Tom Cox	Mexia	pd.
Mrs. T. A. Griffith	Mexia	pd.
Mr. & Mrs. Ernest Watson	Mexia	pd.
Mr. & Mrs. J. E. Woods	Teague	pd.
Harold Wright	Mexia	pd.
Mr. Rado Steele Jr.	Mexia	pd.
Mr. & Mrs. J. M. Vaiden	Mexia	pd.
Mrs. W. A. Keeling	Mexia	pd.
Mrs. Bounds Martin	Mexia	pd.
Mrs. Will Ross Jr.	Mexia	pd.
Mr. & Mrs. R. W. Steen	Groesbeck	pd.
W. H. Reed	Dallas	pd.
N. P. Houx	Mexia	pd.
C. J. Sterling	Mexia	pd.

[Page 278] Moved that exec comd. be instructed to be the head of this ____ Camp. Motion carried.
Election of officers:

Comd.	Mr. T. H. Hayes, elected by acclimation
Lt. Comd.	W. J. Bryant
Quartermaster	Mrs. Allen
Adjutant	Mamie Kennedy

Rado Steele, W. E. Doyle, Scott Reed, Evan Watson, W. J. Bryant, Evan Nelson - Exec. Com. be forced to attend all meetings or be suspended. [Page 279] (continued from Page 277) J. P. Yeldell, C. L. Watson, B. W. Collier, A. J. Cox, Col. Humphries, Mattie Watson, G. W. Plunkett - Wortham, Jackson - Wortham, Sol_ Rasco - Thornton, A. J. Rogers - Lost Prairie, Capt. W. H. Richardson - Austin, Bill Justice - Personville, J. H. Bozeman - Tehuacana, Boone Anderson - Groesbeck, Ben Roberts - Coolidge, Warren Livingston, Jim McKenzie, Mr. Larns - Prairie Hill.
[Page 280]

Miss Ella Bonner	pd.
Miss Ona Young	pd.
Mrs. Emmett Wright	pd.
Harold Wright	pd.

Frank Wilson - Groesbeck
L. Eads - Mexia Rt. 5

[Page 281]
J. C. McDonald - Mexia
Rado Steele - Mexia
Warren Steele - Mexia
J. F. Gilbert - Groesbeck
J. W. Wright - Groesbeck
N. Bert Cox - Fallon
Hampton Steele - Kosse
B. Abb. Waller Mexia
Joshua Wood - Groesbeck
John Maclin - Groesbeck
A. J. Burleson - Kosse
Ralph Hammond - Kosse
W. E. Doyle - Teague
Col. C. G. Carroll - El Campo Route 3 Box 77
Mrs. J. W. Neill
Mrs. Boone Anderson
Mrs. J. W. Thompson - Groesbeck
Mrs. Jno. S. Groover - Mexia
Mrs. Rado Steele - Mexia
Mrs. Geo. Means - Mexia
Mrs. Joe Steele - Mexia
Mrs. C. L. Watson - Mexia
Mrs. S. A. Stitt

[Page 283]

J. P. Brown	2.00
J. A. Jones	.50
N. M. Jones	.50
J. A. Sife	.50
R. W. Dick Payne	.50
Elias East	.50
J. M. Rambo	.50
J. A. T. Richardson	.50
M. P. Reynolds	.50
Axtell Jno. H. Crawford (Lot 78)	5.00
Lot 94 W. L. Powell - Hubbard	5.00
Lot 93 Geo. McNeese - Axtell	5.00
Lot 95 W. C. Poris - Hubbard	5.00
Lot 92 T. W. Skillern [not pd] Frosa	
Lot 81 W. H. Herring	5.00
G. W. Kenny	.50
R. J. Bryant	178.40
Isaac Rayborn	.50

Honorary Members of Joe Johnston Camp
Gen'l. W. L. Cabell
Col. Roger Q. Mills
Col. W. L. Lowrance
Col. G. B. Gerald
Maj. Chas. H. Smith alias "Bill Arp"
Rev. Dr. A. P. Smith

[Page 284]

July 30th 1890
Rec'd of Mr. Jones for Camp ___   5.00
   Rec'd of J. M. Rambaugh for
      Davis Monument fund   5.00

Rec'd from

H. C. Jones	2.50	A. J. Burleson	.50
E. Chambers	.50	J. A. Spruill	.50
J. B. Johnson	.50	J. W. Simmons	.50
W. E. Doyle	.50	Dr. W. L. Corleton	.50

W. L. Powell	.50	M. W. Kemp	.50
Mat Clark	.50	C. H. T. Wood	.50
F. M. Howard	.50	L. E. Camp	.50
T. W. Skillarn	.50	J. H. Goodiman	.50
J. S. Groover	.50	Rado Steele	.50
W. H. Herring	.50	I. E. Wood	.50
W. H. H. Lindsey	.50	J. B. Jordan	.50
A. J. Cox	.50	J. G. Howaze	.50
N. B. Seddenn (see about right name)			.50

[Page 286] List of Parties Contributions

A. M. Kennedy	.50	E. B. Smyth	1.00	
C. H. F. Wood	1.00	J. P. Cook	1.00	
J. H. Harbard	.25	J. M. Berry	1.00	
B. J. Hancock	1.00	Mrs. Stewart	.25	
W. P. Stewart Mrs.	.25	M. P. Fuqua	.25	
J. T. Wright	.50	J. R. Montgomery	.50	
B. W. Turner	.25	W. H. H. Linsey	.75	
J. E. McDonald	.50	G. M. Wood	.25	
J. F. Beaty	.25	A. I. Squyres	.25	
O. D. Walker	1.00	R. L. Smith	.25	Freestone Co.
S. A. J. Richardson	.50	R. E. Davis	.25	
L. E. Camp	.25	J. O. Harper	.50	

[Page 287]
    Rec'd of

Hood	5.00
Herbert	1.50
G. C. Boyle	.50
Barton	.50
M. Groves	.50
Suttles	.50
Y. T. Wright	.50
M. P. Fuqua	.50
A. J. Sloan	.50
J. W. McKinny	.50
M. A. Tucker	.50
W. D. Frazier	.50
L. J. Farrar	.50
R. P. Ward	.50
J. B. Phillips	.50
G. W. Archer	.50
J. M. Storey	.50
C. S. Bates	.50
J. P. Lindley	.50
H. C. Berryman	.50
J. E. Parker	.50
J. G. Corrall	.50
N. F. Hoall	.50
Capt. Gilbert	.50
A. J. Cashion	.50

ADDENDUM

Men buried in Limestone County, Texas that were of the correct age to fight in Civil War or who had CSA markers. Also men from the surrounding counties who fought in CSA.

Armour Cemetery
G. W. Walker 1820-1882
Martin Johansen 10/10/1839 – 7/14/1895
Alexander C. Robbins 5/22/1826 – 10/17/1916
Robert Pierce Merrill 1/1/1834 – 8/29/1913
Jens A. Jenson 1834-1917
Hans Jenson 1844-1926
J. M. Holley 1841-1927 Mason
H. C. Vinson 8/23/1822 – 7/18/1909
Josiah G. Jones 10/29/1823 – 8/12/1885
Henry L. Herring 3/10/1844 – NDD
John N. Lusk – Co. I 17th Mississippi Infantry C.S.A.
W. K. Cundieff 2/15/1847 – 7/20/1895
James N. Roberts 10/28/1845 – 3/21/1921
M. E. Bolen 7/20/1828 – 6/24/1910
Robert Jordon Shanks 4/25/1840 – 9/11/1897
J. H. Bozeman – Co. B 2nd GA. Infantry C.S.A.
Marvin Dee Hopkins 8/12/1845 – 4/27/1904
J. W. Walker 9/5/1846 – 12/22/1912
Bryant B. Blount 9/10/1835 Twiggs Co., GA – 10/25/1880
J. A. Jordan 3/11/1834 – 3/16/1885
T. N. Ganey 8/4/1848 – 2/15/1908 Masonic
James D. Armour 11/16/1835 - 9/5/1884
W. B. Lewis 12/31/1832 – 12/9/1916
J. S. Furlow 3/24/1826 – 4/5/1900
J. J. Riggs 12/27/1837 – 6/5/1891
C. D. Nordyke 6/24/1831 – 2/10/1892
Wilbur Green Lewis – Co. C, 2nd FL Cavalry C.S.A.
Elisha Petty 7/11/1823 – 10/25/1907
J. F. Roan 6/10/1844 – 12/29/1903
T. B. Williams 1/16/1832 – 10/15/1902

Bennett-LeNoir Cemetery
G. W. Jackson 9/25/1826 – 6/2/1889 Mason

Big Hill Cemetery
James C. Kirton 7/4/1848 – 3/3/1916
J. K. Champion 1848 – 1920
Charles Smith 7/29/1842 Scotland – 2/6/1910

Billington Cemetery
E. J. Billington 1/1/1826 – 8/5/1895
Thomas Watson Coker 1847 – 1926

Brown Cemetery
Dr. J. D. Brown 7/12/1845 – 2/10/1877

Ceder Island Cemetery
Hezekial L. DeWitt – A Confederate Veteran 6/22/1829 – 6/10/1862

Cobb Cemetery
J. A. Harris 2/5/1829 - 10/3/1910
J. W. McDaniel 12/27/1847 – 10/26/1948
Pinkney Cobb 3/24/1821 – 4/11/1866
M. O. Bates 3/23/1830 – 6/19/1889
John Lewis 9/26/1829 – 1/18/1897
J. Rogers 11/22/1832 – 10/14/1890
Solon Rasco ND, Co. B, 20th TX Cavalry CSA
E. Hollen 5/14/1844 VA – 8/14/1889
Edmond Reynolds 9/1/1834 – 8/26/1882
John Rasco ND, Co. B, 20th TX Cavalry CSA
Joshua Avery Carrell 1827 – 3/7/1889
J. B. Ellis 11/2/1847 – 2/12/1914
H. V. R. Taylor 2/21/1836 – 5/28/1905
J. S. Wingard ND, Co. A, 1st GA Cavalry CSA
Thomas J. Herod ND, Co. I, 5th MS Cavalry CSA

Coolidge Cemetery
J. A. Sanders 12/31/1842 – 3/24/1926
William M. Vinson 3/23/1848 – 2/6/1943

Cox Cemetery
William H. Brown ND, Co. B, 8th GA Infantry CSA
Houston Henderson 11/22/1847 – 11/22/1936
Obediah Cox 2/17/1841 – 8/9/1914

Criswell Cemetery
M. A. Criswell 6/3/1823 – 5/3/1883
A. Wimberly Eaves 1840 - 1904
M. T. Durhan 2/4/1843 – 6/10/1923
T. J. Sutherland 11/25/1843 – 11/1/1921

Crouch Cemetery
W. H. Langham 11/13/1845 – 1/20/1910

Delia Cemetery
T. J. Boyar 2/7/1822 – 5/31/1913

Dover Cemetery
H. D. Brown 11/11/1828 – 11/22/1905
Jacob F. Jordon 5/13/1829 – 4/16/1902
John Wallace Killough 10/9/1841 – 3/14/1921
G. C. McDonald 7/26/1843 – 1/24/1910
Thomas M. McDonald 6/18/1826 – 3/18/1891
Jasper Moore 3/1/1838 – 6/4/1903
William Roscoe Spruiell 12/8/1843 – 12/6/1927

Eaton Cemetery
Silas Easton 1827 –1871

Ebenezer Cemetery
J. L. Brown 5/4/1848 – 2/9/1931
D. J. Chapman 12/5/1831 – 6/12/1893
William D. Donaldson 9/30/1836 – 3/18/1919
W. S. Cook 11/23/1843 – 9/3/1907
M. E. Cook 4/20/1836 – 4/3/1910
J. T. Cone 4/3/1837 – 4/12/1923
Charles H. Clark 7/2/1845 – 12/9/1927
S. Fulton 1/6/1832 – 3/20/1891
Walter A. Glenn 1837 Clarksville, TN – 1892
Captain T. N. Gray NB – 5/16/1884 CSA
W. M. Harper 10/26/1833 – 12/13/1918
Rev. J. D. Holton 10/31/1830 – 4/13/1900
Thomas C. Holton 1/8/1829 – 4/23/1910
Preston Lawrence 10/19/1840 – 12/20/1922
Sandford Lowery 12/19/1830 – 1/6/1916
D. S. Monachan 7/18/1830 – 5/17/1880
Joseph A. Murff 11/17/1841 – 8/25 1903
John Clingman O'Neal 5/5/1832 – 1/27/1908
Josiah Rasco ND, Co. H, 20th TX Cavalry CSA
John A. Rogers 7/27/1848 – 10/9/1919
L. B. Seale 8l/31/1842 – 12/18/1921
Alonzo Smith 2/5/1843 – 5/5/1927 Co. F, 63rd AL Infantry CSA
R. L. Thompson 2/8/1830 – 12/12/1903
James Knox Polk Truett 1848 – 1933
Dr. W. W. Wilkins 1840 – 1913
Z. T. Williams 2/16/1847 – 5/19/1936

Eutaw Cemetery
William Denning Snowden 6/22/1836 – 6/25/1870
J. R. Irwin 9/5/1847 – 6/16/1914
David Brown 1/25/1834 – 4/3/1885
A. W. McDaniel 8/2/1835 – 6/3/1915
J. H. McDaniel 12/27/1844 – 1/16/1925
William E. Briggs ND, Sgt. Co. K, 27th TX Cavalry CSA
Greene B. Duncan 1/29/1824 – 1/30/1881
Sidney Gumano Hunter 11/20/1831 – 1/17/1897
J. L. Harper 12/25/1841 – 10/11/1891
J. W. Ainsworth 12/16/1839 – 9/24/1927
Elder L. Denson 12/9/1826 – 1/4/1890
W. P. Stephenson 1/16/1835 – 9/30/1913
Robert G. Brown 8/24/1827 GA – 2/13/1878
B. F. Brown 7/27/1843 – 5/12/1904
R. W. Gunn 6/8/1848 – 9/14/1911
J. C. Ainsworth 10/16/1836 – 8/6/1917
T. J. Pillow 2/23/1844 – 5/6/1889
Matthew W. Santry 1837 – 1903
John H. Tillery 1826 – 10/12/1882
W. M. Skipper 11/23/1835 – 1/30/1917
John Z. Adams 4/20/1824 Conecuh Co., AL – 7/4/1881
John H. Welch ND, Co. K, 20th TX Cavalry CSA
William B. McBride 1847 – 1931
D. B. Curry 1843 – 7/8/1905
Benjamin Franklin Foy 1827 – 1/23/1893 No Marker

Faulkenberry Cemetery
Angus V. Jones NB – 4/5/1920, Pvt. 18th MS Cavalry CSA
James Kimbell 4/12/1846 – 12/1/1935 TX Co. H, 1st AR Regt. CSA
William Manuel Franklin 1848 – 1918

Prairie Brodie Whitcomb 6/29/1836 – 3/13/1902
J. W. Stewart 10/16/1847 – 4/1/1918
J. M. Thurmond 10/29/1835 – 5/5/1906
J. D. Whitcomb 5/19/1840 – 1/7/1914
Ales Benson 1833 – 1899 Cpl. Co. K, 7th Regt. TN CSA
W. Winston 12/27/1830 – 2/9/1922
John Harrington 10/11/1840 – 8/1/1899 Pvt. Co. E, 4th TX Infantry CSA
Frank C. Oliver 3/27/1827 – 5/12/1902
T. J. Hayes 11/17/1844 – 4/10/1928
J. D. Shortridge 3/28/1841 – 10/29/1904
A. J. Clancy ND, Co. G, 57th AL Infantry CSA
Joseph Booth Tyus 3/21/1830 – 11/9/1901
A. M. Gleaver 2/12/1847 – 11/27/1899
Allen W. Gleaver 9/7/1839 – 4/15/1918
John Fletcher Cayton 3/3/1847 – 11/13/1918
James W. Wright 3/3/1845 – 9/17/1927
N. T. Popejoy 9/39/1840 – 1/29/11910
Jake Parsons 2/22/1826 – 12/30/1912
Ben Hewitt 11/12/1846 – 6/21/1934
Dr. J. O. A. Daughtry 5/5/1826 – 10/18/1892
Alexander Watson Procter 11/25/1845 – 11/4/1911
Jim McClintock 3/15/1839 – 6/10/1891
A. G. Saunders 12/11/1834 – 2/24/1898
Joseph Scott 1/15/1835 – 1/13/1886
J. T. Davis 8/1/1839 – 6/22/1885
Ed Procter 7/21/1838 – 4/3/1882
R. A. Key 11/4/1832 – 4/3/1889
George Wright 11/4/1846 – 1026/1914
T. H. Sharp 2/9/1840 – 7/1/1917
Samuel Overhiser 6/2/1825 – 5/30/1882
John Howell 1/16/1826 – 6/21/1867
George W. Webb 7/10/1838 – 8/6/1873
D. Faulkenberry 3/12/1845 – 8/30/1867
Richard Andrews 1/2/1823 – 3/10/1881
Green W. Nelson 1/30/1840 – 6/3/1922
L. Ingle 4/8/1822 – 3/25/1887
Dr. A. G. Camp 4/4/1827 – 9/8/1888
William M. Jacobs 10/10/1847 – 8/39/1951
A. Shrivier 10/18/1837 – 12/14/1883
R. P. Cordon 9/25/1827 – 4/4/1891
Felix G. Kennedy 9/15/1840 – 5/21/1887
J. T. Clay 1845 – 1917
G. W. Bennett 7/14/1847 – 5/27/1889
T. C. Kortum 5/16/1840 – 9/29/1894
Frankie Nathan Pelham 1846 – 3/2/1928
James McKenzie 2/25/1825 – 1/6/1920

Ferguson Cemetery
Lee Sandler 10/21/1830 – 12/18/1882
William J. Watson ND, Co. F, 21st TX Infantry CSA
G. Moss 3/26/1833 – 6/27/1907
Milton Oliver Gibson 8/3/1848 ND
J. M. Baldwin 3/12/1847 – 2/10/1905
Johnny A. Hanson 7/7/1837 – 8/19/1878
John McFarlane 3/7/1842 – 9/1926
Charles Roberts 11/13/1823 – 10/4/1900
Levi Whatley 1/6/1830 – 2/17/1906
Henry Sadler 1/11/1844 – 12/9/1887
Joe Allman 2/12/1841 – 1/5/1911
James Allman 1844 – 1950
William Boyd 1845 – 1909

James Benjamin Robertson NB – 1885 [md. 1865]

Forest Glade Cemetery:
T. S. Byrd 1843-1909
William Henry 1840 - 1919
Andrew Gamble 1828-1906
Benjamin L. Speer 1846-1936

Fort Parker Memorial Park Cemetery
James Machon ND, Co. K, 7th LA Inf. CSA
R. Boon Anderson ND, Co. B, 2Nd Battalion, Waul's TX Legion, CSA
C. W. Thompson 1837 – 1914
J. Floyd Gilbert 10/14/1844 – 5/24/1939
P. M. Draper 8/2/1833 – 4/21/1898
Jim S. Burney 11/7/1839 – 9/9/1915
M. L. Priddy 11/3/1835 – 3/31/1914
W. D. Dalton 3/10/1845 – 2/23/1926
John Welch 1/18/1844 – 11/22/1889
John L. Marshall 1/3/1840 – 7/23/1921
Rev. Richard Oden 2/23/1828 – 8/26/1895
W. R. Black 7/24/1845 – 8/15/1908
Abram Bates 2/9/1843 – 4/17/1872
Dr. T. H. Dennis 2/20/1833 – 4/1/1921
W. H. Cargile 1/3/1842 – 8/11/1922
W. A. Biggs 1847 – 2/8/1884
James Carroll Tidwell 2/17/1840 – 3/29/1900
G. W. Seawright 4/20/1844 – 12/11/1873
Robert L. Sharp 12/21/1833 - 2/15/1869
William Wright 5/30/1827 – 6/21/1888
William A. Sharp 6/7/1836 – 12/19/1886
S. C. Foster 10/3/1845 – 4/20/1926
T. F. Sanders 9/2/1837 – 6/3/1911
James M. Sanders 7/16/1823 – 6/22/1893
J. Sanders 3/22/1831 – 5/20/1885
E. W. Sharp 8/4/1826 – 5/16/1870
Dr. J. C. Welch 1827 – 1877
C. R. Waters 6/4/1828 – 9/10/1874
A. J. Runnels 1844 - 1884
H. S. Bynum 5/21/1826 – 6/16/1884
A. G. Davis 4/14/1829 – 9/15/1880
James Anderson 11/24/1835 – 1/16/1904

Gunter Cemetery
J. T. Williams 12/20/1831 – 3/16/1916

Hancock Cemetery
Charles Jackson Hancock 1/18/1823 – 11/20/1903
Lewis Ross Hancock 4/4/1847 – 6/20/1891
A. J. Hayes 5/16/1833 – 12/27/1892

Hewitt Cemetery
William E. Hewitt 9/15/1823 – 2/14/1868 Pvt. TX Green's Div. CSA

Hogan Cemetery
G. I. Hogan ND, Co. K, 12th TX Cavalry CSA

Robert Montgomery 6/24/1824 – 1/12/1872 Mason
W. C. Webb 9/6/1834 – 8/16/1908
John E. Bates 7/28/1841 – 12/10/1881
J. W. Ferrill 7/9/1840 – 6/20/1906
J. L. Goubold 12/25/1827 – 4/1/1882
James E. Carrell 10/13/1844 – 2/14/1937
Henry C. Jackson 3/12/1845 – 2/14/1872
Joseph H. Powell 8/7/1824 TN – 3/11/1912
John Franklin Wilson 1/4/1847 – 8/15/1929

Honest Ridge Cemetery
Henry S. Rennick 11/15/1837 – 3/23/1885
Mc Compton 5/17/1840 – 3/13/1895
H. Van Dyke 8/1/1828 – 4/23/1909
R. S. Barber 6/26/1832 – 4/28/1916 Mason
Neal Davidson 9/10/1843 – 9/16/1878
Bulger Peeples 9/26/1839 – 2/24/1871
William Crawford Zimmerman 6/9/1829 – 3/4/1892
A. B. Smith 7/7/1841 – 7/9/1903
Meredith N. Miller 11/20/1828 – 9/17/1884
Benjamin J. Wilkinson 9/21/1836 – 11/24/1863
L. P. McKnight 4/3/1825 – 2/16/1884

Horn Hill Cemetery
Joe W. Kerley 7/1/1823 – 3/25/1904
T. J. Wilson 1837 – 1/19/1899
R. W. Bevill 7/5/1846 – 9/29/1917
Francis Heflin 1/12/1846 – 4/1922
Eli Posey 3/20/1839 – 1/11/1875
V. A. G. Garrett 10/19/1845 – 6/12/1891
James M. Posey 1/31/1841 – 1/25/1870
Uriah Posey 2/6/1836 – 4/13/1877
Will A. Burris 2/10/1842 – 3/4/1871
J. K. P. Murphey 12/25/1844 – ND
Evans B Hargrove 2/1/1827 – 5/15/1906

Jones Cemetery
Calvin Jones 1833 – 1909 CSA [Picture]

King Cemetery
G. J. Nance 3/1/1844 – 9/11/1916
T. G. Harper 6/14/1844 – 2/4/1884
Franklin W. Harper 2/11/1833 – 2/11/1873
R. M. Cox 11/4/1847 – 9/5/1891
James K. P. Harris 5/25/1845 – 2/17/1928 41st AL Infantry CSA
S. G. Kennedy 3/27/1840 – 12/13/1927
H. J. McCorkille 3/17/1830 – 2/2/1910
Samuel Wacaster 9/16/1827 – 1/21/1897 Co. H, GA Infantry CSA

King-Williams Cemetery
James A. King 11/4/1847 – 12/13/1891

Kirk Cemetery
C. C. Hardwick 6/8/1840 – 10/4/1900
J. V. Hardwick 5/27/1827 – 2/21/1906
Charles H. Richards 8/26/1833 – 10/30/1900

Robert Berton Smith 9/2/1831 – 7/18/1890
Martin S. Sanders 11/12/1830 – 12/23/1892
J. Rose Potts 12/4/1835 – 5/21/1918
M. L. Bass 11/19/1844 – 9/18/1902
David LaGrove 1841 – 1917
J. M. Fortenberry 1/7/1836 – 8/27/1910
Robert Pittman 7/29/1833 – 5/25/1894
J. L. Hudson 2/9/1833 – 1/25/1912
R. C. Cooper 4/4/1833 – 9/12/1913
Riner Christoffer 1844 – 1902
Smauel P. Reid 9/8/1834 – 2/22/1915
Allen M. Drinkard 5/5/1837 – 7/9/1905
Leroy C. Pearce 7/22/1836 – 9/7/1926
Terry Wiley Skillern 6/6/1844 – 2/3/1918
John Eakens 11/23/1842 – 5/3/1909
Benjamin F. Pearce 2/13/1841 – 3/2/1940
W. H. Garrett 1847 – 1927
Thomas H. Hulon ND [Wife 1845-1905]
F. J. Wallace 12/5/1847 – 7/16/1909

Kosse Cemetery
Dr. John R. Taylor 1837-1911
Col. Tillman Ingram 1822-1890
F. G. Ingram 1845-1904
L. L. Reese 1830-1922
Thomas S. Moore, M.D. 1832-1879
J. T. "Kit" Robison ?-1932
Dr. C. C. Davis 1832-1883
Maj. R. C. Robison 1823-1882
Henry Clay Markham 1848-1916
A. E. Hammond 1845-1922
L. M. Bratton 1848-1892
William Jasper Winfield 1845-1930
Albert Willis Pope 1847-1932 Co. I 6th LA Cavalry CSA
Edmond H. Matthews 1834-1884
John Todd 1823-1916
P. Kling 1830-1917
J. H. Snowden 1847-1937
Henry C. Jordan 1844-1925 Co. F 23rd AR Infantry CSA
John Snowden [ND] Co. B 12th TX Cavalry CSA
W. J. Daly 1847-1930
Henry Orum 1827-1910
E. McGee Jolly 1848-1910
G. F. Lloyd 1844-1915 Co. C 3rd Bn. SC Lt. Artillery CSA
A. C. S. Calmes 1822-1898
E. F. Blackmon 1837 –1892
Robert Austin Hearn 1846-1907
Marcus L. Jackson 1828-1882
Thomas Cooper 1833-1910
Burkley B. Brown 1846-1906
W. M. Hunt [ND] Co. A 16th GA Cavalry CSA
D. A. Inmon 1830-1897
W. R. Loper 1845-1906
Thomas B. Reedy 1838-1908
W. G. Ainsworth 1845-1908
J. H. Marett [ND] Co. C 1st SC State Troops CSA
G. W. Kelly 1838-1917
George M. Whitlow 1844-1890
James Benson Hunt 1849-1932
S. E. Dean 1847-1924

LaSalle Cemetery
W. G. Dossey 1849-1926
John W. ? 3/28/1826 - ?
F. M. L. ? 6/10/1837 – 9/21/1874 [Lauderdale?]
Francis M. Campbell [ND] Co. G 13th AL Infantry CSA
Calvin Ferguson 1828-1880

Lindley Cemetery
W. I. Ware 9/39/1848 – 1/1/1892
Joe Harrison Lindley 12/24/1834 – 4/1/1862
John Simon Lindley 1/13/1826 – 9/3/1864 LA [died from wounds]

Lost Prairie Cemetery
Joseph W. Baldwin 12/1/1843 – 8/5/1914
Charlie Blair 8/17/1830 – 5/27/1922
James H. Crider 1847 – 1916
James K. Polk Fitzgerald 4/20/1846 TN – 4/4/1936
James Kennedy 1833 – 1875
Nathaniel Lansford 6/2/1836 – 5/24/1900
J. A. Moore 12/2/1847 – 12/8/1887
Jim Morgan 11/7/1830 – 1/14/1885
J. C. Morton 10/20/1836 – 7/21/1880
Thomas J. Pearce 7/26/1840 – 12/18/1879
W. C. Peters 1/18/1839 – 8/15/11909
J. B.Pollock 5/25/1848 – 12/27/1886
William J. Reeves 9/17/1825 – 4/29/1907 Co. F, 15th TX Cavalry, Sweet's Regt.
J. M. Rogers 2/24/1840 – 12/10/1884
W. F. Sanders 12/12/1848 – ND
Lafayette Shugart 8/27/1845 – 1/17/1917 Pvt. 2nd Batt. TX Cavalry CSA
John S. Sims 6/11/1845 – 3/5/1907
William L. Sims 12/1/18457 - 5/31/1878
William R. Stephens 1840 –1918 Co. F, 3rd AL Infantry CSA
Edward Summers 2/27/1827 – 6/30/1893
M. E. Wayland 1831 – 4/1881
J. C. Wayland 7/15/1827 – 1/27/1875
J. G. Sikes 4/19/1846 – 12/27/1882

Masters Cemetery
G. W. Boatler 6/11/1847 Scott Co., MS – 11/29/1916
F. D. Smith 9/1843 – 5/16/1879
Francis Smith 7/1828 – 9/20/1882
Richard Eslick 7/7/1831 – 11/30/1904
Joseph Chapman 5/22/1822 – 6/1/1882

McKenzie Cemetery
T. A. Duke 1844 – 1923
John Judson, Sr. 1824 – 1893 Pvt. 17th TX Cavalry CSA
Isaiah Shields 12/3/1834 – 2/11/1895 Co. H, 5th TX Infantry CSA
William J. Choate 1833 – 1900 Co. C, 17th TX Cavalry CSA [11/1848 – 7/29/1900]
Jim Thomas 11/9/1847 – 3/3/1934
Rev. W. M. Thomas 8/31/1837 – 2/1/1921 CSA
R. A. McKenzie 11/22/1841 – 4/18/1891 Co. D, 6th TX Cavalry CSA
Paul DeLeon 3/2/1847 Mexico – 1/22/1912
William E. Shipp 7/18/1844 – 9/1/1893

Mexia City Cemetery
Dr. N. E. Hooper 2/11/1844 – 5/10/1902
J. I. Moody 10/4/1847 – 9/18/1899
T. A. Germany 1/15/1834 – 5/12/1901
A. J. Overstreet 11/24/1836 – 3/31/1903 [Mason]
W. F. Moore 1843 – 1903
James H. Pitts 11/23/1830 – 12/15/1914

Jewish Cemetery
Leon Newman 2/14/1845 Montgomery, AL – 9/27/1899
Abraham Mindek 1836 - ?
Abraham Levingston 6/13/1832 – 5/22/1881 [K of H]

Mt. Antioch Cemetery
F. H. Butler 10/21/1839 – 4/21/1914
Charles A. Bryant 6/22/1845 – 7/26/1865 s/o E. R. & W. C.
James E. Bryant 9/28/1834 – 5/10/1885
M. A. Caldwell 1/11/1833 – 10/28/1910
John E. Chaffin 5/30/1831 – 2/3/1870
G. W. Crist 1824 Edgar Co., IL – 10/6/1873
James T. Dunn 1842 – 1933
Sgt. Aaron Estes, 1820 – 1864, Co. B, 10 TX Inf Regt. CSA
Pembroke S. Estes 10/15/1847 – 12/3/1869
S. S. Estes 3/1841 – 4/1886
J. R. Gordon 12/22/1844 – 2/27/1890
Richard C. Horn 9/1830 – 10/1882
William P. Houston 1846 – 1887
Stewart Leathers 1/24/1838 – 11/18/1908
W. M. G. Leathers 9/16/1836 – 5/20/1883
H. M. E. Lewis 6/3/1841 – 7/5/1889
Daniel F. Loyd 7/24/1832 – 4/10/1870
James W. McClellan 3/11/1845 – 12/6/1903
J. S. Nelson 12/27/1847 – 11/3/1905
Pinkney H. Oates 2/25/1848 – 2/2/1871
F. M. Pierce 9/17/1831 – NDD
G. W. Richardson 2/6/1836 – 1/19/1906
John D. Roberts 1/3/1845 – 3/10/1930 Co. A, 7th TX Inf CSA
W. J. Shilling 1832 – NDD
W. M. Whitley 8/3/1833 – 5/3/1907
J. F. Wylie 2/22/1840 – 11/4/1895
W. L. Wylie 6/1/1838 – 12/29/1882

Murphy Cemetery
P. F. Alderman 10/12/1842 – 4/6/1869
W. W. Oliver 1/15/1830 - 2/16/1865

New Hope Cemetery
J. D. Stone 8/18/1840 – 6/24/1904
G. Little 11/24/1837 – 5/27/1911
J. F. Seale 1839 - 8/15/1896
Duncan McKay 7/15/1837 – 4/25/1917
C. E. Story 10/4/1837 - 4/20/1921
S. W. Rogers 8/28/1844 – 6/3/1925

New Hope Cemetery
J. D. Stone 8/18/1840 – 6/24/1904
G. Little 11/24/1837 – 5/27/1911
J. F. Seale 1839 - 8/15/1896
Duncan McKay 7/15/1837 – 4/25/1917
C. E. Story 10/4/1837 - 4/20/1921
S. W. Rogers 8/28/1844 – 6/3/1925

No Name Cemetery located near Kirk
J. M. Cobbs 2/10/1845 – 5/31/1897

Norwegian Cemetery
J. H. Prince 1/19/1840 – 7/24/1915
Martin Johansen 10/10/1839 – 7/14/1895

Nus Cemetery
J. M. Cobb 2/10/1845 – 5/11/1897

O'Neal Cemetery
Warren O'Neal 11/14/1824 – 7/31/1879
L. A. O'Neal 5/8/1827 – 12/3/1881
M. R. Burgess 5/2/1848 – 11/7/1892

Oakes Cemetery
B. F. Martin 3/25/1840 – 5/11/1917
Andrew Oakes 10/27/1844 – 2/19/1919
G. W. Oakes 1843 – 11/22/1917

Oak Hill/Askew/McCoy Cemetery
John William Askew 9/15/1830 – 11/27/1908
James Harvey Reed 3/15/1840 Butler County, KY – 9/22/1911

Oak Island Cemetery
W. P. Means 10/14/1828 – 3/1/1914 Asst. Surgeon 13th Cavalry CSA
William M. Patton 8/12/1828 – 10/22/1855
F. R. Patton, Jr. 5/3/1836 – 1/12/1863
John Marshall Parker 8/5/1843 Monroe Co., AL – 11/3/1878
David Martin 3/3/1824 – 2/12/1877
R. L. Oliver 3/17/1833 – 8/5/1863
James M. Kennedy 8/11/1826 – 2/28/1879
Blueford W. Adamson 11/7/1841 – 11/15/1904

Oklahoma Cemetery
P. W. Scott 3/1/1830 – 7/19/1897
M. D. Anders 4/18/1829 – 3/13/1896
M. M. McDonald 7/27/1823 – 7/5/1897

Old Bethel Cemetery
A. T. Cowan 3/12/1829 – 3/12/1907
Mathew C. Lofland 4/26/1826 – 2/12/1905
J. J. Bower, Sr. 4/22/1825 – 2/6/1875
J. L. Johnson 4/19/1828 – 4/1/1890
John Tompkins [ND] Co. F Bradford's TX Cavalry CSA
O. Whitenton 5/16/1821 – 1/6/1876
A. C. Freeman 8/3/1847 – 1/26/1918
Isaac C. Wheeler 1827-1911
A. R. McBay 4/19/1847 – 12/6/1890
T. H. Mathewson 1845 – 1/9/1910

Sam Bradley 1841-1910 CSA

Old Town Cemetery, Mt. Calm
James Carpenter ND Capt. Co. G, 30th TX Cavalry, CSA
P. H. Burkhalter 5/7/1841 Bibb Co., AL – 12/30/1910
J. B. Cates 1844 – 1920
J. C. Clark, MD 12/21/1847 – 2/9/1909
Humphrey Clarke 8/19/1840 – 6/28/1912
M. P. Coats 10/11/1841 – 11/14/1923
Phillip Coker 6/4/1829 – 6/9/1908
Rev. M. A. Cornelius ND Co. G, 12th AL Cavalry CSA
Lowry Davis 3/15/1834 – 10/17/1870
C. A. Elliott 1835 – 4/13/1887
J. J. Elliott 3/17/1828 – 8/30/1907
Thomas Elliott, Sr. 5/12/1830 – 4/6/1900
Amos Tims Estes 7/15/1846 – 7/8/1909
J. C. Gaunt 1847 – 1918
J. L. Green 6/3/1846 – 12/10/1921 42nd GA Inf CSA
William Marion Jones 1/18/1846 Randolph Co., AL – 3/11/1910
James F. King 1844 – 1867
Kincher Leathers 5/3/1821 – 2/17/1872
B. H. Marlin ND Co. A, TN Cavalry CSA
W. B. Mitchell 5/1/1835 – 4/16/1895
W. O. Morgan 2/22/1829 – 2/4/1871
E. T. Nichels 6/19/1841 – 5/21/1921
J. W. Nicholson 7/23/1834 – 9/12/1903
Jonathan Rice 11/6/1829 – 2/22/1877
Edward Roberts 9/20/1840 – 7/21/1913
Isaiah Rush ND Co. B, 38 MS Inf. CSA
G. W. Sanders 6/10/1840 – 5/2/1908
James T. Sealey 9/10/1844 – 9/25/1921
C.O.X. Shaffer 4/29/1833 – 4/24/1911
W. R. Shaffer 8/17/1842 – 11/25/1903
S. G. Sypert 10/30/1826 – 11/6/1905
James H. White 6/7/1835 – 12/30/1897
George W. Williams 1840 - 1864 Co. G, TX Inf Regt, CSA
Hardy B. Williams 5/12/1847 – 9/5/1925, Co. B, 15th TX Cavalry CSA
L. H. Williams 12/18/1828 – 3/22/1920
Leonard H. Williams 10/10/1828 – 3/22/1920 Co. I, 19th TX Cavalry CSA

Old Union Cemetery
C. E. Roberts ND
Dr. W. M. Cox 12/25/1827 – 6/5/1912 Physician
John Roberts 11/15/1843 – 12/27/1900
William J. Archer 1/28/1838 – 3/15/1918
G. W. Rainer 3/2/1839 – 1/15/1890

Phifer/Forest Chapel Cemetery
Allen Henderson 1/11/1828 – 2/7/1908

Pippin Cemetery
A. L. Pippin 1832 – 1909

Plummer Cemetery
Edward Plummer 12/26/1843 – ND
Wilson Plummer 1/4/1839 – ND

Samuel Lamekin 1829 – 3/29/1869 Mason
N. B. Sikes 9/7/1847 – 3/8/1916

Point Enterprise Cemetery
William Matysiak 1844 – 1922
Alfred L. Brigance 10/23/1822 – 3/6/1899
John O. Gorree 4/24/1828 – 9/12/1901
D. O. Kerzee 8/14/1825 - 8/17/1903
Andrew J. Roberson 1841-1881
B. H. Roberson 9/8/1824 – 12/11/1907
J. D. Barrett 4/8/1844 – ND
B. S. Allphin 1/13/1835 – 3/10/1910
G. W. Williams 4/12/1840 – 9/13/1912
H. D. Brown 8/18/1847 – 1/25/1904
J. F. Brown 7/14/1847 – 1/21/1904
James W. Lear 7/12/1845 – 12/25/1904 Co. A, 1st TN Art. CSA

Polk Cemetery
William E. Polk 11/19/1836 – 1/6/1883 Mason & Confederate Soldier

Pottershop Cemetery
Neverson Deans 5/3/1840 – 1/27/1903 Co. K, 12th Regt. TX Cavalry, CSA
John Fowler 10/31/1845 – 2/10/1910
C. T. Alston 1843 – 12/25/1916

Prairie Grove Cemetery
John Sellers 10/18/1840 – 4/22/1925
A. J. Tibbs 1840 - 1910
A. R. Holt 5/14/1826 – 11/5/1903
J. K. Bailey 1/30/1845 – 6/17/1893
L. McKinnon 9/24/1847 – 3/5/1935
William Henry Kierbow 1847 – 1922
Absalom Hicks 10/5/1822 – 10/2/1888 Mason
John F. Cleveland 9/20/1836 – 7/23/1898
M. E. King 1841 – 1924
W. L. King 1832 – 1892
T. J. Eubanks 7/28/1849 – 2/1/1929
George S. Eubanks 7/28/1849 – 9/28/1926
Thomas W. Wells 10/5/1825- 9/9/1886 Pvt., Co. G, 6th MS Cavalry CSA
J. A. Wright 7/9/1844 – 1/18/1934
M. E. Thompson 9/14/1829 – 1/22/1892
H. L. Williams 9/29/1847 – 12/15/1882
Thomas J. Williams 5/5/1822 – 3/30/1887
Dr. I. Callaway Moody 2/14/1836 – 12/22/1888
J. F. Kennedy 1/25/1848 - 7/29/1932
John Thomas Waller ND, Confederate Solder died AL age 18 yr. 6 mo.
Capt. J. W. Stephens 4/29/1823 – 3/24/1881
David Albert Waller 7/9/1846 – 9/2/1931
Samuel G. McLendon 3/20/1830 – 1/8/1892
W. H. Lansford 11/12/1826 – 1/3/1888 Mason
Charles E. Newsom 4/10/1834 – 6/13/1887 Mason
Martin B. Humphfus 6/17/1848 – 9/21/1937
Pinkney Hawkins 1833 – 1915 Co. F, 15th TX Cavalry CSA
John T. Gardner 2/12/1837 – 11/29/1912
Martin V. Herring 8/30/1840 – 7/6/1876

L. Carroll 1835 - 1900
R. Thurman 1832 – 3/22/1901
Lewis M. Speight 11/10/1831 – 12/1/1903 Co. C, 53rd GA Inf
CSA
William Hammont 4/12/1824 England – 2/8/1905
Frank M. Chilcoat 6/6/1846 – 8/14/1919

Prairie Hill Cemetery
H. C. Arons 8/30/1846 – 9/14/1918
Jahue C. Higgins 7/4/1845 – 1/16/1921 Co. K, 28th TX Cavalry
CSA
A. W. Hitt 5/20/1839 – 11/11/1900
M. M. Mitchell 2/12/1843 – 8/11/1900
John W. Smith 5/20/1837 – 6/5/1908
James L. Weaver 5/3/1840 – 11/7/1911
A. J. Webb 4/17/1846 – 1/23/1902
Armand Wheeler 1837 – 1910
George C. Dromgoole 2/13/1834 – 5/9/1904
Edmond Forrester 5/8/1843 – 1/15/1906
M. A. Hinton 3/18/1843 – 7/15/1922 CSA
Joe G. Jackson 1835 – 1912
James R. McDonald 4/1/1846 – 2/5/1939

Sansom/Wedgeman Cemetery
Dr. J. L. Sansom, Lt. 7/14/1827 – 1/21/1882 Mason
Major William J. Seale ND Co. G, 7th TX Cavalry CSA
Rev. A. L. Bridges, Capt., ND, Co. F, 2nd LA Cavalry CSA
Rev. John Taylor – no marker
Jack Norris – no marker
William Casan Chatman 8/22/1829 3/8/1907 Confederate
Veteran
G. W. Henson 5/14/1828 – 10/12/1904
Harry W. Howard – no marker
Augusta Padgett 3/17/1849 – 11/19/1920 Confederate Soldier
Jim Hinson ND

Shead Cemetery
Jan Beralkovi 1844 – 1909 [inscription in Czech]
Louis B. Fortson 2/27/1828 – 10/2/1884 Mason
John P. Davis 7/31/1836 – 6/5/1896
Louis B. Robison 2/27/1827 – 2/2/1884
J. B. Shead 1840 – 5/24/1882
J. C. Tilman 3/8/1835 – 11/21/1894
Thomas Obediah Wood 10/10/1847 – 6/29/1927

Shiloh Cemetery
William Hunt Weaver 6/16/1848 – 11/17/1928

Sowders Cemetery
Berryv. Sowders 8/9/1838 – 6/20/1897
W. E. Malone 1834 – 1899

Spillers Cemetery
John Clinton McGilvary 5/31/1847 – 6/30/1914

Springfield Cemetery
Ethan Stroud 2/10/1848 – 4/22/1870
John S. Row 5/28/1837 – 12/27/1874
M. D. L. House 7/4/1825 – 3/4/876
William Walker 10/5/1848 – 9/29/1870
Thomas L. Morris 9/17/1823 – 5/30/1891
Ephriam Johnson 1824 – 9/26/1892

Stranger Cemetery
Richard Gassaway 1/1/1833 – 12/7/1913
M. J. Walker 7/16/1835 – 12/19/1909
J. R. Swinnea 11/7/1841 – 3/18/l1925
W. T. Price 3/10/1842 – 6/4/1917
J. H. Price, Jr. 6/3/1838 – 2/22/1870
J. A. Price 9/14/1831 – 2/19/1882
Solomon W. Stephenson ND, Cpl. Co. E, 11th MS Inf. CSA
Andrew J. Fairbairn 9/12/1842 – 10/26/1892
T. J. Hodge 6/6/1842 – 7/16/1922
J. W. Toon 8/7/1847 – 9/2/1905
Thomas D. Harlan 6/1/1831 – 2/4/1910
Simon P. Wolf 1821 – 1886
Dr. L. D. Forbes 1/15/1835 – 4/27/1887
John R. Eddins 11/15/1837 – 12/21/1921 Co. H, 17th AL Inf.
CSA
Thomas J. Hair 1841 – 1927
Hansford Arnett ND, 2nd Lt. Co. I, 21st TX Cavalry CSA
M. L. Rochell 1848 – 9/9/1902
F. R. Noble 3/1/1834 – 12/26/1901
J. E. Vann 5/23/1845 – 12/28/1928
Elias Pool 10/14/1826 – 11/14/1903
W. B. Mathes 3/9/1841 – 4/21/1880
George M. Suttle 1/12/1827 – 12/23/1885
Alexander Smith 2/18/1836 – 12/13/1908
Cater H. Todd 6/17/1839 – 11/27/1871

Tehuacana Cemetery
Newton G. Ferguson 1838 – 1926
Daniel Malloy 8/28/1825 – 10/23/1903
J. S. Schuster 12/25/1825 – 3/28/1901
T. E. Newton 9/22/1846 – 7/29/1893
J. T. Sloan, M.D., 7/2/1840 – 2/9/1905
Seburn Powell 2/22/1838 – 7/26/1904
M. M. Bennett 4/5/1840 – 9/3/1904
Richard W. Payne 5/23/1833 – 2/22/1906
J. W. Thomas 8/20/1835 - 5/25/1915
William Buckholt 7/26/1838 – 5/10/1905
Thomas I. Garrison 3/16/1834 – 8/14/1912
Rev. J. G. Milburn 2/18/1842 – 5/4/1903
Rev. F. S. Tekel 2/14/1844 – 11/4/1907 Mason
A. S. Hendricks 3/6/1847 – 11/11/1905
J. F. Buck 1832 – 1913 Mason
William B. Needham 3/30/1843 – 10/15/1907
W. R. Erskine 4/23/1823 – 1/31/1892
C. J. E. Graham 10/30/1828 – 4/4/1895 Mason
William Rees 1845 – 1937
Cyrus W. Love 10/3/1830 - ND
James A. Love 11/15/1836 - ND
David D. Love 3/24/1840 - ND
John W. Love 1/11/1842 – ND
J. J. Burris 10/15/1848 – 4/17/1911
William L. Mallard 1844 – 1920

Henson Wagley 2/23/1838 Near Pleasant Hill, LA – 1/22/1877
James Hamilton Bell 7/14/1820 – 10/26/1898
Thomas Winmill 1839 – 11/9/1884
G. A. Neill 10/17/1846 – 1/8/1934
D. A. Quaite 3/1/1846 Near Hopkinsville, KY – 7/7/1873
Daniel Washington Cromartie 4/10/1825 – 9/8/1879
Simeon M. Yelverton 1829 – 1876
T. A. Wolfe 1/6/1822 – 12/19/1909
W. E. Beeson, D.D. 10/21/1822 – 9/5/1882
W. P. Gillespie 1826 – 1905
Henry H. Coleman 1828 – 1909
Rev. A. A. Lewis 5/30/1840 – 5/19/1871

Tehuacana Valley Cemetery
J. H. Bounds 2/28/1823 – 1/29/1914
J. M. Wilder 4/4/1840 – 1/2/1876
William Andrews 2/18/1846 – 6/27/1892
L. M. Campbell 12/6/1848 – 8/12/1900

Thornton City Cemetery
George T. Brown 3/10/1841 – 7/15/1918
W. H. Palmer 8/14/1837 – 7/17/1905
J. B. Darwin 7/23/1847 – 10/29/1889
Robert J. Darwin 7/23/1847 – 10/29/1889 Pvt. Co. C, 1st TN Art. CSA
J. E. Barron 8/5/1838 – 1/10/1909
William M. Chisum 6/7/1842 – 9/18/1886
Rev. James Oliver Jorden 3/2/1836 – 12/23/1923
H. J. Cook 9/9/1839 – 3/6/1913
H. H. Stubbs 8/9/1842 – 8/21/1901
John W. Fox 4/3/1829 – 1/16/1888
Rasmus Hansen 2/4/1829 – 5/26/1900
Rasmus P. Hansen 10/27/1847 – 10/16/1935
John Henry Heffner 1833 – 1910
Prichard R. Wray 2/23/1845 – 2/16/1899
W. L. Loftin 4/18/26 – 9/25/1902
J. L. White 11/11/1841 – 6/16/1924
James C. Cayton 3/13/1825 – 12/21/1894
George W. Parten 11/18/1833 – 1/4/1920
John M. Owen ND Co. I, 1st SC Inf. CSA
H. G. Chambless 1836 – 1911 Pvt. Co. K, 11th TX Cavalry CSA
John Sparks 1847 – 1925
James Edgman Foust 1/15/1833 – 1/18/1914
Capt. M. G. Long 11/10/1825 – 3/1/1897
Henry Vansickel 7/24/1842 – 1/17/1925
L. J. McKeehan 11/20/1830 – 2/20/1897
J. C. Neason 8/27/1823 Dublin, Ireland – 8/9/1908
William A. Watson 7/21/1835 – 1/11/1908 Mason
William H. McGuffin 3/27/1839 – 4/20/1902 Pvt. Co. H, 20th TX Regt. CSA
W. G. F. Mayes 10/3/1834 – 2/3/1902 Physician – Mason
William "Buck" Martin 5/12/1847 – 9/27/1930
Albert E. Gardner 8/1/1845 – 1/30/1919
Frank Lown 3/5/1845 – 4/13/1891
Henry G. Fox 1831 – 1919
J. F. Pipkin 8/7/1836 – 1/1/1905
B. P. Sweeney 8/25/1841 – 3/27/1906
Samuel Williams 2/1/1823 – 11/10/1885
B. F. Richardson 11/14/1847 – 3/1/1922
Mason Masters 1847 – 1886
James H. Bradley 3/23/1832 – 4/7/1903

S. M. Carlton 10/1/1830 – 4/2/1913 Physician
A. D. Proctor 11/30/1844 – 11/20/1917
Edward C. Chambers 1831 – 1912
J. S. Milstead 7/9/1823 – 1/10/1900
J. W. Hoover 12/5/1848 – 3/8/1906
B. D. Smith 2/6/1830 – 7/3/1897
Terry Baker 1/25/1842 – 12/8/1927
E. R. Sawyers 6/17/1834 – 3/28/1889 Pvt 9th MS Inf. CSA
Samuel H. Gibson 6/4/1840 - 1/20/1901
Samuel A. Bradley ND Co. B, 2nd KY Cavalry CSA
John Aman 4/2/1833 – 4/24/1887
F. E. Nichols 10/26/1835 – 4/30/1906
R. E. Moore 2/13/1833 – 1/26/1884
Jefferson Spencer 9/13/1842 – 1/30/1908
S. D. Hawkins 1829 – 6/7/1904
J. T. Brady 5/5/1839 – 11/20/1908
James F. Yankee 1836 – 1916

Tidwell Cemetery
J. M. Hodges 6/22/1829 – 10/8/1889
R. H. Barnett 6/10/1824 – 9/21/1900
M. L. Hogan 12/13/1844 – 5/5/1889
J. C. Kilpatrick 11/9/1845 – 12/21/1924
H. V. Tidwell 8/18/1842 – 3/1/1888
T. L. McConnell 2/29/1840 – 2/25/1911/17
John W. Erskine 2/10/1840 – 10/8/1913
A. B. Foster 7/31/1849 – 6/9/1935 Co. K, Texas Infantry C.S.A.
Samuel Beck 10/1/1828 – 5/21/1908
Thomas Lewellen 12/27/1846 – 7/29/1934
Henry Louis Hendrix 12/24/1822 – 9/3/1907 No Marker

Vinson Cemetery
M. J. Hogue 6/10/1839 – 2/12/1903
Robert Vinson 12/18/1845 – 3/30/1876

Walker Chapel Cemetery
W. P. Barron 8/5/1848 – 7/10/1885

Waller Cemetery
J. G. McKinnon 12/31/1824 – 5/3/1864

Whatley Cemetery
John S. Whatley 5/21/1842 – 10/29/1888

Wolverton Cemetery
John B. Wolverton 1/14/1843 Tennessee Colony, TX – 5/27/1875 Hot Springs, AR

Wood Cemetery/Cedar Island Cemetery
Hezekiah L. DeWitt 6/22/1829 – 6/10/1862 Confederate Veteran

Other Limestone Area Men Who Fought But Not Listed on Extant U.V.C. Limestone County Rosters

John Karner, 7th Texas Infantry
William G. Ainsworth, Co. E, 8th MS Infantry
T. A. Germany, 12th Texas under Maj. Farrar, transferred to Ellis' Co.
Carrol N. Brooks, Co. D, Bird's Cavalry Battalion, Trans-Mississippi
Captain Joseph Booth Tyus, 15th Texas Cavalry consolidated with 6th & 10th Infantry
Joshua Wood, 40th AL Infantry, Army of Tennessee
John Askew, Missouri Company, Price's Command, Trans-Mississippi Department
William S. Roberts, Co. D, Hubbard's Regiment, Trans-Mississippi Department
James C. Tidwell, Co. F, 15th TX Cavalry, Trans-Mississippi Department
Benjamin F. Freeman, Capt. Wm. M. Hicks' Co., Young's Regt., Trans-Mississippi Department
Sidney M. Jones, Co. K, Bass' 29th TX Cavalry
Moses Lewis, Texas State Militia
George W. Lewis, Co. K, 5th TX Infantry, Army of Virginia; Co. H, Elmour's Regt., TX Department
James W. Bennett, 1st Lt., Capt., Co. B, 10th TX Regt.
Hampton Steele, Col. Shoolwater's Regt., TX Infantry
J. A. Wright, 31st AL Infantry, Army of Tennessee
Jasper Howard, Co. A, 21st TX Infantry, Texas Department
R. P. Merrill, Speight's Battalion, CSA
C. Herring, O. Sgt., 38th AL Infantry; 36th AL Regt
Berry V. Sowders, Co. I, Speight's Regt., CSA
J. T. Steward, 2nd Sgt., Co. I, Capt. Means, Trans-Mississippi Department
R. E. Steele, 7th TX Infantry, Army of the Tennessee
Sam Lamb, Co. E, 13th TX Infantry, Bayes Regt.
William B. Hill, LA Home Guards
Judge L. D. Bradley, Capt., Col., Waul's TX Legion
Matthew M. Drake, Co. D, 10th TX Infantry, Trans-Mississippi Department, Army of Tennessee
Medicus King, 1st Lt., State Militia
Andrew J. Smith, Co. C, 59th AL Infantry, Army of the Tennessee
Julius Storey, Capt., CSA
Ansel Coleman, Capt. Oliver's Co., Bradford's Cavalry Regt., Texas Department
William G. Blain, Pvt., Co. H, 28th TX Dismounted Cavalry, Lt., Adj. Gen'l, Major of W. H. King's staff of the 3rd Brigade, Walker's Div.
James W. Alderman, Co. E, 29th GA Infantry
David W. Alderman, Walker's Division
James K. Beene, Co. G, Madison's TX Regt, CSA
Egbert G. Beall, Co. C, 5th TX Cavalry, Green's Brigade
George W. Everett, Co. K, 31st LA Infantry
T. B. Grayson, M.D., Charles Pyron's Regt, and Walker's Legion
Garrett K. Beene, Co. G, 3rd TN Cavalry
Jacob A. Womack, Capt. Peck's Co
J. A. Willard, Col. Bartos' Regt, CSA
T. B. Newman, 50th GA Regt. and 3rd Sgt.,Volunteer Guards
William T. Roland, Capt. Moss' TX Infantry Co.
A. W. Sneed, Pvt., 2nd TX Cavalry, Texas Department
P. L. Stubbs, John Oliver's Co., Col. Bradford's TX Regt.
S. H. Smith, Capt. Motley's Co., Shelby's Cavalry Brigade; TX Commissary Department
Dr. J. I. Bonner, Pvt., Timmons' Regt.; Surgeon and Brigade Surgeon of Terrell's TX Regt.
Arthur B. Allison, Co. C, 5th TX Infantry, Col. J. B. Robertson, Army of Virginia
Robert Holleman, Capt. Patrick's Co., Gould's Battalion, Walker's Div., Trans-Mississippi Department
M. B. Smith, Col. Bradford's Cavalry Regt. serving only in Texas
Judge H. B. Pruitt, Provost Marshal of Leon Co.; Col. Baylor's Regt., Wharton's Corps
A. G. Rogers, Lt., Co. E, Gould's Battalion, Walker's Div., Trans-Mississippi Department
Alvin Moore, Co. C, 9th AR Infantry; 12th TX Cavalry, Parson's Brigade
John Richardson, Co. A, O. M. Marsh's Battalion, Speight's TX Regt.

DECEASED MEMBERS OF JOE JOHNSTON CAMP NO. 94

1889
McCain, J. H., Captain

1890
Adams, W. H., Captain [1st Adjutant]
Henry, Jno. R., Colonel
Scott, A. V.

1891
Butler, J. E.
Johnson, J. L.
Kirkpatrick, W. B., Major
Montgomery, J. R.
Stanford, David
Strayhorn, Felix B.

1892
Farnsworth, W. T.
Fitzgerald, J. M.
Stitt, Jno. T.
Walker, S. D.

1893
Guynes, Jno. F.
Hancock, L. Ross
Hunt, Bennett

1895
Gilbert, J. S., Captain
Wallace, B. F.

1896
Armour, James
Bates, Chas. S.
Brown, J. P., Captain
Reed, T. L.
Wilder, J. L.

1897
Raborn, Isaac
Wilder, W. M. [July 6]

1898
Anglin, Jno. A.
Cashion, R. J.

Duncan, N. G. [N.Y.]
Griffis, J.L.
Kemp, M. W.
Stuart, W. P.

1899
Hancock, B. J.
Smyth, E. B.
Suttle, J. M.

1901
Crawford, F. M.
Farrar, L. J., Major
Germany, T. A.
Henry, Wm.
McDonald, Jas. E.
Thomas, John
Waller, N. L.

1902
Moss, G. W.

1903
Buckner, W. A.
Kaufman, M.
Moore, W. F. [Dr.] [Dec. 15]
Rambo, J.M.

1904
Herring, M.
Herring, W. H. [Oct. 22]
Hickman, J. P.
Jayne, A. A. [June 11]
Mahoney, J. T. [Oct. 21]
Michard, J. S. [Dr.]
Wood, C. H. F. [Oct. 11]

1905
Anglin, J.C. [March 21]
Archer, Geo. W. [Sept. 17]
Lindley, J. P. [July 3]
Morgan, H. W., Major
Sloan, J. T. [Dr.]
Watkins, R. L.
Wood, C. H. F.

1906
Boyd, H. A.

Camp, L. E. [March 15]
Ferrill, J. W.
Gordan, Sandy [March 15]
Payne, R. W.
Smith, Jas. L.
Wright, Jno. A.

1907
Barton, W. M. [April 12]
Carroll, Jno. G.

Jones, Jno. A. [July 18]
Ouzts, B. F. [Dr.][Feb. 18]
Reeves, W. J.
Webb, Jno. C.
Welch, J. H.
Wyatt, W. W.

1908
Allen, B. W.
Berryman, H. C.
Humphries, J. W.
Lewis, W. G.
Wilie, T. W.
Wood, E. B.

1909
Beene, R. O.
Byrd, T. S.
Gatlin, T. S.
Gray, H. W.
Ingram, S. C.
Kenney, G. W.
McNeese, G. W.
Patterson, John
Scruggs, S. K. [Sept. 28]
Sherrill, B. F. [Feb. 22]
Thompson, J. W. [Nov. 9]

1910
Allison, A. B.
Arnett, S. T.
Arvin, J. A.
Brown, Geo. T. [July 8]
Burney, Thos. [Sept. 9]
McDonald, M. L. [July 22 in Camp]
Popejoy, N. T. [Jan. 29]
Therrill, J. D.
Wallace, J. D.

1911
Bridges, J. J.
Cook, J. P.
Fortenberry, J. M.
Johnson, T. J.
Parsons, M. J.
Roberts, W. F. [Aug. 7]

1912
Adams, L. A.
Frazier, W. D.
Jennings, G. L. [Rev.]
Jordan, G. L.
Love, S. B.
Risien, Sam'l.
Simmons, H. F.
Simmons, J. W. [April 12]

Storey, J. M.
Walker, S. S. [Nov. 12]

1913
Bond, S. F. [June 16]
Butler, John [Sept. 21]
Doke, F. Y.
Joiner, H. C.
Parsons, Jacob
Ross, Geo. W.
Stedman, Jasper
Ward, R. P.

1914
Adams, M.
Adams, W. L.
Burford, A. W.
Gibson, T. J.
Nabors, A. M.
Archer, J. H.
Prince, J. H.
Thomas, J. W.
Winters, J. S.

1915
Hayes, W. H. [April 9]

1916
Burney, J. S. [Dr.]
Gilbert, C. T. [July 14]
Priddy, M. L.

1917
Collum, George [Feb.]
Farrow, R. E. [Feb. 9]
Lanning, W. D. [Sept. 28]
LaGrone, David [Feb. 14]
Sellers, F. M. [May 22]
Sharp, T. H. [July 1]
Tucker, M. A. [April 24]

1918
Brown, W. P., Captain [Feb. 7]
Brown, Geo. T. [July 8]
Davis, R. E. [June 9]
Deis, Jno. M. [Nov. 10]
Groover, Jno. S. [Feb. 28]
Nash, J. W. [April 9]
Stuart, J. W. [April 1]

1919
Douglass, P. O. [May 20]
Laird, R. S.
McCorkle, James [Jan. 6]
Stanford, J. T. [Feb. 15]
Wood, Ira E.

1920
Brady, J. T.
Clark, M. H.
Gardner, A. E.
Jackson, J. G.
Jones, Nat. M.
Skipper, W. M.
Sowders, J. A.

1921
Bower, C. J.
Brandon, J. A.
Justice, Wm.
Mallard, W. L.
Nelson, T. J.
Reynolds, M. P.
Steele, R. E.
Steward, F. M.
Williams, E. W.
Wright, Z. T.

1922
Hughes, S.
Keeling, B. D.
Lee, G. W.
McClintock, J. F.
McDaniel, J. A.
Sawyer, J. P.
Seale, L. B.

1923
Durham, C. A.
Parker, Jno. E.
Bryant, R. J.
Perdue, B. F.

INDEX

A

Adair, 1, 17, 55
Adams, 1, 28, 34, 42, 43, 55, 89, 90, 91, 102, 108, 109, 115, 122, 130, 131
Adamson, 118, 125
Adkinson. *See* Atkisson
Ainsworth, 122, 124, 129
Alderman, 125, 129
Alford, 1, 56
Allen, 1, 15, 17, 23, 28, 34, 45, 56, 88, 91, 92, 102, 115, 118, 130
Allison, 17, 28, 34, 47, 48, 93, 106, 129, 130
Allman, 122
Allphin, 126
Alston, 126
Aman, 128
Anders, 125
Anderson, 1, 11, 17, 23, 28, 34, 56, 80, 85, 87, 89, 96, 110, 112, 114, 117, 118, 119, 123
Andrews, 122, 128
Anglin, 1, 11, 17, 23, 28, 34, 56, 88, 97, 130
Archer, 1, 17, 23, 28, 34, 40, 42, 43, 45, 47, 48, 52, 56, 76, 87, 99, 111, 120, 126, 130, 131. See . See . See . See . See
Archibald, 1, 11, 15, 56
Armour, 1, 17, 23, 42, 48, 56, 79, 121, 130
Arnett, 1, 23, 28, 56, 106, 117, 127, 130
Arons, 127
Arvin, 1, 23, 28, 56, 80, 106, 130
Askew, 125, 129
Athery, 56
Athey, 1, 56
Atkisson, 1, 11, 56

B

Bachelor, 57
Bailey, 1, 15, 23, 56, 126
Baisden, 15, 56
Baker, 128
Baldwin, 99, 122, 124
Ball, 1, 56, 98
Banks, 1, 56, 116
Barber, 123
Barkwell, 15, 57
Barnard, 1, 56
Barnett, 128
Barrett, 28, 34, 100, 126
Barrey, 1, 57
Barron, 128
Barry, 17, 23, 100
Barton, 1, 11, 17, 23, 28, 34, 47, 49, 55, 57, 79, 80, 81, 83, 88, 94, 95, 98, 99, 100, 120, 130
Bass, 71, 104, 105, 124
Batchelor, 1, 11, 17, 28, 34, 91
Bates, 1, 11, 17, 23, 42, 46, 47, 57, 79, 115, 120, 121, 123, 130
Beall, 129
Beaty, 1, 57, 120
Beauregard, 48
Beaver, 117
Beck, 128
Beene, 17, 23, 28, 34, 57, 99, 101, 102, 103, 104, 106, 107, 108, 109, 129, 130
Beeson, 43, 45, 46, 49, 53, 83, 128
Bell, 1, 11, 15, 57, 97, 108, 128
Bennett, 17, 23, 50, 57, 65, 121, 122, 127, 129
Benson, 122, 124
Benthall, 34
Beralkovi, 127
Berry, 1, 34, 57, 120
Berryman, 1, 11, 23, 28, 57, 102, 120, 130
Berrymore, 17
Bessling, 115
Best, 94, 96
Bevill, 123
Biggs, 123
Billington, 121
Birmingham, 114
Bishop, 1, 23, 48, 57
Black, 1, 57, 123
Blackmon, 1, 57, 115, 116, 124
Blain, 129
Blaine, 49, 50, 88, 89
Blair, 124
Blake, 28, 53, 54, 78
Blount, 121
Boatler, 124
Bolen, 121
Bolton, 15, 57
Bond, 17, 23, 28, 34, 46, 51, 55, 57, 80, 82, 84, 88, 100, 102, 104, 108, 131
Bonner, 115, 117, 118, 129
Boone, 53, 54
Booth, 2, 17, 42, 57
Bounds, 128
Bowder, 23
Bower, 2, 11, 17, 23, 28, 34, 42, 47, 58, 80, 81, 83, 84, 85, 88, 93, 114, 125, 131
Boyar, 121
Boyd, 2, 11, 17, 23, 28, 34, 42, 43, 47, 53, 58, 80, 84, 88, 89, 91, 93, 94, 95, 96, 99, 101, 118, 122, 130
Boykin, 2, 11, 17, 58
Boyle, 2, 17, 28, 52, 55, 58, 85, 120
Bozeman, 34, 118, 121
Bradford, 2, 11, 58
Bradley, 43, 126, 128, 129
Bradshaw, 2, 11, 17, 58
Brady, 28, 34, 113, 128, 131
Brandon, 34, 114, 131
Bratton, 124
Bray, 47
Bridges, 2, 28, 34, 58, 107, 127, 130
Brigance, 126
Briggs, 2, 58, 122
Broadnax, 48
Brooks, 2, 11, 15, 23, 28, 34, 58, 80, 97, 129
Browder, 2, 17, 28, 34, 47, 51, 55, 58, 80, 81, 82, 84, 85, 86, 87, 88, 89, 91, 92, 93, 94, 95, 96, 98, 99, 100, 101, 102, 103, 104, 106, 107, 108, 109, 110, 112, 113, 114, 115, 117
Brown, 2, 11, 17, 23, 28, 34, 42, 43, 44, 45, 47, 53, 54, 58, 76, 82, 84, 86, 88, 89, 90, 91, 92, 95, 96, 98, 102, 104, 113, 117, 119, 121, 122, 124, 126, 128, 130, 131
Bryan, 2, 15, 17, 58, 108, 113
Bryant, 2, 11, 17, 23, 28, 34, 40, 46, 47, 49, 50, 51, 52, 53, 54, 55, 58, 59, 76, 78, 79, 80, 81, 82, 84, 86, 87, 88, 89, 90, 91, 92, 93, 94, 95, 97, 98, 99, 100, 101, 102, 103, 104, 105, 106, 107, 108, 109, 110, 111, 112, 115, 116, 117, 118, 119, 125, 131
Buck, 127, 128
Buckholt, 127
Buckner, 2, 11, 17, 23, 28, 47, 59, 82, 84, 86, 88, 91, 94, 130
Bugg, 2, 59
Bums, 59
Bunn, 23, 28
Burch, 28
Burditt, 2, 59
Burford, 28, 34, 93, 96, 101, 109, 131
Burgess, 17, 23, 125
Burkhalter, 126
Burleson, 17, 23, 28, 34, 47, 48, 49, 50, 53, 55, 59, 80, 83, 84, 85, 88, 91, 95, 101, 103, 104, 110, 116, 119
Burney, 2, 28, 34, 59, 106, 112, 123, 130, 131
Burns, 15, 59
Burris, 123, 127
Burton, 17, 23, 89
Butler, 2, 34, 44, 59, 108, 125, 130, 131
Butrall, 2, 59
Byars, 2, 11, 59
Byers, 28, 34
Bynum, 123
Byrd, 34, 103, 123, 130

C

Cabell, 43, 44, 106, 119
Caldwell, 125
Calhoun, 2, 11, 17, 44, 47, 59
Calmes, 124
Camp, 2, 11, 17, 23, 28, 34, 42, 47, 59, 79, 81, 84, 85, 86, 87, 88, 89, 90, 91, 92, 93, 94, 96, 97, 99, 120, 122, 130
Campbell, 97, 124, 128
Cannon, 95, 115
Capell, 118
Cargile, 123
Carleton, 17, 23, 59
Carlton, 128
Carpenter, 2, 48, 59, 126

Carrell, 121, 123
Carroll, 17, 23, 28, 34, 53, 54, 55, 59, 76, 79, 80, 82, 89, 93, 100, 119, 127, 130
Carruth, 17, 23, 28, 59
Carter, 29, 34
Cashion, 2, 11, 18, 23, 29, 44, 47, 49, 59, 80, 81, 120, 130
Castellow, 2, 59
Castilow, 29
Castles, 105
Castleton, 18
Cates, 29, 126
Cayton, 122, 128
Chaffin, 125
Chambers, 18, 23, 59, 119, 128
Chambless, 128
Champion, 121
Chandler, 2, 34, 59
Chapman, 122, 124
Chatham, 2, 59
Chatman, 127
Chenoweth, 93, 94
Chilcoat, 127
Chisholm, 2, 59
Chisum, 128
Choate, 124
Christoffer, 124
Clanahan, 2, 11, 18, 24, 29, 59
Clancy, 122
Clark, 2, 18, 24, 29, 34, 40, 46, 47, 52, 60, 76, 83, 84, 85, 88, 93, 97, 104, 105, 113, 115, 120, 122, 126, 131. *See*
Clarke, 126
Clay, 122
Cleburne, 103
Cleveland, 126
Cline, 2, 60
Clinton, 2, 11, 60
Coats, 126
Cobb, 68, 70, 121, 125
Cobbs, 125
Cochran, 111
Cockran, 3, 60
Coker, 3, 18, 60, 121, 126
Coleman, 128, 129
Collier, 18, 29, 34, 102, 104, 118
Collins, 3, 60
Collum, 3, 11, 18, 24, 29, 35, 60, 112, 131
Cone, 122
Conley, 24, 60
Connors, 35
Cook, 3, 11, 18, 24, 29, 35, 40, 43, 45, 46, 48, 49, 50, 52, 53, 54, 60, 76, 79, 80, 81, 83, 84, 85, 87, 90, 93, 95, 97, 98, 107, 120, 122, 128, 130
Cooper, 3, 11, 60, 124
Cordon, 122
Corleton, 119
Cornelius, 126
Corrall, 120
Cotton, 3, 11, 18, 60
Cowan, 125
Cowart, 24, 29, 35, 60
Cox, 3, 11, 18, 24, 29, 35, 60, 84, 101, 102, 104, 105, 106, 116, 118, 119, 120, 121, 123, 126
Crawford, 3, 18, 24, 60, 90, 119, 130
Crider, 124
Crist, 125
Criswell, 121
Cromartie, 128
Culberson, 100
Cummings, 95
Cundieff, 121
Currey, 35
Currie, 53
Curry, 3, 11, 29, 35, 60, 122
Curtis, 18

D

Daffan, 91, 92
Dailey, 29, 35
Dallis, 18
Dalton, 123
Daly, 124
Darwin, 128
Daughtry, 122
David, 47, 112, 115, 118, 130, 131
Davidson, 3, 11, 18, 60, 123
Davie, 29, 85
Davis, 3, 11, 18, 24, 35, 40, 42, 43, 45, 47, 49, 52, 60, 79, 87, 95, 99, 103, 107, 109, 110, 111, 113, 120, 122, 123, 124, 126, 127, 131
Day, 3, 11, 60, 79, 81, 83, 107, 108, 111, 114
Dean, 124
Deans, 126
DeCaussey, 24
Deece, 43
DeHart, 35
Deis, 3, 11, 18, 24, 29, 35, 42, 43, 45, 47, 50, 52, 54, 61, 76, 79, 80, 81, 82, 83, 85, 86, 87, 88, 90, 92, 93, 94, 95, 96, 97, 98, 99, 100, 102, 103, 104, 105, 107, 108, 109, 110, 111, 112, 113, 131. *See* Deece
DeLeon, 124
Dellis, 24, 29, 35
Dennis, 123
Denson, 122
DeWitt, 121, 128
Dickson, 29
Dillard, 89
Dillis, 80
Doak, 46. *See* Doke
Doke, 3, 24, 29, 35, 46, 55, 61, 79, 80, 108, 131
Donaldson, 122
Dossey, 124
Douglas, iii, 24, 42, 45, 48, 61, 115, 117
Douglass, 3, 18, 29, 35, 80, 84, 85, 87, 89, 90, 92, 93, 98, 99, 100, 101, 102, 103, 104, 105, 106, 108, 109, 110, 112, 113, 131
Doyle, 3, 11, 18, 24, 29, 35, 46, 48, 49, 51, 52, 53, 55, 61, 79, 80, 81, 82, 84, 85, 88, 91, 95, 96, 97, 98, 99, 100, 101, 102, 104, 106, 107, 110, 116, 118, 119
Drake, 129
Draper, 123
Drinkard, 15, 61, 124
Dromgoole, 127
Duke, 15, 18, 24, 29, 40, 45, 49, 50, 52, 53, 54, 61, 76, 79, 81, 86, 124
Dumis, 15, 61
Dunavan, 92
Dunavant, 92
Duncan, 3, 24, 29, 61, 122, 130
Dunn, 125
Durham, 3, 12, 18, 29, 35, 61, 104, 105, 131
Durhan, 121
Durst, 3, 12, 15, 18, 24, 47, 61
Dyer, 3, 61

E

Eads, 118
Eady, 3, 12, 18, 35, 61, 116
Eakens, 124
Early, 51
East, 18, 24, 61, 96, 113, 119
Easton, 121
Eaton, 47
Eaves, 121
Echols, 88
Eddins, 127
Elliott, 117, 126
Ellis, 121
Ellison, 3, 15, 18, 24, 61
Elzey, 35
Elzy, 3, 15, 18, 61
English, 35
Erschel, 114
Erskine, 127, 128
Erwin, 3, 61
Eslick, 124
Estes, 125, 126
Ethridge, 3, 61
Eubank, Eubanks, 3, 12, 18, 48, 61, 126
Evans, 3, 15, 61
Everett, 129
Ezell, 29, 35

F

Fairbairn, 127
Farmer, 3, 61
Farnsworth, 3, 12, 47, 61, 130
Farrar, 3, 18, 24, 29, 46, 48, 51, 52, 53, 54, 62, 82, 90, 120, 130
Farrington, 3, 62
Farrow, 3, 35, 62, 101, 104, 108, 112, 131
Faulkenberry, 66, 122
Ferguson, 47, 117, 124, 127
Ferrell, 99
Ferrill, 117, 123, 130
Field, 97
Fields, 88
Fife, 18, 24, 35, 62
Fishburn, 115
Fitzgerald, 3, 12, 47, 62, 124, 130
Flanekin, 18, 62
Flanagan, 3, 12
Flaniken, 29
Flanikin, 24
Flannagan, 62
Flint, 48
Flores, 102

Fontinott, 15, 62
Forbes, 127
Forrester, 127
Fortenberry, 35, 107, 124, 130
Fortson, 127
Foster, 3, 12, 15, 62, 123, 128
Foust, 128
Fowler, 126
Fox, 128
Foy, 122
Franklin, 122
Franks, 4, 12, 18, 24, 29, 35, 62
Frazier, 4, 12, 18, 24, 29, 35, 62, 80, 82, 84, 86, 88, 91, 93, 94, 95, 96, 97, 98, 99, 100, 101, 102, 103, 104, 105, 106, 107, 108, 120, 130
Freeman, 125, 129
Friley, 29, 84
Frost, iii, 35, 115, 117
Fullinwider, 4, 12, 18, 62
Fulton, 122
Fuqua, 4, 12, 18, 24, 29, 55, 62, 80, 82, 120
Furguson, 4, 62
Furlow, 121

G

Gamble, 123
Ganey, 121
Gardiner, 4, 62
Gardner, 29, 35, 98, 99, 100, 101, 102, 103, 104, 108, 109, 113, 126, 128, 131
Garner, 15, 62
Garrett, 108, 123, 124
Garrison, 127
Gary, 99
Gassaway, 127
Gatlin, 4, 62, 103, 130
Gaunt, 126
George, 4, 62
Gerald, 45, 46, 47, 119
Germany, 24, 29, 90, 125, 129, 130
Gibson, 4, 12, 15, 18, 24, 29, 35, 42, 43, 44, 45, 46, 47, 48, 49, 50, 51, 52, 53, 54, 55, 62, 79, 81, 82, 83, 84, 86, 87, 88, 89, 90, 91, 92, 93, 94, 95, 96, 98, 99, 100, 101, 102, 103, 104, 105, 106, 107, 108, 109, 116, 117, 122, 128, 131
Gilbert, 4, 12, 18, 24, 29, 35, 44, 47, 49, 50, 53, 55, 62, 63, 78, 79, 80, 112, 116, 117, 119, 120, 123, 130, 131
Gillespie, 128
Gilmore, 4, 12, 43, 63
Glass, 4, 63
Gleaver, 122
Glenn, 122
Goggan, 82, 96
Goodiman, 120
Goodman, 18, 24, 63, 89
Gordan, 130
Gorden, 4, 63
Gordon, 29, 35, 99, 125
Gorree, 126
Goubold, 123
Graham, 4, 15, 19, 63, 127
Granbury, 98
Grasse, 63
Graves, 4, 19
Gravs, 63
Gray, 4, 12, 19, 24, 29, 35, 42, 44, 45, 47, 50, 63, 76, 85, 88, 92, 95, 99, 100, 102, 103, 122, 130
Grayson, 129
Green, 126
Grice, 4, 63
Griffen, 63
Griffin, 15, 63
Griffis, 4, 19, 130
Griffith, 118
Groover, 15, 19, 24, 29, 35, 51, 63, 88, 90, 91, 94, 95, 96, 98, 99, 101, 102, 103, 105, 106, 107, 108, 109, 110, 111, 112, 113, 117, 119, 120, 131
Grooves, 4, 43, 54, 63, 84, 98
Grover, 4
Groves, 4, 12, 19, 24, 29, 63, 120
Gunn, 122
Guy, 15, 19, 63
Guynes, 4, 19, 47, 63, 130

H

Hair, 127
Hall, 4, 63, 90, 117, 118
Hamca, 4
Hamich, 4, 12
Hammond, 4, 29, 35, 63, 116, 119, 124
Hammont, 127
Hancock, 4, 12, 15, 19, 24, 30, 42, 47, 63, 80, 85, 114, 120, 123, 130
Hanica, 63
Hanna, 19, 102
Hannah, 64
Hansen, 128
Hanson, 122
Harbard, 120
Hardin, 42
Hardwick, 30, 123
Hardy, 4, 15, 64, 97, 102, 106
Hargrove, 123
Harlan, 127
Harp, 112
Harper, 4, 64, 106, 120, 122, 123
Harrington, 4, 64, 122
Harris, 15, 19, 24, 30, 35, 47, 49, 64, 84, 92, 97, 98, 99, 115, 117, 121, 123
Hartfield, 24
Harthcock, 4, 12, 64
Harvey, 4, 12, 19, 43, 64
Haskins, 35, 101, 102, 104
Hastons, 117
Hawkins, 47, 126, 128
Hayes, 4, 35, 64, 98, 103, 108, 110, 111, 114, 115, 116, 118, 122, 123, 131
Haynie, 81
Hays, 116
Hearn, 124
Hearne, 108
Heffner, 128
Heflin, 123
Henderson, 4, 64, 117, 121, 126
Hendricks, 127
Hendrix, 128
Henry, 4, 15, 19, 43, 64, 90, 123, 130
Henson, 4, 64, 127
Herbert, 19, 24, 30, 64, 120
Herod, 121
Herring, 4, 12, 19, 24, 30, 35, 40, 48, 49, 50, 52, 53, 54, 64, 76, 80, 81, 83, 84, 85, 87, 89, 95, 96, 97, 119, 120, 121, 126, 129, 130
Hewitt, 122, 123
Hickman, 19, 25, 30, 35, 52, 53, 55, 64, 84, 96, 130
Hicks, 5, 64, 126
Higgins, 127
High, 25, 30
Hill, 79, 97, 129
Hillis, 30
Hillyen, 5, 64
Hinch, 64
Hines, 5, 64
Hinson, 127
Hinton, 127
Hitt, 127
Hoall, 120
Hodge, 127
Hodges, 5, 30, 35, 64, 101, 128
Hogan, 123, 128
Hogue, 30, 128
Holladay, 15, 19, 64
Hollaway, 5, 15, 64
Holleman, 129
Hollen, 121
Holley, 121
Holloway, 5, 25, 64
Holt, 5, 65, 126
Holton, 122
Hood, 19, 25, 30, 65, 120
Hooker, 15, 65
Hooper, 125
Hoover, 128
Hopkins, 121
Hord, 5, 65
Horn, 125
Horton, 56
House, 127
Houston, 125
Houx, 86, 88, 90, 98, 118
Howard, 19, 25, 30, 65, 120, 127, 129
Howaze, 120
Howell, 5, 65, 122
Howze, 5, 19, 25, 36, 65
Hubbard, 83, 84, 87, 98
Hudson, 124
Hughes, 5, 15, 19, 25, 30, 36, 65, 104, 110, 114, 131
Hulon, 124
Humphfus, 126
Humphreys, 113, 114, 115
Humphries, 36, 102, 118, 130
Hunt, 5, 15, 19, 65, 124, 130
Hunter, 5, 65, 122
Hutford, 65
Hyatt, 19

I

Ingle, 122
Ingram, 5, 12, 19, 25, 30, 36, 45, 48, 65, 80, 93, 96, 97, 98, 99, 103, 124, 130

Inmon, 124
Irwin, 5, 12, 65, 122

J

Jackson, 5, 12, 15, 19, 30, 36, 44, 46, 54, 55, 65, 94, 98, 108, 109, 113, 115, 121, 123, 124, 127, 131
Jacobs, 122
Jane, 65
Jayne, 15, 25, 30, 36, 96, 130
Jennings, 5, 15, 19, 25, 30, 36, 42, 46, 48, 66, 79, 80, 81, 83, 84, 85, 86, 87, 88, 90, 92, 93, 94, 95, 96, 97, 98, 99, 100, 102, 103, 105, 107, 108, 130
Jenson, 121
Johansen, 121, 125
Johnson, 5, 12, 19, 25, 30, 36, 44, 45, 47, 66, 107, 114, 115, 119, 125, 127, 130
Johnston, 15, 44, 55, 66, 99, 104, 108, 109, 116, 119
Joiner, 5, 12, 15, 19, 25, 30, 36, 47, 48, 49, 55, 66, 80, 82, 83, 88, 91, 93, 94, 95, 96, 98, 99, 100, 101, 102, 103, 104, 106, 108, 131
Jolley, 25, 30, 36, 66, 84, 88, 104
Jones, 5, 12, 19, 25, 30, 36, 66, 98, 100, 113, 119, 121, 122, 123, 126, 129, 130, 131
Jordan, 5, 19, 25, 30, 47, 66, 108, 120, 121, 124, 130
Jordan, 19
Jorden, 128
Jordon, 121
Jourdan, 5
Judson, 124
Justice, 5, 16, 19, 25, 30, 36, 43, 48, 54, 66, 76, 80, 82, 84, 100, 101, 102, 104, 106, 107, 109, 110, 111, 112, 114, 118, 131

K

Kahle, 114
Kamsler, 5, 19, 25, 30, 36, 53, 66
Karner, 129
Karnes, 84
Kaufman, 5, 12, 19, 25, 30, 42, 66, 82, 85, 88, 94, 130
Kearby, 99
Keeling, 25, 30, 36, 66, 82, 86, 88, 99, 107, 114, 118, 131
Keene, 19, 25
Keirbow, 5, 66
Kell, 30
Kelley, 45, 117
Kelly, 46, 49, 124
Kemp, 5, 12, 25, 30, 43, 45, 46, 47, 48, 49, 51, 52, 53, 66, 81, 120, 130
Kemp, 19
Kemper, 16, 66
Kendall, 5, 66
Kennedy, 5, 45, 66, 83, 106, 115, 116, 117, 118, 120, 122, 123, 124, 125, 126
Kenner, 5, 66
Kenney, 5, 12, 19, 25, 30, 36, 47, 48, 53, 55, 67, 79, 80, 87, 90, 130. See Kinney
Kenny. See Kinny, Kenney
Kerley, 123
Kerzee, 126
Key, 122
Keyes, 115
Keys, 30, 36, 88, 93, 117
Kidd, 30, 36
Kierbow, 126
Killough, 121
Kilpatrick, 128
Kimbell, 36, 112, 113, 114, 115, 116, 122
Kimbrough, 25
Kincaid, 5, 12, 67
King, 118, 123, 126, 129
Kingsberry, 114
Kinney, 19, 103
Kirby, 114, 118
Kirkpatric, 16, 44
Kirkpatrick, 6, 67, 130
Kirley, 83
Kirton, 121
Kirven, 45, 47
Kittrell, 101, 102
Kling, 124
Knott, 30
Knowls, 25, 30, 67
Kortum, 122
Kynerd, 25, 30, 36, 84

L

LaGrone, 36, 112, 131
LaGrove, 124
Laird, 36, 113, 131
Lamb, 129
Lambkin, 25
Lamekin, 126
Lane, 91
Langham, 121
Langston, 6, 67
Lannam, 89
Lanning, 6, 19, 25, 30, 36, 67, 113, 131
Lansford, 6, 25, 67, 124, 126
Larns, 118
Lawrence, 122
Le Noir, 6, 12, 19, 67
Leach, 6, 67
Lear, 126
Leathers, 125, 126
Ledford, 106
Lee, 6, 20, 25, 30, 36, 42, 44, 53, 67, 95, 97, 100, 114, 131
Leonard, 36
Lester, 6, 67
Leverett, 117
LeVert, 107
Levingston, 125
Lewellen, 128
Lewis, 6, 12, 20, 30, 36, 48, 67, 90, 95, 96, 99, 100, 102, 103, 107, 108, 121, 125, 128, 129, 130
Linday, 67
Lindley, 20, 25, 30, 36, 67, 97, 120, 124, 130
Lindly, 6, 12
Lindsay, 6, 12, 67
Lindsey, 20, 25, 120
Lindsley, 6, 67
Linebarger, 6, 12, 67
Lineberger, 20
Linsey, 120
Lippard, 100
Little, 16, 67, 106, 125
Livingston, 36, 110, 118
Lloyd, 124
Lofland, 125
Loftin, 128
Long, 83, 100, 128
Loper, 124
Love, 6, 12, 20, 25, 30, 36, 42, 43, 45, 46, 47, 49, 50, 51, 52, 53, 54, 55, 67, 76, 78, 79, 80, 84, 85, 86, 87, 88, 89, 90, 91, 92, 93, 94, 95, 96, 98, 99, 103, 104, 127, 130
Loventte, 67
Loverette, 20
Loveutte, 6
Loving, 16, 20, 67
Lowe, 102
Lowery, 6, 48, 67, 122
Lown, 128
Lowrance, 44, 46, 47, 76, 80, 81, 82, 106, 108, 119
Loyd, 125
Lumday, 6
Lumpkin, 16, 47, 67
Lumpkins, 106
Lusk, 121

M

Machon, 116, 123
Maclin, 119
Macom, 16, 68
Mahoney, 6, 12, 30, 36, 68, 95, 97, 130
Major, 91, 93, 94, 95, 96, 130
Mallard, 31, 36, 91, 107, 114, 127, 131
Malloy, 127
Malone, 127
Manning, 118
Marett, 124
Markham, 124
Marlin, 126
Marr, 97
Marshall, 31, 36, 123
Martin, 20, 25, 31, 68, 118, 125
Masters, 124, 128
Mathes, 127
Mathewson, 125
Matthews, 36, 124
Matysiak, 126
Mayes, 97, 128
Mc Compton, 123
McAnelly, 6, 68
McBay, 125
McBride, 122
McCain, 6, 49, 68, 130
McClellan, 31, 125
McCleskey, 115
McClinlock, 31
McClintock, 36, 114, 122, 131
McConnell, 128
McCorkille, 123
McCorkle, 25, 31, 36, 68, 102, 113, 131
McCoy, 48
McCullough, 6, 16, 20, 68
McCune, 57
McDaniel, 36, 85, 114, 121, 122, 131

McDonald, 6, 13, 16, 20, 25, 31, 36, 40, 46, 47, 49, 50, 52, 54, 68, 76, 79, 80, 81, 83, 84, 85, 88, 90, 93, 103, 104, 106, 110, 111, 116, 119, 120, 121, 125, 127, 130
McElroy, 16, 68
McFarlane, 122
McGilvary, 127
McGuffin, 128
McKay, 125
McKeehan, 128
McKenzie, 118, 122, 124
McKinney, 6, 13, 16, 20, 25, 31, 36, 43, 45, 47, 48, 49, 51, 55, 68, 80, 82, 84, 86, 88, 91, 93, 94, 101, 102, 104, 106, 107
McKinnon, 126, 128
McKinny, 120
McKnight, 123
McLean, 36
McLendon, 118, 126
McNeece, 98
McNeese, 25, 31, 37, 68, 84, 100, 101, 102, 103, 119, 130
McPherson, 6, 68
McSwane, 118
Meador, 118
Means, 117, 119, 125
Meeks, 6, 68
Menefee, 37
Menifee, 31
Mercer, 48
Merrie, 6, 68
Merrill, 121, 129
Merriwether, 83, 84
Michard, 6, 68, 96, 130
Michum, 16, 68
Milburn, 127
Miller, 6, 20, 25, 31, 37, 68, 123
Milligan, 31
Mills, 44, 119
Milstead, 128
Mindek, 125
Mitchell, 37, 51, 52, 53, 126, 127
Moffett, 6, 68
Monachan, 122
Monroe, 6, 31, 68, 118
Montgomery, 6, 13, 44, 68, 120, 123, 130
Moody, 6, 13, 45, 48, 68, 69, 117, 125, 126
Moon, 69
Moore, 6, 31, 37, 86, 93, 96, 121, 124, 125, 128, 129, 130

Morgan, 6, 13, 31, 69, 124, 126, 130
Moroe, 31
Morris, 6, 16, 69, 127
Morrow, 6, 69, 115, 117
Morton, 7, 20, 26, 31, 37, 69, 117, 124
Moss, 7, 31, 69, 92, 122, 130
Mulley, 31
Mulloy, 37
Mullins, 7, 20, 26, 31, 69
Murff, 122
Murphey, 123
Murphy, 82
Myers, 7, 69

N

Nabors, 37, 101, 102, 104, 109, 131
Nance, 123
Nash, 7, 20, 26, 31, 37, 47, 49, 55, 69, 88, 100, 101, 102, 103, 104, 107, 108, 109, 110, 112, 113, 131
Neason, 128
Neece, 118
Needham, 127
Neill, 31, 37, 86, 115, 117, 119, 128
Nelson, 7, 20, 26, 31, 37, 69, 114, 118, 122, 125, 131
Newberry, 7, 69
Newburn, 88
Newcomb, 7, 69
Newman, 47, 125, 129
Newsom, 126
Newton, 7, 69, 127
Nichels, 126
Nichols, 128
Nicholson, 126
Nickels, 7, 37, 69
Noble, 127
Nobles, 37
Nordyke, 121
Norris, 127
Norwood, 7, 20, 26, 69

O

O'Neal, 7, 69, 122, 125
Oakes, 20, 26, 31, 125
Oaks, 7, 69
Oates, 125
Oden, 123
Oliver, 117, 122, 125
Orum, 124
Ouzts, 7, 26, 31, 37, 69, 82, 83, 84, 86, 88, 89, 91, 95, 96, 98, 100, 130
Overhiser, 122
Overstreet, 125
Owen, 128
Owens, 7, 31, 37, 69

P

Padgett, 127
Palmer, 7, 69, 128
Parker, 7, 13, 20, 26, 31, 37, 45, 46, 48, 49, 52, 53, 69, 80, 86, 87, 92, 101, 120, 125, 131
Parson, 37
Parsons, 31, 37, 107, 108, 122, 130, 131
Parten, 7, 70, 128
Partin, 20
Patterson, 7, 13, 20, 31, 37, 70, 103, 130
Patton, 125
Payne, 7, 13, 20, 26, 42, 43, 45, 48, 70, 80, 99, 119, 127, 130
Pearce, 103, 124
Pearson, 89
Peeples, 123
Pelham, 122
Perdue, 37, 131
Perkins, 7, 37, 70, 97, 118
Persons, 7, 45, 48, 70
Peters, 124
Petty, 121
Phelps, 81, 83
Phillips, 20, 26, 31, 37, 70, 120
Philpott, 83
Pierce, 117, 125
Pillow, 122
Piner, 97
Pipkin, 128
Pippin, 126
Pitman, 96
Pitt, 7, 70
Pittman, 94, 124
Pitts, 125
Pleasant, 7, 70, 108
Plummer, 126
Plunkett, 37, 111, 112, 113, 114, 118
Poindexter, 7, 70
Polk, 7, 13, 43, 44, 45, 70, 126
Polley, 83, 85
Pollock, 124
Pool, 31, 127
Pope, 7, 45, 70, 124
Popejoy, 31, 37, 93, 102, 103, 106, 122, 130

Poris, 119
Posey, 123
Potts, 124
Powell, 7, 8, 13, 20, 26, 31, 70, 119, 120, 123, 127
Powers, 16, 70
Prather, 37, 109, 110
Prendergast, 31, 117
Price, 7, 16, 31, 37, 46, 47, 70, 127
Prichard, 7, 70
Priddy, 37, 109, 117, 123, 131
Prince, 7, 13, 20, 31, 37, 70, 111, 125, 131
Pringle, 7, 70
Procter, 122
Proctor, 128
Pruit, 31
Pruitt, 129
Putnam, 37, 113, 114

Q

Quaite, 128

R

Rabom, 20
Raborn, 26, 31, 70, 82, 130
Rainer, 126
Rainey, 95
Rains, 31
Rambaugh, 119
Rambo, 7, 13, 20, 26, 31, 42, 43, 47, 49, 70, 94, 119, 130
Ramsey, 7, 70
Randall, 47
Rasco, 20, 37, 117, 118, 121, 122
Raseo, 7, 13, 70
Ratliff, 7, 70
Rayborn. *See* Raborn
Rea, 31
Reagan, 98
Red, 37, 107, 108, 109, 110, 111, 112, 115
Reed, 16, 20, 26, 70, 71, 115, 118, 125, 130. *See*
Reedy, 124
Rees, 127
Reese, 124
Reeves, 20, 32, 100, 124, 130
Reid, 124
Rennick, 123

Reynolds, 20, 26, 32, 37, 71, 99, 102, 104, 114, 119, 121, 131
Rice, 126
Rich, 48
Richards, 123
Richardson, 7, 8, 13, 20, 26, 32, 37, 42, 43, 44, 45, 47, 49, 52, 71, 93, 114, 115, 118, 119, 120, 125, 128, 129
Riddle, 8, 16, 20, 71
Riggs, 121
Riley, 20
Risien, 32, 85, 130
Rivers, 8, 71
Roan, 121
Roark, 47
Robbins, 87, 121
Roberson, 32, 126
Roberts, 8, 26, 32, 37, 71, 84, 93, 107, 118, 121, 122, 125, 126, 129
Robertson, 91, 114, 123
Robison, 124, 127
Rochell, 127
Rodgers, 8, 71, 93
Rogers, 8, 13, 20, 21, 32, 37, 71, 117, 118, 121, 122, 124, 125, 129
Roland, 129
Roller, 89, 94
Roper, 71
Ross, 8, 13, 21, 26, 32, 37, 71, 81, 82, 108, 118, 130, 131
Row, 127
Royen, 71
Rucker, 8, 13, 21, 71
Ruff, 8, 71
Runnels, 123
Rush, 126
Russell, 37, 109, 110

S

Sadler, 47, 122
Salter, 21
Sanches, 21, 37
Sanders, 8, 21, 71, 72, 121, 123, 124, 126
Sanderson, 21
Sandifer, 8, 71
Sandler, 122
Sansom, 127
Santry, 122
Satterwhite, 37
Saunders, 122
Sawyer, 8, 13, 21, 26, 32, 37, 71, 111, 112, 113, 114, 131
Sawyers, 128

Saxon, 32
Sayers, 85, 87
Scarborough, 8, 13, 21, 26, 32, 72
Schluter, 93, 94
Schuster, 127
Scott, 8, 43, 72, 122, 125, 130
Scroggin, 8, 72
Scruggs, 32, 37, 103, 130
Seale, 37, 43, 107, 114, 122, 125, 127, 131
Sealey, 126
Seawright, 123
Seay, 118
Seddenn, 120
Sellers, 8, 13, 21, 26, 38, 43, 49, 72, 101, 102, 104, 106, 107, 108, 109, 110, 111, 112, 126, 131
Seventt, 115
Sexton, 32
Shaffer, 8, 72, 126
Shanks, 121
Sharp, 26, 32, 38, 112, 122, 123, 131
Shaw, 91
Shead, 8, 72, 127
Shelby, 80
Shell, 8, 48, 72
Shelton, 16, 72
Sherman, 104
Sherrill, 32, 38, 103, 130
Shields, 124
Shilling, 8, 72, 125
Shipp, 124
Shortridge, 32, 122
Shriver, 8, 16, 21, 26, 32, 38, 72, 96, 113, 114, 115, 117
Shrivier, 122
Shugart, 124
Shultz, 115
Sife, 119
Sikes, 126
Sikes 4/19, 124
Simmons, 8, 13, 21, 26, 32, 38, 40, 43, 44, 45, 46, 47, 48, 49, 50, 51, 52, 53, 54, 55, 72, 79, 80, 81, 82, 83, 84, 85, 86, 87, 88, 89, 90, 91, 92, 93, 94, 95, 96, 97, 98, 99, 100, 101, 104, 119, 130
Sims, 8, 13, 21, 72, 124
Sinclair, 117
Skillarn, 120
Skillern, 8, 13, 21, 26, 32, 38, 72, 109, 119, 124
Skipper, 32, 38, 104, 113, 122, 131

Skruggs, 8, 72
Sloan, 8, 21, 26, 32, 72, 97, 120, 127, 130
Smith, 8, 32, 38, 46, 47, 49, 57, 58, 61, 62, 66, 72, 83, 84, 86, 99, 119, 120, 121, 122, 123, 124, 127, 128, 129, 130
Smyth, 21, 26, 32, 42, 44, 53, 54, 55, 72, 85, 120, 130
Smythe, 8
Sneed, 129
Snowden, 122, 124
Sowders, 38, 113, 127, 129, 131
Sparks, 128
Speer, 123
Speers, 38
Speight, 127
Spencer, 54, 128
Spikes, 117
Spruiell, 121
Spruill, 21, 26, 72, 119
Squyres, 8, 72, 120
Stafford, 8, 72
Stamford, 72
Stanford, 8, 9, 13, 21, 38, 44, 47, 48, 72, 73, 96, 99, 113, 130, 131
Starkey, 9, 73
Starley, 32, 38, 92, 94
Statesman, 73
Stedman, 38, 108, 131
Steddum, 21, 26, 32
Steeddum, 73
Steele, 9, 13, 16, 21, 26, 32, 38, 43, 46, 47, 48, 49, 50, 53, 55, 73, 76, 79, 80, 81, 82, 83, 84, 85, 86, 88, 89, 90, 91, 92, 93, 94, 95, 96, 97, 98, 99, 100, 101, 102, 103, 104, 105, 106, 107, 108, 109, 110, 111, 112, 113, 114, 115, 116, 117, 118, 119, 120, 129, 131
Steen, 92, 118
Stephens, 9, 73, 124, 126
Stephenson, 122, 127
Sterling, 118
Stevens, 91, 94
Steward, 38, 114, 129, 131
Stewart, 9, 65, 68, 71, 73, 91, 95, 120, 122
Stitt, 9, 13, 47, 73, 117, 118, 119, 130
Stone, 91, 125
Storey, 9, 13, 21, 26, 32, 38, 42, 46, 49, 50, 51, 52, 55, 73, 80, 81, 83, 84, 85, 86, 87, 88, 89, 90, 91, 92, 93, 95, 98, 99, 100, 104, 107, 117, 120, 129, 131
Story, 125
Strahorn, 9, 73
Strayhorn, 44, 130
Strother, 89
Stroud, 127
Stuart, 32, 38, 96, 113, 130, 131
Stubbs, 128, 129
Sturdivant, 9, 13, 21, 26, 32, 38, 73
Stutesma, 16
Stutesman, 21, 73
Stutts, 97
Summers, 124
Sutherland, 121
Suttle, 9, 13, 21, 26, 32, 40, 42, 43, 45, 46, 47, 48, 49, 51, 52, 53, 55, 73, 79, 80, 82, 85, 127, 130
Suttles, 120
Swaim, 16, 48, 73
Swain, 26, 73
Sweeney, 128
Sweet, 73
Sweth, 116
Swinnea, 127
Swinney, 16, 73
Sypert, 126

T

Tackett, 9, 73
Talley, 32
Taylor, 9, 13, 21, 38, 73, 82, 101, 121, 124, 127
Teakell, 9, 73
Tekel, 127
Tennison, 26, 32
Terry, 38
Tew, 38, 112, 113
Therrell, 88, 106
Therrill, 32, 38, 130
Thomas, 9, 13, 21, 26, 32, 38, 47, 73, 84, 88, 90, 111, 124, 127, 130, 131
Thompson, 9, 13, 21, 26, 32, 38, 49, 55, 73, 74, 80, 84, 85, 86, 88, 91, 93, 95, 96, 99, 101, 106, 117, 119, 122, 123, 126, 130
Thornton, 21, 26, 32, 42, 74
Thurman, 127
Thurmond, 122

137

Tibbs, 126
Tidwell, 13, 74, 123, 128, 129
Tiles, 9, 74
Tillery, 122
Tilman, 127
Tipton, 16, 74
Todd, 124, 127
Tomkins, 21
Tompkins, 125
Toon, 127
Trammell, 9, 16, 21, 26, 45, 47, 48, 74
Tribble, 9, 74
Truett, 122
Tubb, 13, 21, 74
Tucker, 9, 13, 21, 27, 32, 38, 74, 112, 120, 131
Tunnell, 44
Turner, 9, 74, 117, 120
Tyns, 45, 46, 47, 117
Tyus, 73, 122, 129

U

Ushe, 9, 74
Usry, 9, 21, 74

V

Vaiden, 115, 118
Van Dyke, 123
Van Zandt, 89, 91
Vann, 127
Vansickel, 128
Vaughan, 32
Vestal, 38
Vickers, 9, 13, 21, 27, 74
Vincen, 43
Vinson, 9, 13, 74, 121, 128

W

Wacaster, 9, 16, 74, 123
Wade, 9, 21, 74
Wadkins, 74
Wagley, 128
Wait, 9
Waite, 21
Walk, 52
Walker, 9, 13, 21, 27, 32, 38, 43, 44, 45, 47, 49, 50, 51, 52, 53, 54, 55, 74, 76, 79, 80, 82, 84, 85, 91, 92, 93, 96, 98, 120, 121, 127, 130, 131
Wallace, 9, 14, 21, 27, 38, 43, 44, 45, 47, 48, 55, 74, 106, 124, 130

Waller, 9, 32, 38, 74, 90, 116, 119, 126, 130
Walling, 9, 14, 21, 27, 33, 38, 40, 42, 43, 45, 46, 50, 52, 53, 54, 55, 75, 76, 78, 79, 80, 82, 84, 85, 86
Ward, 9, 14, 21, 27, 33, 38, 46, 48, 75, 80, 82, 88, 106, 108, 120, 131
Ware, 124
Washam, 9, 75
Washum, 27
Waterman, 87
Waters, 123
Watkins, 9, 16, 22, 27, 33, 75, 97, 130
Watly, 14
Watson, 10, 14, 22, 27, 33, 38, 42, 43, 44, 45, 46, 47, 48, 49, 50, 51, 52, 53, 55, 75, 76, 79, 80, 81, 82, 83, 84, 85, 86, 88, 89, 90, 91, 92, 93, 94, 95, 96, 98, 99, 100, 101, 102, 103, 104, 105, 106, 107, 108, 109, 110, 111, 112, 113, 114, 115, 116, 117, 118, 119, 121, 122, 128
Watty, 75
Wayland, 124
Weaver, 127
Webb, 10, 33, 75, 100, 122, 123, 127, 130
Welch, 27, 33, 38, 100, 122, 123, 130
Wells, 115, 118, 126
West, 91
Whatley, 22, 122, 128
Whattley, 16, 75
Wheeler, 125, 127
Whitcomb, 122
White, 10, 14, 38, 75, 126, 128
Whitenton, 125
Whitfield, 33
Whitley, 125
Whitlow, 124
Wickder, 22, 33, 80
Wickdir, 27
Wilder, 10, 14, 22, 27, 33, 42, 75, 79, 82, 128, 130
Wiley, 14, 22, 27, 33, 38, 43, 44, 45, 46, 47, 53, 75, 76, 80, 85, 88
Wilie, 33, 38, 101, 102, 130
Wilkins, 122
Wilkinson, 123
Willard, 129

Williams, 10, 14, 22, 27, 33, 39, 40, 43, 45, 46, 47, 48, 49, 50, 51, 52, 53, 54, 55, 75, 76, 79, 80, 81, 82, 83, 84, 85, 86, 87, 88, 89, 90, 91, 92, 93, 94, 95, 96, 97, 98, 99, 100, 101, 102, 103, 104, 105, 106, 107, 108, 109, 110, 111, 112, 113, 114, 115, 121, 122, 123, 126, 128, 131
Wilson, 10, 75, 116, 118, 123
Winfield, 39, 124
Wingard, 121
Winmill, 128
Winston, 122
Winters, 39, 131
Wolf, 127
Wolfe, 128
Wolverton, 39, 128
Womack, 117, 129
Wood, 10, 14, 22, 27, 33, 39, 43, 45, 46, 47, 54, 55, 64, 72, 74, 75, 76, 79, 82, 83, 84, 85, 86, 88, 89, 91, 92, 93, 96, 97, 102, 104, 113, 116, 119, 120, 127, 129, 130, 131
Woods, 33, 118
Wooldridge, 33, 39, 96, 97, 98, 99, 100, 102, 103, 104, 105, 107, 108, 109, 110, 111, 112, 113, 114, 115, 116
Wootan, 10, 76
Wooten, 22, 50
Word, 10, 76
Wray, 128
Wright, 10, 14, 22, 27, 33, 39, 48, 76, 82, 95, 96, 99, 102, 104, 107, 109, 114, 115, 116, 117, 118, 119, 120, 122, 123, 126, 129, 130, 131
Wyatt, 22, 27, 33, 55, 100, 130
Wylie, 10, 125

Y

Yankee, 33, 128
Yankie, 39
Yates, 10, 76
Yeldell, 27, 33, 39, 100, 101, 102, 103, 104, 105, 106, 107, 108, 109, 110, 111, 114, 115, 116, 118
Yelverton, 128
Young, 115, 117, 118
Yowell, 117

Z

Zimmerman, 123

Patricia Bennett McGinty

About The Author

Patricia Bennett McGinty is a seventh generation Texan through her maternal line and has been married to a third generation Houstonian, Thomas Dreaper McGinty, for over thirty-six years. She is the mother of a daughter, Kathleen McGinty Shumate, and a son, Timothy Dreaper McGinty. Having a life long romance with history and especially Texas history, she has been involved with the genealogical field for over forty years either teaching, or researching in almost all of the Southern States.

www.ingramcontent.com/pod-product-compliance
Lightning Source LLC
Chambersburg PA
CBHW080403170426
43193CB00016B/2800